HOW 6

A Handbook for Office Workers

KENT Series in Business Education

Arntson, *Word/Information Processing: Concepts, Procedures, and Systems,* Second Edition

Arntson/Auvil, *MS/PC DOS on the IBM PC and Compatibles: Concepts, Exercises, and Applications*

Arntson/Todesco, *Word/Information Processing: Exercises, Applications, and Procedures,* Second Edition

Carbone, *Modern Business English: A Systems Approach*

Clark/Clark, *HOW 6: A Handbook for Office Workers,* Sixth Edition

Clark/Clark, *Universal Transcription*

Guffey, *Business English,* Third Edition

Guffey, *Essentials of Business Communication,* Second Edition

Himstreet/Baty, *Business Communications: Principles and Methods,* Ninth Edition

Kupsh/Rhodes, *Automated Office Systems for Managers and Professionals*

Lee, *Self-Paced Business Mathematics,* Fourth Edition

Lundgren/Lundgren, *Records Management in the Computer Age*

McCready, *Business Mathematics,* Sixth Edition

McCready, *Office Machines: Electronic Calculators,* Seventh Edition

Penrose/Rasberry/Myers, *Advanced Business Communication*

Quinn/Arntson, *WordPerfect 5.0*

Rittman/Gonzalez, *Effective Business Communication*

Ruch/Crawford, *Business Reports: Written and Oral*

Swindle, *Business Math Basics,* Fourth Edition

Tedesco, *Telecommunications for Business*

Wells, *Communications in Business,* Fifth Edition

HOW 6

A Handbook for Office Workers

Sixth Edition

James L. Clark

Chairman, Business Department
Pasadena City College

Lyn R. Clark

Professor, Office Administration Department
Los Angeles Pierce College

PWS-KENT Publishing Company
Boston, Massachusetts

PWS-KENT
Publishing Company

PWS-KENT Publishing Company is a division of Wadsworth, Inc.

Printed in the United States of America

3 4 5 6 7 8 9 — 95 94 93 92

Library of Congress Cataloging-in-Publication Data

Clark, James Leland
HOW 6 : a handbook for office workers / James L. Clark, Lyn R. Clark.—6th ed.
p. cm.
Rev. ed. of: HOW 5. 5th ed. c1988.
Includes index.
ISBN 0-534-92556-1
1. Commercial correspondence—Handbooks, manuals, etc.
I. Clark, Lyn. II. Clark, James Leland HOW 5. III. Title.
HF5726.C55 1991
808'.06665—dc20 90-21183
CIP

International Student Edition ISBN 0-534-98465-7

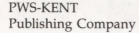

Editor: Rolf Janke
Editorial Assistant: Marnie Pommett
Production Editor: Pamela Rockwell
Interior Designer: Pamela Rockwell
Cover Design and Art: Piñeiro Design Associates
Manufacturing Coordinator: Marcia Locke
Typesetting: Modern Graphics Inc.
Cover Printer: John P. Pow Company
Print and Bind: R.R. Donnelley & Sons Company

CONTENTS

PREFACE

How 6: A Handbook for Office Workers, Sixth Edition, is designed to assist students, office personnel, and business writers in preparing written business communications. Detailed and precise information for writing, formatting, and transmitting business documents may be found in this manual.

The primary function of *HOW 6* is to act as a reference book—to answer specific questions regarding punctuation, grammar, capitalization, number usage, word usage, forms of address, abbreviations, format, and document transmission as they relate to the preparation of business letters, memorandums, bulletins, reports, manuscripts, and meeting minutes.

New to the sixth edition are expanded and more detailed materials on grammar and language usage with a separate glossary of grammatical terms. In addition, the chapters on report preparation and document formats have been expanded and/or revised extensively to incorporate the advances that have occurred in high-end word processing programs and desktop publishing.

HOW 6 may be employed as a classroom text or supplement for instructing potential office employees, administrative assistants, business writers, and managers—anyone who deals with the preparation of written business documents. By using the *Workbook for HOW 6,* the instructor may teach and reinforce the major principles contained in the reference manual. Exercises are coordinated specifically with sections in *HOW 6* and are designed to provide students with realistic learning applications, not just isolated sentence exercises. In this edition the workbook has been augmented with an extensive section on words most often misused and confused.

The *Instructor's Manual and Key* includes over 120 instructional transparency masters that contain the major punctuation, grammar, capitalization, and number-usage principles in *HOW 6* and correspond directly with the exercise applications in the workbook. All transparency masters in the instructor's manual have been revised and reproduced in a print format. Other teaching materials in the instructor's manual include a familiarization exercise, a series of business letter and memorandum problems, and a complete set of dictation and/or transcription materials.

Special Features

Several features, in addition to the table of contents and the index, have been included to increase the functional use of *HOW 6* as a reference book.

1. **Solution Finders**—comprehensive topic indexes at the beginning of each chapter so that solutions to problems may be found easily
2. **Two-color format**—rules printed in red and examples printed in black for ease in locating, reading, and understanding principles
3. **Example headings**—italicized headings that differentiate aspects of each rule so that specific examples and applications may be located immediately
4. **Chapter indexers**—edge-of-page printed tabulators so that major sections may be reached quickly
5. **Spiral binding**—a lie-flat feature so that readers may readily compare their problems with the examples

Finding Solutions to Problems

Information you need may be located easily and quickly in *HOW 6* by using a four-step process:

1. Find the chapter you need by turning to the list of contents shown on the outside back cover.
2. Turn to the Solution Finder at the beginning of that chapter by using the printed tabulators that appear on the outside edges of the pages.
3. Locate the information you need in the Solution Finder. Each main topic is listed alphabetically followed by subsections of that topic and their corresponding rule numbers.
4. Turn to the appropriate section within the chapter by referring to the page guide references (the rule numbers shown at the top right corner of the odd-numbered pages).

If information cannot be located through surveying the contents listed on the back cover, use the comprehensive index at the end of the book to find the appropriate section. Then use the printed tabulators on the outside edges of the pages to locate the appropriate chapter and the page guides to find the specific section.

Acknowledgments

We wish to thank the following reviewers for their assistance in the preparation of this edition:

Hazel Gee
Tarrant County Community College

Edna Jellesed
Lane Community College

Jan Larson
Pikes Peak Community College

Jim Scott
Utah State University

Theresa Zimmer
McNeese State University

CHAPTER 1

Punctuation

Punctuation Solution Finder

Punctuation Solution Finder (continued)

Dash

Punctuation Solution Finder (continued)

Diagonal

Ellipses

Exclamation Mark

Parentheses

Period

Question Mark

Quotation Marks

Semicolon

Punctuation Solution Finder (continued)

Underscore

1

Comma

1–1. Series

a. **In a sentence containing a series of three or more equally ranked parts (words, phrases, or short clauses), place a comma after each part except the last one. Be sure to use a comma before the conjunction *(and, or, nor).*[1]**

words

Today's luncheon special consists of soup, salad, beverage, and dessert for only $3.99.

Our branch office advertised for an accountant, an administrative assistant, and a word processing specialist in yesterday's newspaper.

phrases

A new manager was hired to supervise office services, improve our management of records, and implement more cost-effective procedures.

short clauses

I signed the contract, Karen Jones mailed it, and Ralph Harris initiated computer installation procedures.

b. **Commas are not used when the parts of a series are all joined by conjunctions.**

words

Neither cameras *nor* jewelry *nor* appliances were stolen from the store.

phrases

For several years we have employed custodians to clean the building *and* gardeners to maintain the grounds *and* special crews to perform painting and electrical maintenance.

c. **Although generally avoided, *etc.* is sometimes used to indicate "and so forth" at the end of a series. If it is used, *etc.* is set off by commas; it is never preceded by the word *and.***

within a sentence

Staples, paper clips, fasteners, rubber bands, etc., were placed on our last supplies order.

end of a sentence

We plan to visit all our branch offices this year--New York, Los Angeles, San Francisco, Chicago, etc.

---

[1]Some literary writers prefer to omit the comma before the conjunction in a series. For business writing, however, always use the comma before the conjunction to promote ease of reading and clarity.

d. **A comma is not used before an ampersand (&) in an organizational name unless the organization officially uses the comma in its name.**

no comma

Her first interview is with Gates, Hamilton & Gates.

comma

Augner, Haight, Liggett, & Phelan is a new accounting firm in the Chicago area.

1–2. Parenthetical Expressions

a. **Transitional words and expressions that are considered unnecessary for the grammatical completeness of a sentence and that *interrupt its natural flow* are set off with commas. A partial list of such parenthetical expressions follows:**

according to our records
accordingly
after all
all in all
all things considered
also
as a matter of fact
as a result
as a rule
at any rate
at the same time
besides
between you and me
by the way
consequently
even so
finally
for example
fortunately
furthermore
hence
however
in addition
incidentally
in conclusion
indeed
in effect
in essence
in fact
in general
in my opinion
in other words
instead
in summary
in the first place
in the meantime
likewise
moreover
namely
needless to say
nevertheless
no
no doubt
obviously
of course
on the contrary
on the other hand
on the whole
otherwise
perhaps
periodically
secondly
so
that is
then
therefore
thus
too
under the circumstances
unfortunately
what is more
without a doubt
yes

beginning of sentence

Needless to say, he is planning to attend the meeting.

end of sentence

The store will be closed over the Labor Day weekend, *without a doubt.*

within a sentence

A large crowd, *nevertheless,* attended the exhibit.

b. Sometimes words and phrases used as parenthetical expressions *do not interrupt* the flow of a sentence. In such cases no commas are used with the expression.

beginning of sentence

Perhaps the package will arrive in Dallas by Monday.

end of sentence

My boss is planning a trip to New York City *too.*

within a sentence

She was *indeed* concerned about the omissions in the financial analysis.

c. Exclamations at the beginning of a sentence are parenthetical expressions that require a comma.

Oh, what a surprise to see Mrs. Hilton at the Christmas party!

Ah, it will not be easy to transfer these holdings into liquid assets!

d. Enumerations or explanations used as parenthetical expressions *within a sentence* are set off by commas, dashes, or parentheses. Use commas when the enumerated or explanatory information has no internal commas, dashes when the information contains commas within it, or parentheses when the information is considered to be only incidental to the rest of the sentence.

commas

Only one company, *namely, Consolidated Enterprises,* bid on the contract.

dashes

He had invited several relatives--*namely, his parents, his sister, and his aunt and uncle*--to attend the company picnic.

parentheses

Our vice president toured several Ohio cities *(Cleveland, Columbus, and Toledo)* to find a suitable plant site.

e. A parenthetical expression introducing an enumeration or explanation *after a complete thought* may be set off with either (1) commas or (2) a semicolon and a comma. If the enumeration or explanation itself is a complete thought or contains internal commas, use a semicolon and a comma. Otherwise, use just commas.

commas

We are expecting two exceptionally large orders next week, *namely,* from Reed's Department Store and Payco.

There are a number of ways we can cut our expenses during the next quarter, *for example,* by reducing our advertising budget.

semicolon and comma

This customer ordered new furniture for her living room; *namely,* a sofa, two chairs, two lamp tables, and an occasional table.

Your present insurance policy does not cover all hazards; *i.e.,* any losses resulting from earthquake damage are not recoverable.

f. **Short introductory prepositional phrases essential to the meaning of the sentence should not be mistaken for parenthetical expressions. These phrases answer specifically questions such as *when, where, why,* or *how.* Introductory prepositional phrases containing fewer than five words (but not containing a verb form) generally flow smoothly into the sentence and are *not* followed by a comma.**

when?

In the future please place your orders with our Eastern Washington office.

At your convenience please fill out and return the enclosed form.

where?

At the conference we met agents from all parts of the United States.

In this case we are able to grant only a partial refund of the purchase price.

why?

For that reason we have turned over your account to our attorney for collection.

On this basis we have decided to expand our operations in the South.

how?

In this way you will be able to cut your travel costs by 20 percent.

With this program you can speed up the operation of any computer that uses a hard disk.

g. **Parenthetical expressions used as adverbs do not require commas.**

However brilliant his work may be, Mr. Rogers will not be promoted until his disposition improves.

Obviously concerned with Ms. Jones's illness, the supervisor phoned her home.

Too many managers were absent yesterday.

1–3. Direct Address

Names, titles, or categories of people employed *in speaking directly* to individuals or groups are set off by commas because they are used in direct address. Capitalize only (1) proper nouns and (2) personal and professional titles appearing in direct address.

beginning of sentence

Ladies and gentlemen, it is a pleasure to address you this evening.

Mrs. Phelps, you are the winner of a Thanksgiving turkey.

within a sentence

Will you please, *Dr. Jones,* send us your check for $50 by March 30.

The book you have ordered, *Professor,* is presently out of stock.

Please examine for yourselves, *ladies and gentlemen,* how this proposal will affect you.

You, *fellow golfer,* will now be able to cut strokes from your game with this new Leading-Edge driver.

end of sentence

You are certainly a competent assistant, *Ms. Boyer.*

You also should be concerned about this issue, *fellow American.*

1–4. Appositives

a. **Appositives are word groups that rename or explain the nouns or pronouns they follow. These descriptive words usually add extra information and are set off by commas. (See 1–4b and 1–4c for exceptions.)**

within a sentence

All the reports were submitted to Ms. Hartford, *our sales manager,* for approval.

Our vice president, *Mr. Vodden,* will be in Denver all next week.

end of sentence

At your suggestion we contacted a representative in your nearest branch office, *the Hillsdale Office.*

She had reservations on the 5:30 p.m. flight, *the last flight to San Francisco that day.*

b. **Restrictive appositives—descriptive word groups that are *needed to identify* the person or thing further described—are not set off by commas. These restrictive appositives tell *which one* or *which ones* and are essential to the meaning of the sentence.**

necessary for identification—tells which one or which ones

The book *Terminology for the Automated Office* will be released next week.

Your student *Larry Green* has an appointment to see you tomorrow.

We *board members* are responsible for ensuring that each child in our community receives a quality education.

unnecessary for identification

His latest book, College English, was released last December.

Your best student, *Ann Freeman,* has an appointment to see you next week.

c. Closely related one-word appositives or those forming parts of proper names do not require commas.

closely related one-word appositives

My sister *Ellen* has received two promotions within the last year.

I *myself* plan to attend the organizational meeting in Memphis.

In this area the state legislation sets forth only general guidelines for us *teachers.*

proper name

His last two novels dealt with the lives of Alexander *the Great* and Richard *the Lionhearted.*

d. Abbreviations, Roman numerals, and college degrees written after individuals' names are set off by commas. Abbreviations after company names are also set off by commas. However, Roman numerals and the abbreviations *Inc., Ltd., Jr.,* and *Sr.* are not set off by commas if a particular company or individual elects to omit them.

abbreviations with commas after individual and company names

Mr. Lowell T. Harrison, *Jr.,* has just been promoted to executive vice president.

Our firm will be represented by Alan Moskley, *Esq.*[2]

Caroline R. Ryan, *Ph.D.,* is the author of Executive Decision Making.

Hargrave & Lyons, *Inc.,* was awarded the equipment contract.

Roman numeral with commas after name of individual

Donald J. Ellington, *III,* has just been appointed Secretary of State.

college degree after name of individual

Marilyn Drengson, *Doctor of Divinity,* will deliver the main graduation address.

omission of commas

Clothiers *Ltd.* is one of the largest jobbers on the West Coast.

Please send copies of the contract to David Warburton *Jr.* and the other names listed in the attached letter.

Only Robert T. Link *II* has access to the safety deposit box.

---

[2]Courtesy titles are not used with the term *Esq.*

e. **Words or expressions referred to simply as words or expressions should be underscored or placed in quotation marks rather than set off by commas.**

underscored

The word convenience is often misspelled in business letters.

quotation marks

The phrase "Thanking you in advance" is an outdated expression that should be avoided in business letters.

1–5. Dates and Time Zones

a. **Dates containing combinations of weekday, calendar date, and year require commas. Place a comma *after each element* used unless, of course, the element concludes a sentence. Remember *always* to place a comma *after* the year when a calendar date and year appear within the sentence.**

Commas are not used with a calendar date expressed alone.

calendar date expressed alone

On *February 28* our books were audited by the Internal Revenue Service.

calendar date and year

On *February 28, 1991,* our books were audited by the Internal Revenue Service.

weekday and calendar date

On *Tuesday, February 28,* our books were audited by the Internal Revenue Service.

weekday, calendar date, and year

On *Tuesday, February 28, 1991,* our books were audited by the Internal Revenue Service.

b. **Expressions of month and year may be written with or without commas, but the same form must be used throughout a document. Remember also that a comma *must* be used after the year if one is used before it, unless the year appears at the end of the sentence.**

with commas

In *March, 1993,* we will release our new line of products.

without commas

In *March 1993* we will release our new line of products.

c. **Set off by commas any time zones used with clock times.**

Our flight will leave Denver at 9:35 a.m., *MST,* and arrive in New York at 3:18 p.m., *EST.*

Your message arrived in San Diego at 8:40 a.m., *PDT.*

1–6. Addresses

a. **The parts of an address written in sentence form are separated by commas.**

name and complete address

Please send the check to *Ms. Harriet Buckley, 14832 Ventura Boulevard, Encino, California 91316,* after May 1.

complete address only

Mr. Livingston may be reached at *740 Gayley Avenue, Los Angeles, California 90025.*

b. **Use commas to set off a state following the name of a city. Remember to use the second comma after the state name when it appears in the middle of a sentence.**

within a sentence

The letter was sent to Kansas City, *Missouri,* in error.

end of sentence

On our tour we will visit Boston, *Massachusetts.*

1–7. Coordinating Conjunctions

a. **The words *and, but, or,* and *nor* are coordinating conjunctions. Place a comma before any of these words that separates two independent clauses (complete thought units) in a compound sentence. No comma is used if both clauses are not totally independent and could not stand alone as separate sentences. (See Section 1–18 for use of semicolon instead of comma.)**

two independent clauses

Several of our staff should reach their sales goals by the end of this month, and they will then be eligible to receive a bonus vacation to Hawaii.

There are still 43 orders to fill, but we will close for vacation as scheduled.

You can have the interest added to your account, or we can send you a monthly check for the interest earned.

We have not purchased any appliances from this distributor within the past three months, nor have we requested an extension of our credit line.

no second independent clause

I plan to complete this project by Wednesday but cannot promise that it will reach your desk before Monday.

We are aware that sales have increased in your district and that another salesperson should be assigned to your territory.

b. In imperative sentences (command statements) the subject *you* is understood. Separate with a comma two independent clauses, whether one or both are in the imperative form.

Ship the books to me at Eastern High School, but send the bill to the bookstore manager of Grant High School.

Please call Dr. Greenberg's office tomorrow morning, and his nurse will let you know what time the doctor is expected to finish surgery.

c. When a simple adverb, introductory phrase, or dependent clause precedes and applies equally to two clauses, these clauses are not independent. Consequently, no comma is used between them.

simple adverb

Please call the doctor's office tomorrow morning and arrange to have your appointment changed to next week. (The adverb *please* refers to both *call* and *arrange.* Therefore, the two clauses are not independent of each other and no comma is used.)

introductory phrase

During the next month the board will visit several sites in Memphis and it will make a decision regarding the location of our new branch office. (*During the next month* applies equally to both clauses. Consequently, they are not independent and are not separated by a comma.)

dependent clauses

When Mr. Howard calls, ask him for his new address and send him 100 copies of our revised price list. (Subject *you* is understood in both clauses. *When Mr. Howard calls* applies to both clauses. Therefore, they are not independent and no punctuation mark is used.)

As soon as we receive your response, we will notify our distributor and he will ship your order immediately. (In this case *As soon as we receive your response* applies to both clauses; therefore, no punctuation mark is needed between the last two clauses.)

d. Omit the comma in short compound sentences connected by *and.* For simplicity, "short" in these cases *may be* interpreted as describing those compound sentences containing up to 12 or 13 words.

Format these disks and take them to Ms. Wilson.
John wrote the letter and his supervisor signed it.
I received the inquiry yesterday and my assistant contacted the client immediately.

1–8. Independent Adjectives

Use commas to separate two or more independent adjectives that modify a noun. No commas are needed, though, when the first adjective modifies the second adjective and the noun as a unit. To identify independent adjectives, (1) reverse the adjectives, (2) read the adjectives independently, and (3) read the sentence with the word *and* between the adjectives. If the sentence makes sense and means the same thing with the

adjectives read in these ways, then commas should be placed between them.

independent adjectives

He enclosed a *stamped, addressed* envelope.

The president had surrounded herself with *efficient, intelligent* assistants.

We received a *demanding, discourteous, unprecedented* letter from your company.

first adjective modifies second adjective and noun

The posters were lettered in *large* bold print.

He received several *attractive* business offers.

The room was filled with *old* local newspapers dating back to the 1950s.

Be sure the press release describes thoroughly Liza's *dazzling* blue evening gown.

1–9. Introductory Clauses

a. **An introductory dependent clause is separated from the rest of the sentence by a comma. Introductory dependent clauses contain a subject and a verb and usually begin with one of the words listed below.**

as if when	} are most common	after although because before	provided since so unless	until whenever while

When Mr. Jones received his $10,000 inheritance, he invested the money in mutual funds.

So that we may reach a decision by March 14, please submit the papers immediately.

b. **A shortened form of an introductory clause is separated from the rest of the sentence by a comma.**

If so, the delivery of these materials will be delayed. (If that is so, ...)

As agreed, he will be dismissed. (As we agreed, ...)

Whatever the reason, I would like to have the error corrected immediately. (Whatever the reason may be, ...)

c. **Occasionally an introductory clause may follow another introductory word group. In these cases place a comma only after the introductory clause.**

Mrs. Jones said that *when these accounts are paid,* we will reinstate their credit privileges.

I hope that *before you file your income tax return,* you will check with our tax attorneys on this issue.

d. When an introductory clause is followed by two main clauses, place a comma only after the introductory clause.

When Gerald answers the telephone, he speaks clearly and he answers all questions courteously.

If you wish employment with our company, fill out the enclosed application form and mail it in the enclosed envelope.

1–10. Introductory Phrases

a. An introductory infinitive phrase (a verb preceded by *to*) is followed by a comma.

To arrive at an immediate decision, the Board of Directors called an emergency meeting of the stockholders.

To carry out the original plans, Ms. Morii hired two additional employees.

b. An introductory participial phrase (a verb form used as an adjective) is followed by a comma.

Hoping to obtain several large orders, Mr. Irwin embarked upon a selective advertising campaign.

Concerned about the sudden decrease in sales, Ms. Alexander flew to the West Coast office.

c. An introductory prepositional phrase (a group of words that includes a preposition and an object) is separated from the rest of the sentence by a comma if it contains a verb form *or* five or more words.[3] After an introductory prepositional phrase that contains no verb form and fewer than five words, use a comma only if the comma is necessary for clarity.

A partial list of prepositions used to begin introductory prepositional phrases follows:

about	among	behind	during	on	until
above	around	below	for	over	up
after	at	between	from	through	upon
along	before	by	in	under	with

verb form

Upon receiving the papers, Swift & Company filed suit against its former parent company.

After reviewing the case, the judge decided in favor of the defendant.

By enrolling today, you are assured of receiving a place in the class that begins on March 1.

After calling you, I notified our insurance company of the theft.

---

[3]Some authorities suggest four words.

five or more words

During the past few days of litigation, concessions were made by both sides.

Between July 1 and August 31, all our stores will be closed on Mondays.

Within the next few days, you should receive a written confirmation from the Hawaiian Village Hotel.

no verb form and fewer than five words

About three months ago our laboratories released several new medical discoveries to the press.

Through your efforts we have been able to locate new customers for our towels and linens.

For over two weeks our offices have been without air-conditioning.

On September 30 we will open our new branch office in Boise.

comma necessary for clarity

After the class, discussion on this issue will continue until 3 p.m. in Conference Room 14.

In my office, files dating back to 1980 are stored in three of the cabinets.

Until next Monday, morning deliveries will be accepted only between 8:30 and 10 a.m.; afternoon deliveries, between 3 and 5 p.m.

d. An introductory phrase that follows another introductory word group is treated as if the opening introductory word group were not included. In other words, mentally omit the opening expression, and punctuate the introductory phrase according to the rules in Section 1–10a-c.

infinitive phrase

Mr. Wilson explained that *to meet our production deadline,* we would have to work overtime the remainder of the week.

participial phrase

Mrs. Winston expressed concern over the poor telephone techniques used by our receptionist; and *speaking clearly and distinctly,* she demonstrated how Ms. Davis should handle incoming calls.

prepositional phrase, fewer than five words

We were notified that *on Monday* we will resume our regular schedule.

You may be sure that *within the next week* your order will be shipped from our warehouse.

prepositional phrase, five or more words

I hope that *in view of the urgency of the situation,* we will obtain the full cooperation of our staff.

We expect that *during this rapid growth period,* many investors will attempt to acquire our company.

e. Any phrase that acts as the subject or is part of the predicate is not followed by a comma.

phrase that acts as subject

To answer your question would require several days' research on the part of our staff.

Helping his employees prepare for advancement does not rank high among Mr. Green's management attributes.

phrase that is part of the predicate

From the police's intensive investigation came some new evidence that led to the apprehension of the suspected arsonists.

1–11. Restrictive and Nonrestrictive Phrases and Clauses

Restrictive phrases and clauses modify and contribute substantially to the main idea of a sentence and are essential to its meaning. They tell *who, what,* or *which one* and are not set off with commas.

Nonrestrictive phrases and clauses add an additional idea and do not significantly change or contribute to the main idea of a sentence. They are unessential word groups; that is, they are not needed by the main clause to tell *who, what,* or *which one*. Set off nonrestrictive phrases and clauses from the rest of the sentence with commas.

a. Relative clauses (those beginning with *who, whose, whom, which,* or *that*) are either restrictive (no comma) or nonrestrictive (comma required).

restrictive and essential to meaning

Office employees *who possess computer application skills* can obtain well-paying jobs. (Tells *which kind* of office employees.)

nonrestrictive and not essential to meaning

Ms. Kennedy, *who possesses computer application skills,* can obtain a well-paying job. (Additional idea.)

In the first example the clause "who possess computer application skills" limits the type of office employees who "can obtain well-paying jobs." In the second example "who possesses computer application skills" is of no assistance in *identifying* Ms. Kennedy but is merely an additional idea. Therefore, this is a nonrestrictive clause and is set off by commas.

restrictive and essential to meaning

All students *who are enrolled in history classes* will take part in organizing World Affairs Day. (Tells *which* students.)

nonrestrictive and not essential to meaning

Joseph, *who is enrolled in a history class,* will take part in organizing World Affairs Day. (Additional idea.)

b. Careful writers will use *that* for restrictive clauses (no comma) and *which* for nonrestrictive clauses (comma required).

restrictive

The stores *that are located in the Flintridge Mall* are sponsoring a free parking lot carnival this weekend.

He has written a new book *that will be released next December.*

nonrestrictive

Her new book, *which was scheduled for spring publication,* will be released next December.

We have canceled our winter sales meeting, *which was scheduled from December 11–13 in Miami.*

c. **Dependent adverbial clauses (ones that begin with words such as *if, as, when, since, because,* etc.) that follow the main clause may be restrictive (no comma) or nonrestrictive (comma required). Restrictive clauses (1) answer such questions as *when, why, how,* or *whether* or (2) limit the main idea of the sentence. Nonrestrictive clauses, however, add an additional idea that does not alter the meaning of the main clause.**

restrictive and essential to meaning

We will ship your order *as soon as your account is approved.* (Tells *when.*)

National Food Products has doubled its monthly sales *since the advertising campaign began.* (Tells *when.*)

Please send us this information by March 1 *so that we may bring your records up-to-date.* (Tells *why.*)

Our company president retired last month *because his doctor recommended a six-month leave of absence.* (Tells *why.*)

You can receive this handsome carrying case free of charge *if you will fill out and return the enclosed questionnaire.* (Tells *how.*)

We can still promise you the discount price *if we receive your order on or before July 15.* (Tells *whether.*)

We cannot install the additional equipment you requested *unless we receive an authorization from your main office.* (Limits main idea.)

You may order additional items at the advertised sale prices *as long as our current supply of merchandise lasts.* (Limits main idea.)

nonrestrictive and not essential to meaning

He has written his letter of resignation, *although I do not believe he will submit it.* (Additional idea.)

She will continue with her plans for introducing a new product, *whatever the competition might be.* (Additional idea.)

Next week our Board of Directors will tour our new South Haven plant, *where we will be hiring several hundred new employees.* (Additional idea.)

d. **A dependent clause or a short independent clause used to provide an extra idea within a sentence is nonrestrictive and is set off with commas (or dashes for emphasis).**

interrupting dependent clause

Sales figures for last year, *as you can see from the financial reports,* were nearly 10 percent higher than we had projected.

On Tuesday morning, *when you arrive for the meeting,* please give the manuscript to my secretary.

We can, *as I see the situation,* complete this project at least a month before its deadline date.

This year's line of holiday greeting cards--*although the cards are larger and more exquisite*--is less expensive than last year's.

interrupting short independent clause

Ms. Moore is, *I believe,* the only applicant who presently resides out of the state.

We will, *I hope,* be able to supply you with this information by August 1.

e. Participial, infinitive, or prepositional phrases appearing within a sentence may be restrictive (no comma) or nonrestrictive (comma required), depending whether or not they tell *who, what, what kind,* or *which one.* Phrases that answer these questions are restrictive (no comma).

participial restrictive

All employees *planning to attend the picnic* must sign up by July 1. (Tells *which ones.*)

participial nonrestrictive

The entire accounting staff, *planning to attend the picnic,* arranged for car pools. (Additional idea.)

infinitive restrictive

We are planning *to attend the company picnic* on July 1. (Tells *what.*)

infinitive nonrestrictive

The picnic will be held on July 4, *to mention only one company social function.* (Additional idea.)

prepositional restrictive

The announcements *for the company picnic* will be ready June 15. (Tells *which ones.*)

Manufacturers *like us* find themselves in financial difficulty today. (Tells *what kind.*)

Clients *like the Atkinsons* make the real estate business a pleasure. (Tells *what kind.*)

prepositional nonrestrictive

We are planning, *in response to numerous requests,* an annual company picnic. (Additional idea.)

Small appliance manufacturers, *like us,* are in financial difficulty today. (Additional idea.)

1–12. Contrasting, Limiting, and Contingent Expressions

Contrasting, limiting, or contingent expressions are set off with commas. Words often used to introduce contrasting and limiting expressions include *not, never, but, seldom,* and *yet.*

contrasting expression

She had considered selling her stocks, *not her rental property,* to increase her liquid assets.

limiting expression

The association will give us four tickets, *but only for members of our sales staff.*

contingent expression

The sooner we are able to contact our investors in Chicago, *the sooner* we will be able to finance this new project.

The more money you can invest, *the greater the return* you can expect.

1–13. Omitted Words

Commas are often used to indicate the omission of words when the context of the sentence makes the omitted words clearly understood.

Four new secretaries were hired in the Accounting Department; three, in the Policy Issue Department. (Three *new secretaries were hired* in the Policy Issue Department.)

Last week Mr. Higgins dictated three complete reports; this week, two complete reports. (This week *Mr. Higgins dictated* two complete reports.)

Our B-124 contract expired on June 14; the B-127 contract, June 16; and the B-132, June 21. (The B-127 contract *expired on* June 16, and the B-132 *contract expired on* June 21.

1–14. Punctuation for Clarity

a. **Two identical verbs that appear together in a sentence are separated by a comma.**

Whoever *wins, wins* a trip to Hawaii.

Whoever *travels, travels* at his own risk.

Whatever irregularities *occurred, occurred* without the knowledge of the president.

b. **Words repeated for emphasis are separated by a comma.**

Many, many years ago this company was founded by Bernard Harris.

It has been a *long, long* time since one of our vice presidents has visited the East Coast offices.

c. **A word or phrase at the beginning of a sentence that could be read incorrectly with the words that follow is set off by a comma.**

Ever since, she has been employed by the Hirschell Corporation of Boston.

The week before, the corporation expanded its operations to Brazil.

From the beginning, students are expected to proofread their own work accurately.

In our business, letters are written primarily to sell goods and services and to collect money.

d. **A name written in inverted form is separated by a comma between the last name and the first name.**

Irwin, Carl   Luers, Barbara R.

1–15. Short Quotations

a. **A short quoted sentence is set off from the rest of the sentence by a comma. When the quoted sentence is broken into two parts, commas are required before and after the interjected thought.**

beginning quotation

"All employees will receive two days' vacation after the contract is completed," said Mr. Adams.

interrupted quotation

"All employees will receive two days' vacation," said Mr. Adams, *"after the contract is completed."*

ending quotation

Mr. Adams said, *"All employees will receive two days' vacation after the contract is completed."*

b. **Unless a beginning quotation is interrupted, omit any separating commas when the quoted sentence is a question or an exclamation.**

question

"When will the vacation period begin?" asked Ms. Snow.

interrupted question

"When," asked Ms. Snow, *"will the vacation period begin?"*

exclamation

"What a wonderful opportunity you have given our staff!" exclaimed Mr. Stevens.

interrupted exclamation

"What a wonderful opportunity," exclaimed Mr. Stevens, *"you have given our staff!"*

c. **No comma is needed to set off a quotation or part of a quotation that is woven into a complete sentence or one that is not a complete thought.**

woven into sentence

The chairperson operated on the premise that *"A stitch in time saves nine."*

John is reported to have said that *". . . no one will be able to take a vacation until June."*

incomplete sentence

Please mark this package *"Fragile."*

The personnel manager advised me *"to submit my application as soon as possible."*

He merely answered *"yes"* to all the questions.

d. **When a comma and a quotation mark fall at the same point in a sentence, *always* place the comma inside the closing quotation mark. Periods, too, are *always* placed inside the closing quotation mark.**

"Please arrive at the airport by 9 p.m.," requested Mrs. Chambers.

Her last magazine article, *"Western Travel,"* appeared in the Automotive Digest.

John said, *"Be sure to mail your report by June 11."*

e. **For placement of question marks and exclamation marks with closing quotation marks, see Sections 1–44a and 1–44b.**

1–16. Numerals

a. **Numerals of more than three digits require commas.**

1,320	1,293,070
51,890	23,092,946
963,481	

b. **Two independent figures appearing consecutively in a sentence are separated by a comma.**

Two consecutive numbers that act as adjectives modifying the same noun are *not* separated by a comma. Instead, express one number in figures and the other one in word form. Generally express the first number in word form and the second one in figure form. Only if the second number can be expressed in *fewer words* than the first one is it expressed in word form while the first number is written in figures.

independent figures

Of this *$23,000, $12,000* is secured by real property.

During *1990, $876,000* worth of sales were financed through this plan.

By October *1, 43* people had submitted applications.

two numbers modifying a noun, word form-figure form

I will need *thirty 12-inch* rulers for my accounting class.

Each package contains *twelve 2-inch* nails.

Be sure to order *twenty-four 100-watt* bulbs for the lamps in the doctors' waiting rooms.

two numbers modifying a noun, figure form-word form

When you are at the post office, please purchase *100 seventeen-cent* stamps.

The prescription was for *250 ten-milligram tablets.*

When the carton fell, *27 forty-watt* bulbs were broken.

c. Commas are omitted in years, house numbers, zip codes, telephone numbers, decimal fractions, metric measurements, and any word-numeral combinations. In metric measurements use a space to separate groups of numerals in all numbers containing more than four digits.

year

1989 1776 2003

house number

9732 Porter Street 19573 Bestor Boulevard

zip code

Northridge, CA 91324 Bothell, WA 98041-3011

telephone number

(212) 482-9768, Ext. 4412

decimal fraction

.2873

metric measurement

1200 kilometers *(but)* 10 200 kilometers

word-numeral combination

Serial No. 83621 page 1276 Room 1890

d. Volume numbers and page references are separated by commas.

Please refer to Volume XI, page 9.

The article appeared in Volume X, July 1991, page 23.

e. **Measurements (such as weights, capacities, dimensions, etc.) are treated as single elements and are not interrupted by commas.**

weight

Their new baby weighed *8 pounds 7 ounces.*

dimension

He is *5 feet 10 inches* tall.

The room measurements are *20 feet 6 inches* by *18 feet 4 inches.*

time period

Our flight time was estimated to be *2 hours 40 minutes.*

Semicolon

1–17. Independent Clauses Without Coordinating Conjunctions

a. **A semicolon is used between two or more closely related independent clauses (complete thoughts that could stand alone as separate sentences) that are not connected with a coordinating conjunction *(and, but, or, nor).***

two independent clauses

Several orders were delayed in the Milwaukee office last month; Ms. Williams will check into our shipping procedures there.

Plan to attend the next American Management Association meeting; you will certainly find it to be well worth your time.

three independent clauses

Mr. Horowitz drafted the contract specifications last week; Ms. Aames consulted the firm's attorneys on Monday; Mr. Dotson signed and mailed the company's offer on Wednesday.

b. **Short and closely related independent clauses may be separated by commas.**

two short independent clauses

She collated the copies, I stapled and stacked them.

three short independent clauses

The vase teetered, it fell, it shattered.

I came, I saw, I conquered.

1–18. Independent Clauses With Coordinating Conjunctions

a. **Two independent clauses linked by a coordinating conjunction *(and, but, or, nor)* are normally separated with a comma. If either or both clauses**

contain one or more internal commas, however, they should generally be separated by a semicolon.

no comma within clauses

She planned to attend the Chicago meeting, but several important matters interfered with her plans.

commas in one clause

Several large orders were recently placed through the Dayton office; and Ms. Baca, our national sales manager, has commended the sales staff for its diligent efforts in making such rapid progress in a new office.

commas in both clauses

You, of course, need not attend the committee meeting on June 4; but I believe, Mr. Plotkin, you will find reading the minutes of this meeting helpful before you address the Board of Directors.

b. A comma *may* be used before a coordinating conjunction that separates two *short* independent clauses containing internal commas.

Yes, Mr. Dale, we have on hand your current order, but it will be shipped only after your account is brought up-to-date.

We were pleased with the results of the survey, and you will, of course, receive a copy of the summary.

Yes, you may mail in your monthly payment, or you may take it to one of our fast, convenient pay stations.

1–19. Independent Clauses With Transitional Expressions

Two independent clauses (complete thoughts) separated by a transitional expression require a semicolon. A partial list of common transitional expressions follows. In addition, those words and phrases listed in Section 1–2 may be considered transitional expressions when they separate two closely related complete thoughts.

accordingly	indeed	notwithstanding	still
besides	in fact	on the contrary	then
consequently	in other words	on the other hand	therefore
furthermore	likewise	otherwise	thus
hence	moreover	so	yet
however	nevertheless		

A comma is used after a transitional expression of more than one syllable or where a strong pause is needed after a one-syllable expression.

transitional expression with one syllable

The library will have difficulty obtaining a budget increase this year; *thus* members of your staff should not plan to receive all the books specified on this requisition.

transitional expression containing more than one syllable

New catalogs will be shipped to our customers the first week in February; *therefore,* we anticipate a 20 percent sales increase for the months of February, March, and April.

1–20. Series Containing Internal Commas or Complete Thoughts

a. **Items in a series are usually separated by commas. When, however, one or more of the parts contain internal commas, use semicolons to separate the items.**

Representatives from Boston, Massachusetts; Los Angeles, California; and Denver, Colorado, were not present at the conference.

Among those present at the convention were Mr. Harmon Fieldcrest, president of Fieldcrest Steel Industries; Dr. Joyce Morton, research director for the University of Wisconsin; Mr. Garland Hansen, vice president of Wisconsin State Bank; and Ms. Georgia Fillmore, secretary-treasurer of CRA Consultants, Inc.

b. **Three or more independent clauses (complete thoughts) comprising a series are separated by semicolons. Only very short clauses are separated by commas.**

series of independent clauses

Nearly 7,000 circulars were mailed to prospective clients in 1984; over 15,000 circulars were mailed in 1989; and next year we plan to mail over 10,000 new brochures as well as 20,000 circulars.

series of independent clauses with internal commas

Mr. John Harris, our company president, will arrive Saturday; Mrs. Olga Williams, one of our vice presidents, will arrive Monday; and Ms. Carol Watson, our company treasurer, will arrive Tuesday.

series of short independent clauses

The tenant called yesterday, we investigated his complaint immediately, and the roof will be repaired tomorrow.

1–21. Enumerations and Explanations

a. **Certain words and phrases are used to introduce enumerations or explanations that follow an independent clause (complete thought). Some common introductory expressions follow:**

for example (e.g.)	for instance	that is (i.e.)
namely (viz.)	that is to say	

If the enumeration or explanation following the introductory expression *contains commas* or *forms another complete thought,* use a semicolon after the opening independent clause and a comma after the introductory expression.

enumeration containing commas

Many factors have contributed to the sharp increase in production costs during the last three months; namely, *price increases in raw materials, wage increases for electrical workers, and overtime salaries for the entire production staff.*

explanation forming another complete thought

To open its Syracuse office, Caldwell Industries advertised for a number of new employees; that is to say, *not all the staff members were willing to transfer to the new location.*

b. **Some independent clauses followed by expressions that introduce enumerations and explanations require a comma, not a semicolon, after the independent clause. If the enumeration or explanation that follows the introductory expression does *not* contain commas or form another complete thought, use commas after the independent clause and the introductory expression.**

enumeration without internal commas

As a member of our user group, you are eligible to purchase additional computer peripherals through our discount program, for instance, *an automatic control panel or a modem.*

explanation forming an incomplete thought

You may wish to call Ms. Hendrix for further advice, for example, *to inquire which filing system would be more efficient for your office.*

c. **Enumerations or explanations used as parenthetical expressions within a sentence are not set off by semicolons. Use commas when the enumerated or explanatory information has no internal commas; use dashes or parentheses when the information contains internal commas.**

commas

Your accounting procedures, *for example, posting customer deposits,* can be streamlined with our new computer system.

dashes

Because of current economic conditions, we must find new vendors for some of our audiovisual equipment--*e.g., cassette tape recorders, video playback units, and carousel projectors*--to stay within our budget allocations.

parentheses

Your recommendations *(namely, increasing our staff, improving our hiring procedures, and revamping our testing program)* were approved unanimously by the board.

d. **Complete thoughts that introduce enumerations or explanations without an introductory expression are followed by a colon, not a semicolon.**

Several new items were introduced in this popular line: gloves, scarves, and hosiery.

The following people were present at the sales managers' meeting: Roberta Adams, Horace Brubaker, Phillip Haledon, and Susan McCloskey.

Only 82 teachers attended the ARTA state conference: apparently many of our members did not receive their brochures in time to plan for this event.

1–22. Semicolon Placement

Always place the semicolon outside closing quotation marks and parentheses.

quotation marks

Last month Mr. Harrison promised, "I will mail you a check the 1st of next month"; but we have received no money or explanation from him.

parentheses

Several of our staff from the Accounting Department were out ill (with the flu); consequently, the end-of-the-month reports will be a week late in reaching the home office.

Colon

1–23. Formally Enumerated or Listed Items

a. Use a colon after an independent clause (complete thought) that introduces a formal listing or an enumeration of items. Words commonly used in introductory independent clauses include *the following, as follows, these,* and *thus*. Sometimes, however, the introduction is implied rather than stated directly. Use a colon following both direct and implied introductions.

direct introduction

Mrs. Robinson ordered the following furniture and equipment for her offices: three desks, six chairs, two sofas, two electronic typewriters, and one microcomputer.

These rules should be observed for a successful job interview:

1. Dress appropriately.
2. Appear interested in the company and the job.
3. Answer questions courteously.
4. Thank the interviewers for their time.

implied introduction

Several kinds of microcomputers were on display: IBM, DEC, Apple, Commodore, TRS, and Xerox.

In determining whether to use a colon or semicolon for introducing enumerated items, use the colon when the enumeration is not preceded by a transitional introductory expression such as *namely, for example, e.g., that is,* or *i.e.* If an introductory expression immediately precedes the listing, use a semicolon before the expression and a comma after it. (See Section 1–21a for examples.)

b. **The colon is *not* used to introduce listings of items in the following situations: (1) when an intervening sentence separates the introductory sentence and the enumerated items, (2) when the enumerated items are introduced by a *being* verb or a preposition, and (3) when the listing is immediately preceded by an enumerating expression.**

no colon: intervening sentence

The following new silverware patterns will be available January 1. They will be introduced to our dealers next month.

1. Fantasia
2. Sunburst
3. Apollo
4. Moonglow

no colon: listing after "being" verb

The words most commonly misspelled *were* convenience, occasionally, commodity, consequently, and accommodate.

no colon: listing after preposition

Sales meetings are scheduled *for* January 3, February 4, March 7, and April 9.

no colon: listing after enumerating expression

Please order some additional supplies; *namely,* 8½- by 11-inch plain bond paper, legal-sized envelopes, and letter-sized manila file folders.

1–24. Explanatory Sentences

Separate two sentences with a colon when the second sentence explains, illustrates, or supplements the first.

explanation

During the next three months, we will gross approximately 50 percent of our annual sales: major toy purchases occur during September, October, and November.

illustration

Our new advertising campaign will be directed to buyers of economy cars: we will stress efficient gas mileage, low maintenance costs, and reliability.

supplement

Several new customers complained about the delay in receiving their charge account plates: they wished to have them in time to complete their holiday shopping.

1–25. Long Quotations

Long one-sentence quotations and quotations of two or more sentences are introduced by a colon.

Long quotations of two or more sentences (and usually more than three typewritten lines) omit the quotation marks and appear as separate paragraphs. They are indented from the left and right margins and separated from the main text by single blank lines at the beginning and the end of the quotation.

long one-sentence quotation

Ms. Judy Dolan, personnel manager of Higgins Corporation, reported in her annual summary: "Graduates from the University of Southern California's School of Business have been placed in a number of our divisions, and they have risen to middle-management positions within a three-year period."

long quotation of two or more sentences

One item of importance was noted from the board minutes of March 16:

> Two new products, which will revolutionize word processing, will be introduced on July 1. Trade journal publicity and direct mail advertising will be the major vehicles for distributing information about these products. Efforts by the sales staff for August and September will be directed specifically at marketing the Model AB 1781 and the Model AB 2782 communications networks.

As you can see from the board minutes, we will soon be involved. . . .

1–26. Special-Purpose Uses for Colon

a. **In business letters a colon is placed after the salutation when the mixed punctuation format is used (see Section 10–19).**

Dear Bill: Dear Ms. Corrigan: Gentlemen:

b. **Use the colon to separate hours and minutes in expressions of time.**

We will arrive at *8:30 a.m.* on Tuesday, March 24.

At *12:15 p.m.* Ms. Hardesty is scheduled to address the Compton Chamber of Commerce.

c. **In expressing ratios, use the colon to represent the word *to*.**

The label instructions recommend proportions of *4:1*.

The union members voted *2:1* against accepting the new contract.

d. The colon is often used to separate items in literary references.

between place of publication and publisher

Clark, James L., and Lyn R. Clark. *HOW 6: A Handbook for Office Workers.* Boston: PWS-KENT Publishing Company, 1991, 448 pp.

between title and subtitle

William C. Himstreet and Wayne Murlin Baty, *Business Communications: Principles and Methods,* 9th ed. (Boston: PWS-KENT Publishing Company, 1990), p. 237.

biblical citation

As an introduction to his sermon, the minister quoted Psalm *23:1* (Chapter 23, verse 1).

1–27. Colon Format and Use With Other Punctuation Marks

a. In *typewritten* or *word processing-generated* copy, leave two blank spaces after a colon.

May I please have the following documents by next week: copies of the rental agreement, the returned check, and the 30-day notice to move.

b. Place the colon outside closing quotation marks and parentheses.

closing quotation mark

Several staff members have already read her latest article, "Closing the Sale Effectively": they had received advance copies last week.

closing parenthesis

Several contractors were being considered for the new project (Mountain Hills): Wyeth and Sons, Burnside Developers, and Hartman Associates.

c. In vertical listings introduced by a colon, conclude each item in the listing with a period only if the items are complete sentences.

Single-space the items in a vertical listing. If any item in the listing contains more than one line, double-space between the items. If all the items in the listing consist of a single line, you may either leave one blank line between each item or just single-space the listing. Always place one blank line before and after a listing.

In business letters and memorandums, vertical listings may be indented from the left and right margins *or* may assume the margins of the main text.[4] Items in a listing may or may not be numbered. If they are numbered, space twice after the period in the introductory numeral.

[4]See Section 12–9 for guidelines governing the format and preparation of horizontal and vertical listings in reports and manuscripts as well as in business letters and memorandums.

complete sentences, numbered items, standard margins

We have discontinued manufacturing our Model 1040A microwave oven for the following reasons:

1. The popularity of our smaller ovens has decreased continually during the last eighteen months.

2. Manufacturing costs and price differ only slightly from those for our standard-sized ovens.

3. Two other models smaller than our standard-sized ones have been more popular.

incomplete sentences, unnumbered items, indented margins

Effective July 1 new rates will be in force for the following types of policies:

> Jewelry riders on home owners' policies
> Liability coverage for drivers under 25 years of age
> Earthquake riders on all casualty policies
> Term life insurance for males 65 and older

1–28. Capitalization With Colons

a. When a colon is used to introduce a horizontal listing of items, the first letter after the colon is not capitalized unless it begins a proper noun. Capitalize the first letter of each item in a vertical listing.

lowercase letter in horizontal listing

Place the following items in the tray: the original invoice, the duplicate invoice, and the shipping copy.

proper noun capitalized

Four employees were promoted last week: Teresa Caruana, Sue Rigby, Lloyd Bartholome, and Arthur Rubin.

capitalized letters in vertical listing

You may pay for your Empress Vacation Time-Share package in a number of ways:

> Personal check
>
> Credit card--Visa, MasterCard, or American Express
>
> Eighteen monthly installments of $637.50

Do not miss the opportunity to get in on the ground floor of this . . . .

b. Do not capitalize the first letter after a colon when the second sentence explains or supplements the first unless the letter begins a proper noun.

lowercase letter begins second sentence

Your account has been temporarily closed: outstanding bills for $327 still remain unpaid.

proper noun capitalized

The $1,000 award was given to Mary Ellen Guffey: Dr. Guffey's essay was the most original one submitted.

c. **Capitalize the first word after a colon when the colon introduces a formal rule or principle stated as a complete sentence.**

You should be able to apply the following rule in preparing all your business correspondence: Always place commas and periods inside closing quotation marks.

Mr. Wilson emphasized the importance of strict adherence to the following policy: In case of absence all employees must notify their immediate supervisors by 8:30 a.m. that day.

d. **When two or more sentences follow a colon, capitalize the first letter of each sentence.**

Several suggestions emerged from the discussion: To begin with, an engineering firm should be consulted to determine the extent of damage to the property. Then a building contractor should be contacted for estimates to repair the damage. Finally, financial institutions should be surveyed to obtain the best terms for reconstructing the property.

e. **Capitalize the first letter of sentences or phrases introduced by words such as *Note, Attention,* or *For Sale.***

Warning: All cars parked illegally will be towed away at owners' expense.

Caution: Please hold children by hand.

For Rent: Large three-bedroom home with family room, fireplace, air-conditioning, and pool. Phone (617) 555-3542.

f. **Capitalize the first word of quoted material that follows a colon.**

Mr. Rosen informed the board of expansion plans for this year: "Since property has already been purchased on the corner of Tampa and Nordhoff, construction of our new branch office will begin early this spring so that we can open this office in September or October."

Dash

1–29. Parenthetical Elements and Appositives With Internal Commas

a. **Parenthetical elements and appositives are usually set off from the rest of the sentence by commas. When the parenthetical element or appositive contains internal commas, however, substitute dashes (or parentheses) for the separating commas. Use dashes when the parenthetical element requires emphasis.**

In typewritten or word processing-generated material, a dash is formed by typing two hyphens with no space before, between, or after; in printed or desktop publishing-generated material, a dash appears as a solid line.

parenthetical element with internal commas

Last month Ms. Arntson--with the hope of increasing sales, recruiting new employees, and establishing sources of supply--made several trips to the East Coast.

appositive with internal commas

Three state dignitaries--Governor Charles Inacker, Attorney General Marilyn Satterwaite, and Secretary Ralph Spanswick--attended the opening session of the convention.

b. Use a dash to set off a brief summary from the rest of the sentence.

Thanksgiving, Christmas, and New Year's Day--these are the only holidays the store will be closed.

White, black, navy, red, and tan--you have your choice of these five colors.

c. To achieve greater separation, use dashes instead of commas to set off abrupt parenthetical elements or those requiring emphasis. Appositives requiring emphasis may also be separated from the rest of the sentence with dashes instead of commas.

abrupt parenthetical element

Her only concern--notwithstanding her interest in job security--was finding employment in an organization where opportunities for advancement were numerous.

emphatic parenthetical element

Several orders were rerouted to the Milwaukee office--not to the Salt Lake City branch.

emphatic appositive

Additional heavy-duty equipment--bulldozers and graders--was needed to complete the project.

d. For emphasis use a dash in place of a comma or a semicolon to introduce an example or explanation.

example requiring emphasis

Insurance coverage adequate five years ago may no longer fulfill the purpose for which it was designed--for example, if current inflationary trends continue, fire and theft insurance may not cover the replacement costs of the insured properties.

explanation requiring emphasis

Our sales of greeting cards have increased 25 percent since 1989--namely, from $1 million to $1.25 million.

e. Afterthoughts or side thoughts generated from the text, but not necessarily part of it, may be separated from the rest of the sentence by dashes.

side thought

All members of our staff were invited to the conference on simplifying communication procedures--only Ms. Harris was unable to attend the session.

afterthought

Mrs. Wilson had planned to finish the correspondence this afternoon--at least John thought she had planned to do it then.

1–30. Hesitations in Verbal Reports

Use dashes to indicate hesitations, falterings, or stammering in reports of conversations, testimonies, or speeches.

Ms. Morrow: Yes, Mr. President--we expect perhaps a--oh--35 percent increase in sales during the next year.

Mr. Schatz: Well--perhaps a new inventory-control system will solve some of the current problems.

1–31. Source of Quotations

A dash is placed before the source of a quotation when the source is listed after the quotation.

"We can expect a great decrease in our unemployment rate during the next ten months."

--H. J. Scott

"The difference between the right word and the almost right word is the difference between lightning and the lightning bug."

--Mark Twain

1–32. Format and Placement of Dash

a. **Form the dash by typing two hyphens consecutively; leave no space before, between, or after the hyphens. A dash never begins a new line, but it may appear at the end of a line.**

end of line

Our contract negotiations--after reaching an impasse on December 20--
were resumed on January 5.

within line

Several influential community organizations--the Kiwanis Club, the Chamber of Commerce, and the Rotary Club--sponsored Marian C. Crawford for the vacant seat on the board of education.

b. **The only punctuation mark that may precede an opening dash is a period in an abbreviation. Closing dashes may be preceded by a period in an abbreviation, a question mark, or an exclamation mark.**

opening dash after abbreviation

Prices quoted on all Eastern furniture were f.o.b.--freight charges from Pennsylvania to Los Angeles amounted to $834.

closing dash after question mark

A new kind of after-dinner mint--do you know which one I mean?--was introduced by the Sweitzer Candy Company last month.

Period

1–33. End of Sentence

Place a period at the end of a declarative sentence, an imperative statement or command, an indirect question, and a polite request. Polite requests end with a period even though they may appear to have the format of a question. A polite request (1) asks the reader to perform a specific action and (2) is answered by the reader's compliance or noncompliance with the request.

declarative sentence

Several new products were introduced to the stockholders at the April 5 meeting.

imperative statement

Answer the telephone before the third ring.

indirect question

She asked who would be attending the conference scheduled for next week.

1–34. End of Independent Phrase

Independent phrases, those phrases representing implied complete thoughts not directly connected with the following thought, are concluded with a period.

Now, to get to the point. Will you be able to accept responsibility for conducting a sales campaign during June?

Yes, for the most part. Our salespeople have increased their sales since the new incentive program was established.

1–35. Abbreviations and Initials

a. **Abbreviations are usually concluded with periods. However, after abbreviations for business and governmental organizations, associations, radio and television stations, federal agencies, and certain professional designations *(CLU, CPA, CPS, PLS),* the periods are omitted. (See Section 1–39a for spacing following the period.)**

period after abbreviation

Fletcher, Hagan, Ross, and Company, *Inc.,* released several new stock issues.

periods after abbreviations

Mr. Haynes requested that all orders be sent on a *c.o.d.* basis.

Most of these products were manufactured in the *U.S.A.*

no periods with certain abbreviations

I hope the educational project director for *NASA* will be able to address our convention.

Did you purchase additional *IBM* stock?

b. Place a period after an initial. Leave one space between the period and the next word.

Ms. Roberta *D.* Holt accepted the invitation to address the convention participants.

We have tried for several days to contact *A. F.* Elliot.

1–36. Outlines

a. Use periods after letters and numbers in alphanumeric outlines, except those enclosed in parentheses. Leave two blank spaces before beginning the contents of the item.

Use periods after whole numbers in decimal outlines. Leave two blank spaces after the last typed character before beginning the contents of the item.

alphanumeric outline

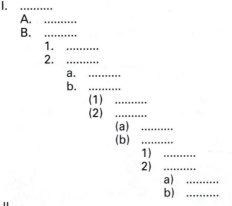

```
I.  ..........
    A.  ..........
    B.  ..........
        1.  ..........
        2.  ..........
            a.  ..........
            b.  ..........
                (1)  ..........
                (2)  ..........
                     (a)  ..........
                     (b)  ..........
                          1)  ..........
                          2)  ..........
                              a)  ..........
                              b)  ..........
II.  ..........
```

decimal outline

1. ....
    1.1 ....
    1.2 ....
        1.21 ....
        1.22 ....
            1.221 ....
            1.222 ....
                1.2221 ....
                1.2222 ....
                    1.22221 ....
                    1.22222 ....
                        1.222221 ....
                        1.222222 ....
2. ....

b. Use periods after complete sentences in outlines and listings. No punctuation mark is placed after an incomplete thought.

periods—complete sentences

A. Two new processes were developed as a result of the experiments.

1. Lamination of fiberglass to wooden surfaces contributes to vessel buoyancy.
2. Sealing of surfaces prevents excessive moisture absorption.

no periods—incomplete sentences

A. New Processes

1. Lamination of fiberglass to wooden surfaces
2. Sealing of surfaces

1–37. Decimals

Periods are used to signify decimals.

The fact that *34.7* percent of the students failed the final examination was hard to believe.

Last year Mr. Phoenix paid $120 for the 2,000 sales announcements; this year he paid *$145.50* for the same kind and number.

1–38. Emphasis and Omission

An ellipsis (a series of three periods with a space before, between, and after the series) is used for emphasis in advertising material or for showing omissions in quoted material. In showing omissions, indicate the completion of a thought with an additional period or other appropriate closing mark of punctuation. (See Section 1–52 for further information on the use of ellipses.)

emphasis

Place your order today . . . for relief from tension headaches . . . for ending miserable aches and pains . . . for a happier, tension-free you.

omission

The president read from the consulting company's report: "Basically, operations should be conducted according to the attached plan. . . . Several new operations personnel should . . . implement the recommended procedures."

1–39. Period Format

a. No space is placed between a decimal point and a number or after a period within an abbreviation. However, within a sentence one space follows an initial or the concluding period in an abbreviation. In typewritten copy or copy prepared on a word processor, allow two spaces after a period at the end of a sentence.

decimal—no space

Since 1988 costs of manufacturing materials have risen *18.5* percent.

period within abbreviation—no space

All prices quoted are *f.o.b.*

initial—one space

John *R.* Gardner was elected chairman of the committee.

abbreviation within sentence—one space

Dr. Sussman has scheduled Mrs. Johnson for surgery at 9 *a.m.* in Encino Hospital.

end of sentence—two spaces

Please begin transcribing your notes after the morning session. I believe the committee wishes to have the minutes by tomorrow morning.

b. Use only one period to end a sentence, even though the sentence may end with an abbreviation.

She is scheduled to arrive between 9 and 10 a.m.

Mr. Kirk's mail is to be forwarded to his Washington, D.C., address: 1938 South Harvard Street, N.W.

c. A period is always placed inside the closing quotation mark.

Ms. Allison promptly replied, "No funding requests will be honored after July 1."

Joseph was pleased with your magazine article, "New Ideas for Home Builders."

d. **A period is placed inside the closing parenthesis when the words in parentheses are a complete sentence. When words in parentheses are not a complete thought and are part of another sentence, place the period outside the closing parenthesis.**

complete sentence in parentheses

Several executives left the company after the merger. (They were disappointed with the leadership of the new company.)

incomplete sentence in parentheses

Only three items were discontinued after the consulting analysts completed their investigation (last March).

Question Mark

1–40. Direct Questions

Conclude a direct question that requires an answer with a question mark.

How many times have you tried to contact Ms. Cates?

Of all the people at the board meeting, how many would you estimate were antagonistic toward the salary proposal?

1–41. Statements With Questions

a. **When a sentence contains a statement followed by a direct question, conclude the sentence with a question mark. Separate the statement from the question with a comma, dash, or colon, depending upon the nature of the statement.**

question mark with comma

I would recommend that we contact at least three other vendors before selecting a permanent source of supply, wouldn't you agree?

question mark with dash

They were satisfied with the report--weren't they?

question mark with colon

Each of us should consider the following question: what can we do to improve the profit picture for next year?

b. **Conclude a statement that contains a short, direct question with a question mark.**

You have filed your income tax return, have you not, for the last taxable year?

Mr. Bradley called--or was the call from Mrs. Bradley--to request additional information about your bid?

c. **A statement that is meant as a question is concluded with a question mark.**

You still expect to leave for Cleveland tomorrow morning?

The conference has been delayed until April?

d. **A period, rather than a question mark, is placed after an indirect question.**

Mr. Joyner asked when we expected our Albany office to release the information.

Ms. Schmidt inquired about the possibility of her placing several students in our Accounting Department as trainees in a cooperative work-experience program.

Most of the telephone calls have been inquiries asking where we have moved our store.

e. **Polite requests phrased as questions are followed by periods rather than question marks because they are considered to be commands. A polite request (1) asks the reader to perform a specific action and (2) is answered by having the reader either take or ignore the action requested instead of responding with a "yes" or "no." Both components *must* be present for a period to be used; otherwise, a question mark is correct.**

polite request requiring period

Will you please send us three copies of your latest financial report.

May I please have this information by the end of the month.

Won't you take a few minutes now to fill in the enclosed questionnaire and return it in the self-addressed envelope.

May we count on your support with a "yes" vote on Proposition 11.

direct question requiring question mark

Would you be willing to address envelopes for the Senator's reelection campaign? (Requires "yes" or "no" answer.)

May we call on you next week for a demonstration? (Requires "yes" or "no" answer.)

Wouldn't you like to be the proud owner of a new Supra 28 personal computer? (Does not require reader to return a "yes" or "no" answer, but no *specific* action is requested.)

May we have your support in the future? (Does not require reader to return a "yes" or "no" answer, but no *specific* action is requested.)

May I compliment you on your outstanding performance in meeting this year's sales quota? (No "yes" or "no" answer required; however, no *specific* action is requested.)

1–42. Expressions of Doubt

Doubt in expressing statements of fact may be signified by enclosing a question mark in parentheses.

His last visit to the South was in 1988(?).

She earns $2,400(?) a month.

1–43. Series of Questions

When a sentence contains a series of questions, place a question mark at the end of each question. Only the first letter of the sentence is capitalized unless a question in the series begins with a proper noun or is a complete thought. Leave one space after a question mark that appears within a sentence; leave two spaces after the concluding question mark.

series of incomplete questions

What are the primary responsibilities of the president? the executive vice president? the treasurer?

Who requested copies of the report--the judge? the insurance company? the plaintiff's attorney?

series of proper noun questions

Will the new flight routes stop in San Diego? Los Angeles? San Francisco?

series of independent questions

Several important issues were discussed at the conference last week: What style trends will be popular during the next decade? What comfort demands will the public make on furniture manufacturers? How much will price influence consumer furniture purchases?

1–44. Question Mark Placement and Format

a. Question marks may be placed either inside or outside the closing quotation mark or parenthesis.

When a complete question is contained within the quotation or parenthetical remark, place the question mark inside the closing quotation mark or parenthesis. If the entire sentence, not just the quotation or parenthetical remark, comprises the question, place the question mark outside the closing quotation mark or parenthesis.

Use only one concluding mark at the end of a sentence.

complete question contained in parentheses

We received official notification last week *(did your notice arrive yet?)* that we must vacate our offices by the 1st of the month.

The committee informed me that J. Wilson Edwards has been appointed manager of the Phoenix office. *(Did you approve this appointment?)*

complete question contained in quotation marks

"Will the entire original cast be present for the opening night in Philadelphia?" asked a local reporter.

The Governor then inquired, *"Who is in charge of this committee?"*

question encompasses entire sentence whole sentence is a question

Will you be able to ship this order by May 15 (earlier if possible)?

Have you finished reading the article "Hidden Magic"?

b. **If an entire sentence and a quotation within the sentence are both questions, use only the first question mark—the one appearing inside the closing quotation mark.**

Did the president ask, "When will the directors hold their next meeting?"

c. **In typewritten and word processing-generated copy, leave one space after a question mark that appears within a sentence and two spaces after a question mark that appears at the end of a sentence.**

one space

Shall I place these supplies on the desk? in the cabinet? in the storeroom?

two spaces

What time shall we leave for the airport? When is your flight scheduled to depart? What time do you expect to arrive in Atlanta? May I please have answers to these questions by this afternoon.

Exclamation Mark

1–45. Use of Exclamation Mark

To express a high degree of emotion, use an exclamation mark after a word, phrase, clause, or sentence.

word

What! You mean the materials will not arrive until next week?

phrase

How beautiful! The designer certainly used a great deal of color and imagination in creating this pattern.

clause

If he comes! He'd better come, or Mr. Ramirez will get a new assistant.

sentence

So, she finally answered my question!

1–46. Exclamation Mark Placement and Format

a. **In typewritten and word processing-generated copy, leave two spaces after the exclamation mark before beginning the next word.**

b. **The exclamation mark should be used sparingly in business correspondence, and one exclamation mark directly following another should be avoided. Instead, use commas, periods, or question marks to complete an exclamatory thought.**

exclamation with comma

Oh, I don't see how we can possibly meet the contract deadline without working overtime!

exclamation with period

No! Mr. Jones has not resigned.

exclamation with question mark

What! You expected the completed analysis last week?

c. **Exclamation marks may be placed before or after the closing quotation mark or parenthesis.**

When a complete exclamatory remark is a quotation or is enclosed in parentheses, place the exclamation mark inside the closing quotation mark or parenthesis. If the entire sentence, not just the quotation or parenthetical element, comprises the exclamatory expression, place the exclamation mark outside the closing quotation mark or parenthesis.

Use only one concluding mark at the end of a sentence.

complete exclamatory expression in quotation marks

At the time of the emergency, one of the employees shouted, *"Break down the door!"*

complete exclamatory expression in parentheses

He obtained the help of several advisors *(what a mistake that was!)* to assist him in selecting the project subcontractors.

Management was shocked at the employees' reactions to the new process. *(Only 4 percent of the staff welcomed the new procedures!)*

exclamatory expression encompasses entire sentence

If you wish to take advantage of these bargains, you will have to act now (today)!

I cannot believe Marie Huffinger's statement, "Only 3 percent of the merchandise was returned"!

Quotation Marks

1–47. Direct Quotations

Direct quotations contain the exact wording used by a writer or speaker. Place one-sentence quotations and short two-sentence quotations within quotation marks.

Use commas to introduce most one-sentence quotations. Long one-sentence quotations and quotations of two or more sentences are introduced by a colon.

Quotation marks are not used for indirect quotations that do not use the exact wording of the reference.

direct quotation

"The economy cannot help slowing down by next year," said Dr. Roger Watson, a renowned economist.

"Although this stock has split three times since 1971," explained Ms. Mooneyhan, "you cannot anticipate that it will continue to do so."

One of the reporters shouted, "Look out! The building is collapsing."

Mr. Goldman explained in his February 8 memo: "Because my wife became ill Monday morning and was hospitalized that afternoon, I was unable to attend the meeting. Please send me a copy of the minutes."

indirect quotation

Kriss Powell, our production manager, said that our manufacturing costs per unit will increase at least 30 percent within the next year.

1–48. Long Quotations

Long quotations of two or more sentences (and usually more than three typewritten lines) are written without the quotation marks and appear as separate paragraphs. They are indented from the left and right margins and separated from the main text by single blank lines at the beginning and the end of the quotation.

The speaker brought out the importance of management communication when she made the following statement:

> To exercise the function of leadership, there must be effective communication. If a leader cannot communicate, there is no leader because information cannot pass between the two groups. For instance, in management one cannot delegate duties and authority without effective communication.

Effective communication remains paramount to effective leadership. . . .

1–49. Short Expressions

a. **When short expressions—such as words used in humor, technical words used in a nontechnical way, or slang words—need to be emphasized or clarified for the reader, they are placed in quotation marks. These same words are often shown in italics when they appear in print.**

slang words

My secretary was certainly "on the ball" when she discovered the error in the contract.

technical words used in nontechnical way

Mr. Rollins announced that "all systems are go" for the new golf course and condominium project in Scottsdale.

b. **Place in quotation marks the definitions of words or expressions. Underscore the word or expression defined.**

defined word

According to some economists, a recession is actually a "little depression."

defined expression

The French term faux pas means "a social blunder."

c. **References to words marked or stamped are placed in quotation marks.**

Be sure to mark all packages "Glass--Handle With Care."

The envelope was stamped "Addressee Unknown, Return to Sender."

1–50. Literary Titles

Titles of various kinds of literary or artistic works such as magazine or newspaper articles, chapters of books, movies, television shows, plays, operas, concerts, poems, lectures, songs, and themes are placed within quotation marks. Names of books, magazines, pamphlets, and newspapers, however, are underscored or typed in all capital letters.

chapter and book title

The chapter "Principles of Office Organization" contained in Office Management and Automation was helpful in implementing our office reorganization.

movie title

Disney's "Cinderella" has been a favorite of children for many years.

lecture title

Her last lecture, "Combating Inflationary Trends," was very well attended.

song title

Although late, we arrived at the musical just in time to hear "With a Little Bit of Luck."

1–51. Quotations Within Quotations

Use single quotation marks to signify a quotation within a quotation. Single quotation marks are formed by using the apostrophe key.

The report stated, "According to the U.S. Chamber of Commerce, 'The problem of air and water pollution must be solved within the next decade if our cities are to survive.' "

1–52. Ellipses

An ellipsis (a series of three periods with a space before, between, and after the series) is used to show an intentional omission of quoted material:

(1) If the omission begins the quoted sentence, use an ellipsis to begin the quotation.

(2) If the omission occurs within a sentence, use an ellipsis to substitute for the omitted words.

(3) If the omission occurs at the end of a sentence, use an ellipsis and then add the closing punctuation mark for the sentence.

(4) If one or more sentences have been omitted after the quoted sentence or sentences, first conclude the last sentence with the appropriate punctuation mark and then follow with an ellipsis to show the omission.

omission at beginning of quotation

The instructions stated, " . . . and turn knob in clockwise direction." (Remember to leave one space between the opening quotation mark and the first period in the ellipsis.)

omission within sentence

The new sign was worded to discourage nonresidents from parking in the private lot: "Violators will be towed . . . cars will be released only upon payment of a $50 fine."

end-of-sentence omission

The guarantee reads: "All repairs that are not covered under the warranty will be made at a 25 percent discount of regular cost . . . ."

One of the directors inquired, "How many miles is the home office from our various branch offices; i.e., Houston, Dallas, Oklahoma City, Atlanta, . . . ?"

one or more sentences omitted

The directive specifically stated: "Please ship our foreign orders by September 1. . . . Our European distributors must have their merchandise by October 1." (Double-space after the final period in the ellipsis before beginning the next sentence.)

The marketing manager wrote in her August 1 memo, "Will you be able to attend the conference in Baltimore? . . . We will need to set up our display booths on September 9." (Double-space after the final period in the ellipsis before beginning the next sentence.)

1–53. Capitalization With Quotation Marks

a. **Capitalize the first word of a complete sentence enclosed in quotation marks.**

"Please call me before 10 a.m. tomorrow," requested Mrs. Edwards.

Andrew replied, "Yes, I will be able to attend the conference on July 28."

b. Capitalize incomplete thoughts enclosed in quotation marks only if the quoted words themselves are capitalized. Quoted expressions preceded by "stamped" or "marked" are usually capitalized.

capitalized

His check was returned from the bank marked "Insufficient Funds."

"Handle With Care" was stamped on the package.

Did you mark the invoice "Paid in Full"?

not capitalized

Mrs. Atkins asked us to spend "as little time as possible" on this project.

1–54. Quotation Mark Placement

a. Periods and commas are always placed inside the closing quotation mark; semicolons and colons, outside the closing quotation mark.

period

The purchase requisition stipulates, "Cancel this order if the merchandise cannot be delivered by the 1st of the month."

comma

"Our operating costs must be lowered," said Mr. Collins.

semicolon

The consultant's report stated emphatically, "A thorough analysis of the company's data and information processing system should be undertaken"; however, no steps have been taken to initiate such an analysis.

colon

Mrs. Cox recommended the following vacation policy "unless a better one can be found": (1) Employees should select their vacation time on the basis of seniority and (2) conflicts should be resolved by the employees themselves, whenever possible.

b. When a complete question or exclamation is contained within the quotation, place the question mark or exclamation mark inside the closing quotation mark. If the entire sentence comprises the question or exclamation, then place the appropriate mark outside the closing quotation mark. If both the quotation and the entire sentence are questions, use only the first question mark.

complete question within quotation

He asked, "Where are the annual reports filed?"

entire sentence comprises question

Do you have a copy of her latest article, "Air Pollution Control"?

complete exclamation within quotation

"Do not," exclaimed Mr. Rey, "leave the lights burning all night again!"

entire sentence comprises exclamation

Our new sales manager is a real "go-getter"!

question within a question

Did Mr. Heinze inquire, "What time will our flight depart?"

Apostrophe

1–55. Possessives

a. When a noun, singular or plural, does not end with a pronounced *s,* add an apostrophe and *s ('s)* to form the possessive case.

singular noun

Yes, I found the request on my *assistant's* desk.

Lisa's father owns the company.

plural noun

Women's fashions are much more colorful this year.

This garment is made from 100 percent *sheep's* wool.

b. When a noun, singular or plural, ends with a pronounced *s,* generally add an apostrophe *(')* to form the possessive case. However, an apostrophe and *s ('s)* may be added to singular nouns ending in a pronounced *s* if an additional *s* sound is also pronounced.

singular noun—add ' only

Mrs. Simons' attendance record has been perfect during the last five years.

Most of these museum pieces were found among *Athens'* ruins.

plural noun—add ' only

Customers' accounts must be reviewed every 90 days.

The Simonses' home was burglarized earlier this week.

singular noun with additional "s" sound—add 's

We have been invited to our *boss's* home for dinner on April 15.

The *class's* scores are unusually low this session.

Ask *Mr. Jones's* secretary for a copy of the report.

Were you present in court during the *witness's* testimony?

c. **Possessives are generally formed on nouns that represent people or animals (animate objects) or nouns relating to time, distance, value, or celestial bodies. For other types of nouns (inanimate objects), show possession by an *of* phrase.**

animate possessive

The *employees'* picnic is scheduled for next Saturday.

Our *company's* declining profits eventually caused bankruptcy.

time possessive

This *year's* profit and loss statement showed a gain of nearly 12 percent.

Enclosed is a check for three *months'* rent.

value possessive

She ordered several thousand *dollars'* worth of continuous-form paper.

You owe me 50 *cents'* change.

celestial possessive

During the summer months the *sun's* rays can be extremely harmful if one is not careful.

Is *Mars'* atmosphere suitable for human survival?

distance possessive

He came within a *hair's* breadth of hitting the parked car.

The thief rushed by within an *arm's* length.

inanimate possessive

The *terms of the loan* were extended another six months.

Who broke the *base of the pot?*

d. **Form the possessive of compound nouns by having the last word show possession.**

She was designated her *father-in-law's* beneficiary.

Our next Christmas party will be held at the *chairman of the board's* home.

My two *sisters-in-law's* business is doing well.

e. **When two or more nouns have joint possession, only the last noun shows possession. When the nouns represent individual ownership, however, each noun must show possession.**

joint possession

Bill and Sheryl's new assistant has worked at ABCO Corporation for three years. (Bill and Sheryl share the same assistant—joint possession.)

The Harrises and the Bradys' new boat was damaged in the storm. (The Harrises and the Bradys own the same boat—joint possession.)

1

individual possession

Mary's and Henry's new secretaries had worked in the clerical pool for over a year. (Mary and Henry have different secretaries—individual possession.)

The Schaeffers' and the Gonzalezes' houses are on the same street. (The Schaeffers and the Gonzalezes live in different houses—individual possession.)

f. **The possessive of indefinite pronouns such as *anyone, everyone, someone, anybody, everybody, somebody,* and *nobody* is formed by using the same rules that apply to possessive nouns.**

It is *anyone's* guess when we will be able to resume production.

Somebody's car is blocking the entrance to the parking lot.

g. **The possessive forms of personal or relative pronouns (such as *its, theirs, whose,* or *yours*) do not include apostrophes. These pronouns are often confused with verb contractions, all of which contain apostrophes.**

possessive pronoun

I met Ralph, *whose* father has a large account with our organization.

Although the company had *its* greatest sales volume last year, it still failed to show a profit.

contraction

I met Sara, *who's (who is)* going to apply for a job with our firm.

It's (It is) one of our best-selling products.

h. **Possessives of abbreviations are formed by using the same rules that apply to possessive nouns.**

abbreviation not ending with "s"

The *CPA's* report was comprehensive.

NASA's new space project is scheduled for a 1993 launching.

abbreviation ending with "s"

Barker Bros.' annual sale will be held next week.

All *R.N.s'* badges are to be turned in at the end of each shift.

You may wish to follow the *IRS's* advice in this instance. (Use *'s* instead of *'* because of the extra pronounced syllable.)

i. **Use the possessive case of a noun or a pronoun before a gerund (an *-ing* verb used as a noun).**

noun

Don's accounting of the convention expenses was incomplete.

pronoun

We would appreciate *your* returning the enclosed form by March 31.

j. **When a possessive noun is followed by an explanatory expression (an appositive), use an apostrophe only in the explanatory expression. When this form of writing sounds awkward, as it does in most cases, show possession by using an *of* phrase.**

apostrophe

Ms. Madden, our *production manager's,* office is being remodeled.

"of" phrase

The office *of our production manager,* Ms. Madden, is being remodeled.

k. **Many organizations with plural possessives in their names have omitted the apostrophe; organizations with singular possessives have tended to retain the apostrophe. The precise format used by the organization itself should be followed.**

plural possessive

We have just been granted a loan from the *Farmers* Bank and Trust Company.

singular possessive

The contract was issued to *Linton's* Manufacturing Company.

l. **Sometimes the possessed item is not explicitly stated in a sentence, but it is understood or clearly implied. In such cases the ownership word still uses an apostrophe to show possession.**

This year the holiday party will be at *Sandy's.*

Be sure to meet me at the *doctor's* by 2 p.m.

The wallet found in the corridor was *Mr. Lopez's.*

Deliver this floral arrangement to the *Briggses'.*

This month's sales are considerably higher than last *month's.*

1–56. Additional Uses of the Apostrophe

a. **Use the apostrophe to form contractions.**

single-word contraction

acknowledged *ack'd*

two-word contraction

is not *isn't*

b. **The apostrophe is used for clarity to form the plural of all isolated lowercase letters and the single capital letters *A, I, M,* and *U.***

plural of lowercase letter

Be sure to dot your *i's* and cross your *t's.*

How many times have I reminded you to watch your *p's* and *q's?*

plural of capital letters "A," "I," "M," and "U"

Mr. Craig's daughter received three *A's* on her report card.

Avoid using too many *I's* in the business letters you write.

Parentheses

1–57. Nonessential Expressions

Parentheses are used to set off and subordinate nonessential expressions that would otherwise confuse the reader because (1) they give supplementary information that has no direct bearing on the main idea or (2) they call for an abrupt change in thought. References and directions are examples of expressions that are often enclosed in parentheses.

abrupt change in thought

I wrote to Mr. Furstman *(I tried to call him, but there was no answer)* and asked him to contact us before October 4.

reference

All major repairs over $3,000 must first be cleared through proper channels. *(See Bulletin 8 dated March 2.)*

directions

Please reproduce 100 copies of this form by tomorrow. *(Center the material and use yellow paper.)*

1–58. Numerals

Numerals in legal, business, and professional documents are often shown in parentheses to confirm a spelled-out figure.

All work is guaranteed for ninety *(90) days.*

Compensation for services rendered will not exceed three thousand dollars *($3,000).*

The committee cannot consider any bid over nine thousand nine hundred ninety-nine dollars *($9,999).*

On March 4 our client received a check for two thousand eight hundred forty-three dollars and seventy-five cents *($2,843.75).*

1–59. Enumerated Items

Enclose in parentheses numbers or letters when they are used to enumerate lists of items within a sentence.

See Section 1–36a for the use of parentheses with alphanumeric outlines.

numbers

I need the following information for the current year: *(1)* the number of people hired, *(2)* the number of people retired, and *(3)* the number of people terminated.

letters

Please send us the following information: *(a)* current salary trends, *(b)* unemployment statistics, and *(c)* placement requests.

1–60. Parentheses Use With Other Punctuation Marks

a. **Words, phrases, and clauses enclosed in parentheses in the middle of a sentence function as part of the sentence in applying rules of punctuation and capitalization.**

word

We will fly to Fort Lauderdale *(Florida)* for our annual convention.

phrase

Ms. Haven will gross nearly $800,000 *(as compared to a $500,000 average)* in sales this year.

clause

Our new manager *(several members of our staff met him last week)* will conduct a communications seminar in the spring.

b. **When an incomplete thought enclosed in parentheses ends a sentence that requires a period, place the period outside the closing parenthesis.**

According to our latest reports, this procedure violates state laws (Minnesota and Wyoming).

Several members of the committee will meet in Kansas City this weekend (if possible).

c. **When a complete thought enclosed in parentheses ends a sentence that requires a period, the two elements are treated separately. Place a period at the end of both thoughts, with the final period appearing inside the closing parenthesis.**

Yes, your order is on its way. (I mentioned this fact to your assistant yesterday.)

Several members of our staff attended the ATLW conference this year. (This year's conference was held in Hawaii.)

d. **If a word, phrase, or clause shown in parentheses requires a question mark or exclamation mark, use such a mark of punctuation only if the sentence ends with a different mark.**

parenthetical question

Our new manager (do you know Marsha Karl?) will arrive in Los Angeles tomorrow.

Were you informed that our new price list (has your copy arrived yet) will go into effect on October 1?

parenthetical exclamation

Have you heard about the enormous price increases (I can scarcely believe them!) in single-family dwellings?

Living conditions (you can scarcely call them that) are absolutely deplorable in this section of the city!

e. **Place commas, semicolons, and colons outside the closing parenthesis.**

comma

If you plan to attend the company party (on May 16), please send your reservations to Terry Thomsen by Monday, May 12.

semicolon

His report dealt with the importance of our country's major transportation systems (railroads, inland waterways, motor trucks, pipe lines, air transportation, and parcel post); therefore, little emphasis was given to rising transportation costs.

colon

On February 15 Ms. Satterlee will introduce two new product lines (for women's fashion departments): the Sportswoman Series and the Sun and Surf Coordinates.

Brackets

1–61. Use of Brackets

a. **Brackets are generally used to insert remarks or set off editorial corrections in material written by someone else. In addition, use brackets to enclose the term *sic* (meaning *thus* or *so*) to show that an error in quoted material appeared in the original document.**

In his report Mr. Gilmer stated: "With new equipment to speed up the production process *[he did not specify what new equipment was needed]*, substantial savings can be mad *[sic]* in both material and labor costs."

b. Brackets may be used within parentheses to indicate even another subordinate idea.

The auction of Rita Rothchild's possessions (including jewelry, furs, furniture, movie costumes *[from 1940 through 1970],* china, silverware, and other memorabilia) is scheduled for July 17 and 18.

1–62. Use With Other Punctuation Marks

The placement of other punctuation marks with brackets follows the same principles outlined for parentheses in Section 1–60.

Asterisk

1–63. Use of Asterisk

Asterisks may be used to call the reader's attention to footnotes in a document when the footnotes appear infrequently and occur at widely spaced intervals; otherwise, superior arabic numbers are used. The asterisk generally follows other punctuation marks, except when it is used with a dash or with a complete thought enclosed in parentheses.

after most punctuation marks

A recent government report states, "Air traffic is expected to double within the next decade."*

before dash or closing parenthesis

We are studying the works of Ray Bradbury*--one of today's leading science fiction writers.

Good results have been obtained by companies that have hired outside consultants to develop cost-cutting procedures. (Several articles attesting to this fact have recently appeared in leading professional journals.*)

Diagonal

1–64. Use of Diagonal

Use a diagonal (also called a "solidus," "slash," or "virgule") between (1) letters in some abbreviations, (2) numerals in fractions, and (3) the expression *and/or* to indicate the terms are interchangeable. No space is left before or after the diagonal.

abbreviation

Please address the envelope as follows: Mrs. Maureen Smith, *c/o* Mr. George Martin, Display Manager, Wilson Disc Company, 1141 Western Avenue, Los Angeles, California 90024.

fraction

Costs have increased *1/2* percent since last week.

and/or

Authorizations for future purchases may be obtained from Ms. Jorgensen *and/or* Mr. Kline.

Underscore

1–65. Use of the Underscore

The underscore is used to emphasize such items as headings; words that would normally be italicized in print; and titles of books, magazines, newspapers, or pamphlets. Continuous lines, with no spacing between words, are used for underscoring. Except for periods with abbreviations, punctuation marks immediately following underscored material are not underscored.

word italicized in print

He always misspells the word convenience.

magazine title

According to an article in Business Week, most movies are currently being filmed outside the United States.

abbreviation

Be sure to place a.m. in lowercase letters.

punctuation mark following standard underscored material

Did the bookstore order sufficient copies of Webster's Ninth New Collegiate Dictionary?

Ampersand

1–66. Use of the Ampersand

The ampersand (&), a symbol that represents the word *and,* is used primarily to express the official name of some business organizations.

ampersand in company name

Johnson & Johnson was the subcontractor for the project.

use of "and" in company name

All merger talks with Merritt *and* Sons have been delayed until the end of our fiscal period.

CHAPTER 2

Hyphenating and Dividing Words

Hyphenating and Dividing Words Solution Finder

Hyphenating and Dividing Words Solution Finder (continued)

Hyphenating Words

2

2–1. Compound Nouns and Verbs

Often two or more words act as single thought units. Nouns and verbs in this category may be written as separate words, written as single words, or hyphenated. Consult an up-to-date dictionary to determine the exact form of compound nouns and verbs.[1]

separate words, nouns

sales tax	notary public	editor in chief
charge account	life insurance	word processing
air conditioner	work force	high school

single words, nouns

bookcase	checkbook	lawsuit	heavyweight
airline	salesperson	paycheck	newlywed

hyphenated words, nouns

life-style	brother-in-law	attorney-at-law	trade-off
by-product	light-year	hole-in-the-wall	stand-in

single words, verbs

to upgrade	to keyboard	to downgrade	to landscape
to videotape	to download	to handpick	to mastermind

hyphenated words, verbs

to tape-record	to air-condition	to triple-space	to free-lance
to ill-treat	to jury-rig	to double-check	to piece-dye

2–2. Compound Adjectives

When two or more words appearing together act as a unit to describe a noun or pronoun, these words form a single-thought modifier and function as a compound adjective. In many cases these compound adjectives are hyphenated; in other cases they are not. Use the following guidelines to determine whether or not a compound adjective should be hyphenated.

a. A number of compound adjectives are listed and shown hyphenated in the dictionary. These adjectives may be considered *permanent* compounds. They are hyphenated whenever they are used as adjectives in a

---

[1]All spellings and hyphenations used in this manual are based upon *Webster's Ninth New Collegiate Dictionary* (Springfield, Mass.: Merriam-Webster Inc., 1989).

sentence, no matter where they appear in the sentence—before or after the nouns or pronouns they modify.

permanent compound before noun or pronoun

up-to-date	*up-to-date* reports
well-known	*well-known* reporters
part-time	*part-time* employment
snow-white	*snow-white* clouds
smooth-tongued	*smooth-tongued* salesperson
small-scale	*small-scale* operation
hands-off	*hands-off* policy
machine-readable	*machine-readable* text
no-fault	*no-fault* insurance
public-spirited	*public-spirited* citizens

permanent compound following noun or pronoun

None of these files are *up-to-date.*
If your job is *part-time,* please fill out the enclosed form.
These clothing brands are *well-known* throughout the country.
Almost all mailing addresses on envelopes from major corporations are *machine-readable.*
You cannot deny that this community is *public-spirited.*

b. Sometimes compound nouns are used as single-thought adjectives to describe other nouns or pronouns. When these combinations are shown as *open compounds* (not hyphenated) in the dictionary, they are not hyphenated when they are used as compound adjectives.

compound noun	*compound noun used as compound adjective*
word processing	*word processing* center
dot matrix	*dot matrix* printer
life insurance	*life insurance* policy
money market	*money market* account
data base	*data base* management
early bird	*early bird* special
finance company	*finance company* records
charge account	*charge account* customer
high school	*high school* teacher
data processing	*data processing* equipment
income tax	*income tax* return
department store	*department store* personnel
mobile home	*mobile home* sales
real estate	*real estate* commission

c. Many single-thought word groups that function as compound adjectives are not shown in the dictionary. Such word groups are known as *temporary compounds.* These temporary compounds are hyphenated when

they appear *before* the nouns or pronouns they describe. They are not hyphenated, however, when they appear after the words they modify.

2

temporary compound before noun or pronoun

Capture that *never-to-be-forgotten* moment with pictures by Mardell!

The Holtzes are interested in purchasing a *four-bedroom* home.

The Walters' *7-pound-12-ounce* son was born yesterday at 5 a.m.

We did not believe the Senator's opponent would resort to such *low-level* tactics.

All *city-owned* property is exempt from these state taxes.

A *well-established* legal firm has been retained to represent our interests.

All vehicles are expected to abide by the *55-mile-an-hour* speed limit on this freeway.

The mayor's *not-too-cordial* attitude toward the press was evident.

temporary compound following noun or pronoun

Your wedding should be a day that is *never to be forgotten.*

The Holtzes' new home has *four bedrooms.*

The Walters' baby weighed *7 pounds 12 ounces* at birth.

Who would believe that our opponent's tactics could be so *low level!*

None of the properties on this block are *city owned.*

This firm has been *well established* in the Chicago area for nearly thirty years.

The speed limit on this highway is *55 miles an hour.*

Mr. Simms' greetings this morning were certainly *not too cordial.*

d. When *two separate* proper nouns or *two separate* common nouns are combined to form single-thought adjectives before other nouns or pronouns, these compounds are hyphenated.

separate proper nouns used as an adjective

This morning's issue of the newspaper carried several articles on *Sino-American* relations.

Your *Chicago-New York* flight has been delayed until tomorrow.

separate common nouns used as an adjective

This morning's scheduled training session will deal with *union-management* relations.

Most of the classes offered by our institute maintain a 15 to 1 *student-teacher* ratio.

e. The components of a *single* proper noun are not hyphenated when they are used as an adjective.

We have been negotiating with a *Far Eastern* firm for the last three months.

How many *University of Nebraska* alumni have you been able to locate in Salt Lake City?

f. Adverbs ending in *ly* that are combined with adjectives to form a single modifier are not hyphenated.

I understand that your suggestion was the most *hotly debated* issue discussed at the conference.

Dr. Stevens is an *exceptionally gifted* nuclear physicist.

g. Two separate colors stated in a compound modifier are hyphenated. Other adjectives, however, used in conjunction with colors are not hyphenated unless the combination is a permanent compound shown in the dictionary.

two separate colors

This *blue-green* fabric was selected for upholstering the sofas in the hotel lobby.

The artist used *red-orange* hues effectively in portraying the Hawaiian sunset.

adjective combined with color

The *bluish green* water magnified the size of the iridescent, colorful fish.

The *bright red* flag can easily be seen from a distance.

Ask all our sales representatives to wear *dark gray* suits to the exhibition.

The *emerald green* cover of your new book stands out quite visibly.

Place these artists' prints against a *snow-white* background to accentuate their deep color contrasts. (The adjective *snow-white* is shown hyphenated in the dictionary.)

h. When a series of hyphenated adjectives has a common ending, use suspending hyphens.

Have these announcements printed on *8½- by 11-inch* bond paper.

Please order a supply of *1/16- and 1/8-inch* drills.

Most of the awards were given to *tenth- and eleventh-grade* students.

All construction bids for this hillside are based on *one-, two-, and three-level* family dwellings.

i. Dollar amounts in the millions and billions, percentages, and nouns used with numerals or letters are *not* hyphenated when they function as compound adjectives.

dollar amounts in the millions and billions

How will the President deal with the projected *$1 billion* decline in the Gross National Product?

Nearly *2.5 million* people in the United States use our soap.

percentages

You will receive a *10 percent* discount on all orders placed before October 1.

There will be a ½ percent increase in our state sales tax effective July 1.

nouns used with numerals or letters

Will our new employee be rated in as a *Grade 1* word processor?

How many *Vitamin C* tablets are in each container?

Please ship these *Model 85A* wall units by October 1.

j. **Simple fractions are hyphenated *only* when they are used as compound adjectives.[2]**

compound adjective

John sold his *one-third* ownership in the company for $575,000.

Amendments to our bylaws require a *two-thirds* majority approval by our voting membership.

simple fraction as noun

Only *one third* of the stockholders responded to the questionnaire.

The Board of Directors voted to reinvest *one half* of this year's profits in additional research and development projects.

2–3. Prefixes

a. **Words beginning with *ex* (meaning "former") and *self* are hyphenated, and those beginning with *pre, re*[3], and *non* are generally not hyphenated. Words beginning with *co* and *vice* may or may not be hyphenated. Use your dictionary to check the hyphenation of words with these two beginnings.**

"ex" and "self"

The *ex-baseball* hero is now in the real estate business.

Our *ex-chairman* still has all the committee records in his files.

She is very *self-confident* about her work.

Employee *self-satisfaction* contributes to morale and productivity.

---

[2]*Webster's Ninth New Collegiate Dictionary* (Springfield, Mass.: Merriam-Webster Inc., 1989), page 810.

[3]The words *re-collect* meaning to collect again, *re-cover* meaning "to cover anew," *re-create* meaning "to create again," *re-lease* meaning to lease again, *re-present* meaning to present again, *re-press* meaning to press again, *re-sign* meaning to sign again, *re-sort* meaning to sort again, and *re-tread* meaning to tread again are exceptions to this rule. Note that without the hyphens these words would have completely different meanings.

"pre," "re," and "non"

All disposable diapers are *prefolded.*

Where will the *preemployment* interviews be held?

Please *recheck* all the total columns carefully.

Please have the wheels on the truck *realigned.*

Tuition *reimbursements* will not be made to *nonaccredited* educational institutions.

Please initiate legal proceedings against Phillips Bros. for *nonpayment* of its account.

"co"

co-edition
co-owner
co-occurrence

coauthor
codefendant
copilot

"vice"

vice-chancellor
vice-consul
vice-chairman

vice admiral
vice president

b. **When a prefix is added to a proper noun, place a hyphen between the prefix and the proper noun.**

We found that many firms operating in the South today date back to *pre-Civil War* times.

If you cannot promise a *mid-September* delivery date, cancel the order.

To some people a 4th of July without fireworks would be *un-American.*

2–4. Numbers

a. **Compound numbers from *21* to *99* are hyphenated when they appear in word form.**

Ninety-six of our agents responded to the questionnaire, but we are still awaiting replies from *twenty-four* more.

b. **In numbers over *100*, components other than compound numbers are not hyphenated.**

The lessee shall pay a sum of *Two Thousand Eight Hundred Seventy-five Dollars and Twenty-four Cents* ($2,875.24) to the lessor.

c. **Simple fractions are expressed in word form. These fractions are hyphenated *only* when they function as compound adjectives.**

simple fraction used as noun

Nearly *two thirds* of our employees voted to ratify the new contract.

Can you believe that over *three fourths* of the computers purchased in our industry last year were microcomputers?

2

simple fraction used as compound adjective

Our company wishes to purchase a *one-fourth* interest in the new shopping mall planned for the Pinehurst area.

A *two-thirds* majority vote is needed to pass this proposition, which will appear on the November ballot.

d. When a number-noun combination functions as a *single unit* (a compound adjective) to describe another noun, separate the words in the compound adjective with a hyphen. Only in percentages, dollar amounts in the millions and billions, and capitalized noun-number combinations are the hyphens omitted.

hyphen—number-noun compound adjective

We have a *three-year* lease on this building.

Our freeways have a *55-mile-an-hour* speed limit.

She was charged a *25-cent* toll for using the speedway.

He just started a *$1,500-a-month* job.

The Joneses' *7-pound-8-ounce* baby girl was born on December 25.

no hyphen—percentage

We have had a *25 percent* sales increase during the past year.

no hyphen—dollar amount in the millions

Ridgewood, Inc., announced a *$3 million* profit for the year.

no hyphen—capitalized noun-number combination

Your Evansdale *Model 380* curio cabinet should arrive in our store within the next three weeks.

e. The hyphen may be used to replace the terms *to* or *through* between two numerals.

Your vacation will be July *3-18* this year.

Refer to pages *70-75* for further instructions.

End-of-Line Word and Word-Group Divisions

Where possible, avoid dividing words at the end of a typewritten or computer-printed line because complete words are easier to read, easier to understand, and neater in appearance. Sometimes, however, word divisions at the end of a line are necessary because to avoid them would result in awkward line lengths and unbalanced paragraph constructions.

Particular rules need to be observed to divide words and certain word groups correctly at the end of a line. Some of these rules should be adhered to strictly; others are flexible in their application. The following sections address (1) words and word groups *never* to be divided, (2) word

divisions to be avoided, if possible, and (3) rules and guidelines for proper end-of-line word and word-group divisions.

2

2–5. Words and Word Groups Never to Be Divided

Some words and certain word groups may not be divided under any circumstances:

a. **Do not divide one-syllable or one-syllable "ed" words.**

one-syllable words

straight   threats   thought   through   bread

one-syllable "ed" words

changed   weighed   planned   striped   shipped

b. **Do not set off a single-letter syllable at either the beginning or the end of a word.**

beginning of a word

a warded   e nough   i dentify   o mitted   u niform

end of a word

radi o   bacteri a   health y   photocop y

c. **Do not set off a two-letter syllable at the end of a word.**

present ed   compa ny   month ly
build er   week ly   debt or

d. **Unless a hyphen already appears within an abbreviation, do not divide capitalized abbreviations. Hyphenated abbreviations may be divided after the hyphen. Do not divide abbreviations of academic degrees.**

not divided

UNESCO   U.S.A.   UCLA   Ph.D.

may be divided

AFL-CIO   KMET-TV   NBEA-WBEA

e. **Do not divide a day of the month from the month, *a.m.* or *p.m.* from clock time, percentages from the word *percent*, page numbers from the word *page*, or other such closely related word-and-number groups.**

month from day

November 25   August 30   January 5

"a.m." or "p.m." from clock time

10 a.m.   2:45 p.m.   12 midnight   12 noon

percentage from the word "percent"

1 percent 43 percent 20 percent 100 percent

page number from page reference

page 23 page 241 page 1073

other word-and-number combinations

7 ounces Room 341 Model 4A No. 437892

f. **Do not divide contractions or numerals.**

contractions

wouldn't doesn't haven't shouldn't isn't

numerals

$15,487 1,240,500 3 billion 4,500 $2.5 million

g. **Do not divide the last word of more than two consecutive lines.**

h. **Do not divide the *last word in a paragraph* or *the last word on a page.***

2–6. Words to Avoid Dividing, If Possible

Although adherence to the following rules is desirable, situations may occur where end-of-the-line word divisions are unavoidable. Observe these rules—unless doing so would result in an extremely ragged right margin.

a. **Avoid dividing words containing six or fewer letters.**

forget person better number ratio

b. **Avoid dividing a word after a two-letter prefix.**

en large im portant un necessary de pendent

c. **Avoid dividing proper nouns.**

Boulevard Washington Fernando
Corporation Lieutenant Mississippi

d. **Avoid dividing a word at the end of the first line of a paragraph.**

e. **Avoid dividing a word at the end of the last full line of a paragraph.**

2–7. Rules and Guidelines for Dividing Words

Divide words *only* between syllables. Use an up-to-date dictionary or a word division manual to locate the correct syllabication of words to be divided. All word divisions shown in this reference manual are based on the syllabication shown in *Webster's Ninth New Collegiate Dictionary,* the 1989 printing, published by Merriam-Webster Inc.

Words containing several syllables often require forethought to determine the appropriate place to separate the word. Use the following guidelines to determine where to divide a word:

a. **Divide hyphenated and single-word compounds at their natural breaks.**

hyphenated compound

vice-/chancellor   self-/esteem   Governor-/elect   stepping-/stone

single-word compound

common/place   hand/made   break/down   sales/person

b. **Where possible, divide words after a prefix or before a suffix.**

prefix

anti/body   mis/fortune   dis/crepancy   sub/stantiate

suffix

evasive/ness   inspira/tion   oversell/ing   unemploy/ment

c. **Divide words between double letters *except* when the root word itself ends with the double letters and is followed by a suffix.**

divided between double letters

accom/modate   bul/letin   suc/cess   oscil/late   neces/sarily

divided after double letters

business/like   fulfill/ment   helpless/ness   install/ing

d. **Divide words between two vowels pronounced separately.**

continu/ation   gradu/ation   extenu/ating   insinu/ation

e. **Divide words *after,* not before, a single vowel pronounced as a syllable except when the vowel is part of a suffix.**

single vowel

congrat u/lations   assim i/late   ben e/ficial   clar i/fication

suffix vowel

accept/able   collaps/ible   forc/ible   collect/ible   allow/able

2–8. Guidelines for Dividing Word Groups

Certain word groups may be divided only in specific places. Use the following guidelines to separate dates, names of individuals, addresses, numbered items, and copy containing dashes.

a. **Divide dates between the day and the year, but *not* between the month and the day.**

January 7,/ 1991 *not* January/ 7, 1991

April 15,/ 1992 *not* April/ 15, 1992

b. **Full names of individuals appearing with titles are ideally divided directly before the last name. However, names preceded by long titles *may be* separated between the title and the first name.**

divided before last name

Mr. William / Harrison

Dr. Robert P. / Rosenberg

divided before first name

Lieutenant / Harvey Petrowski

Professor / Alice H. Duffy

c. **Street addresses may be broken between the street name and the street designation (*Street, Avenue, Boulevard, Lane,* etc.). If the street name contains more than one word, the address may also be broken between words in the street name.**

single-word street name

1138 Monogram / Avenue	849 North 73 / Street
218 East Hawes / Street	3624 59th / Place

street name containing more than one word

6800 Coldwater / Canyon Avenue

17325 San Fernando / Mission Boulevard

d. **Geographical locations in addresses should be divided only between the city and state, not between the state and zip code.**

Dubuque, / Iowa 52001 Poughkeepsie, / New York 12601

e. **Divide a numbered or lettered horizontal listing directly before the number or letter, but not directly after.**

An affirmative action officer gave these reasons: (1) fewer openings in the profession, (2) enrollment declines in the student population, and (3) an increase in the mandatory retirement age for teachers.

f. **A sentence with a dash may be broken after the dash, but not directly before it.**

The board will surely agree that your new policies are excellent--
a step in the right direction.

When our peak sales subside at the end of this year--in early December--
we plan to take a Caribbean cruise.

CHAPTER 3

Capitalization

Capitalization Solution Finder

Capitalization Solution Finder (continued)

General Format

3–1. Beginning Words

a. Capitalize the beginning words of sentences, quoted sentences, independent phrases, lines of poetry, and items in an outline.

3

sentence

All employees are requested to work overtime until the inventory has been completed.

quoted sentence

The guarantee states, "*Defective* parts will be replaced free of charge."

independent phrase

Now, to the important point.

poetry

By the rude bridge that arched the flood,
Their flag to the April's breeze unfurled,
Here once the embattled farmers stood,
And fired the shot heard round the world.
--Emerson

outline

1. *Specific* instructions
   a. *Type* of correspondence
   b. *Number* of copies
   c. *Special* mailing notations

b. The initial letter of an incomplete quoted thought is not capitalized unless the first word (1) is a proper noun, (2) is preceded by identification words such as *marked* or *stamped,* or (3) is capitalized because of another rule of capitalization.

lowercase

Mr. Reyes was directed to "*t*ake care of this situation immediately."

proper noun

Mr. Stone's curt answer was "*G*eorge's car."

preceded by identification words "marked" or "stamped"

This package should be stamped "*P*riority Mail."

Your check was returned by the bank marked "*I*nsufficient Funds."

rule of capitalization

My favorite song in the production is "*M*y Boy Bill."

c. **In standard salutations used for correspondence, capitalize the first word and any nouns contained in the salutation. For salutations directed to undetermined individuals, capitalize the first word and all *main* words that follow. Capitalize only the first word of a complimentary close.**

standard salutation—first word and all nouns

Dear Mr. Jones: *Gentlemen:* *My* dear *Friend:*

Dear fellow *American:* *Ladies* and *Gentlemen:*

salutation to undetermined individual—first word and all main words

To Whom It May Concern: *To Stockholders* of *Record* on *May* 9, 1991:

complimentary close

Sincerely yours, *Cordially* yours, *Yours* very truly,

d. **Capitalize the first word after a colon when the following material (1) presents a formal rule, (2) consists of two or more sentences, (3) begins a vertical listing, (4) begins with a proper noun, or (5) requires emphasis. In other cases do not capitalize the first word following a colon.**

formal rule following colon

Please use the following procedure in preparing all our office correspondence: *Format* all letters in the modified-block letter style with blocked paragraphs and mixed punctuation.

two or more sentences following colon

Here are two important questions to consider: *Will* enlarging our facilities at this time be economically feasible? *Is* the current market able to assimilate any increased production?

vertical listing following colon

Please send us copies of the following items:

1. *Lease* agreement with Property Management Associates
2. *Statement* of rental income for 1991
3. *List* of projected expenses for 1992

proper noun following colon

Three colleges are involved in the project: *DeKalb* Community College, MiraCosta College, and the City College of New York.

item of special emphasis following colon

Note: *Several* of our employees were listening to the World Series during working hours.

Wanted: *Student* to work weekends and holidays.

first word not capitalized

We need to order the following garden supplies: *lawn* seed, liquid fertilizer, and insect spray.

Our production schedule is experiencing a two months' delay: *the* warehouse fire set us back considerably.

e. Unless the word is a proper noun, the first word of a complete thought contained in parentheses *within a sentence* is not capitalized. A complete thought contained in parentheses that appears immediately after a sentence is treated as a separate unit, and the first word is capitalized.

first word not capitalized within sentence

Several minor changes (*these* were recommended by Mr. Lloyd) will be made in the final draft.

proper noun capitalized within sentence

Your recommendations (*Ms.* Williams approved all of them) will be incorporated into the marketing survey.

first word capitalized at end of sentence

A group of marketing students wishes to tour our main plant in Atlanta, Georgia. (*The* students will arrange for their own transportation.)

3–2. Proper Nouns and Adjectives

a. Proper nouns (words that name a particular person, place, or thing) and adjectives derived from proper nouns are capitalized. Capitalize the names of persons, cities, states, countries, rivers, mountains, streets, parks, colleges, buildings, shopping centers, malls, developments, organizations, ships, airplanes, specific events, etc.

proper noun

We have opened a new branch office in *Austin, Texas.*

I will meet you at the top of the *Empire State Building.*

The *Orange County Fair* will be held in *Petit Park* this year.

When will the *Brownsville Shopping Mall* be ready for occupancy?

We flew to *Florida* on a *Boeing 747* to meet our cruise ship, the *Song of Norway.*

Next month *John* and *Lisa* will take a raft down the *Colorado River.*

How much is the toll for the *Golden Gate Bridge,* which crosses *San Francisco Bay?*

adjective derived from a proper noun

Football and baseball are typical *American* sports.

Be sure to order *Roquefort* dressing and *Swiss* cheese for the salad bar.

The *Socratic* method is often used in debates.

Your decorator selected *Vandyke* brown carpeting for the executive offices.

How much *Canadian* money do you have in your wallet?

The use of the *Heimlich* maneuver has saved many people from choking.

According to a recent *Gallup* poll, the President's foreign policy is looked upon favorably by more than 60 percent of those Americans eligible to vote.

Our store, The Furniture Guild, always carries an extensive inventory of *Victorian* furniture.

b. **When well-known descriptive terms, such as nicknames, are used in place of proper nouns, they are capitalized.**

My territory includes sales districts west of the *Rockies.* (Rocky Mountains)

Most of his business trips have been to the *Windy City.* (Chicago)

Old Hickory was particularly popular with the frontiersmen. (Andrew Jackson)

Several of our colleagues from the *Big Apple* will attend the convention. (New York City)

c. **Sometimes proper nouns, such as widely used commercial products, acquire common noun meanings through popular usage.[1] As a result, they are not capitalized. Always capitalize, however, specific brand or trade names of products. Any words that describe the type or kind of product (such as *refrigerator, vacuum cleaner, video cassette recorder*) are not capitalized unless they represent a coined derivative that is considered part of the trade name.**

common noun meaning

Be sure that each address on this mailing list has a *zip code.*

Yes, *india* ink was included in the order.

Our restaurant serves *french* fries with all sandwiches.

Copies of the *braille* alphabet may be obtained from the Foundation for the Junior Blind.

This statue is made from plaster of *paris.*

How many *china* patterns does Regency carry in its line?

The old-fashioned *venetian* blinds in your office should be replaced with a more attractive window covering.

Did the *thermos* break when it fell off the shelf?

---

[1]Check an up-to-date dictionary to determine which proper nouns have acquired common noun meanings and are no longer capitalized. The examples shown here are based on entries from *Webster's Ninth New Collegiate Dictionary* (Springfield, Mass.: Merriam-Webster Inc., 1989).

3

brand or trade name with common noun product

Did you order a *Sony portable television set?*

Our new *Frigidaire freezer* was delivered today.

Please deliver this *Macintosh computer* to Dr. Ianizzi's home.

The *Xerox copier* in our office enables us to copy forms on colored paper.

Does your drugstore chain carry *Kleenex tissues* exclusively?

product name part of trade name

Your *Amana Radarange* will give you many years of service.

Next week we will install a *Griffin Mail-O-Meter* in our office.

The *IBM Personal Computers* in our office have been replaced by IBM Personal System 2 computers.

Almost every day Mr. Rosen orders a *Filet-O-Fish* and *Chicken McNuggets* for lunch from McDonald's.

3–3. Abbreviations

Most abbreviations are capitalized only if the words they represent are capitalized. Exceptions to this rule are the abbreviations of academic degrees and certain coined business expressions. Refer to Section 5–10 for the proper format for commonly used abbreviations.

lowercase words represented by lowercase abbreviations

Please send 5 *doz.* hammers *c.o.d.* (*dozen* and *collect on delivery*)

You may contact me any time after 5:30 *p.m. (post meridiem)*

capitalized words represented by capitalized abbreviations

She sat for the *CPS* examination last May. *(Certified Professional Secretary)*

Mrs. Johnson was awarded a bachelor of arts degree from *UCLA* in 1986. *(University of California, Los Angeles)*

exceptions

Our university offers *B.S.* and *M.S.* degrees in psychology through the College of Letters, Arts, and Sciences. (*bachelor of science* and *master of science*)

On this application form please include any other names by which you may be known and precede them with the initials *AKA. (also known as)*

3–4. Numbered or Lettered Items

Nouns followed by numerals or letters are capitalized except in the case of page, paragraph, line, size, and verse references. The word *number* is abbreviated except when it appears at the beginning of a sentence.

capitalized nouns

A reservation is being held for you on *Flight 487* to Chattanooga.

Please check *Invoice B3721* to verify that all items have been shipped.

Did you receive our order for your *Model 23D* china case?

The meeting is scheduled to be held in *Room 132* of the Business Building.

3

lowercase nouns

Refer to *page 3, paragraph 2,* of the contract for the schedule of project completion.

We are sold out of *size 10* in our Style 483 blazer.

the word "number" abbreviated within a sentence

Have you had an opportunity to restock our supply of *No. 10* white envelopes?

I believe that my policy, *No. 68341,* covers this kind of injury.

the word "number" written out at beginning of sentence

Number 145-MD has been out of stock for over three months.

Titles

3–5. People

a. **Capitalize the courtesy titles *Mr., Ms., Mrs., Miss, Master,* and *Dr.* when they precede and are used in conjunction with persons' names.**

Capitalize also a title representing a person's profession, company position, military rank, service rank, or political office when it precedes and is used directly with a person's name in place of a courtesy title.

A title representing family relationship is capitalized when it appears before the name of an individual and is used directly with the name.

courtesy title

Please send copies of this report to *Mr.* Donald Curry and *Dr.* Scot Ober.

Both *Ms.* Bielich and *Mrs.* Scher-Padilla have agreed to serve on the selection committee for this position.

Please inform *Master* Todd Jaffarian that he has been selected as one of the finalists in the "eight-year-old" category of our children's contest.

professional title

The meeting will be conducted by *Professor* Wanda Stitt.

title indicating company position

Although *President* Newton attended the stockholders' meeting, he asked *Vice President* Eleanor Chu from our Minneapolis branch to present the earnings report for this year.

political title

We are looking forward to meeting *Mayor* Don Busche next Friday.

Please ask *Senator* Rhodes to authorize payment of this invoice.

military or service rank title

All medical problems should be referred to *Major* Kenneth Zimmer.

These kinds of police matters are under *Captain* Murillo's jurisdiction.

title showing family relationship

When *Aunt* Elizabeth's house is sold, her attorney will set up the trust fund.

These U.S. Savings Bonds were given to the children by *Grandpa* Fairbanks.

b. When a title follows a person's name, it is not capitalized except in cases pertaining to high-ranking government officials (President of the United States, Vice President of the United States, Cabinet members, members of Congress, and governors).

regular title

Carl Irwin, *comptroller* of A & I Enterprises, wrote the report.

You may wish to subpoena Janet Horne, *president* of AMCO Products, to appear in court on May 11.

title of high-ranking government official

Robert Haller, *Senator* from Georgia, received an award for outstanding service.

Tonight at 8 p.m., EST, George Bush, *President* of the United States, will appear on national television.

c. A person's title is not capitalized when it is followed by an appositive.

I went to see the *executive vice president,* F. Ross Byrd.

She consulted with her *doctor,* Linda Montgomery, about the accident.

d. When a person's title is used in place of his name, it is generally not capitalized. However, in cases of direct address and in references to high-ranking government officials (President of the United States, Vice President of the United States, Cabinet members, members of Congress, and governors), capitalize the title if it replaces the name.

Do not capitalize common nouns such as sir, ladies, or gentlemen used in direct address or the titles of high-ranking government officials used in plural form.

regular title

The *auditor* indicated that our books were in order.

After the meeting the *president* directed his *executive assistant* to inform all the department managers that the *director of marketing* had resigned.

direct address

Did I pass the test, *Professor?*

Yes, *Doctor,* we have your reservation for May 8.

I believe, *ladies and gentlemen,* that all our sales personnel will meet their quotas this year. (Common nouns.)

title of high-ranking government official

I was pleased to be able to meet the *Secretary of State* last week.

Please invite the *Governor* to attend the conference.

Only three *governors* responded to our invitation. (Plural form.)

e. **A person's title is always capitalized in business correspondence when it appears in the inside address, signature line, or envelope address.**

Mrs. Delieu Scopesi, *Personnel Director*

Dr. Donald Phelps, *Chancellor*

f. **When the title of an executive officer is used in that organization's minutes, bylaws, or rules, it is capitalized.**

The *Treasurer's* report was read and approved.

The *President* will be responsible for the negotiation of all labor contracts.

g. **Descriptive terms such as *ex, elect, late,* and *former* are not capitalized when they are combined with a title.**

"ex"

Since *ex*-President D. J. Morgan was appointed chairman of the board, our company has prospered.

"elect"

Councilman-*elect* Norman Rittgers will be sworn in on January 2.

"late"

The *late* President Eisenhower was an avid golfer.

"former"

A copy of the report was sent to *former* President Reagan.

3–6. Literary or Artistic Works

a. **Capitalize the principal words in titles and subtitles of publications and other literary or artistic works such as movies, plays, songs, poems, and**

lectures. Articles *(a, an, the)*, conjunctions *(and, but, or, nor)*, and prepositions with three or fewer letters (*for, of, in, out, on, to, up,* etc.) are not capitalized unless they appear as the first or last words of the title or subtitle.

The titles of books, magazines, pamphlets, and newspapers are underscored or typed in all capital letters. Titles of other literary or artistic works are placed in quotation marks.

3

book

I learned a great deal from the book The Art of Readable Writing.

DuPont, the Autobiography of American Enterprise will be available in June.

The best-seller UP AND BEYOND OUR GALAXY has sold over 1 million copies.

book with subtitle

The students are using Sociology: An Introduction as their basic textbook.

This information is on page 81 of HOW 6: A Handbook for Office Workers, Sixth Edition.

magazine

We have ordered the Journal of Abnormal and Social Psychology for our reference library.

play

Andre Conway's new production, "Who Is Molly Burns?" will open on Broadway next week.

movie

"Snow White and the Seven Dwarfs" is scheduled for screening in neighborhood theaters next month.

b. **Capitalize the main words and place in quotation marks the titles of subsections contained in books, magazines, pamphlets, or newspapers. Also capitalize the main words and place in quotation marks the titles of typewritten or computer-generated reports.**

chapter of book

Please review carefully the chapter "Supervision of Office Personnel" in our book entitled The Electronic Office: Organization and Management.

magazine article

Did you read "Word Processing Shortcuts" in the latest issue of The Executive Secretary's Journal?

newspaper column

"Jim Elwood Reports" in yesterday's Vista Daily Journal covered extensively the city council's feud with the mayor.

typewritten or computer-generated report

Here is your copy of "Research Personnel Available."

All our staff is presently working on "An Analysis of Advertising Costs in Relationship to Sales Increases," a report that is scheduled for presentation to the Board of Directors on June 2.

3–7. Academic Subjects, Courses, and Degrees

a. The names of numbered courses and the specific titles of courses are capitalized, but the names of academic subject areas are not unless the subject area name contains a proper noun.

names of numbered courses

How many students are enrolled in *Computer Science 43?*

To fulfill your degree requirements, you must complete the following courses: *Psychology 182, Anthropology 1,* and *Music 30.*

specific course title

You are scheduled to teach two sections of *Survey of Business Law* next semester.

Last year Tina took *Speech 125, Introduction to Public Debate.*

subject area

Please encourage Ms. Harris to take an *accounting* class this spring.

Our college offers over 20 different *history* classes.

subject area containing proper noun

I earned an "A" in my *business English* class.

Perhaps you should take a course in *conversational French* before you leave for Paris.

b. References to academic degrees are generally not capitalized unless they are used after and in conjunction with the name of an individual.

general reference

Bill Clark will be awarded a *bachelor of science* degree this June.

after person's name

Joyce Mooneyhan, *Doctor of Divinity,* will deliver the opening address.

c. **Capitalize abbreviations of academic degrees appearing after a person's name. Remember, though, that the *h* in *Ph.D.* appears in lowercase form.**

James Bennett, *D.D.S.,* is an excellent dental surgeon.

We have asked Louise Peebles, *D.B.A.,* to be our speaker.

Make your check payable to Lawrence W. Erickson, *M.D.*

Marcia McKenzie, *Ph.D.,* will join our clinic in June as a staff psychologist.

Groups, Places, Dates

3–8. Organizations

a. **Principal words in the names of all organizations—business, civic, educational, governmental, labor, military, philanthropic, political, professional, religious, and social—are capitalized.**

Boston Chamber of Commerce
Los Angeles Board of Education
Arizona Department of Motor Vehicles
Tactical Air Command
American Cancer Society
Illinois Bar Association
Young Republican Club
National Council of Churches
Porter Valley Country Club
Stanford Research Institute
Foundation for the Junior Blind
United States Department of Defense

b. **When the word *the* precedes an organizational name and is officially part of the name, it must be capitalized.**

We received two letters from *The* Prudential Insurance Company.

c. **When the common noun element of an organization's name is used in place of the full name, it is generally not capitalized. In formal documents and in specific references to national government bodies, however, capitalize the shortened form.**

general communication

All employees of the *company* are allowed ten days' sick leave each year.

The *board of education* convened for a special meeting yesterday to consider the budget crisis.

Two members from our local *chamber* received Presidential appointments.

So far only two members of the *city council* have agreed to support our rapid transit proposal.

formal communication

As agent for the *Association,* I am authorized to sign the convention contracts.

On July 15, 1991, the *Company* acquired several additional holdings.

national government bodies

The bill is now before the *House.* (United States House of Representatives)

Three *Cabinet* members were interviewed by the press. (President's Cabinet)

When will *Congress* reconvene? (United States Congress)

Who is presently majority leader of the *Senate?* (United States Senate)

This issue is now before the *Supreme Court.* (United States Supreme Court)

d. **Governmental terms such as *federal, government, nation,* and *constitution* are often used in place of their respective full names. Because they are used so often and are considered terms of general classification, they are not capitalized.**

"federal"

Veterans Day is a holiday for all *federal* employees.

"government"

The *government* is concerned about inflation and its effect on the economy.

Loans such as these are fully guaranteed by the *federal government.*

"nation"

The *nation* has been able to overcome a number of crises.

"constitution"

Interpretation of the *constitution* is the Supreme Court's responsibility.

e. **The official name of a division or department within a business organization is capitalized. When a division or department is referred to by its function because the official or specific name is unknown, do not capitalize this reference.**

Always capitalize a division or department name used in a return address, an inside address, a signature block, or an envelope address.

official or specific name

Please notify the *Personnel Department* when you are going to be absent from work.

This contract must be signed by two members of the *Board of Directors.*

A check for this amount must first be approved by the manager of our *Accounting Department.*

We will send a copy of our official findings to your *Department of Research and Development.*

Will you be able to send a member from your *Information Processing Department* to the conference?

official or specific name unknown

The efficiency of your *accounting department* can be increased by using our computer system.

A member of your *advertising department* may wish to contact one of our account executives to take advantage of this rare opportunity.

return address, inside address, signature block, or envelope address

Mr. Gary Packler, Manager, Credit Department

f. Capitalize the names of departments, bureaus, divisions, offices, and agencies in governmental organizations.

We will forward this information to the *Department of Health and Human Services* within the next week.

Have you contacted the *Bureau of Indian Affairs* about this matter?

You may obtain copies of the proposed freeway route from the *Division of Highways.*

This case is under investigation by the *Office of Internal Affairs.*

To work for the *Federal Bureau of Investigation,* you must first receive a security clearance.

g. Capitalize the names of specific departments, divisions, and offices within educational institutions. The names of schools or colleges within universities are also capitalized.

educational departments, divisions, or offices

Each year the *Music Department* of Banning High School sponsors a spring music festival.

Does Professor Joyce Arntson teach in the *Social Science Division?*

All such budget requests must be submitted to the *Office of Educational Services* by June 30.

Please submit your application for admission to the *Admissions Office* by March 1.

university schools or colleges

I am presently taking courses in the *School of Business and Economics* at Kentview State University.

The major in which you are interested is offered in the *College of Letters, Arts, and Sciences.*

3–9. Geographical Locations

a. The names of places—for example, specific continents, countries, islands, states, cities, streets, mountains, valleys, parks, oceans, lakes, rivers, canals, bays, and harbors—are capitalized. When a geographical term (such as *city, bay,* or *island*) appears directly after a place name, it is considered part of the name and is capitalized.

A geographical term appearing before the name of a place is generally not capitalized. Capitalize the term only if (1) it is part of the official name or (2) it is used by the governing bodies of that place as part of an official name.

Do not capitalize geographical terms appearing in plural form.

specific places

Our products are distributed throughout *North America.*

Does any airline have a direct flight from *Kansas City* to *New York City?*

Customers in the *Hawaiian Islands* will soon be serviced by their own branch office in *Honolulu.*

The magazine article dealt mainly with camping facilities on the *Colorado River.*

We have a number of tours that take foreign visitors to *Yellowstone National Park.*

Many of our shipments are brought here through the *Panama Canal.*

Property taxes in *Ventura County* have risen steadily during the past five years.

geographical term appearing before specific place—not capitalized

Most of our business is conducted within the *state* of Utah.

Will your tour include the *city* of London?

The *city* of Los Angeles was selected as the site for our next convention.

The estimated 1989 population for the *county* of Ventura is 653,609.

geographical term appearing before specific place—capitalized

Most of our suppliers are located in the *City of Industry.* (geographical term part of city name)

The *City of Los Angeles* has approved a new budget plan. (geographical term used by governing bodies as part of official name)

Did the *State of California* adopt a new automobile insurance plan for low-risk drivers? (geographical term used by governing bodies as part of official name)

geographical term in plural form

The excursion will include trips on both the Mississippi and Missouri *rivers.*

Most of our discoveries have been in the San Bernardino and San Gorgonio *mountains.*

The new shopping mall is located on the corner of 59th and State *streets.*

b. Capitalize nicknames of geographical locations and names of regional areas that have evolved as a result of usage.

geographical nickname

All our pineapples come directly from the *Aloha State.* (Hawaii)

When were the Olympics held in the *City of the Angels?* (Los Angeles)

How many times each year must you go to the *Big Apple?* (New York City)

This year our convention will be held in the *Windy City.* (Chicago)

regional names emerging from usage

Many of our clients are from *Upper New York State.*

Police reports indicate that the *Lower East Side* has the highest crime rate in our city.

Merchants from the *Greater Los Angeles Area* have banded together to support this worthwhile project.

Many residents in the *Bay Area* are concerned about the pollution occurring in San Francisco Bay.

c. Points of the compass are capitalized when they are used as simple or compound nouns to designate *specific regions*. Points of the compass are not capitalized, however, when they are used to indicate *direction* or *general localities*.

specific regions

Firms connected with the aerospace industry are heavily concentrated in the *West* and *Southwest.*

Our company has increased its trade to the *Far East.*

The festival was held in *East Los Angeles.*

The sales of our *Southern Region* have increased 25 percent during the past year.

Within the next month we will expand our operations into *East Texas.*

direction

My territory includes all states *east* of the Mississippi River.

The study recommended that our new plant be located just *northwest* of Baltimore.

To avoid the harsh winter weather, many retirees move *south* or *west* during the snow season.

By taking the *eastbound* on-ramp, you will get to the center of Madison.

general localities

The *southern* part of our state is suffering a severe drought.

Our delivery service is restricted to the *east* side of Miami.

Customers from the *northwest* section of the city have registered more complaints than customers from any other sector.

Did you survey most of the *western* states?

This new weather stripping is guaranteed to protect you against the severity of *northern* winters.

d. Words derived from simple or compound nouns representing *specific* regions are capitalized.

Many of my friends tell me that I am a typical *Midwesterner.*

Southern Californians are known for their casual life-style.

This survey includes responses only from *Easterners.*

Your city is known for its *Southern* hospitality.

3–10. Dates, Time Periods, and Events

Capitalize days of the week, months of the year, holidays (including religious days), specific special events, and historical events or periods.

The names of seasons, decades, and centuries are generally not capitalized. If, however, a season is combined with a year, capitalize the season.

month and day of week

Our committee will meet the first *Monday* in *March, June, September,* and *December.*

holiday

Will our store be closed on *New Year's Day* this year?

Each year *Veterans Day* is observed on a different date.

specific special event

Our company will celebrate its *Silver Anniversary* next year.

During April many employers and their secretaries observe *National Secretaries' Week.*

This year the *Maricopa County Fair* will be held from September 4 through September 27.

How many of your staff members will be attending the *NBEA Convention* this year?

historical event or period

The *Apollo 10 Moon Landing* was the most dramatic event of this century.

The stock market crash of 1929 brought the *Roaring Twenties* to a dismal end and catapulted our country into the *Great Depression.*

During the *Industrial Revolution* children were often forced to work long hours under intolerable conditions.

season

Our biggest sales item during this *spring* season has been the Model 550 patio set.

None of the *winter* coats we ordered have arrived yet.

If you wish to enroll for the *fall* semester, please submit your application by August 15.

We have received your application for admission for the *Winter 1992* quarter.

decade

During the last year a number of movies portraying life in the *sixties* have been released.

This company was founded in the early *fifties* by Jonathan Hunt.

century

Technological developments during the *twentieth century* have advanced the human race further than all other developments during our previous history.

Many of Mr. Ryan's critics believe that he operates his business on *nineteenth-century* principles.

3–11. Ethnic and Religious References

a. Ethnic-related terms (references to a particular language, race, or culture) are capitalized. Generic terms such as *black, white,* and *brown* when used in reference to race are not capitalized.

language

A knowledge of both *German* and *English* is required for the job.

race

The census indicated that many *Orientals* are living in this area.

Courses in *Afro-American* history and culture are taught in many major colleges and universities throughout the United States.

Several *black* leaders have requested to address the city council on this issue.

culture

Cinco de Mayo is observed with many festivities in the *Mexican-American* community.

The predominant native language of *Hispanics* is Spanish, but a significant number claim Portuguese as their native tongue.

b. Capitalize references to specific religious groups.

Massive opposition from *Catholic, Protestant,* and *Jewish* clergy led to the defeat of this proposed legislation.

A *Mormon* temple will be built on this site in 1993.

3–12. Celestial Bodies

The names of celestial bodies are generally capitalized except for the terms *earth, sun,* and *moon.* Since the capitalization of *earth* is shown in the dictionary as a secondary spelling, this term may be capitalized when it is used in conjunction with the names of other planets in its solar system.

lowercase

Television broadcasts of the first *moon* landing were viewed by millions of Americans.

None of the pieces from the satellite found their way back into *earth's* atmosphere.

capitalized

We have been studying the orbital paths of *Mars* and *Earth.*

Can you pick out the *Big Dipper* among the many stars in the sky?

CHAPTER 4

Numbers

Numbers Solution Finder

General Format

4–1. General Rules for Numbers

a. A number that begins a sentence *must be* expressed in word form. When the number cannot be written in one or two words, however, change the word order of the sentence so that the number does not begin the sentence. Then write the number in figures. This number rule takes precedence over all others.

number written in words

Twenty-four people responded to our advertisement for a secretary.

sentence order rearranged for figure form

The questionnaire was answered by *260* respondents. (Not: *Two hundred sixty* [or *260*] respondents answered the questionnaire.)

b. Numbers *one* through *ten* used in a general way are written in words. Write such numbers above *ten* in figures, except those used to begin a sentence (See Section 4–1a).

number "ten" or below

Would you please send us *four* additional copies of this software program.

number above "ten"

We have received *12* letters of complaint about service in our Springfield office during the last month.

Thirty-three of our present employees will not be moving with us to our Santa Maria location.

c. Approximations above *ten* that can be expressed in one or two words may be written in either figures or words. Keep in mind that figures are more emphatic and conform to the rule for the use of general numbers.

approximation written in figures

Nearly *300* people sent telegrams to the mayor.

approximation written in words

He expected over *fifty* people for the conference.

d. Round numbers in the millions or billions are expressed in a combination of figures and words. *One million* used as an approximation is usually written in all word form; otherwise, it is written *1 million.*

round number

Captain Maez has flown nearly *2 million* miles since he earned his wings.

round number with fraction

Our company manufactured over *3½ billion* pens last year.

round number with decimal

Will we exceed our production quota of *1.2 million* automobiles?

"one million" as an approximation

Look to establish additional locations in cities with populations of more than *one million.*

"1 million" as an exact figure

We will recover all development and marketing costs once we have sold *1 million* of these special bolts.

4–2. Related Numbers

a. **Numbers used similarly in the same document are considered related numbers and should be expressed in the same form. Therefore, write numbers *one* through *ten* in figures when they are used with related numbers above ten.**

Of the *130* items inspected, only *2* were found to be defective.

Next week we will deliver the *3* reams of bond paper, the *24* boxes of envelopes, and the *2* file trays that were back ordered for you. (Note that items appearing in a series are always considered to be related.)

b. **Round numbers in the millions or billions are expressed in figures when they are used with related numbers below a million or with related numbers that cannot be expressed in a combination of words and figures.**

combined with number below 1 million

Our production of umbrellas rose from *970,000* to *2,000,000* this year.

combined with number over 1 million written in figures

During the past two years, our circulation has risen from nearly *3,000,000* copies to *3,875,500* copies.

c. **Unrelated numbers used in the same sentence are considered individually to determine whether they should be expressed in words or figures.**

unrelated numbers in same sentence

Please send each of the *four* vice presidents *15* copies of our monthly report.

For this banquet each of the *14* tables should seat *eight* people.

combination of related and unrelated numbers in same sentence

Our warehouse inventory of *22* dishwashers, *17* refrigerators, and *8* washing machines must be distributed among our *three* stores.

These new packing boxes hold *four* cartons that contain *12* bottles each whereas the old boxes held *six* cartons that contained *6* bottles each.

4–3. Number Format

a. **Numbers expressed as figures are separated into groups of three by commas. Exceptions include years, house numbers, telephone numbers, zip codes, serial numbers, page numbers, decimal fractions, and metric measurements. Metric measurements of five or more digits are separated into groups of three by the use of spaces.**

commas in figures with more than three digits

4,782 17,750 385,450 2,865,000 1,567,874,500

no commas in certain figures

1987 Serial No. 14896-AN 1111 Figueroa Street page 1032

.7534 (805) 555-6132 Evansville, IN 47701-1957 1000 kilometers

space in metric measures with five or more digits

Our dairy delivers over *45 000* liters of milk daily to homes in this city.

b. **When two independent figures appear consecutively (one directly after the other) in a sentence, separate the figures with a comma.**

By *1991, 52* homes had been built around the golf course.

Of the *325, 72* questionnaires were not returned.

c. **When two numbers appearing together both modify a following noun, use figure form for one number and word form for the other. Use word form for the one that may be expressed in the *fewest* number of words. If both numbers have an equal word count, spell out the first number and place the second one in figures.**

word form for number expressed in fewer words

We processed your order for *twelve 48-inch* glass table tops yesterday.

Our contract calls for *three 25-second* commercials during this broadcast.

Please purchase *150 twenty-five*-cent stamps from the post office.

The contractor plans to build *36 five*-bedroom houses on this land.

The bank has agreed to finance your purchase of a *1991 thirty*-foot mobile home.

numbers with an equal word count

Each package contains *twenty 3*-inch nails.

Did you order *seventy 50*-watt bulbs?

Each box contains *twelve 6*-pack cartons of Coke.

d. **Separate volume numbers and page references by commas. Weights, capacities, and measures that consist of several words are treated as single units and are not separated by commas.**

volume and page number

This information can be found in *Volume IV, page 289.*

weight as a single unit

The Millers' newborn weighed *7 pounds 3 ounces* at birth.

capacity as a single unit

In conventional terms the capacity of the pitcher is *2 quarts 1 cup.*

4

measure as a single unit

Mr. Knight verified that the room length measured *28 feet 4 inches.*

The flight time has been calculated to be *4 hours 20 minutes.*

e. **The plural of a figure is formed by adding *s*.**

How many *7s* do you see in this serial number?

The *1900s* will be noted for man's first successes in space travel.

Figure Form

4–4. Money

a. **Amounts of money *$1* or more are expressed in figures. Omit the decimal and zeros in expressing whole dollar amounts, even if they appear with mixed dollar amounts.**

money expressed in figures

We paid *$484.95* for this new electronic typewriter.

omission of decimal and zeros

The list of purchases included items for $6.50, *$3,* $79.45, *$200,* and *$265.*

b. **Amounts of money less than *$1* are expressed in figures combined with the word *cents* unless they are used in conjunction with related amounts of *$1* or more. Unrelated amounts of money appearing in the same sentence, however, are treated separately.**

amounts less than $1

Last week the basic bus fare was increased from *60 cents* to *75 cents.*

related amounts of money

To mail the three reports, I paid *$.85, $1.40,* and *$2* in postage.

unrelated amounts of money

The tax on this *$8* item was *52 cents.*

c. **Round amounts of money in millions or billions of dollars are expressed in combined figure and word form except when they are used with related dollar figures below a million or related amounts that can be expressed in figures only.**

round amount

The cost of the new building was over *$12½ million.*

Nearly *$2.5 billion* in assets provides the customer confidence that has made Liberty Fed the largest savings and loan bank in the country.

4

related to amount less than $1 million

We estimate that *$850,000* will be needed to equip the Wilmington plant and *$2,000,000* will be needed for the Van Nuys plant.

related to amount that can be expressed in figures only

Our sales decreased from *$12,450,000* last year to less than *$12,000,000* this year.

d. **Amounts of money in legal documents are expressed in words followed by the figure amount contained in parentheses. The word *and* is used only to introduce cents included in a money amount written in word form.**

The Company shall pay up to *One Thousand Dollars ($1,000)* within 90 days upon receipt of a valid release statement.

The amount of indebtedness incurred by the defendant during this period was *Ten Thousand Five Hundred Eighty-three Dollars ($10,583).*

A check for *Two Thousand Four Hundred Sixty-one Dollars and Forty-eight Cents ($2,461.48)* was received from Westin Industries on May 3.

4–5. Decimals and Percentages

a. **Numbers containing decimals are expressed in figures. To prevent misreading, place a zero before a decimal that does not contain a whole number or begin with a zero.**

decimal with whole number

Our trucks average *12.843* miles per gallon of gasoline.

decimal beginning with 0

The part must be made within *.002* inch of specifications.

decimal not containing whole number or beginning with 0

Only *0.4* percent of all the items manufactured this year were rejected because of defective workmanship.

b. **Write percentages in figures followed by the word *percent.* The percent symbol (%) is used for statistical or technical tables or forms.**

"percent" used in sentence format

Last month we were able to decrease our energy consumption by only *1 percent.*

This year's travel expenses are up *8 percent* over last year's.

A *12½ percent* pay increase was granted to all office employees.

We anticipate a *0.5 percent* increase in sales tax this year--from *6 percent* to *6.5 percent.*

4

% used in statistical tables or forms

32.5% 80% 99.9% 4.3% 6%

4–6. Standard Weights and Measures

For quick comprehension express in figures the amount something weighs or measures. Units of weight and measure (inches, feet, yards, miles, kilometers, ounces, pounds, tons, grams, pints, quarts, gallons, liters, each, dozen, gross, reams, degrees, etc.), however, are written out fully in words. Abbreviations or symbols representing these units are limited to use in business forms or statistical materials.

general use

This carton is *3 pounds 6 ounces* in excess of the U.S. Postal Service limitations.

Over *2 tons* of waste material leave the plant daily.

Place the *8 reams* of copy paper in the storeroom.

Approximately *150 square yards* of carpeting will be needed for this office.

Use *3-inch* screws for this job.

use for forms and statistical materials

4 doz. 12 yds. 84° 9# 9 ft. 85 lb. 12 ea.

4–7. Metric Weights and Measures

a. **The basic metric measurements consist of meters, grams, and liters. Prefixes indicating fractions and multiples of these quantities follow:**

fractions

deci (1/10) centi (1/100) milli (1/1000)

multiples

deka (× 10) hecto (× 100) kilo (× 1000)

b. **Express metric measurements in figures. Use a space to separate numbers of five or more digits into groups of three. No space or comma is used with four-digit figures.**

regular metric measures

We will be using *1.75-liter* bottles for our large-sized apple juice.

Our new package of pie crust sticks weighs 11 ounces, which is equal to *311 grams* or *3.11 hectograms.*

four-digit figures

The distance to Boston is over *2000 kilometers.*

Our bakery chain ordered *1500 kilograms* of flour and *1200 kilograms* of sugar to be delivered to our bakeries throughout the state.

4

five-digit figures

His 5 acres is equal to approximately 2 hectares, that is, approximately *20 000 square meters.*

c. **For general correspondence spell out units of measure. Abbreviate units of measure only in technical writing, medical reports, or any kind of forms.**

general correspondence

10 millimeters   4 liters   80 kilometers

technical writing, medical reports, or forms

60 mm   6 mg   25 km   100 cc

d. **The following tables provide equivalents for metric and standard measures. Equivalents for length, weight, and capacity are shown.**

Measure of Length

1 km = 0.6214 mi. = 5/8 mi.	1 mi. = 1.609 km = 8/5 km
1 m = 1.0936 yd.	1 yd. = 0.9144 m (Exact)
1 m = 39.37 in.	1 ft. = 0.3048 m (Exact)
1 cm = 0.3937 in. = 2/5 in.	1 in. = 2.54 cm (Exact)

Measure of Mass (Weight)

1 ton (or tonne) (t) = 1.1023 ton	1 ton = 0.90721 t
1 kg = 2.2046 lb.	1 lb. = 453.592 g
1 kg = 11/5 lb.	1 oz. (avdp.) = 28.35 grams (g)
1 kg = 35 oz.	
1 gram (g) = 0.035 oz. (avdp.)	

Measure of Capacity

1 hectoliter (hl) = 2.838 bushels	1 bushel = 35.239 liters
1 liter (L) = 0.264 liquid gal.	1 liquid gal. = 3.785 liters
1 liter (L) = 1.057 liquid qt.	1 liquid qt. = 0.946 liters
1 liter (L) = 0.908 dry qt.	1 dry qt. = 1.101 liters
1 milliliter (ml) = 1 cm^3 (cc) = 0.034 fluid oz.	1 fluid oz. = 29.573 milliliters

4–8. Numbers Used With Nouns, Abbreviations, and Symbols

a. **Numbers used directly with nouns are placed in figures. Page numbers, model numbers, policy numbers, and serial numbers are just a few of the instances in which numerals are used with nouns. The words preceding the numerals are usually capitalized except for page, paragraph, line, size, and verse references. (See Section 3–4 for capitalization format.)**

model number

We ordered *Model 3* for our Information Processing Center.

4

policy and serial numbers

Please return your copy of *Policy 1284691D* to the home office.

Our IBM Personal Computer, *Serial No. A32-74603552,* was reported missing from the office.

page number

You will find a picture of this economy unit on *page 21* of our current catalog.

b. **Direct reference to the word *number* is the most common instance in which figures are used with an abbreviation. The word *number* is abbreviated in this case except when it appears at the beginning of a sentence.**

We expect to replace this office furniture with your *No. 378* series.

The following checks were returned by your bank: *Nos. 487, 492, and 495.*

Numbers 381, 1209, and 1628 were the winning raffle tickets.

c. **The use of symbols is generally avoided in business writing. However, for preparing forms (such as invoices and orders), charts, tables, and other documents where space is limited, symbols are used liberally. Numbers expressed with symbols are written in figures.**

2/10, N/30 8% #455

Time

4–9. Dates

a. **When the day is written after the month, use cardinal figures (1, 2, 3, etc.). Ordinal figures (1st, 2nd, 3rd, etc.) are used for expressing days that appear before the month or that stand alone.**

month followed by day

March 23, 1993, is the deadline for filing your claim.

Your *October 15* payment is now 30 days past due.

day appearing before month

We expect payment in full by the *10th of April.*

Our new offices should be ready for occupancy by the *3rd of June.*

day used alone

Your reservations for the *9th* and the *24th* have been confirmed.

Please send us your rental payment by the *1st* of each month.

b. Dates used in most business correspondence are expressed in terms of month, day, and year. Dates used in military and foreign correspondence are generally expressed day, month, and year, with no intervening comma.

4

business correspondence

November 27, 1992

military or foreign correspondence

27 November 1992

4–10. Clock Time

a. Figures are used with *a.m., p.m., noon,* or *midnight* to express clock time. Omit the colon and zeros with even times, even if they appear in conjunction with times expressed in hours and minutes.

The terms *noon* and *midnight* may be used with or without the figure *12.* When these terms are used with other clock times containing *a.m.* and/or *p.m.,* however, include the figure *12.* Never use *a.m.* or *p.m.* following *noon* or *midnight.*

"a.m.," "p.m.," "noon," "midnight" with figures

His plane was scheduled to arrive at *1 p.m.,* but the actual arrival time was *1:27 p.m.*

Our next plant tour will begin at *10:30 a.m.* and conclude by *12 noon.*

The afternoon shift is scheduled from *4 p.m.* until *12 midnight.*

"noon" and "midnight" with the figure "12"

She left promptly at *12 noon.*

The new shift starts at *12 midnight.*

This postal station is open Saturdays from *8 a.m.* until *12 noon.*

New hours for our coffee shop are from *8 a.m.* until *12 midnight* daily.

"noon" and "midnight" without the figure "12"

May we please have your answer before *noon* on July 30.

All envelopes containing tax payments must be postmarked before *midnight,* April 15.

b. **Either word or figure form may be used with *o'clock*.**

We must leave here by *eight o'clock* (or *8 o'clock*) if we are to arrive at the meeting on time.

c. **Phrases such as "in the morning," "in the afternoon," or "at night" may be used with *o'clock* but not with *a.m.* or *p.m.***

Coffee breaks are scheduled at *10 o'clock in the morning* and at *3 o'clock in the afternoon.*

By *two o'clock in the afternoon,* our campus is almost empty; but by *seven o'clock in the evening,* it is filled with students attending night classes.

4

d. **When even clock hours of the day are expressed without *a.m., p.m.,* or *o'clock,* use word form. Either word or figure form may be used, however, when both hours and minutes are expressed.**

exact hour

The party is scheduled to begin at *eight* tonight.

hour and minutes

The meeting was not adjourned until *6:30* (or *six-thirty*).

The power went off at *9:05* (or *five after nine*) this morning but resumed operation before 10 (or ten).

4–11. Periods of Time

a. **Periods of time relating to *days, weeks, months,* or *years* that can be expressed in one or two words are usually written in word form when they are used in a general way. Periods of time that cannot be expressed in one or two words are written in figure form.**

General references to clock hours, minutes, or seconds are treated as general numbers: numbers *ten* and below are written in word form and numbers above *ten* are written in figure form.

Business Terms use numerals

general time periods—days, weeks, months, or years

During the last *sixteen months,* we have shown a slight profit.

We have been in this location for *thirty-two years.*

The auto workers' strike lasted *117 days.*

general references to clock time

Each candidate's speech is limited to *five* minutes.

We offer *24-hour* repair service to all our subscribers.

b. **Time-period data related to specific loan lengths, discount rates, interest rates, payment terms, credit terms, or other such information dealing with definite business contracts are expressed in figures.**

This loan must be paid in full within *90 days.*

We give a 2 percent discount on all invoices paid within *10 days* of the invoice date.

You have been granted a 9 percent loan for *6 months.*

4–12. Ages and Anniversaries

Ages and anniversaries that can be expressed in one or two words are generally written in word form; those that require more than two words are written in figures. Figures are also used when an age (1) appears directly after a person's name; (2) is used in a legal or technical sense; or (3) is expressed in terms of years, months, and sometimes days. (Note that no commas are used to separate the years, months, and days in the expression of ages.)

4

general expression of ages and anniversaries

David will be *twenty-seven* on August 9; his son John will be *three* on the same day.

The staff brought a cake as a surprise for Mrs. Wong's *fifty-first* birthday.

We plan to give a party for Larry to celebrate his *twenty-fifth* anniversary with the company.

Our city will celebrate its *150th* anniversary in 1994.

age after name

Ms. Soderstrom, *47,* was promoted to office manager last week.

age used in technical or legal sense

Employees no longer must retire at the age of *65.*

The legal voting age is *18.*

At *25* you will be eligible for these reduced insurance rates.

age in years, months, and days

According to our records, the insured was *35* years *5* months and *28* days of age upon cancellation of the policy.

Addresses and Telephone Numbers

4–13. Addresses

a. **House numbers are expressed in figures except for the house number *One.* No commas are used to separate digits in house numbers.**

One Alpha Street

18817 Clearview Avenue

b. **Street names that are numbered *ten* or below are expressed in words. Street names numbered above *ten* are written in figures and expressed in cardinal form when separated from the house number by a compass direction. Use the ordinal form *(st, nd, rd, th)* when the street name directly follows the house number.**

street name "ten" or below

All visitors to New York City must stroll down *Fifth* Avenue.

street name above "ten" with a compass direction—cardinal form

His new address was listed as 3624 West *59* Place.

street name above "ten" without a compass direction—ordinal form

Please send this order to 1111 *23rd* Street.

c. **Apartment numbers, suite numbers, box numbers, and route numbers are expressed in figure form.**

1883 Creek Avenue, Apt. *4*

Plaza Medical Building, Suite *102*

Post Office Box *1584*

Rural Route *2*

d. **Zip codes are expressed in figures (without commas) and typed a single space after the state.**

sentence format

Ms. Reynolds requested that the refund be sent to her at Pasadena City College, 1570 East Colorado Boulevard, Pasadena, California *91106.*

inside address or envelope address

Mr. Arthur M. Manuel
5565 1/2 Eighth Avenue
Inglewood, CA *90305*

Mrs. Judy Dolan
1073 83rd Street, Apt. 2
Moonachie, NJ *07074*

e. **Address lines containing zip + 4 are written in the same manner as those containing regular zip codes. The only difference is that the four extra digits are separated from the zip code by a hyphen.**

sentence format

Redirect this order to Palmer Enterprises, 1586 Cicero Avenue, Chicago, Illinois *60651-4827.*

inside address or envelope address

Ms. Eleanor Chu, Personnel Director
Parke-Dunn Pharmaceutical Company
21654 Grand Boulevard
Detroit, MI *48211-1853*

4–14. Telephone Numbers

Telephone numbers are expressed in figures. When the area code is included, place it in parentheses before the number. Extension numbers, preceded by the abbreviation *Ext.,* follow telephone numbers. If an extension number concludes a sentence, use a single comma to separate it from the telephone number. However, if an extension number appears in the middle of a sentence, use commas before and after it.

telephone number

You may reach our representative at *728-1694.*

area code with telephone number

Do not hesitate to call me collect at *(714) 555-5235.*

area code, telephone number, extension

You may reach me any weekday at *(617) 555-7139, Ext. 3712.*

We were requested to call *(213) 347-0551, Ext. 244,* within an hour.

Special Forms

4–15. Fractions

a. **Simple fractions that can be expressed in two words are written in word form. Fractions written in word form are not hyphenated unless they are used as compound adjectives.**[1]

simple fraction used as a noun

We have already met *three fourths* of our production quota for this year.

Only *one third* of our agents returned the questionnaire.

simple fraction used as a compound adjective

A *two-thirds* majority vote is needed to ratify the contract.

Our investment syndicate wishes to purchase a *one-fourth* interest in the proposed new shopping center.

b. **Figures are used to express (1) long and awkward fractions, (2) fractions combined with whole numbers, or (3) fractions used for technical purposes.**

long and awkward fraction

The study indicated that *21/200* of a second is needed for people to begin reacting in emergency situations.

---

[1]*Webster's Ninth New Collegiate Dictionary* (Springfield, Mass., Merriam-Webster Inc., 1989), p. 810.

fraction combined with whole number

Our new plant is located *3 1/2* miles from here.

fraction for technical use

Our department is temporarily out of stock of *5/8*-inch round-head metal screws.

4

c. **Fractions written in figures that are not found on the computer or typewriter keyboard are formed by using the diagonal to separate the two parts. Leave one space between the fraction and any whole number used with the fraction. When fractions located on the keyboard are used with those not found on the keyboard, type all fractions by using the diagonal construction.**

fraction not on keyboard

We shipped *7 2/3* tons of beef last week.

combination of fraction on keyboard with fraction not on keyboard

Our employees averaged *31 1/2* hours sick leave last year as compared to *24 3/4* hours this year.

4–16. Ordinals

a. **Ordinal numbers (*first, second, third,* etc.) that can be written in one or two words are generally expressed in word form except those appearing (1) in dates before the month or standing alone and (2) in numbered street names above *ten.***

general use

Mr. Cox was elected to represent the *Thirty-fourth* Congressional District.

Mrs. Lang was criticized for managing the company according to *nineteenth*-century policies.

dates

Our next audit is scheduled for the *1st of August.*

Your order will be shipped by the *15th* of this month.

Please submit your report by the *1st* of the year.

numbered streets

Our new store is located at 820 West *Third* Avenue.

I plan to meet Mr. Siegel at noon on the corner of Main and *42nd* streets.

b. **Ordinals expressed in figure form end in *st, nd, rd,* or *th.***

This note is due the *1st* of March.

May we have your response by the *22nd* of November.

This year marks the *123rd* anniversary of our city.

Our new offices are located at 1560 *12th* Avenue.

4–17. Roman Numerals

a. **When typing Roman numerals for chapter or outline divisions, use capital letters to form the numbers. Also use capital letters for expressing years written in Roman numerals.**

Arabic Numeral	*Roman Numeral*	*Arabic Numeral*	*Roman Numeral*
1	I	16	XVI
2	II	17	XVII
3	III	18	XVIII
4	IV	19	XIX
5	V	20	XX
6	VI	30	XXX
7	VII	40	XL
8	VIII	50	L
9	IX	60	LX
10	X	70	LXX
11	XI	80	LXXX
12	XII	90	XC
13	XIII	100	C
14	XIV	1,000	M
15	XV		

b. **The preliminary sections of a report such as the letter of transmittal, the table of contents, and the list of tables are numbered with lowercase Roman numerals. Number the pages consecutively using *i, ii, iii, iv, v,* etc.**

CHAPTER 5

Abbreviations and Contractions

Abbreviations and Contractions Solution Finder

Abbreviations

5–1. Titles

a. **The abbreviations *Mr., Ms., Mrs.,* and *Dr.* are used for courtesy titles.**

Mr. Peter Miller

Ms. Frances Cates

Mrs. Carole Eustice

Dr. Ella Butler

b. **Spell out civil, educational, military, or religious titles used before and in conjunction with a person's full name or the last name only. Lengthy titles (those containing more than one word) may be abbreviated, however, when they appear before a person's *full* name and brevity is required.**

written out—full name

I believe *Professor* Sharlene Pollyea is in charge of the project.

written out—last name only

Dear *Governor* Reece:

Address the letter to the attention of *Lieutenant Governor* Richards.

abbreviated—full name

Please invite *Lt. Col.* Donald Curry to the meeting.

5

c. **Abbreviate and capitalize personal titles (*Jr., Sr., Esq.,* etc.), professional designations (*CPA, CLU, R.N., R.P.T.,* etc.), or academic degrees (*M.D., Ph.D., Ed.D, L.L.B., M.L.S.,* etc.) that follow a person's name. A comma is used before and after an abbreviation appearing within a sentence but only before an abbreviation appearing at the end of a sentence.**

Abbreviations of academic degrees and professional designations are separated by periods except for the designations *CPA* (Certified Public Accountant), *CPS* (Certified Professional Secretary), *PLS* (Professional Legal Secretary), and *CLU* (Chartered Life Underwriter).

personal title

John A. Wrigley, *Jr.,* was elected to the Lynwood City Council.

Please send a copy of the report to Robert Lucio, *Esq.*

professional designation

Cynthia Armstrong, *CPA,* was present at the meeting.

The person in charge during that shift is Eric Blake, *R.N.*

academic degree

Our new college president, David Wolf, *Ph.D.,* met with the Board of Trustees yesterday.

First fill the prescriptions written by Dorothy Salazar, *M.D.*

5–2. Organizations

a. **The names of well-known business, educational, governmental, military, labor, philanthropic, professional, and other organizations or agencies may be abbreviated. No periods or spaces are used to separate the individual letters.**

A & P	AMA	FCC	NBC	SAC
AAA	CBS	NAACP	NCR	TWA
AFL-CIO	FBI	NASA	NYU	UN

5

b. **In the names of business firms, abbreviations such as *Co., Corp., Inc., Ltd.,* and *Mfg.* are used only if they are part of the official organizational name.**

We ordered the parts from Corway *Mfg. Co.*

Johnson Products, *Inc.,* will receive the contract.

5–3. Dates and Time

a. **Spell out days of the week and months of the year. Abbreviate them only in lists, tables, graphs, charts, illustrations, or other such visual presentations where space is limited.**

spelled out in text

Our next committee meeting will be held on *Monday, January 18.*

Next *Tuesday, October 8,* will mark the company's fifth anniversary.

abbreviated in graphics

Sun.	Mon.	Tues. (Tue.)	Wed.
Thurs. (Thu.)	Fri.	Sat.	

Su M Tu W Th F Sa

Jan.	Feb.	Mar.	Apr.
May	June (Jun.)	July (Jul.)	Aug.
Sept. (Sep.)	Oct.	Nov.	Dec.

b. **The abbreviations *a.m. (ante meridiem)* and *p.m. (post meridiem)* are used for expressing clock time. They are typed in lowercase letters separated by periods.**

Would you prefer to take the flight at 8:45 *a.m.* or the one at 2 *p.m.*?

He arrived at 3:30 *p.m.*

c. **United States time zones—*EST* (eastern standard time), *CST* (central standard time), *MST* (mountain standard time), and *PST* (Pacific standard time)—are usually abbreviated. Time zones for daylight saving time are abbreviated *EDT, CDT, MDT,* and *PDT.***

According to the latest report, his plane will arrive in Denver at 6:05 p.m., *MST.*

The new schedules are based on *EDT.*

d. **The abbreviations *B.C. (before Christ)* and *A.D. (anno Domini)* are sometimes used in expressing dates. Both follow the year and are typed in capital letters with periods. In formal writing, however, *A.D.* may appear before the year.**

B.C.

Professor Farhood claims that the statue dates back to 400 *B.C.*

A.D. after the year

Ms. Lopez's thesis deals with the rise of Christianity from 200 to 350 *A.D.*

A.D. before the year

The Spanish legions, under the leadership of Galba, conquered Rome in *A.D.* 68.

5–4. Standard Units of Measure

Common units of measure such as distance, length, temperature, volume, and weight are usually spelled out in business documents. Abbreviations, however, may be used on invoices, packing slips, and other business forms where space is limited. In abbreviating units of measure, place periods after one-word abbreviations. Omit the periods in abbreviations representing more than one word.

general business documents

All perishable goods shipped over *100 miles* should be kept below *40 degrees* Fahrenheit.

business forms, one-word abbreviations

12 *ft.* 2 *in.* (12 feet 2 inches)   3 *lb.* 2 *oz.* (3 pounds 2 ounces)

business forms, multiple-word abbreviations

80 *wpm* (80 words per minute)   55 *mph* (55 miles per hour)

5–5. Metric Units of Measure

a. **In regular business documents metric units of measurement are generally written out. However, in business forms and tables and in scientific and technical writing, they are often abbreviated. These abbreviations are**

written without periods, and the singular and plural forms are the same. Common abbreviations for measurements related to distance, weight, and volume follow:

prefixes

deci *d* (1/10)
centi *c* (1/100)
milli *m* (1/1000)

deka *da* (× 10)
hecto *h* (× 100)
kilo *k* (× 1000)
mega *m* (× 1 000 000)

common units of measure

meter *m*
gram *g*
liter *L*

centimeter *cm*
kilogram *kg*
milliliter *ml*

kilometer *km*
milligram *mg*

5

square meter *sq m*
cubic centimeter *cc*

kilobyte *KB*
megabyte *MB*

b. **The abbreviation for *liter* is a capital *L* because the lowercase letter "l" and numeral "1" (one) on many typewriters are typed with the same key. Therefore, to avoid confusion, the capital *L* is used instead.**

1 *L* milk *but* 1 *ml* vaccine (abbreviation is clear)

c. **Temperatures in the metric system are expressed on the Celsius scale. This term is abbreviated *C*.**

37°*C* 25°*C*

d. **Express abbreviations relating to kilometers per hour with a diagonal.**

The maximum speed permitted on this highway is *90 km/h* (55 mph).

Slow down to *40 km/h* (25 mph) in the school crossing zone.

5–6. Business and General Terms

a. **When the word *number* is not followed by a numeral, spell it out. The abbreviation *No.*, however, is used when a numeral directly follows the term unless the term begins the sentence.**

The stock *number* of the item you requested is *No. 4-862.*

Please ship us three *Model No. 17A* electric motors.

Number 18-A part is no longer stocked in our warehouse.

b. **Most commonly abbreviated business and computer terms are typed in all capital letters with no spaces or periods separating the letters. A few business terms, when used in business correspondence, however, are written in lowercase letters separated by periods.**

capitalized abbreviation of business term

PERT (program evaluation and review technique)
GNP (gross national product)
LIFO (last in, first out)
FIFO (first in, first out)
SOP (standard operating procedures)

capitalized abbreviation of computer term

RAM (random-access memory)
CPU (central processing unit)
CRT (cathode-ray tube)
EDP (electronic data processing)
OCR (optical character recognition)

lowercase letters for abbreviation in correspondence

c.o.d. (collect on delivery)

f.o.b. (free on board)

c. **Capitalize and abbreviate the word *extension (Ext.)* when it appears in conjunction with telephone numbers.**

You may reach me at 987-9281, *Ext.* 1201, any weekday between 10 and 11 a.m.

Please call me collect at (714) 555-3827, *Ext.* 248.

d. **Some commonly abbreviated terms are derived from foreign expressions. They are generally typed in lowercase letters and are followed by a period at the close of each abbreviated word.**

foreign abbreviations

e.g. (for example)
et al. (and others)
i.e. (that is)
etc. (and so forth)
cf. (compare)
viz. (namely)
ibid. (in the same place)
loc. cit. (in the place cited)
op. cit. (in the work cited)

5–7. Plurals

Apostrophes are not used to form the plurals of abbreviations; most plural abbreviations are formed by adding only *s* to the singular form. Some words, however, use the same abbreviation for the singular and plural form.

plural formed by adding "s"

hr., *hrs.*
mgr., *mgrs.*
c.o.d., *c.o.d.s*
IOU, *IOUs*
CPA, *CPAs*
R.N., *R.N.s*

singular and plural form identical

deg., *deg.* ft., *ft.* in., *in.*

5–8. Addresses and Geographical Expressions

a. For addresses in business correspondence, street designations such as *Boulevard, Street, Avenue, Lane, Place,* and *Road* are spelled out. *Boulevard,* however, may be abbreviated *(Blvd.)* if space is limited in expressing long street names.

street designation spelled out

Ms. Lila Green
462 Olive *Avenue*
Iowa City, IA 52240

Woodcutt Escrow Company
5700 Jefferson *Boulevard*
Columbus, OH 43266-0309

"Boulevard" abbreviated with long street name

Mr. James F. Campenelli
1873 San Fernando Mission *Blvd.*
San Francisco, CA 94127

b. Terms indicating direction (North, South, East, West) that precede a street name are spelled out. Compound directions such as *N.E.,* however, are abbreviated when they are used after the street name.

direction before street name

851 *East* Lake Street

compound direction after street name

7059 Capitol Avenue, *S.W.*

c. The U.S. Postal Service recommends that on all mailings the names of states be abbreviated by using the official zip code designations. (They are typed in capital letters with no periods or spaces.) These two-letter state abbreviations are shown on pages 129 to 130 and on the page opposite the inside back cover.

However, since modern optical scanning equipment no longer requires the use of the two-letter abbreviations, either the full state name or the two-letter zip code designation may be used, depending on which form more nearly balances with the other lines of the address. If both forms provide balance, use the zip code designation.

zip code designation

Mrs. Marjory Clark, PLS
Los Angeles Pierce College
6201 Winnetka Avenue
Woodland Hills, *CA* 91371

state spelled out fully

Fielder Publishing Company
9836 West Seventh Avenue
Ridgewood, *New Jersey* 07541

d. **Since 1974 the U.S. Postal Service has recommended a format for addressing envelopes that uses all capital letters, abbreviations, and no internal punctuation marks. As yet, this format has not been widely accepted for individually typed correspondence or even computer-generated form correspondence; its use has been mainly with standard bulk mailings. This format is described fully in Section 11–27.**

e. **A period is placed after each abbreviated word in geographical abbreviations. Only with the two-letter state abbreviations recommended by the U.S. Postal Service are the periods omitted.**

5

capital letters

U.S.A. (United States of America)
U.S.S.R. (Union of Soviet Socialist Republics)
U.K. (United Kingdom)
G.B. (Great Britain)

capital and lowercase letters

So. Nev. (Southern Nevada) Ire. (Ireland)

postal service abbreviation

MT (Montana) IA (Iowa)

5–9. Abbreviation Format

a. **The capitalization of abbreviations is generally governed by the format of the original word or words. Proper nouns are always capitalized while common nouns generally appear in lowercase letters. Some common noun abbreviations, however, are capitalized.**

capital letters for proper noun

His father is a member of the *AFL-CIO.*

lowercase letters for common noun

Please send the order *c.o.d.*

capital letters for some common nouns

How many *VCRs* did our sales staff sell during the holiday season?

Be sure to ask the *TV* repair service to send the bill to our home address.

b. **Abbreviations that appear in all capital letters are generally typed without periods or spaces. Exceptions are (1) geographic expressions, most professional designations, and academic degrees, which are typed with periods but no spaces and (2) initials in a person's name and most abbreviations containing capital and lowercase letters, which are typed with both periods and spaces.**

general rule—no periods and no spaces

We heard the news from an *NBC* reporter.

Be sure to turn your dial to *KBIG* for beautiful music.

geographical expressions—periods with no spaces

Their travel agency sponsored several trips to the *U.S.S.R.* last summer.

Please submit these completed forms to the *U.S.* Department of Agriculture.

Our new store location is 800 Tufts Avenue, *S.W.*

professional designations—periods with no spaces

Jodi Myers, *R.P.T.,* is the physical therapist who is handling this case.

Will Robert Soto, *R.N.,* be the new director of our nursing program?

academic degrees—periods with no spaces

Mr. Fujimoto was granted an *M.A.* in business last June.

Sharon Lund O'Neil, *Ph.D.,* was awarded the position.

initials—periods and spaces

Please deliver this report to Ms. *J. T.* Kelley.

Only Gerald *H.* Monroe applied for the position.

abbreviations with capital and lowercase letters—periods and spaces

So. Calif. (Southern California)   *N. Mex.* (New Mexico)

c. In abbreviations beginning with lowercase letters, a period is generally placed after each letter or group of letters representing a word. No space appears between periods and letters in compound abbreviations. Periods are not used, however, in abbreviations of metric measurements and compound abbreviations representing "measures per time."

general rule—periods

c.o.d. (collect on delivery)
a.m. (ante meridiem)
ft. (foot or feet)
mgr. (manager)
qt. (quart)
amt. (amount)

metric measurements—no periods

mm millimeter
cm centimeter
cc cubic centimeter
ml milliliter
kg kilogram

measurements per time—no periods

rpm revolutions per minute
wpm words per minute
wam words a minute
mph miles per hour

d. If an abbreviation containing a period falls at the end of a sentence that requires a period, use only a single period. In a question or an exclamation, place a closing question or exclamation mark directly after the period appearing in the abbreviation.

period

The hotel clerk awakened Mr. Sykiski at *8 a.m.*

question mark

Did you send the order *c.o.d.?*

exclamation mark

The plane was three hours late arriving in the *U.S.A.!*

5

5-10. Abbreviations of Terms Commonly Used in Business

Term	*Abbreviation*
account	acct.
accounts payable	AP
accounts receivable	AR
additional	addnl., add'l
administration, administrative	adm., admin.
advertisement	advt., ad
affidavit	afft.
agency	agcy.
agent	agt.
also known as	a.k.a., AKA
American Standard Code for Information Interchange	ASCII
amount	amt.
anno Domini	A.D.
answer	ans.
ante meridiem	a.m.
approximately	approx.
April	Apr.
as soon as possible	ASAP
assistant	asst., ass't.
association	assn., assoc.
attachment	att.
attention	attn.
attorney	atty.
audiovisual	AV
August	Aug.
avenue	ave.
average	av., avg.
back order	BO
balance	bal.
bale, bales	bl.
barrel, barrels	bbl.
before Christ	B.C.

5

Abbreviations of Terms Commonly Used in Business *(continued)*

Term	*Abbreviation*
bill of lading	B/L, BL
bill of sale	B/S, BS
binary digit	bit
bits per second	bps
brothers	bros.
building	bldg.
bushel, bushels	bu.
by way of	via
capital	cap.
carbon copy	cc, CC
courtesy copy	cc, CC
care of	c/o
carton	ctn.
cathode-ray tube	CRT
Celsius	C
centigram	cg
centimeter	cm
central processing unit	CPU
central daylight time	CDT
central standard time	CST
certified public accountant	CPA
characters per inch	cpi
characters per second	cps
charge	chg.
chief executive officer	CEO
chief financial officer	CFO
chief operating officer	COO
collect on delivery	c.o.d., COD
colonel	Col.
commission	comm.
Common Business Oriented Language	COBOL
company	co., Co.
computer-aided instruction	CAI
computer-aided transcription	CAT
computer output microfilm	COM
continued	cont.
corporation	corp., Corp.
cost, insurance, and freight	c.i.f., CIF
cubic	cu.
cubic centimeter	cc
credit	cr.
data base management system	DBMS
data processing	DP
daylight saving time	DST
December	Dec.
department	dept.
depreciation	depr.
destination	dstn.
discount	disc., dis.

Abbreviations of Terms Commonly Used in Business *(continued)*

Term	*Abbreviation*
distributed, distribution, distributor	distr.
district	dist.
dividend	div.
division	div.
doctor, doctors	Dr., Drs.
doing business as	d.b.a., DBA
dozen	doz., dz.
duplicate	dup.
each	ea.
eastern daylight time	EDT
eastern standard time	EST
electronic data processing	EDP
enclosure	enc., encl.
end of month	e.o.m., EOM
esquire	esq., Esq.
estimated time of arrival	ETA
expense	exp.
extension	ext., Ext.
facsimile	fax
Fahrenheit	F
February	Feb.
fiscal year	FY
first in, first out	FIFO
foot, feet	ft.
for example	e.g.
FORmula TRANslator	FORTRAN
for the benefit of	f.b.o., FBO
for your information	FYI
forward	fwd.
free on board	f.o.b., FOB
freight	frt.
Friday	Fri.
gallon	gal.
garbage in, garbage out	GIGO
general	gen., Gen.
general manager	GM
gram	g
gross	gr.
gross national product	GNP
handling	hdlg.
headquarters	HQ, hdqtrs.
horsepower	HP, hp
hour, hours	hr., hrs.
hundredweight	cwt.
identification data	ID
inch, inches	in.
inches per second	ips
includes, including	incl.
incorporated	inc., Inc.

5

5

Abbreviations of Terms Commonly Used in Business *(continued)*

Term	*Abbreviation*
insurance	ins.
intelligence quotient	IQ
interest	int.
international	intl., intnl.
inventory	invt.
invoice	inv.
January	Jan.
kilobyte, kilobytes (thousand bytes)	KB
kilogram, kilograms	kg
kilometer, kilometers	km
kilometers per hour	km/h
last in, first out	LIFO
less-than-carload lot	l.c.l., LCL
lieutenant	Lt.
limited	ltd., Ltd.
lines per minute	lpm
liter	L
local area network	LAN
mail order	MO
major (military rank)	Maj.
manager	mgr.
manufacturer, manufacturers	mfr., mfrs.
manufacturing	mfg.
March	Mar.
master of ceremonies	emcee (represents *MC*)
maximum	max.
megabyte	MB
memorandum	memo
merchandise	mdse.
meter	m
miles per gallon	mpg
miles per hour	mph
milligram, milligrams	mg
milliliter, milliliters	ml
millimeter, millimeters	mm
minimum	min.
minute, minutes	min.
miscellaneous	misc.
Mister	Mr.
Misters	Messrs.
Mistress	Mrs.
mistress of ceremonies	emcee (represents *MC*)
Monday	Mon.
money order	MO
month, months	mo., mos.
mountain daylight time	MDT
mountain standard time	MST
net weight	nt. wt.
no date	ND

Abbreviations of Terms Commonly Used in Business *(continued)*

Term	*Abbreviation*
not applicable	NA
not available	NA
November	Nov.
number, numbers	No., Nos.
October	Oct.
okay	OK
optical character recognition	OCR
optional	opt.
organization	org.
original	orig.
ounce, ounces	oz.
overdraft	o.d., OD
out of stock	OS
over-the-counter	OTC
Pacific daylight time	PDT
Pacific standard time	PST
package	pkg.
page, pages	p., pp.
paid	pd.
pair, pairs	pr., prs.
parcel post	PP
postage and handling	p and h, P/H
postpaid, prepaid	ppd.
program evaluation and review technique	PERT
pint, pints	pt., pts.
port of entry	p.o.e., POE
post meridiem	p.m.
post office	P.O.
postscript	P.S., PS
pound, pounds	lb., lbs.
president	pres.
private automatic branch exchange	PABX
private branch exchange	PBX
profit and loss	P & L, P/L
programmable read-only memory	PROM
public relations	PR
purchase order	P.O., PO
quantity	qty.
quart, quarts	qt., qts.
quarter, quarterly	qtr.
quire, quires	qr., qrs.
railway	rwy., ry.
random-access memory	RAM
read-only memory	ROM
ream, reams	rm., rms.
received	recd.
registered	reg.
requisition	req.
respond, if you please	R.S.V.P., RSVP

5

Abbreviations of Terms Commonly Used in Business *(continued)*

Term	*Abbreviation*
retail	ret.
retired	ret.
returned	retd.
revised	rev.
revolutions per minute	rpm, RPM
rural free delivery	RFD
Saturday	Sat.
second, seconds	sec.
secretary	sec., secy., sec'y
section	sect.
self-addressed, stamped envelope	SASE
September	Sept., Sep.
sergeant	Sgt.
shipment	shpt.
shipping order	S.O., SO
shortage	shtg.
square	sq.
standard	std.
standard operating procedure	SOP
statement	stmt.
storage	stge.
Sunday	Sun.
television	TV
that is	i.e.
thousand (in reference to computer disk or memory capacity)	K
Thursday	Thurs., Thu.
treasurer	treas.
Tuesday	Tues., Tue.
versus	vs., v.
vice president	V.P.
volume	vol.
Wednesday	Wed.
week, weeks	wk., wks.
weight	wt.
Western Union Teleprinter Exchange Service	TWX
What you see is what you get.	WYSIWYG
wholesale	whsle.
wide area network	WAN
Wide Area Telephone Service	WATS
word processing	WP
words a minute	wam
words per minute	wpm
yard, yards	yd., yds.
year, years	yr., yrs.
Zone Improvement Plan	zip, ZIP

5–11. Abbreviations of States and Territories

State or Territory	Two-Letter Abbreviation	Standard Abbreviation
Alabama	AL	Ala.
Alaska	AK	——
Arizona	AZ	Ariz.
Arkansas	AR	Ark.
California	CA	Calif., Cal.
Canal Zone	CZ	C.Z.
Colorado	CO	Colo., Col.
Connecticut	CT	Conn.
Delaware	DE	Del.
District of Columbia	DC	D.C.
Florida	FL	Fla.
Georgia	GA	Ga.
Guam	GU	——
Hawaii	HI	——
Idaho	ID	——
Illinois	IL	Ill.
Indiana	IN	Ind.
Iowa	IA	——
Kansas	KS	Kans., Kan.
Kentucky	KY	Ky.
Louisiana	LA	La.
Maine	ME	——
Maryland	MD	Md.
Massachusetts	MA	Mass.
Michigan	MI	Mich.
Minnesota	MN	Minn.
Mississippi	MS	Miss.
Missouri	MO	Mo.
Montana	MT	Mont.
Nebraska	NE	Nebr., Neb.
Nevada	NV	Nev.
New Hampshire	NH	N.H.
New Jersey	NJ	N.J.
New Mexico	NM	N. Mex.
New York	NY	N.Y.
North Carolina	NC	N.C.
North Dakota	ND	N. Dak.
Ohio	OH	——
Oklahoma	OK	Okla.
Oregon	OR	Oreg., Ore.
Pennsylvania	PA	Pa., Penn., Penna.
Puerto Rico	PR	P.R.
Rhode Island	RI	R.I.
South Carolina	SC	S.C.
South Dakota	SD	S. Dak.
Tennessee	TN	Tenn.
Texas	TX	Tex.

Abbreviations of States and Territories *(continued)*

State or Territory	*Two-Letter Abbreviation*	*Standard Abbreviation*
Utah	UT	——
Vermont	VT	Vt.
Virgin Islands	VI	V.I.
Virginia	VA	Va.
Washington	WA	Wash.
West Virginia	WV	W. Va.
Wisconsin	WI	Wis., Wisc.
Wyoming	WY	Wyo.

5

5–12. Two-Letter Abbreviations for Canadian Provinces

Canadian Province	*Abbreviation*
Alberta	AB
British Columbia	BC
Labrador	LB
Manitoba	MB
New Brunswick	NB
Newfoundland	NF
Northwest Territories	NT
Nova Scotia	NS
Ontario	ON
Prince Edward Island	PE
Quebec	PQ
Saskatchewan	SK
Yukon Territory	YT

Contractions

5–13. Contractions

a. **Contractions are similar to abbreviations in that they are shortened forms. Unlike abbreviations, however, contractions always contain an apostrophe to indicate where letters have been omitted. The use of single-word contractions is generally limited to business forms and tables. Some common single-word contractions follow:**

ack'd (acknowledged)
ass't (assistant)
gov't (government)
nat'l (national)
rec't (receipt)
sec'y (secretary)
'92 (1992)

b. **A second kind of contraction occurs with verb forms. By using an apostrophe to indicate where letters have been omitted, two words may be combined into one. The use of verb contractions is generally limited to**

informal business writing. A sampling of commonly used verb contractions follows:

aren't	(are not)	shouldn't	(should not)
can't	(cannot)	should've	(should have)
couldn't	(could not)	that's	(that is)
didn't	(did not)	there's	(there is)
doesn't	(does not)	they're	(they are)
don't	(do not)	wasn't	(was not)
hasn't	(has not)	we'll	(we will)
haven't	(have not)	we're	(we are)
he's	(he is)	weren't	(were not)
I'll	(I will)	what's	(what is)
I'm	(I am)	where's	(where is)
isn't	(is not)	who's	(who is)
it's	(it is)	won't	(will not)
I've	(I have)	wouldn't	(would not)
let's	(let us)	you'd	(you would)
she's	(she is)	you're	(you are)
		you've	(you have)

CHAPTER 6

Literary and Artistic Titles

Literary and Artistic Titles Solution Finder

Punctuation

Titles

Titles

6–1. Published Works

a. **Underline or place in all capital letters the titles of published books, magazines, newspapers, and booklets or pamphlets. In underlined titles capitalize the first letter of the principal words in the title. Articles (a, an, the), conjunctions (and, but, or, nor), and prepositions with three or fewer letters (of, in, on, to, for, etc.) are not capitalized unless they appear as the first or last words of the title or as the first word of a subtitle following a colon.**

book

A copy of The Random House Dictionary of the English Language arrived yesterday.

This question is answered on page 26 of HOW 6: A Handbook for Office Workers, Sixth Edition.

Copies of COMPUTERS AND THE ELECTRONIC AGE are available at your local bookstore.

magazine

Use the enclosed coupon to renew your subscription to the Journal of Higher Education.

Have you read the latest issue of BETTER HOMES AND GARDENS?

newspaper

An article in The Wall Street Journal yesterday discussed sales trends in our industry.

We will place an advertisement in the LOS ANGELES TIMES for nurses and nurses' assistants.

booklet or pamphlet

Your Attitude Is Showing is a publication that should be distributed to our new employees.

Be sure to print at least 500 copies of our new booklet, EMPLOYEE PROGRAMS AND BENEFITS, for distribution to all our employees.

b. **Place in quotation marks the titles of chapters, sections, units, lessons, and other such subdivisions of published books or pamphlets. Capitalize the first letter of the principal words in the title.**

chapter in a book

The final chapter, "Application of Information Processing Procedures," contributed immeasurably to the success of Office Systems and Management.

6

section in a pamphlet

Please review the section "Filling Out the Application" before you apply for a job.

c. **Place in quotation marks the titles of articles, regular features, and columns in magazines or newspapers. Capitalize the first letter of the principal words in the title.**

article in a magazine

Did you read "Successful Ideas for the Indoor Gardener" in last month's issue of Ladies' Home Journal?

column in a newspaper

Potter's "Financial Outlook" predicted a rising stock market during the next quarter.

6

d. **Capitalize the first letter of subdivisions such as *preface, contents, appendix,* and *index* when they refer to a specific work.**

specific work

The rule for punctuating words in a series can be found in the *Appendix.*

Consult the *Index* to see on which page the explanation of molecular theory begins.

general reference

The *index* generally follows any *appendixes* that may be included in a book.

6–2. Unpublished Works

Place the titles of unpublished manuscripts, reports, theses, and dissertations in quotation marks. Capitalize the first letter of the principal words in the title.

title of a report

Copies of "Report on Progress in Areas of Public Concern" were distributed to the board members last week.

6–3. Artistic Works

Place in quotation marks the titles of movies, television and radio shows, plays, musicals, operas, poems, albums, songs, paintings, essays, lectures, and sermons. Capitalize the first letter of the principal words in the title.

movie

"Gone With the Wind" is a classic that is still enjoyed by movie viewers.

lecture

Dr. Zimmer's dynamic presentation, "Politics and Education," was concluded with a challenge the audience could not overlook.

television series

Rerun marathons of "The Twilight Zone" still entertain today's young adults.

Punctuation

6–4. Punctuation Format

a. **Titles of literary and artistic works are often used in appositive expressions; that is, they are used to rename a previously mentioned noun. In cases where the title is not needed to identify the work, set it off from the rest of the sentence with commas. Where the title is needed for identification, no commas are used.**

title unnecessary to determine which article

His latest article, "Marketing Changes in the Automotive Industry," recommended a startling departure from current practices.

title necessary to determine which book

The book Escape to Riches should soon make the best-seller list.

b. **Periods and commas are *always* placed before the closing quotation mark; semicolons and colons *always* follow the closing quotation mark.**

period and comma before closing quotation mark

Hawaii is the location of our new movie, "Mousetrap."

Your last article, "Computerized Accounting Procedures in the Banking Industry," was certainly helpful to me in planning our new procedures.

semicolon and colon after closing quotation mark

Yesterday we saw the last performance of "Les Miserables"; on Saturday "Phantom of the Opera" will open.

The following performers have been selected to star in the new television series, "New York Strike Force": Rod Whitcomb, Erika Lovejoy, Steve Markham, and Lisa Darnell.

c. **Question or exclamation marks appearing with and at the end of quoted titles are placed before the closing quotation mark. If the question or exclamation mark in a title appears at the end of the sentence, no other form of punctuation is required. On the other hand, if the sentence, not the title, is a question or exclamation, place the ending punctuation mark outside the closing quotation mark.**

6

quoted question in middle of sentence

The movie "Who's Afraid of Virginia Woolf?" was shown on television last week.

quoted question at end of sentence

Last week we saw the movie "Who's Afraid of Virginia Woolf?"

Have you seen the movie "Who's Afraid of Virginia Woolf?"

quotation separate from question

When will you be able to purchase tickets for "Fiddler on the Roof"?

6

CHAPTER 7

Words Often Misused and Confused

All entries in this chapter appear in alphabetical order.

7

A/An
A (used before a word beginning with a consonant sound or a long $\bar{u}$ sound)—Please call *a* technician to service the photocopier. A *u*nion representative met with us yesterday.
An (used before a word beginning with a vowel sound other than long $\bar{u}$)—Please make *an* appointment for me with Dr. Carlson.

A while/Awhile
A while (an adjective-noun combination meaning "a short time")—He will be here in *a while.*
Awhile (used as an adverb meaning "*for* a short time")—Exercise *awhile* each day to maintain your good health.

Accede/Exceed
Accede (to agree or consent)—I will *accede* to this request only if the tenants sign a one-year lease.
Exceed (to surpass a limit)—Many accidents occur when people *exceed* the posted speed limit.

Accept/Except
Accept (to take or receive)—We do not *accept* checks written on out-of-state banks.
Except (with the exclusion of, but)—No one else *except* you knows about the proposed merger.

Access/Excess
Access (admittance or approachability)—Everyone in the office should have *access* to these files.
Excess (beyond ordinary limits; a surplus)—You may return all *excess* flooring materials for full credit within 60 days of purchase.

Ad/Add
Ad (abbreviated form of *advertisement*)—We have filled most of our personnel needs by running an *ad* in the local newspaper.
Add (to increase by uniting or joining)—This new computer will *add* to the efficiency of our office staff.

Adapt/Adept/Adopt
Adapt (to adjust or modify)—We must readily *adapt* ourselves to new situations in this rapidly changing market.
Adept (skilled)—The person hired for this position must be *adept* at dealing with the public.
Adopt (to take and follow as one's own)—We will *adopt* Mrs. Williams' proposal to computerize our accounting system.

Add: see Ad.

Addict/Edict
Addict (one who is habitually or obsessively dependent; devotee)—Our clinic has noted success with the rehabilitation of drug *addicts.* Many of today's teenagers are rock music *addicts.*
Edict (order or command)—When did our manager issue this *edict?*

Addition/Edition
Addition (the process of uniting or joining)—The increased production quotas require the *addition* of factory floor space in all our facilities.
Edition (a particular version of printed material)—Only the second *edition* of this book is now available.

Adept: see Adapt.

Adherence/Adherents
Adherence (a steady attachment or loyalty)—A strict *adherence* to all safety procedures is required of all personnel.
Adherents (loyal supporters or followers)—There are many *adherents* to the space program and its importance to the human race.

7

Adopt: see Adapt.

Adverse/Averse
Adverse (opposing; antagonistic)—Rising interest rates have had an *adverse* effect on real estate sales and new home developments.
Averse (unwilling; reluctant)—Carol is a valuable employee because she is not *averse* to working overtime.

Advice/Advise
Advice *n.* (a suggestion, an opinion, or a recommendation)—He would have avoided the problem if he had followed his attorney's *advice.*
Advise *v.* (to counsel or recommend)—We had to *advise* her not to sign the contract in its present form.

Affect/Effect
Affect *v.* (to influence)—Large pay increases throughout the country will *affect* the rate of inflation. Increased costs will *affect* our pricing policies on all merchandise.
Effect *v.* (to bring about or cause to happen; to create)—Our government plans to *effect* a change in the rate of inflation by tightening bank credits. Rising costs of raw materials will *effect* large price increases in May.
Effect *n.* (a result or consequence)—Inflation usually has a negative *effect* on our economy. The new vacation policy had no apparent *effect* on company morale.

Aid/Aide
Aid (to help or assist; assistance)—The United States *aids* many foreign countries. Your application for financial *aid* is currently being processed.
Aide (a person who assists another)—Please ask your *aide* to deliver these papers to Dr. Powell's office by Friday afternoon.

7

Aisle/Isle
Aisle (a passageway for inside traffic)—After the show the *aisles* of the theater were cluttered with empty popcorn containers and candy wrappers.
Isle (a piece of land surrounded by water; island)—This script centers around two teenagers marooned on a tropical *isle.*

Allowed/Aloud
Allowed (permitted)—We are *allowed* to sell our products only through contracted retail outlets.
Aloud (to speak audibly)—The president's resignation was read *aloud* to all board members present.

All ready/Already
All ready (prepared)—We are *all ready* to initiate the new procedures as soon as the equipment arrives.
Already (by or before this time)—Orders for our August sale have *already* been placed with the suppliers.

All right/Alright
All right (approving or agreeable)—It is *all right* with our supervisor if you wish to change your vacation dates from June to July.
Alright (an informal spelling of *all right* that is not appropriate for business writing).

All together/Altogether
All together (everyone in a group)—We must work *all together* if the company is to survive this crisis.
Altogether (wholly; entirely)—*Altogether,* 20 families signed up for the company picnic.

Allude/Elude
Allude (to mention or refer to)—As proof of Americans' concern for economy, I *allude* to the increased popularity of small cars during recent years.
Elude (to evade or escape)—The Senator has been able to *elude* severe criticisms of his program by anticipating and counteracting objections.

Allusion/Delusion/Illusion
Allusion (an indirect reference)—Several *allusions* were made to Mr. Reed's apparent laziness.
Delusion (a false belief)—Many people invested heavily in these oil stocks because the company propagated the *delusion* that its wells were active producers.
Illusion (a misconception or misapprehension)—Many of our employees had the *illusion* that this new equipment would reduce our staff by one half.

All ways/Always
All ways (by all methods)—We must try *all ways* possible to solve the problem.
Always (at all times; continually)—Our company is *always* on the lookout for qualified office personnel.

Almost/Most
Almost (an adverb meaning "nearly")—Our company *almost* reached its sales quota this year.
Most (an adjective or subject complement meaning "the greatest in amount or number")—Ellen Reynolds received the *most* votes in the election for faculty senate treasurer.

Aloud: see Allowed.

Already: see All ready.

Alright: see All right.

Altar/Alter
Altar (a structure used for worship)—The wedding flowers made the *altar* look particularly beautiful.
Alter (to change)—The plane had to *alter* its altitude to avoid hitting the mountain.

Altogether: see All together.

7

Always: see All ways.

Among/Between
Among (refers to more than two persons or things)—Distribute the supplies equally *among* the three departments.
Between (refers to two persons or things)—The final selection for the position is *between* Ms. Claffey and Mr. Thompson.

Amount/Number
Amount (used with singular nouns and mass items that cannot be counted)—Only a small *amount* of the pie was eaten. Because of the power failure, a significant *amount* of the frozen food had deteriorated and was discarded.
Number (used with plural nouns and items that can be counted)—Only a small *number* of spaces have been allotted for visitor parking. This year the *number* of children in each classroom has been reduced by three.

An: see A.

Anecdote/Antidote
Anecdote (a story of a brief account of an event)—We all had to laugh at Tom's *anecdote* about the customer who insisted upon returning a product our store doesn't even sell.
Antidote (a remedy that counteracts a harmful substance or circumstance)—Dr. Martin has consented to write an article about the new *antidote* he developed to counteract five different poisons.

Annual/Annul
Annual (yearly)—The company's *annual* report will be mailed to all stockholders next week.
Annul (to void or abolish)—We had to *annul* the contract because of unexpected legal complications.

Antidote: see Anecdote.

Any one/Anyone
Any one (any one person or thing in a group [always followed by "of"])—Please hand me *any one* of those pencils.
Anyone (any person)—If you know of *anyone* who has these qualifications, please have that person contact our personnel manager.

Any time/Anytime
Any time (an unspecified *point* in time; an amount of time)—Please let us know *any time* you have questions about our products or services. *Any time* we can be of service, just call our toll-free number and a telephone representative will assist you. We do not have *any time* to review this case.
Anytime (at any time *whatsoever*)—Drop by our offices *anytime.* For an emergency you may call Dr. Mulcahy *anytime,* day or night. During the last quarter of the year, you may take your vacation *anytime.*

Any way/Anyway
Any way (any method)—Is there *any way* we can step up production to advance our July 1 release date?
Anyway (in any case)—Considering the low bids of our competitors, I don't believe we would have received the contract *anyway.*
Anyways (an informal form of *anyway* that is not appropriate for business writing).

Appraise/Apprise
Appraise (to estimate)—Before we can liquidate this company, we must hire an outside firm to *appraise* its assets.
Apprise (to inform or notify)—Please *apprise* all employees immediately of this change in policy.

As/Like
As (used as a conjunction at the beginning of a clause)—I will get the material to you by Friday, *as* (not *like*) I promised. Our manager always acts *as if* (not *like*) he knows more than anyone else.
Like (used when the sentence requires a preposition [followed only by a noun or pronoun and its modifiers])—This new adhesive feels *like* wet cement. I have never met anyone *like* him.

Ascent/Assent
Ascent (rising or going up)—The recent *ascent* of stock market prices is an encouraging sign for the economy.
Assent (to agree or consent)—Everyone at the meeting will surely *assent* to the plan you have outlined in this report.

Assistance/Assistants
Assistance (help or aid)—The project could not have been completed on time without your *assistance.*
Assistants (people who aid or help a superior)—The consultant's staffing report indicates that our general manager should have three *assistants.*

Assure/Ensure/Insure
Assure (to promise; to make a positive declaration)—I *assure* you that the loan will be repaid according to the terms specified in the note. Please *assure* the patient that this procedure is not painful.
Ensure (to make certain)—To *ensure* the timely completion of this project, please hire additional qualified personnel.
Insure (to protect against financial loss)—We *insure* all our facilities against earthquake damage.

Attendance/Attendants
Attendance (being present or attending)—At least two thirds of the members of this committee must be in *attendance* before the meeting can be called to order.
Attendants (one who attends with or to others)—The *attendants* had difficulty parking all the cars for such a large crowd.

7

Averse: see Adverse.

Awhile: see A while.

Bad/Badly
Bad (an adjective or subject complement used after such intransitive or nonaction verbs as *is, was, feel, look,* or *smell*)—I feel *bad* that your transfer request was denied. Profits for the first quarter of this year look *bad* in view of the additional expenses incurred by our sales staff. The air in this office smells *bad.*
Badly (an adverb used with transitive or action verbs)—We *badly* need the advice of a tax attorney before we invest further in this project. The defeated candidate behaved *badly* before thousands of television viewers.

Bail/Bale
Bail (guarantee of money necessary to see a person free from jail until the trial)—*Bail* in your client's case has been set at $5,000.
Bale (a large bundle)—One *bale* of used clothing was lost in transit.

Bare/Bear
Bare (uncovered, empty, plain, or mere)—The paint had chipped and peeled so badly that the *bare* wood was showing. After the break-in two offices were *bare* of furniture and equipment. Every summer our family spends two weeks in a *bare* wooden cabin in the mountains. I had time to cover only the *bare* facts involved in this issue.
Bear (to support, carry, or bring forth)—Unfortunately, he had to *bear* the brunt of the losses. Our travel agency will secure for you guides who have donkeys to *bear* the luggage and provisions. As a result of the surgery, the patient was able to *bear* children.

Base/Bass
Base (bottom part of something; foundation)—When did the *base* of this marble column crack?
Bass (a low-pitched sound; musical instrument having a low range)—We could use his *bass* voice in our quartet. Do you play the *bass* violin?

Bear: see Bare.

Beside/Besides
Beside (by the side of)—Please put the new file cabinet *beside* the one in the corner.
Besides (in addition to)—Who else *besides* Ms. Graham was awarded a bonus?

Between: see Among.

Biannual/Biennial
Biannual (occurring twice a year)—The stockholders' *biannual* meetings are held in January and July.
Biennial (occurring once every two years)—According to our society's constitution, the *biennial* election of officers should be held in November.

Billed/Build
Billed (charged for goods or services)—You will be *billed* on the 10th of each month.
Build (to construct)—We plan to *build* a new plant in Texas.

Bolder/Boulder
Bolder (more fearless or daring)—Perhaps we need a *bolder* person as president of the university.
Boulder (a large rock)—Damage to the insured's left-front tire was apparently caused by a *boulder* in the road.

Born/Borne
Born (brought forth by birth; originated)—This patient was *born* on February 14, 1935. One can hardly believe that this multimillion-dollar industry was *born* in a garage just two decades ago.
Borne (past participle of *bear*)—Mrs. Talbert has already *borne* six children, and she is currently expecting her seventh. Our school district has *borne* these financial burdens for over six years.

Bouillon/Bullion
Bouillon (a clear soup)—For the first course I have ordered beef *bouillon.*
Bullion (uncoined gold or silver in bars or ingots)—Mr. Reece had hidden in his home nearly $25,000 in gold *bullion.*

Boulder: see Bolder.

Breach/Breech
Breach (a violation of a law or agreement; a hole, gap, or break)—The judge ruled that a *breach* of contract existed when the building was not finished by the date agreed upon. If contract negotiations are to continue, we must narrow the *breach* between union and management negotiators.
Breech (part of a firearm or cannon that is located behind the barrel)—They had difficulty firing the old cannon because the *breech* would not work properly.

Build: see Billed.

Bullion: see Bouillon.

Callous/Callus
Callous (insensitive; without feeling)—Everyone on the committee agreed that Mr. Bush's *callous* remark concerning Ms. Wright's attire was in poor taste.
Callus (hard, thick skin)—Pointed-toe shoes can cause permanent *calluses* on your feet.

Can/May
Can (the ability to do something)—Pauline *can* convert our manual accounting system to a computerized one.
May (permission)—Yes, you *may* take a day's vacation tomorrow.

7

Canvas/Canvass
Canvas (a firm, closely woven cloth)—Use these *canvas* coverings to protect the new cars as they arrive.
Canvass (to survey or solicit in an area)—Do you have a volunteer who will *canvass* the residences on Jersey Street?

Capital/Capitol
Capital *n.* (a city in which the official seat of government is located; the wealth of an individual or firm)—The *capital* of Wisconsin is Madison. Much of our *capital* is tied up in equipment.
Capital *adj.* (punishable by death; foremost in importance)—Treason in many countries is a *capital* crime. The forthcoming election is *capital* in the minds of the school board members.
Capitol *n.* (a building used by the U.S. Congress [always capitalized])—Senator Reece must be in the *Capitol* by 9 a.m. for the hearings. The United States *Capitol* is a major tourist attraction in Washington, D.C.
Capitol *n.* (a building in which a state legislature convenes [capitalized only when used in full name of building])—The *capitol* was surrounded by angry pickets waving placards. Is this office located in the California State *Capitol?*

Carat/Caret/Carrot/Karat
Carat (a unit of weight for gems)—Her engagement ring has a 2-*carat* diamond surrounded by six 20-point diamonds.
Caret (a symbol similar to an inverted *v* that is placed at the bottom of a line to show where something is to be inserted)—Our editor asked us to use a *caret* to show any insertions or additions in the manuscript.

Carrot (a vegetable)—A *carrot* can be just as delicious raw as it is cooked.
Karat (a unit of weight for gold)—The chain was made of 18-*karat* gold.

Cease/Seize
Cease (come to an end; stop)—Please *cease* shipment of any further orders to the Hogan Company until its current account has been paid.
Seize (to take possession of; to take)—Will the Internal Revenue Service *seize* all the company's assets for the payment of back taxes? You may wish to *seize* this opportunity to ask Mr. Rodriguez for a salary increase.

Censor/Censure
Censor (to examine materials and delete objectionable matter; one who censors)—We will need to *censor* scenes from this movie for television viewing. When will the *censor* finish reviewing the script?
Censure (to criticize or condemn; condemnation)—The city council *censured* the mayor for awarding the contract to his brother-in-law's firm. After the facts were disclosed, Senator Dillon was subjected to public *censure.*

Census/Senses
Census (an official count of a country's population)—The United States takes an official *census* every ten years.
Senses (the specialized functions of sight, hearing, smell, taste, and touch)—Our client's *senses* of hearing and touch were altered as a result of the accident.

7

Cent/Scent/Sent
Cent (a coin known as a "penny")—Your tallies always balance to the last *cent.*
Scent (a distinctive smell or odor)—Because Webby Bakery is located in our industrial complex, the *scent* of freshly baked bread permeates the area each morning.
Sent (the past tense and past participle of *send*)—Your order was *sent* by United Parcel Service yesterday.

Cereal/Serial
Cereal (a breakfast food made from grain)—Your diet calls for a daily serving of wheat *cereal.*
Serial (arranged in a series)—The *serial* numbers of all our vehicles should be on file in your office.

Choose/Chose
Choose (to select or make a choice)—We do not know whom he will *choose* for his executive assistant.
Chose (past tense of "choose")—The new president *chose* Ms. Randall to be his executive assistant.

Cite/Sight/Site
Cite (to quote or mention; to summon)—Dr. Rosenthal can *cite* many authorities who have studied the problem of pollution in major United States cities. Did the police officer *cite* you for speeding?

Sight (to see or take aim; a view or spectacle)—Luckily the salesperson did not *sight* Ms. Brown leaving the office. The Statue of Liberty is a frequently visited tourist *sight* in New York City.
Site (a location)—This 20-acre land parcel is a perfect *site* for the proposed housing project.

Coarse/Course
Coarse (rough texture)—This material is too *coarse* for our use.
Course (a particular direction or route; part of a meal; a unit of learning)—We are now committed to a *course* of action that we hope will increase our sales volume. Which menu item have you selected for the main *course?* You need only three more *courses* to graduate.

Collision/Collusion
Collision (a crash)—Fortunately, no one was hurt in the *collision.*
Collusion (an agreement to defraud)—No one suspected them of *collusion.*

Command/Commend
Command (to order or direct; an order)—The sergeant *commanded* his troops to return to base by 0600. This dog has been trained to obey only its owner's *commands.*
Commend (to praise or flatter)—Please *commend* the staff for the fine job it did in promoting our line at the San Francisco convention.

Complement/Compliment
Complement (that which completes or makes perfect)—The paintings you have selected for the office reception area will *complement* the remainder of the decor. You may wish to select one of our fine wines to *complement* your meal.
Compliment (to praise or flatter)—Mr. Rose did *compliment* me on the fine job I had done.

Complementary/Complimentary
Complementary (serving mutually to blend, fill out, or complete)—Both these wall coverings are *complementary* to the carpeting you have selected.
Complimentary (favorable; given free)—We appreciate receiving your *complimentary* letter about the service you received in our Fifth Avenue store. To receive a *complimentary* copy of this textbook, merely fill out and return the enclosed postcard.

Confidant/Confident
Confidant (a trusted friend)—He has been his closest *confidant* for years.
Confident (sure of oneself)—Mrs. Allen was *confident* she would get the position.

Conscience/Conscious
Conscience (the faculty of knowing right from wrong)—In the last analysis, his *conscience* required him to release the funds.
Conscious (aware or mentally awake)—Yes, we are *conscious* of the new marketing opportunities available to our firm. Most of our patients are *conscious* during this type of surgery.

Console/Consul
Console (a cabinet)—The popularity of our Model 4750 stereo may be attributed to its attractive *console.*
Consul (an official representing a foreign country)—Travel information can often be obtained by contacting the *consul* of the country one wishes to visit.

Continual/Continuous
Continual (a regular or frequent occurrence)—These *continual* telephone calls are disrupting my routine.
Continuous (without interruption or cessation)—The *continuous* humming of the new air conditioner is disturbing everyone in the office.

Cooperation/Corporation
Cooperation (working together)—The full *cooperation* of all employees is needed to reduce our high rate of absenteeism.
Corporation (one type of business organization)—We are looking into the possibility of forming a *corporation.*

Corespondent/Correspondence/Correspondents
Corespondent (person named as guilty of adultery with the defendant in a divorce suit)—Who was named as *corespondent* in this divorce case?
Correspondence (letters or other written communications)—Our last *correspondence* from Mr. Flores was dated October 14.
Correspondents (letter writers or news reporters)—Be sure to have one of our *correspondents* answer these customers' letters within the next three days. African *correspondents* have reported that several countries are now suffering severe food shortages.

7

Corporation: see Cooperation.

Corps/Corpse
Corps (a body of persons having a common activity or occupation)—A *corps* of students have been soliciting funds for the stadium lights. Representatives from the Marine *Corps* will visit our campus next week.
Corpse (a dead body)—The identity of the *corpse* is still unknown.

Correspondence: see Corespondent.

Correspondent: see Corespondent.

Council/Counsel
Council (a governing body)—We will present the proposal to the city *council* in the morning.
Counsel (to give advice; advice)—Our staff *counsels* at least eight students each day. In this situation the president received good *counsel* from his advisors.

Course: see Coarse.

Credible/Creditable
Credible (believable or reliable)—The excuses offered by Ms. Day for her many absences are hardly *credible.*
Creditable (bringing honor or praise)—Ms. Kawakami's perfect attendance record is certainly *creditable.*

Decent/Descent/Dissent
Decent (in good taste; proper)—The *decent* solution to the problem would have been for the salesperson to apologize for his rude behavior.
Descent (moving downward; ancestry)—The view of the city was breathtaking as the plane began its *descent* into the Denver airport. Mr. Sirakides is of Greek *descent.*
Dissent (differences or disagreement)—There was no *dissent* among the council members concerning the resolution to expand our city's parking facilities.

Defer/Differ
Defer (to put off or delay)—Our company has decided to *defer* this project until next spring.
Differ (to vary or disagree)—Doctors *differ* in their views as to the optimum treatment for this particular virus.

Deference/Difference
Deference (yielding to someone else's wishes)—In *deference* to many shoppers' requests, the store remained open until 9 p.m. during the summer months.
Difference (state of being different; dissimilarity)—There is little *difference* between these two product brands.

Delusion: see Allusion.

Deprecate/Depreciate
Deprecate (to disapprove or downgrade)—His speech did nothing but *deprecate* the present zoning system.
Depreciate (to lessen the value)—We will *depreciate* this new equipment over a ten-year period.

Descent: see Decent.

Desert/Dessert
Desert (an arid, barren land area)—Palm Springs was once a *desert* area occupied only by California Indians.
Dessert (a sweet course served at the end of a meal)—Apple pie and ice cream is a traditional American *dessert.*

Device/Devise
Device (an invention or mechanism)—The *device* worked perfectly during the demonstration.
Devise (to think out or plan)—Were you able to *devise* an overtime plan that would be equitable to all employees?

Dew/Do/Due
Dew (drops of moisture)—The heavy morning *dew* caused the airport officials to delay our flight.
Do (to perform or bring about)—We must *do* everything possible to ship the order by June 17.
Due (immediately payable)—All payments are *due* by the 10th of each month.

Differ: see Defer.

Difference: see Deference.

Disapprove/Disprove
Disapprove (to withhold approval)—Our manager will *disapprove* any plan that is not properly justified.
Disprove (to prove false)—We must *disprove* the rumor that we are cutting back production next month.

Disburse/Disperse
Disburse (to pay out; to distribute methodically)—A new system has been devised to *disburse* commissions more rapidly. The property will be *disbursed* according to the provisions set forth in Mr. Williams' will.
Disperse (to scatter; to cause to become widely spread)—The crowd *dispersed* rapidly after the ball game. Those factories that *disperse* pollutants into the environment will continue to be subject to heavy fines. Please *disperse* this information to consumers nationwide.

Disprove: see Disapprove.

Dissent: see Decent.

Do: see Dew.

Done/Dun
Done (past participle of *do*)—Our company has not *done* any further research in this area.
Dun (to make persistent demands for payment; a variable drab color, usually a neutral brownish gray)—Ms. Green's main responsibility is to *dun* slow-paying customers. One of our tasks is to repaint these *dun*-colored walls to achieve a more cheerful atmosphere.

Due: see Dew.

Dun: see Done.

Edict: see Addict.

Edition: see Addition.

Effect: see Affect.

Elicit/Illicit
Elicit (to draw out or bring forth)—Was the speaker able to *elicit* questions from the audience?
Illicit (unlawful)—One of our agents was cited for *illicit* business practices.

Elude: see Allude.

Emigrate/Immigrate
Emigrate (to move from a country)—The Johnsons *emigrated* from Norway in 1979.
Immigrate (to enter a country)—How many Canadians were permitted to *immigrate* to the United States last year?

Eminent/Imminent
Eminent (prominent; distinguished)—Mr. Mendez is an *eminent* authority on labor relations.
Imminent (impending; likely to occur)—There is *imminent* danger of equipment breakdown unless periodic service checks are made.

Ensure: see Assure.

Envelop/Envelope
Envelop (to wrap, surround, or conceal)—Each tamale is *enveloped* in a corn husk before it is cooked. The chief said his fire fighters would *envelop* the fire by morning. Each day a layer of early morning fog *envelops* the city.
Envelope (a container for a letter)—Please send me your answer in the return *envelope* provided for your convenience.

Every day/Everyday
Every day (each day)—I will call you *every day* and give you a status report on the new project.
Everyday (ordinary)—Sales meetings seem to be an *everyday* occurrence in this office.

Every one/Everyone
Every one (each person or thing in a group [always followed by "of"])—*Every one* of our secretaries is proficient in the use of our word processing and spreadsheet programs.
Everyone (all people in a group)—*Everyone* is expected to be on time for the stockholders' meeting.

Exceed: see Accede.

Except: see Accept.

Excess: see Access.

Executioner/Executor
Executioner (one who puts to death)—The *executioner*-style murders still remain unsolved.
Executor (person appointed to carry out the provisions of a will)—Whom have you named as *executor* of your will?

Expand/Expend
Expand (to enlarge)—The plan to *expand* our storage facilities was approved.
Expend (to use up or pay out)—Ms. Smith *expends* too much time dealing with insignificant matters. If you do not *expend* these moneys by June 30, they will revert to the general fund.

Expansive/Expensive
Expansive (capable of expanding; extensive)—An *expansive* commercial development is planned for this area.
Expensive (costly)—The consultant's recommendations were too *expensive* to implement.

Expend: see Expand.

7

Expensive: see Expansive.

Explicit/Implicit
Explicit (expressed clearly)—The accompanying booklet gives *explicit* instructions for assembling this piece of equipment.
Implicit (implied)—By reading between the lines, one can discern an *implicit* appeal for additional funds.

Extant/Extent
Extant (currently or actually existing)—Please provide me with a three-year budget for all *extant* and projected programs.
Extent (range, scope, or magnitude)—Unfortunately, we will be unable to assess the *extent* of the damage until next week.

Facetious/Factious
Facetious (humorous or witty, often in an inappropriate manner)—His seemingly *facetious* remark contained a kernel of truth.
Factious (creating a faction or dissension)—A series of *factious* disputes eventually led to the dissolution of the partnership.

Factitious/Fictitious
Factitious (artificial)—One manufacturer created a *factitious* demand for copper alloy by spreading rumors of shortages.
Fictitious (nonexistent; imaginary; false)—Many people believe that the reported UFO sightings are *fictitious.* This suspect has been known to operate under a number of *fictitious* names.

Fair/Fare
Fair (marked by impartiality and honesty; an exhibition; mediocre)—Further legislation was passed recently to enforce *fair* employment practices. Our annual county *fair* is usually held during the first week of September. He did a *fair* job.
Fare (get along or succeed; price charged to transport a person)—Our company did not *fare* well in its last bidding competition. How much is the first-class airline *fare* from Chicago to New York?

Farther/Further
Farther (a greater distance [always a measurable amount of space])—The trip from the warehouse to the plant is *farther* than I thought.
Further (additional; to help forward)—Refer to my July 8 memo for *further* details. The Truesdale Foundation has contributed $5 million to *further* research in spinal cord injuries.

Feat/Fete
Feat (an act of skill, endurance, or ingenuity)—Under stress human beings have been known to perform *feats* beyond their normal capabilities.
Fete (to honor or commemorate; a large elaborate party)—A large banquet is being planned to *fete* our company president upon his retirement in September. The *fete* to honor our company president will be held on August 19.

Fewer/Less
Fewer (used with items that can be counted and plural nouns)—We had *fewer* sales this month. Reserve this checkout for customers with ten or *fewer* items. *Fewer* than half the apples had been eaten.
Less (used with mass items that cannot be counted and singular nouns)—You will get by with *less* work if you follow my suggestions. *Less* than half the pie had been eaten.

Fictitious: see Factitious.

Finally/Finely
Finally (in the end)—The missing part was *finally* delivered.
Finely (elegantly or delicately; in small parts)—We all admired the *finely* embroidered tapestry. This engine has been *finely* tuned by our expert mechanics. You may purchase these *finely* chopped nuts in 8- and 16-ounce packages.

Flagrant/Fragrant
Flagrant (glaring; scandalous)—His behavior was a *flagrant* violation of company policy.
Fragrant (sweet smelling)—She received a *fragrant* bouquet of flowers from the staff.

Flair/Flare
Flair (a natural talent or aptitude)—Ms. Strehike has a *flair* for making people feel at ease when they enter the office.
Flare (to blaze up or spread out)—The gusty winds could easily cause the fire to *flare* out of control.

Flaunt/Flout
Flaunt (to make a gaudy or defiant display)—Although Mrs. Paige is recognized as one of the most affluent people in Hartford, she does not *flaunt* her wealth.
Flout (to mock or show contempt for)—As a new driver, the young man continued to *flout* the posted speed limit.

Flew/Flu/Flue
Flew (past tense of *fly*)—The plane *flew* to the West Coast in record time.
Flu (abbreviated form of *influenza*)—Nearly 30 percent of our employees are absent because of the *flu.*
Flue (a duct in a chimney)—If the *flue* is closed, smoke from a burning fire cannot escape through the chimney.

Flout: see Flaunt.

Flu: see Flew.

Flue: see Flew.

7

Formally/Formerly
Formally (in a formal manner)—At our next meeting you will be *formally* initiated into the organization.
Formerly (in the past)—Marie Martin was *formerly* the president of a large metropolitan area community college.

Former/Latter
Former (first of two things or belonging to an earlier time)—Your *former* suggestion appears to be the better one. As a *former* employee, Lois Oliver is always invited to our annual company picnic.
Latter (second of two things or nearer to the end)—Of the two proposals the *latter* one seems to be more economical. Mail deliveries in your area are scheduled for the *latter* part of the day.

Forth/Fourth
Forth (forward)—The president requested that any objections to his plan be brought *forth* at this time.
Fourth (a numeric term; the ordinal form of *four*)—The *fourth* member of our group never arrived.

Fragrant: see Flagrant.

Further: see Farther.

Good/Well
Good (an adjective that describes a noun or pronoun)—Mr. Collins writes *good* letters.
Well (an adverb that describes a verb, an adjective, or another adverb; a person's well-being and health)—The majority of our nursing graduates do *well* on their state board examinations. My secretary did not look *well* today.

Grate/Great

Grate (to reduce to small particles by rubbing on something rough; to cause irritation; a frame of parallel or crossed bars blocking a passage)—In the future please use a food processor to *grate* the cheese for our pizzas. His continual talking could *grate* on anyone's nerves. Be sure to place a *grate* over this excavation when you have finished removing the dirt.
Great (large in size; numerous; eminent or distinguished)—From the cruise ship we often sight a *great* white shark. A *great* many people have expressed an interest in purchasing our Model No. 47A videocassette recorder. Many *great* performers from stage and screen will be present at our annual benefit.

Guarantee/Guaranty

Guarantee (assurance of the quality or length of service of a product; an assurance for the fulfillment of a condition)—All our cars have a one-year or 50,000-mile *guarantee.* I *guarantee* that your children will enjoy immensely the adventures Disneyland has to offer.
Guaranty (an assurance to pay the debt of another in case of default; to agree to pay the debt of another in case of default)—John Fletcher's car loan will be approved as soon as we receive his parents' signed *guaranty.* The federal government will *guaranty* all loans made under this new student loan program.

7

He/Him/Himself

He (the subject of a clause or a complement pronoun)—*He* is the one I interviewed for the job. The person in our family with the best singing voice has always been *he.*
Him (a direct object, an indirect object, or an object of a preposition)—The president asked *him* to head the project. Doris Waters gave *him* the results of the study yesterday. The choice is between you and *him.*
Himself (a reflexive pronoun used to emphasize or refer back to the subject)—He *himself* had to solve the problem. Rick Bogart addressed the envelope to *himself.*

Hear/Here

Hear (to perceive by the ear)—Yes, I can *hear* you clearly.
Here (in this place or at this point)—Install the telephone *here.*

Her/Herself/She

Her (a direct object, an indirect object, or an object of a preposition)—When Paulette arrived, Mr. Schultz asked *her* for the information. Barbara offered *her* a chair. The check is for *her.*
Herself (a reflexive pronoun used to emphasize or refer back to the subject)—Wendy *herself* wrote and dictated the entire audit report. Kristen often talks to *herself.*
She (the subject of a clause or a complement pronoun)—*She* went to lunch about 15 minutes ago. It was *she* who designed this spreadsheet.

Here: see Hear.

Herself: see Her.

Hew/Hue
Hew (to cut with blows of a heavy cutting instrument)—Which famous faces have been *hewed* on Mt. Rushmore?
Hue (color or gradation of color; aspect)—The *hues* of the rainbow glistened in the sunlight. Persons from every political *hue* criticized the President for not informing the American public of his actions.

Him: see He.

Himself: see He.

Hoard/Horde
Hoard (to store or accumulate for future use)—Please do not *hoard* stationery and other supplies.
Horde (a multitude)—A *horde* of people were waiting for the doors to open.

Hole/Whole
Hole (an opening or open place)—Burglars had entered the jewelry store by cutting a *hole* through the outer wall.
Whole (complete; entire)—Too many inexperienced managers make decisions before knowing the *whole* story.

Holy/Wholly
Holy (sacred)—This place is considered *holy* by some people.
Wholly (completely)—Do you agree *wholly* with the committee's recommendations?

Horde: see Hoard.

Hue: see Hew.

Human/Humane
Human (characteristic of people)—Please remember that all of us are guilty of possessing *human* frailties.
Humane (marked by compassion, sympathy, or consideration)—The treatment of elderly people in this convalescent home is certainly less than *humane.*

Hypercritical/Hypocritical
Hypercritical (excessively critical)—Many believe Mr. Reed to be *hypercritical* of new employees.
Hypocritical (falsely pretending)—*Hypocritical* people have difficulty keeping friends.

I/Me/Myself
I (a subject of a clause or a complement pronoun)—*I* finished the report last night. If you were *I,* what would you do under these circumstances?
Me (a direct object, an indirect object, or an object of a preposition)—Jolene Mack telephoned *me* this morning. Pat gave *me* the report this morning. None of this material is for *me.*

Myself (a reflective pronoun used to emphasize or refer back to the subject)—I wrote the entire report *myself.* I can blame only *myself* for losing this sale.

Ideal/Idle/Idol
Ideal (perfect; model)—Your proposal outlines an *ideal* solution to the problem.
Idle (doing nothing)—The production line was *idle* for almost a week.
Idol (an object for religious worship; a revered person or thing)—One of the church *idols* had been vandalized. Money is often the *idol* of ambitious, greedy people.

Illicit: see Elicit.

Illusion: see Allusion.

Immigrate: see Emigrate.

Imminent: see Eminent.

Implicit: see Explicit.

7

Imply/Infer
Imply (to suggest without stating)—Does that statement *imply* that I have made a mistake?
Infer (to reach a conclusion)—From the results of this independent survey, we can only *infer* that our advertising campaign in the Pittsburgh area was ineffective.

Incidence/Incidents
Incidence (occurrence)—There has yet to be an *incidence* of theft within the company.
Incidents (events or episodes)—Several *incidents* have occurred recently that require us to review our safety policies and practices.

Incite/Insight
Incite (to urge on or provoke action)—The speaker attempted to *incite* the audience to take action. Poverty, depression, and starvation *incited* riots throughout the country.
Insight (keen understanding)—Bob's *insight* and patience prevented the situation from developing into a major problem.

Indigenous/Indigent/Indignant
Indigenous (native of a particular region)—I believe that this tree is *indigenous* only to the Northwest.
Indigent (poor; needy)—My parents were *indigent* farmers.
Indignant (insulting; angry)—Successful store managers must know how to deal with *indignant* customers.

Infer: see Imply.

Ingenious/Ingenuous
Ingenious (marked by originality, resourcefulness, and cleverness)—This *ingenious* plan could save our company thousands of dollars annually.
Ingenuous (showing innocent or childlike simplicity; natural)—Mr. Warren's *ingenuous* smile and warm personality have contributed immeasurably to his successful political career.

Insight: see Incite.

Insure: see Assure.

Interstate/Intrastate
Interstate (between states)—Since expanding operations to New Jersey, we must abide by all laws governing *interstate* commerce.
Intrastate (within a state)—This firm, an Illinois corporation, is primarily concerned with *intrastate* product sales.

Isle: see Aisle.

7

Its/It's
Its (possessive form of *it*)—The company had *its* stockholders' meeting in Atlanta last week.
It's (contraction of *it is*)—Although this model microwave oven has become very popular, *it's* not our best-seller.

Karat: see Carat.

Later/Latter
Later (after the proper time)—The shipment arrived *later* than we had anticipated.
Latter (the second thing of two things mentioned)—Your *latter* suggestion is more likely to be adopted. [See also *Former.*]

Lay/Lie
Lay (to put or place; a transitive verb that needs an object to complete its meaning; *lay, laid, laid,* and *laying* are the principal parts of this verb)—Please *lay* the message on my desk. I *laid* the message on your desk. I have *laid* several messages on your desk from Fred Obermiller. We are *laying* the foundation for the new building today.
Lie (to recline; an intransitive verb that does not have an object; *lie, lay, lain,* and *lying* are the principal parts of this verb)—May I *lie* down? He *lay* in the hospital waiting room for over three hours before a doctor saw him. These papers have *lain* on your desk since Monday. Mrs. Hartman is *lying* down.

Lean/Lien
Lean (to rest against; to be inclined toward; not fat)—Do not *lean* against these railings. I believe that most of our employees *lean* toward accepting increased medical benefits rather than greater salaries. We use only first-quality *lean* ground beef in our hamburgers.

Lien (a legal right or claim to property)—If he refuses to pay, we will be forced to obtain a *lien* on his house.

Leased/Least
Leased (property rented for a specified time period)—The building has been *leased* for three years.
Least (smallest; slightest; lowest)—This year we showed the *least* profit since our company was founded in 1966.

Lend/Loan
Lend *v.* (to give for temporary use with the understanding that the same or equivalent will be returned)—Has the bank agreed to *lend* us additional funds for expansion?
Loan *n.* (something given for a borrower's temporary use)—Your $3,000 *loan* will be fully paid with your October 1 payment.

Less: see Fewer.

Lessee/Lesser/Lessor
Lessee (one to whom a lease is given)—As specified in the lease agreement, the *lessee* must pay a monthly rent of $650 to the landlord.
Lesser (smaller or less important)—Although the decision was not wholly satisfactory, it was the *lesser* of two evils.
Lessor (one who grants a lease)—The *lessor* for all our company cars is Allied Car Rental Service.

Lessen/Lesson
Lessen (to make smaller)—Chris Timmins recommended that we *lessen* our efforts in the manufacturing area.
Lesson (a unit of study; something from which one learns)—The experience was a good *lesson* in how miscommunication can cause problems.

Lesser: see Lessee.

Lessor: see Lessee.

Levee/Levy
Levee (the bank of a river or a boat landing)—The river overflowed the *levee.*
Levy (an order for payment)—To pay for the flood damage, the governor ordered a 1 percent *levy* on gasoline sales.

Liable/Libel
Liable (legally responsible; obligated)—The court ruled that the company was *liable* for all damages resulting from the accident.
Libel (a false or damaging written statement about another)—Don refused to include the statement in his article because he feared he would be sued for *libel.*

Lie: see Lay.

Lien: see Lean.

Lightening/Lightning
Lightening (illuminating or brightening; lessening or alleviating)—Please select colors that will result in *lightening* the reception area. Only by *lightening* her workload can we expect to retain Ms. Burton.
Lightning (the flashing of light produced by atmospheric electricity)—During the storm *lightning* flashes streaked across the sky.

Like: see As.

Loan: see Lend.

Local/Locale
Local (limited to a particular district)—Only persons living in the *local* area were interviewed.
Locale (a particular location)—This parcel of land is an ideal *locale* for a shopping center.

Loose/Lose
Loose (not fastened, tight, or shut up)—A *loose* connection was the probable cause of the power failure.
Lose (to fail to keep; to mislay)—Please be careful not to *lose* this bank statement.

Magnate/Magnet
Magnate (a powerful or influential person)—As the first *magnate* of the auto industry, Henry Ford changed the lifestyle of many Americans.
Magnet (something that has the ability to attract)—Picking up the spilled paper clips with a *magnet* was an easy task.

Main/Mane
Main (principal or most important part)—Our *main* selling feature is still customer service.
Mane (the heavy hair on the neck of a horse or lion)—The horse's *mane* had become entangled in the wire fence.

Manner/Manor
Manner (method; a customary or particular way)—Unless the company changes its *manner* of doing business, it will lose many more customers. Chancellor Phelps' congenial *manner* has endeared him to both faculty and students alike.
Manor (a main house or mansion)—Although the decor of the *manor* dated back to the early years of the twentieth century, it was still beautiful.

Marital/Marshal/Martial
Marital (pertaining to marriage)—Use "*marital* bliss" as the primary appeal in your advertising copy for this client.
Marshal (a military or law enforcement rank; the head of a ceremony)—If you wish to have a *marshal* serve these papers, there is an additional $25 fee. Jack Ritter was asked to act as honorary *marshal* of the parade.

Martial (warlike; military)—Several bands played selections of *martial* music at the concert.

May: see Can.

May be/Maybe
May be (a verb phrase [a helping verb and a main verb] derived from the infinitive "to be")—This *may be* the last year we will be able to lease these facilities.
Maybe (an adverb meaning "perhaps")—*Maybe* the new carpeting will reduce the noise level in the office.

Me: see I.

Medal/Meddle
Medal (a metal disk; an award in the form of a metal disk)—This gold religious *medal* was found lying on the sidewalk outside the church. He should receive a *medal* for his heroic efforts.
Meddle (to interfere)—This argument was one in which he dared not *meddle.*

Miner/Minor
Miner (a person who works in a mine)—He listed his last job as that of coal *miner.*
Minor (a lesser thing; a person under legal age)—Your forgetting to mail the proposal proved to be only a *minor* error. Please post a sign that reads "No *minors* allowed."

Mode/Mood
Mode (style or preferred method)—What *mode* of transportation will you use to reach the airport?
Mood (feeling or disposition)—Before you ask Mr. Smith for a salary increase, be sure he is in a good *mood.*

Moral/Morale
Moral (pertaining to right and wrong; ethical)—She made the decision on a *moral* rather than on a practical basis.
Morale (a mental condition)—Announcement of an across-the-board 7 percent pay increase instantly boosted employee *morale.*

Morning/Mourning
Morning (the time from sunrise to noon)—Would you be able to schedule a Friday *morning* appointment for me to see Dr. Rose?
Mourning (a period of time during which signs of grief are shown)—Please allow the family to observe this period of *mourning* without any interruptions concerning business matters.

Most: see Almost.

Mourning: see Morning.

Myself: see I.

Naval/Navel
Naval (relating to a navy)—Last week Mr. Marsh's son accepted an assignment with *naval* intelligence.
Navel (a depression in the middle of the abdomen)—According to Dr. Chin, the incision will leave a small scar directly below the *navel.*

Number: see Amount.

Ordinance/Ordnance
Ordinance (a local regulation)—The city has an *ordinance* banning excessive noise after 10 p.m.
Ordnance (military weapons)—We should know by the end of the month whether we will receive the army *ordnance* contract.

Overdo/Overdue
Overdo (to exaggerate)—Exercise is healthful if one does not *overdo* it.
Overdue (late)—Your payment is 15 days *overdue.*

Pair/Pare/Pear
Pair (two of a kind; made of two corresponding parts)—The *pair* of ski gloves I bought for my sister's birthday present was too small.
Pare (to reduce in size or trim)—I hope you can *pare* this budget at least 15 percent.
Pear (a fruit)—Our market carries three brands of canned *pears.*

Partition/Petition
Partition (something that divides)—Office efficiency increased substantially after each computer station was separated by a *partition.*
Petition (a formal written request)—Have you signed the *petition* to create curb cutouts at major intersections in the downtown business district?

Passed/Past
Passed *v.* (past tense or past participle of *pass,* meaning "to go by" or "circulate")—Once you have *passed* the intersection, look for our store on the right side of the street. Lisa *passed* around the announcement to everyone in the office.
Past *n.* or *adj.* (time gone by or ended)—Our weak profit picture is all in the *past.* From *past* experience we have learned not to extend credit to this company.

Patience/Patients
Patience (calm perseverance)—Your *patience* in working with these handicapped children is certainly to be admired.
Patients (people undergoing medical treatment)—I am one of Dr. Hedge's *patients.*

Peace/Piece
Peace (truce; tranquillity)—As long as the hostilities exist, there can be no *peace* among these nations. Since Ms. Seraydarian began the project, she has not had a moment's *peace.*
Piece (a part of a defined quantity)—Each of us had a *piece* of the birthday cake.

Peal/Peel
Peal (a loud sound or succession of sounds)—The bells *pealed* from the church tower.
Peel (skin or rind; to remove by stripping)—Do any of these recipes require the use of lemon *peel?* Ask the customer to *peel* off the mailing label and affix it to the enclosed postcard.

Pear: see Pair.

Peel: see Peal.

Peer/Pier
Peer (one belonging to the same societal group; gaze)—Most teenagers imitate the behavior of their *peer* group. Do customers often *peer* into the bakery shop window before entering the store?
Pier (a structure extending into navigable waters)—No fishing is allowed from this *pier.*

Persecute/Prosecute
Persecute (to harass persistently)—If your supervisor continues to *persecute* you, please contact your union representative at Ext. 3543.
Prosecute (to start legal proceedings against someone)—We are not sure whether the district attorney will *prosecute* the case.

Personal/Personnel
Personal (private; individual)—Each full-time employee has been assigned a *personal* parking place.
Personnel (employees; relating to employment)—All *personnel* are requested to work overtime until the inventory has been completed. Your annual performance evaluation will be placed in your *personnel* file.

Perspective/Prospective
Perspective (a mental picture or outlook)—His *perspective* is distorted by greed.
Prospective (likely; expected)—Last week we interviewed several *prospective* candidates for our Accounting Department.

Petition: see Partition.

Piece: see Peace.

Pier: see Peer.

Plaintiff/Plaintive
Plaintiff (one who commences a lawsuit to obtain a remedy for an injury to his or her rights)—Who is the attorney for the *plaintiff?*
Plaintive (expressive of suffering or woe)—In a *plaintive* voice the witness explained how the gunmen executed the robbery.

Pole/Poll
Pole (a long, slender object that is usually cylindrical)—The teachers will need a *pole* to open the top row of windows in these classrooms.
Poll (counting of opinions or votes cast; place where votes are cast [usually *polls*])—Our latest *poll* shows that consumers prefer Revel toothpaste over any other. Be sure to urge all registered voters to go to the *polls* next Tuesday.

Populace/Populous
Populace (masses; population)—The winning candidate must have the support of the *populace.* After the earthquake the *populace* of Evansville was evacuated.
Populous (densely populated)—At present we have restaurants only in *populous* areas.

Pore/Pour
Pore (to read studiously or attentively; a small opening in a membrane)—How long did the auditors *pore* over these books? Hot water will open the *pores* of your skin, and cold water will close them.
Pour (to dispense from a container; to move with a continuous flow)—Please ask the waiters to *pour* the water before the guests are seated. Even before the game ended, spectators began to *pour* out of the stadium.

Practicable/Practical
Practicable (an idea or plan that in theory seems to be feasible or usable)—The plan to build a car that runs on electricity seems to be a *practicable* one.
Practical (an idea or plan that is feasible or usable because it has been successfully tried or proved by past experience)—Once gasoline prices began to rise, many people found small cars to be the *practical* solution to reducing transportation costs.

Pray/Prey
Pray (to make a request in a humble manner; to address a god)—I *pray* that these bureaucrats will listen to my request. Children may not be required to *pray* in public schools.
Prey (victim; to have an injurious or destructive effect)—Do not become *prey* to the quick-rich schemes of such con artists. Ms. Rice should not let this experience constantly *prey* on her thoughts.

Precede/Proceed
Precede (to go before)—Mrs. Andrews' presentation will directly *precede* the convention's first general session.
Proceed (to go forward or continue)—Please *proceed* with your analysis of the financial statements.

Precedence/Precedents
Precedence (priority)—Please give *precedence* to Mr. Wilson's application for funds.
Precedents (things done or said that can be used as an example)—There are no legal *precedents* in our state for this particular case.

Presence/Presents
Presence (condition of being present; stately or distinguished bearing of a person)—Please ensure the *presence* of all supervisors and managers at this meeting. Everyone was impressed by the confidence and *presence* with which the new president addressed the faculty.
Presents (gifts or things given)—Company employees donated a record number of *presents* to needy children this year.

Prey: see Pray.

Principal/Principle
Principal *n.* (a capital sum; a school official)—Both the *principal* and the interest paid are shown on your loan statement each month. As *principal* of Lindberg High School, Mrs. Brereton was proud that so many seniors attended college upon graduation.
Principal *adj.* (highest in importance)—The *principal* reason for changing our promotion procedures was to encourage all employees within the company to upgrade themselves.
Principle *n.* (an accepted rule of action; a basic truth or belief)—Her knowledge of accounting *principles* is questionable. Our country was founded on the *principle* that all men are created equal.

Proceed: see Precede.

Propose/Purpose
Propose (to suggest)—I *propose* that we borrow money to purchase the new equipment.
Purpose (a desired result)—The *purpose* of this meeting is to discuss ways of increasing our productivity and sales.

Prosecute: see Persecute.

Prospective: see Perspective.

Purpose: see Propose.

Quiet/Quite
Quiet (peaceful; free from noise)—The *quiet* operation of this printer is one of its main sales features.
Quite (completely or actually)—Our salespeople seem to be *quite* satisfied with the new commission plan.

Raise/Raze/Rise
Raise (to lift something up, increase in amount, gather together, or bring into existence; a transitive verb that needs an object to complete its meaning; *raise, raised, raised,* and *raising* are the principal parts of this verb)—Please do not *raise* your voice. The company *raised* our quota 30 percent last month. We have *raised* $200 for Mrs. Morgan's retirement gift. A number of our stockholders are *raising* questions about the proposed merger.

Raze (to destroy to the ground)—When does your company plan to *raze* this old warehouse?
Rise (to go up or to increase in value; an intransitive verb that does not have an object; *rise, rose, risen,* and *rising* are the principal parts of this verb)—Our sales should *rise* beyond the $1 million mark this quarter. The rocket *rose* 30,000 feet before it exploded. Our sales have *risen* for the third month in a row. Production has been *rising* steadily since the new equipment was installed.

Real/Really
Real (an adjective meaning "great in amount or number")—The new accounting program was a *real* help in getting out our monthly statements.
Really (an adverb meaning "actually" or "truly")—Wilma Carroll was *really* disappointed that Robert did not accept the position.

Reality/Realty
Reality (that which is real; that which exists)—Our problems began when the general plant manager would not face *reality* in negotiating with the employees' representatives.
Realty (real estate)—The last *realty* company that tried to sell my property could not find a qualified buyer.

7

Receipt/Recipe
Receipt (a written acknowledgment for receiving goods or money)—No refunds can be made without a *receipt.*
Recipe (a set of instructions)—He has always kept secret the *recipe* for his delicious spaghetti sauce.

Residence/Residents
Residence (a place where one lives)—This house has been Mrs. Scott's *residence* for the past twenty years.
Residents (people who live in a place)—One of the retirement home *residents* reported that the heater in her room emits only cold air. The *residents* of Nashville have elected a new mayor.

Respectably/Respectfully/Respectively
Respectably (in a correct or decent manner)—The vagrant was dressed *respectably* for his court appearance.
Respectfully (used in the body or complimentary close of a letter to show high regard or respect for the reader; a manner denoting high regard)—We *respectfully* submit that the contract calls for all work to be completed by April 1. Please remember to treat all our customers *respectfully.*
Respectively (each in turn or in order)—Janice Jackson, John Zelinsky, and Al Turnbull were first-, second-, and third-prize winners, *respectively.*

Rise: see Raise.

Role/Roll
Role (a part or character assumed)—Mr. Hayworth is very successful in his *role* as mediator for grievances within the company. What *role* will you play in this theater production?

Roll (to move by turning or rotating; something wound around a core; a list of names)—Be sure to *roll* back the bathroom carpeting before attempting any plumbing repairs. Please order 3 dozen *rolls* of transparent packaging tape from Hillsbrough Stationers. How many students are on your *roll?*

Rote/Rout/Route
Rote (mechanical or repetitious learning)—All fourth-grade children are expected to learn the multiplication tables for *one* through *ten* by *rote.*
Rout (a disorderly assembly or disastrous defeat)—The game turned into a *rout* after the opposing team scored 30 points in the first quarter.
Route (a course taken in traveling from one point to another)—Most of our delivery *routes* were changed based upon the consultant's recommendations.

Scene/Seen
Scene (a place of an occurrence; an exhibition of anger)—The police arrived at the *scene* of the robbery shortly after the security guard telephoned them. How would you handle a hostile customer who was creating a *scene?*
Seen (past participle of *to see*)—I have not *seen* our sales manager for three days.

Scent: see Cent.

Seize: see Cease.

Senses: see Census.

Sent: see Cent.

Serial: see Cereal.

Set/Sit
Set (to place, position, or arrange; a transitive verb that generally needs an object to complete its meaning; *set, set, set,* and *setting* are the principal parts of this verb)—Please *set* the calculator on my desk. He *set* the clocks ahead one hour for daylight saving time. I have *set* the times for all your medical appointments this week. We are *setting* higher quotas for all our sales personnel this year.
Sit (to be seated or occupy a seat; an intransitive verb that does not have an object; *sit, sat, sat,* and *sitting* are the principal parts of this verb)—*Sit* here, Ms. Brown. I *sat* for over an hour awaiting his return. He has *sat* in that chair all day watching television. If Mr. Weaver calls, tell him I am *sitting* in on a meeting of the department heads.

Sew/So/Sow
Sew (to fasten by stitches with thread)—I can't find anyone who will *sew* a button on my coat.
So (in a way indicated; to that degree; therefore)—*So* that we may update our files, please complete the enclosed form and mail it to us in the return envelope. She was *so* upset over the incident that she accidentally tore the paper. Our company is moving its offices to Columbus, Ohio; so now we are in the process of recruiting new personnel in this city.

Sow (to scatter seed)—This machine can *sow* more seed in a day than any 15 farmhands.

Shall/Will
Shall (used in formal writing when the first person is employed)—I *shall* give your request the utmost consideration. We *shall* initiate legal proceedings on November 1.
Will (used with all three persons except in formal writing)—I (or We) *will* call you tomorrow. You *will* receive your refund when you return the merchandise. He (or She or They) *will* finish the project according to schedule unless he (or she or they) encounter(s) bad weather conditions.

She: see Her.

Shear/Sheer
Shear (to cut, strip, or remove)—We had to *shear* off the bolts before we could remove the wheel.
Sheer (transparently thin; utterly; steep)—None of the *sheer* fabrics are suitable for the kind of draperies we have in mind. This conference was a *sheer* waste of time. Did any of the prisoners attempt to scale the *sheer* cliffs?

Shone/Shown
Shone (past tense and past participle of *shine*)—If only the flashing red lights had *shone* through the dense fog, the accident might have been avoided.
Shown (past participle of *show*)—The computer-generated slide presentation describing our new products has been *shown* to all our salespeople.

Should/Would
Should (used in formal writing when the first person is employed)—We *should* appreciate your returning the signed contracts by Friday, March 23.
Would (used with all three persons except in formal writing)—I (or We) *would* appreciate receiving a copy of that report. She (or He or They) said that she (or he or they) *would* be willing to work overtime if the report isn't finished by 5 p.m. Did you say that you *would* be interested in having a demonstration of our new Model 1100 copier?

Shown: see Shone.

Sight: see Cite.

Sit: see Set.

Site: see Cite.

So: see Sew.

Soar/Sore
Soar (to fly aloft or about; to rise or increase dramatically)—These miniature aircraft are built to *soar* through the sky without motor or battery power. News of the merger will cause the price of our stock to *soar.*
Sore (painfully sensitive)—If you overdo an exercise program, your muscles will become *sore.* Last year's financial losses have become a *sore* point for our company president.

Sole/Soul
Sole (the undersurface of a foot; being the only one)—Distribute your weight evenly between the *sole* and the heel of your foot. John is the *sole* heir to his father's fortune.
Soul (the immaterial essence of an individual; exemplification of personification)—Most contemporary religions believe that the *soul* of an individual continues on after his or her physical death. Mr. Perry is the *soul* of honesty and integrity.

Some/Somewhat
Some (an adjective meaning "an indefinite amount")—The report revealed that we will have to make *some* structural changes when we move into our new offices.
Somewhat (an adverb meaning "to some degree")—Most of our sales force feels that your sales projections for next year are *somewhat* optimistic.

Some time/Sometime
Some time (a period of time)—Our staff will need *some time* to review your proposal before we can make a decision.
Sometime (an indefinite time; anytime)—Your order should be delivered *sometime* during the early part of next week.

Somewhat: see Some.

Sore: see Soar.

Soul: see Sole.

Sow: see Sew.

Staid/Stayed
Staid (sedate; composed)—A more *staid* individual is needed to fill this position.
Stayed (past tense and past participle of *stay*)—She *stayed* long after regular hours to finish the report.

Stationary/Stationery
Stationary (not movable)—Only two of the interior walls in this suite are *stationary.*
Stationery (writing material)—Mr. Troy wants this letter prepared on his personal *stationery.* Our order for additional *stationery* supplies was placed last week.

Statue/Stature/Statute
Statue (a carved or molded image of someone or something)—Meet me in front of the *statue* of Lincoln at 2 p.m.
Stature (the height of an object; status gained by attainment)—The *stature* alone of the pyramids is overwhelming. Dr. Sunayama is a person of great *stature* within the community.
Statute (law enacted by a legislature)—There is a *statute* in this state that prohibits gambling in any form.

Stayed: see Staid.

Straight/Strait
Straight (free of bends, curves, or angles)—Ms. Torti always seems to be able to go *straight* to the source of the problem.
Strait (a narrow space or passage connecting two bodies of water)—The ship and its cargo were damaged while going through the *strait.*

Suit/Suite
Suit (an action filed in court; a set of garments)—A & Z Computer Corporation has already filed *suit* against Compco for patent infringements. Be sure to wear a three-piece gray business *suit* for the interview.
Suite (a group of things forming a unit; a set)—Were you able to reserve a *suite* for the week of March 25 at the Americana Hotel? (refers to a group of rooms) How many pieces are featured in this bedroom *suite?* (refers to pieces of furniture in a set)

Sure/Surely
Sure (an adjective or subject complement meaning "certain" or "positive")—Nancy was *sure* she had made the right decision.
Surely (an adverb meaning "certainly" or "undoubtedly")—The employees believed that they would *surely* get a raise this year.

Tare/Tear/Tier
Tare (the weight of goods after the weight of the container is deducted)—The *tare* cost of our merchandise has increased over 15 percent in one year.
Tear (to pull apart or rip; a rip)—When you open the envelope, be careful not to *tear* the contents. The customer complained about a *tear* in the sweater she had purchased.
Tier (things placed one above the other)—Our season tickets are on the third *tier* of the stadium.

Than/Then
Than (a conjunction used to show comparison)—Ms. Espinoza has more experience *than* I in writing contract proposals.
Then (an adverb meaning "at that time")—Once all the data has been gathered, you may *then* begin organizing the report.

That/Which

That (introduces a restrictive or essential subordinate clause)—We have in stock, Mr. Harrington, all the merchandise *that* you requested. All dogs *that* are found wandering in the streets will be impounded. This is the telephone *that* has been out of order since this morning.
Which (introduces a nonrestrictive or nonessential subordinate clause)—The security staff recommended that we acquire a watchdog, *which* would be kept inside the plant at night. Our new credit system, *which* will be installed next week, will cost over $50,000.

Their/There/They're

Their (the possessive form of *they*)—As a result of *their* recommendation, we installed an Apex Security System in our main warehouse.
There (at that place or at that point)—Please be *there* promptly at ten o'clock in the morning.
They're (contraction of *they are*)—Although the union representatives rejected our first offer, *they're* willing to consider our second proposal.

Them/They

Them (a direct object, an indirect object, or an object of a preposition)—I asked *them* to please wait outside. I sent *them* a bill last week. I waited for *them* all morning.
They (subject of a clause or a complement pronoun)—*They* are meeting with the Board of Directors this afternoon. The two persons who cochaired the committee were *they*.

7

Then: see Than.

There: see Their.

They: see Them.

They're: see Their.

Threw/Through

Threw (past tense of *throw*)—Mr. Samuels accidentally *threw* away the report on equipment purchases for the current year.
Through (in one end and out the other; movement within a large expanse; during the period of; as a consequence of)—May I give you a tour *through* our plant? The messenger pigeons flew gracefully *through* the air. This sale will be in progress *through* June. You may order this software at a 15 percent discount from June 15 *through* June 30. We have retained this account *through* your diligent efforts.

Tier: see Tare.

To/Too/Two
To (a preposition; the sign of an infinitive)—Please return these materials *to* me when you have finished reviewing them. She wanted *to* see for herself the condition of the plant cafeteria.
Too (an adverb meaning "also" or "to an excessive extent")—I was there *too.* Because the office was *too* noisy, I had difficulty hearing you on the telephone.
Two (a number)—There was just too much work for the *two* of us to finish by five o'clock.

Us/We
Us (a direct object, an indirect object, or an object of a preposition)—The vice president took *us* on a tour of the plant. The manager gave *us* a copy of the report. This party was planned for *us.*
We (the subject of a clause or a complement pronoun)—*We* must decide upon a definite course of action by 3 p.m. The singers selected to perform for this special broadcast were *we.*

Vain/Van/Vane/Vein
Vain (unduly proud or conceited)—Tom would be more popular with his fellow workers if he were not so *vain.*
Van (a covered truck)—Our hospital *van* is used primarily for transporting patients.
Vane (a thin object used to show wind direction)—The weather *vane* indicated that the wind was coming from a westward direction.
Vein (a tubular vessel that carries blood to the heart; mode of, style)—The laboratory technician had difficulty finding a *vein* from which to obtain a blood sample. Although Mr. Bates had been warned about his unfriendly attitude toward other employees, he continued to behave in that *vein.*

Vary/Very
Vary (to change)—The new office manager said she would not request us to *vary* any procedures at the present time.
Very (extremely)—These figures are *very* difficult to type accurately.

Vein: see Vain.

Vice/Vise
Vice (immoral habit; personal fault)—Drug abuse by America's populace is a *vice* that must be curtailed. Cigar smoking is his only *vice.*
Vise (a clamp; to hold or squeeze)—He shook my hand with a *vise*-like grip.

Waive/Wave
Waive (to relinquish; to refrain from enforcing)—Do you *waive* your right to a jury trial? You must petition the dean of academic affairs to *waive* this requirement.
Wave (to swing something back and forth or up and down)—The angry customer was determined to *wave* his bill in everyone's face.

Waiver/Waver
Waiver (the relinquishment of a claim)—Please sign the enclosed *waiver* to release our company from any further responsibility for your injury.
Waver (to shake or fluctuate)—I believe he is beginning to *waver* concerning my request for an early vacation.

Wave: see waive.

Waver: see waiver.

We: see Us.

Weather/Whether

Weather (the state of the atmosphere; to bear up against)—Today's *weather* forecast predicted a cold, rainy day. We are glad to learn that you were able to *weather* the high rate of employee turnover during the summer months.
Whether (an introduction of alternatives)—We will not know until next week *whether* our company will be awarded the contracts.

Well: see Good.

Whether: see Weather.

Which: see That.

Who/Whom

7

Who (the subject of a subordinate clause or a complement pronoun)—I was the one *who* asked you to attend. I cannot tell you *who* it was at the door.
Whom (a direct object, an indirect object, or an object of a preposition)—*Whom* have you hired as my assistant? *Whom* did he send the book? Here is the address of the person with *whom* we met for legal assistance. [See Section 8–7j for a further explanation of how to use *who* and *whom*.]

Whole: see Hole.

Wholly: see Holy.

Whom: see Who.

Who's/Whose

Who's (a contraction of *who is*)—Please let me know *who's* taking over for you during August.
Whose (possessive form of *who*)—He is the fellow *whose* position was abolished.

Will: see Shall.

Would: see Should.

Your/You're

Your (possessive form of *you*)—*Your* secretary told me that you had invited the mayor to the reception.
You're (contraction of *you are*)—So *you're* the one who has been trying to reach me.

CHAPTER 8

Grammar and Usage

Grammar and Usage Solution Finder

Grammar and Usage Solution Finder (continued)

Sentences

8–1. Complete Sentences

a. **Use complete sentences to express your ideas. A complete sentence (1) contains a verb (a word showing action or describing a condition), (2) has a subject (a noun or pronoun that interacts with the verb), and (3) makes sense (comes to a closure). A complete sentence is an independent clause.**

Verbs appear by themselves or in a verb phrase. The last verb in a verb phrase is considered the main verb.

Subjects are either simple or compound. *Simple subjects* consist of a single noun or pronoun whereas *compound subjects* contain two or more nouns or pronouns linked by *and, or,* or *nor.*

statements

(simple subject) (verb)
Last week several *employees* in our Production Department *increased* their standard output by 10 percent. (Makes sense)

(compound subject) (verb phrase)
Karen and Richard, as a result of their hard work, *have been promoted* to senior analysts. (Makes sense)

8

(subject) (verb)
This latest *manuscript* by Kym Freeman *is* excellent. (Makes sense)

questions

When *may I expect* your reply? (Simple subject, *I*; verb phrase, *may expect;* makes sense)

How many *members* of your staff *plan* to attend the convention? (Simple subject, *members;* verb, *plan;* makes sense)

requests or commands

Please *return* the questionnaire by March 31. (Simple subject, the word *you* understood; verb, *return;* makes sense)

Do not *litter* in the parks or on the highways. (Simple subject, the word *you* understood; verb, *do litter* [*not* is an adverb]; makes sense)

b. **Simple sentences consist of a single independent clause that contains a subject and a verb or verb phrase. They express only one complete thought.**

The *manager* of our Springfield branch *has been* in our employ for over ten years. (Simple subject, *manager;* verb phrase, *has been*)

Partnerships and corporations in this state *are* not eligible for this tax deduction. (Compound subject, *Partnerships and corporations;* verb, *are*)

c. **Compound sentences contain two independent clauses (each with a subject and a verb or verb phrase) that are usually joined by a coordinating conjunction—*and, but, or,* or *nor.***

Our regional *representative will call* on you next week, *and she will demonstrate* our new line of Creation III cosmetics. (Simple subjects, *representative* and *she;* verb phrases, *will call* and *will demonstrate;* coordinating conjunction, *and*)

Neither of our vice presidents *is* in the office this week, *but* our *general manager* for East Coast operations *will be able* to answer your questions. (Subjects, *neither* and *general manager;* verb and verb phrase, *is* and *will be able;* coordinating conjunction, *but*)

d. Other compound sentences contain two independent clauses (each containing a subject and a verb or verb phrase) that are joined by either a semicolon or a semicolon coupled with a transitional expression such as *therefore, however, nevertheless, for example,* or *of course.*

joined by a semicolon

The *loan* on your home *has been transferred* to Certified Home Mortgage Corporation; *you should receive* a new payment booklet from them within the next ten days. (Simple subjects, *loan* and *you;* verb phrases, *has been transferred* and *should receive*)

joined by a semicolon and a transitional expression

Professors and administrators at our college *are covered* under the same retirement program; *therefore, administrators* also *are* eligible for retirement at age 55. (Compound and simple subjects, *professors and administrators* and *administrators;* verb phrase and verb, *are covered* and *are;* transitional expression, *therefore*)

8

e. Complex sentences include an independent clause and a dependent clause, each of which contains both a subject and a verb or verb phrase. The independent clause can stand alone as a complete sentence because it makes sense, but the dependent clause cannot. Dependent clauses begin with (1) relative pronouns such as *who, whom, that,* or *which* or (2) conjunctive adverbs such as *if, when, as, since* or *because.* The dependent clause may begin, interrupt, or conclude the sentence.

complex sentence with a relative pronoun clause

Mr. Johnson asked me *who won the grand prize in our drawing.*

None of the people *whom we interviewed* were willing to accept the position at the salary offered.

The book *that you recommended* is no longer available in our bookstore.

Chris is habitually absent, *which may be the reason for his dismissal.*

complex sentence with a conjunctive adverb

As soon as we receive your check, we will begin processing your application.

In the future you may, *if you wish,* send all your orders directly to our Springfield office.

Our sales have increased substantially *since the new advertising campaign began.*

f. Compound-complex sentences contain two independent clauses and one dependent clause.

We are discontinuing our present line of mattresses *because deliveries from the manufacturer have been slow in reaching our customers,* but we expect to replace this line with one of equal or better quality.

We received nearly thirty applications for this opening; but *after I read all the resumes,* I realized that not one of the candidates was qualified for the position.

8–2. Sentence Fragments

a. Use only sentence fragments that *represent* a complete thought. Such usages should be confined to informal business writing.

And now to the point.

If only I had known!

What a relief!

b. For the most part, use concluding punctuation marks (periods, question marks, and exclamation marks) only after complete sentences. Avoid these marks after sentence fragments except in those instances in informal writing where the fragment represents a complete thought (Section 8–4a).

8

NOT: *In the near future.*
BUT: *In the near future* we will expand our operations.

NOT: *Although the present contract has expired.*
BUT: *Although the present contract has expired,* both management and union are governed by its provisions until a new contract is negotiated.

NOT: *The biggest money-saving event of the year.*
BUT: We look forward to seeing you at our annual clearance sale, *the biggest money-saving event of the year.*

Nouns[1]

8–3. Nouns

a. Nouns are words that name something—for example, persons, animals, places, things, objects, time, feelings, qualities, actions, concepts, measures, and states of being.

person

Please have your *attorney* call me.

Did you refer this *client* to me?

[1]The rules and spellings in this chapter are based on *Webster's Ninth New Collegiate Dictionary* (Springfield, Mass.: Merriam-Webster Inc., 1989).

animal

We have been interested in purchasing another *horse.*

This *fish* is too old to eat.

place

The new *park* will be located in our *suburb.*

When will you visit our *city?*

thing

Your *business* seems to be doing well.

Have the *company* and the *union* reached an *agreement?*

object

Did you find your *purse?*

Place the *computer* on this *table.*

time

We signed the contract *yesterday,* and it will become effective in 30 *days.*

The balloon payment is due next *month.*

feeling

I could detect his *anger* as he spoke.

We should sympathize with his *sorrow* and *grief.*

quality

I appreciate your *thoughtfulness* and *generosity.*

Such *irresponsibility* cannot be tolerated.

action

Do you enjoy *swimming?*

Golfing is an individual sport.

concept

Our country was founded on *freedom* of *expression.*

Please report any *progress* you have made.

measure

Our company's assets total nearly *$23 million.*

Three *yards* of fabric will be needed for each chair.

state of being

Her *illness* has not yet been properly diagnosed.

Complacency in this rapidly changing industry could easily lead to *bankruptcy.*

b. **Any noun that names a particular entity is capitalized. These capitalized nouns are known as *proper nouns.* Nouns that do not name specific entities are known as *common nouns,* and they are not capitalized.**

proper nouns

Last month the *Columbus City Council* approved a 4 percent increase in property taxes.

Repairs on the *Golden Gate Bridge* are still in progress.

We must make a decision by *December 1.*

common nouns

Last month the *city council* approved a 4 percent increase in property taxes.

Repairs on the *bridge* are still in progress.

We must make a decision by the *1st* of next *month.*

c. **Although most common nouns consist of single words, many contain two or even three words. These *compound nouns* appear as regular entries in the dictionary and are defined as nouns. Some are hyphenated, but most are separate words without hyphens *(open compounds).***

hyphenated compound nouns

This business is operated by the mayor's *brother-in-law.*

The *vice-principal* of our local high school is in charge of the project.

open compound nouns

Please have the *vice president* approve this purchase.

Our local *high school* is sponsoring this event.

8–4. Noun Plurals[2]

a. **Most nouns form their plurals by adding *s.* However, nouns ending in *s, sh, ch, x,* or *z* form their plurals by adding *es.***

nouns adding "s"

account accounts
executive executives
letter letters

[2]Noun plurals, other than those regular ones ending in *s* or *es,* are shown in the dictionary immediately after the singular form of the word.

nouns adding "es"

business	businesses
wish	wishes
branch	branches
tax	taxes
waltz	waltzes

b. **Common nouns ending in *y* form the plural in one of two ways. If the letter preceding the *y* is a vowel, just add *s*. However, if the letter preceding the *y* is a consonant, drop the *y* and add *ies*.**

"y" preceded by a vowel add s

attorney	attorneys
money	moneys
valley	valleys

"y" preceded by a consonant add ies

company	companies
secretary	secretaries
reply	replies

8

c. **Musical terms ending in *o* form the plural by adding *s*. Other common nouns ending in *o* may form the plural by adding *s* or *es*; the correct plural forms are shown in the dictionary after the singular forms of the words.**

musical terms add s

sopranos concertos cellos solos pianos

common nouns ending in "os"

zeros mementos dynamos portfolios ratios

common nouns ending in "oes"

cargoes heroes potatoes embargoes vetoes

d. **Nouns ending in *ff* form the plural by adding *s*. Nouns ending in just *f* or *fe* may add *s*, or they may drop the *f* or *fe* and add *ves*. The plurals of those nouns taking the irregular form *ves* are shown in the dictionary. If the dictionary does not show the plural form, just add *s*.**

plural nouns ending in "ffs"

sheriff	sheriffs	plaintiff	plaintiffs
cliff	cliffs	bailiff	bailiffs

plural nouns ending in "fs" or "fes"

proof	proofs	belief	beliefs	roof	roofs
safe	safes	chief	chiefs	strife	strifes

plural nouns ending in "ves"

wife	wives	shelf	shelves	knife	knives
half	halves	thief	thieves	self	selves

e. The plurals of proper nouns are formed by adding *s* or *es*. Those proper nouns ending in *s, sh, ch, x,* or *z* form the plural by adding *es*. All others form the plural by adding *s*.

proper noun plurals ending in "es"

Winters	the Winterses	Rodriguez	the Rodriguezes
Bush	the Bushes	Bendix	the Bendixes
Finch	the Finches		

proper noun plurals ending in "s"

Halby	the Halbys	Russo	the Russos
Dixon	the Dixons	Kelly	the Kellys
Wolf	the Wolfs	Griffin	the Griffins

8

f. Many nouns of foreign origin have both an English plural and a foreign plural. Consult your dictionary and use the one that appears first.

foreign nouns with English plurals

memorandum	memorandums	formula	formulas
index	indexes	appendix	appendixes

foreign nouns with foreign plurals

alumna	alumnae	analysis	analyses
alumnus	alumni	basis	bases
stimulus	stimuli	crisis	crises
terminus	termini	criterion	criteria
curriculum	curricula	medium	media
datum	data	parenthesis	parentheses

g. Some nouns form their plurals by changing letters within the word or adding letters other than *s* or *es*. These irregular plurals are shown in the dictionary.

tooth	teeth	mouse	mice
man	men	foot	feet
child	children	woman	women

h. Some nouns have the same form in both the singular and the plural. Other nouns are used only with singular verbs while still others are used solely with plural verbs. These unusual constructions are explained in the dictionary in the entry that defines the word.

nouns with the same singular and plural forms

fish	politics	Chinese	moose
scissors	measles	Japanese	cod
gross	series	corps	vermin
Vietnamese	species	sheep	odds
headquarters	deer	salmon	mumps

nouns always used with singular verbs

news	mathematics	economics (course)
genetics	aeronautics	statistics (course)

nouns always used with plural verbs

earnings	proceeds	goods	winnings
premises	thanks	belongings	credentials

i. Hyphenated or open compound nouns containing a main word form their plurals on the main words. Those hyphenated compounds not containing a main word and compound nouns consisting of only one word form the plural at the end.

plural formed on main word

personnel manager*s*	sister*s*-in-law
leave*s* of absence	notarie*s* public
lieutenant colonel*s*	vice-principal*s*
attorney*s* at law	co-owner*s*

plural formed at end

follow-up*s*	trade-in*s*
go-between*s*	stand-in*s*
teaspoonful*s*	bookshel*ves*
workm*en*	stockholder*s*

j. The plurals of numerals, most capital letters, words referred to as words, and abbreviations composed of initials are formed by adding *s* or *es*. For clarity, though, all isolated lowercase letters and the capital letters *A, I, M,* and *U* are made plural by adding an apostrophe before the *s*.

plural formed with "s" or "es"

I have difficulty distinguishing between his *1s* and his *7s.*

Can you list the five *Cs* of good letter writing?

Ms. Smith, our new copy editor, does not use her *whiches* and *thats* correctly.

On the last ballot the *noes* outnumbered the *yeses.*

Mr. Wilson wants this assignment completed without any further *ifs, ands,* or *buts.*

Make a list of *dos* and *don'ts* for the care and maintenance of this equipment.

There are two vacancies for *R.N.s* on our team.

How many of your graduates became *CPAs* last year?

All our *c.o.d.s* still need to be sent out.

Type the *"a.m.s"* and *"p.m.s"* in lowercase letters.

plural formed with an apostrophe and "s"

We were asked to watch our *p's* and *q's* while the dignitaries were in the building.

To improve your penmanship, be sure to dot your *i's* and cross your *t's.*

Your son received three *A's* on his last grade report.

Why are the *M's* smudged on this document?

k. **When referring to two or more individuals with the same name and title, make either the name or the title plural, but never both.**

the *Messrs.* Johnson or the Mr. *Johnsons*

the *Drs.* Clark or the Dr. *Clarks*

the *Mses.* Smith or the Ms. *Smiths*

the *Mesdames* Jones or the Mrs. *Joneses*

the *Misses* Fry or the Miss *Frys*

8–5. Noun Possessives[3]

a. **All nouns not ending with a pronounced *s,* whether singular or plural, form the possessive by adding *'s.***

office of the *attorney*	*attorney's* office
toys belonging to the *children*	the *children's* toys
books belonging to *Judy*	*Judy's* books
lounge for *women*	*women's* lounge
tribal customs of the *Iroquois*	the *Iroquois's* tribal customs
paycheck of *Ms. DuBois*	*Ms. DuBois's* paycheck
car belonging to *Francois*	*Francois's* car

(Note: The final *s* in *Iroquois, DuBois,* and *Francois* is not pronounced; therefore, *'s* is used with these possessive forms.)

[3]See Section 1–55 for additional examples.

b. **Nouns ending with a pronounced *s* form the possessive by simply adding an apostrophe unless an additional syllable is pronounced in the possessive form. In the latter case, *'s* is added.**

no extra pronounced syllable

clothing for *girls*	*girls'* clothing
the efforts of two *cities*	two *cities'* efforts
the home belonging to the *Foxes*	the *Foxes'* home
the pen belonging to *Mr. Simons*	*Mr. Simons'* pen

extra pronounced syllable

grades of the *class*	the *class's* grades
the briefcase belonging to *Mr. Harris*	*Mr. Harris's* briefcase
testimony of the *witness*	the *witness's* testimony

c. **In the case of joint ownership, possession is shown only on the last noun. Where individual ownership exists, possession is shown on each noun.**

joint ownership

Mary and *Alice's* apartment has been newly painted.

The Rodriguezes and the *Martinsons'* mountain cabin was sold last week.

Mr. Stewart and *Ms. Ross's* partnership agreement was drawn up over two weeks ago.

Clark and *Clark's* handbook is required for this class.

individual ownership

My *mother's* and *father's* clothes were destroyed in the fire.

Bob's and *John's* payroll checks were lost.

Mr. Granados' and *Ms. Stone's* stores are both located on Tampa Avenue in Westfield.

All the *accountants'* and *secretaries'* desks have been moved into the new offices.

d. **The possessive form of compound nouns is shown at the end.**

investments of my *father-in-law*	my *father-in-law's* investments
the report for *stockholders*	the *stockholders'* report
convention of *attorneys at law*	*attorneys at law's* convention
report of the *personnel manager*	*personnel manager's* report

e. **Use the possessive form before a gerund.**

We would appreciate *Lisa's helping* us with the audit.

There is no record of the *witness's being* subpoenaed.

8

f. Use an apostrophe with the possessives of nouns that refer to time—minutes, hours, days, weeks, months, and years.

singular

peace for a *minute*	a *minute's* peace
work for a *day*	a *day's* work
delay for a *week*	a *week's* delay
notice of a *month*	a *month's* notice
mail from this *morning*	this *morning's* mail
calendar for *tomorrow*	*tomorrow's* calendar

plural

work for four *hours*	four *hours'* work
interest for two *weeks*	two *weeks'* interest
trial for three *months*	three *months'* trial
experience for five *years*	five *years'* experience

g. Use an apostrophe with the possessive of nouns that refer to distance.

He lives just a *stone's* throw from the office.

The truck missed hitting our car by just an *arm's* length.

h. Do not use an apostrophe to form possessives for inanimate objects, except for time or distance. Instead, use a simple adjective or an *of* phrase.

adjective

The *table* top is scratched. (Not: The table's top is scratched.)

The *computer* monitor needs to be cleaned. (Not: The computer's monitor needs to be cleaned.)

"of" phrase

The door *of the supply cabinet* is jammed. (Not: The supply cabinet's door is jammed.)

The stipulations *of the will* were presented by the attorney. (Not: The will's stipulations were presented by the attorney.)

i. In some possessive constructions the item or items owned are not stated explicitly or do not directly follow the ownership word. The ownership word, however, still shows possession with an apostrophe.

The only desk to be refinished is *Mary's.*

On Tuesday we will meet at the *Culleys'* to discuss the sale of their property.

Mr. Ardigo left the *attorney's* over an hour ago.

Pronouns

8–6. Pronouns

a. **Pronouns are noun substitutes; they take the place of a noun. Business writers use pronouns to add variety and interest to their writing.**

b. **Pronouns perform one of four functions: they may (1) substitute for a person or thing, (2) refer back to a noun used previously in the sentence, (3) substitute for an unspecific person or thing, or (4) act as an adjective by modifying a noun.**

substitute for a noun or pronoun (personal pronoun)

Michael has been ill for three days; *he* should schedule an appointment with a doctor.

Because Mrs. Scher-Padilla is in charge of this program, please give the forms to *her.*

The board members can only blame *themselves* for this error.

reference to a noun named previously in the sentence (relative pronoun)

Please send me the *book that* Tony recommended.

Brian recommended three *students who* are enrolled at Fillmore College.

8

substitute for an unspecific person or thing (indefinite pronoun)

Do you know *someone* who meets these qualifications?

Neither of these plans is acceptable to the committee.

personal pronoun used as an adjective

His computer needs a new disk drive.

This account is *hers.*

8–7. Personal Pronouns

a. **Each personal pronoun may be expressed in three ways; these ways are referred to as *case forms.* The three case forms for personal pronouns are the *subjective,* the *objective,* and the *possessive.***

b. **The subjective case[4] pronouns are the following:**

I	she	we	who
he	you	they	it

[4]The subjective case is also known as the *nominative case.*

Use a subjective case pronoun (1) for the subject of a sentence, (2) for the complement of a "being" verb *(am, is, are, was, were, be, been),* and (3) after the infinitive "to be" when this verb does not have a subject (a noun or pronoun directly preceding it).

subject of a verb

She has applied for the position.

They will arrive at 10 a.m.

Mark, Ellen, and *I* have been appointed to the committee.

complement of a "being" verb

The person who answered the telephone was not *I.*

This is *she.*

The visitors could have been *they.*

infinitive "to be" without a subject

Deanna was thought to be *I.*

The doctor on duty at that time had to be *he.*

c. The objective case pronouns are the following:

me	her	us	whom
him	you	them	it

The objective case is used when the pronoun is (1) the direct or indirect object of a verb, (2) the object of a preposition, (3) the subject of any infinitive, (4) the object of the infinitive "to be" when it has a subject, and (5) the object of any other infinitive.

direct object of a verb

Mr. Reslaw will meet *her* at the airport tomorrow.

You may ask *him* for this information.

Ms. Orsini asked Ken and *me* to provide her with this information by June 15.

indirect object of a verb

Please mail *me* a receipt as soon as possible.

We will send Marie or *him* these copies before Friday.

object of a preposition

When was the shipment sent *to us?*

Two of the customers asked *for her.*

Between you and me, I do not believe the plan will be approved.

subject of an infinitive

Our department manager expects *her* to complete the audit by December 1.

We thought *them* to be somewhat overconfident.

object of "to be" with a subject

I wanted the *candidate* to be *her.*

Ms. Stapleton thought *them* to be *us.*

They expected *Mary* to be *me.*

object of an infinitive other than "to be"

Our office will not be able to mail *them* until Monday.

We asked her to help *us* with the decorations.

d. The possessive case pronouns are the following:

my	mine	their	theirs
his, her	his, hers	its	its
your	yours		whose
our	ours		

All pronoun possessive case forms are written without apostrophes. They should not be confused with contractions.

possessive pronouns—no apostrophes

Its wrapping had been torn.

Is this *your* sweater?

The idea was *theirs.*

Whose briefcase was left in the conference room?

contractions—apostrophes

It's (It is) still raining very heavily here on the West Coast.

Let us know if *you're* (you are) going to the convention.

If *there's* (there is) a logical reason for the delay, please inform the passengers.

Who's (Who is) in charge of ordering supplies for our personal computers?

e. Use the possessive case immediately before a gerund.

His leaving the company was quite a surprise.

We would appreciate *your returning* the enclosed card by Friday, March 18.

f. A pronoun after *than* or *as* may be expressed in either the subjective or objective case, depending on whether the pronoun is the subject or object of the following stated or implied verb.

subjective case

Are you as concerned about this matter as *I* am? (Stated verb *am*)

He has been with the company two years longer than *I.* (Implied verb *have*)

objective case

Our editor admires my coauthor more than he admires *me.* (Stated subject and verb *he admires*)

She works for Mr. Reece more often than *me.* (Implied subject, verb, and preposition *she works for*)

g. Pronouns used in apposition take the same case as those nouns or pronouns with which they are in apposition.

We, Barbara and *I,* will appear in court tomorrow.

Barry told Ms. Larsen to submit her expenses to one of our accounting clerks, John or *me.*

h. Pronouns followed by an identifying noun (such as *we employees* or *us employees*) are treated as if the noun were not there in determining the proper case form. Therefore, mentally omit the noun in such pronoun-noun combinations (restrictive appositives) to select the correct form.

subjective case

Within the next week *we* ~~employees~~ must decide whether or not we will move with the company to Columbus. (Subject of verb phrase *must decide*)

The victims in this case are *we* ~~students~~. (Complement of being verb *are*)

objective case

The company just gave *us* ~~employees~~ the opportunity to purchase stock at prices below the market value. (Indirect object of verb *gave*)

None of *us* ~~students~~ have yet received any enrollment information. (Object of preposition *of*)

i. Pronouns ending in *self* or *selves* emphasize or reflect a noun or pronoun used previously. They should not be used in place of objective case pronouns.

emphasizes previous noun or pronoun

Wendy herself was not pleased with the results of the advertising campaign.

They themselves could not justify their exorbitant budget requests.

reflects a previous noun or pronoun

Jim addressed the envelope to *himself.*

They agreed to vote *themselves* monthly salary increases of $100.

objective case pronoun used correctly

None of these packages are for *me.* (Not: None of these packages are for *myself.*)

These contracts will be sent directly to *you* after they have been signed by our president. (Not: These contracts will be sent directly to *yourself* after they have been signed by our president.)

j. **The same rules apply to the pronouns *who, whoever, whom, whomever,* and *whose* as apply to the other personal pronouns. *Who* and *whoever* are used for the subjective case; *whom* and *whomever,* for the objective case; and *whose,* for the possessive case.**

***Isolate the clause in which the pronoun appears;* and apply the rules outlined for the subjective, objective, and possessive case pronouns in Sections 8–7b, c, and d. Mentally substitute *he* for *who* and *him* for *whom* to help you distinguish between the subjective and objective cases. Be sure to eliminate mentally any extra clause that may appear in the *who, whom,* or *whose* clause and arrange the clause, if necessary, in normal subject-verb order to insert the appropriate pronoun.**

subjective case—"who" or "whoever"

Who delivered these contracts to my office? (Subject of verb—*[he]* delivered)

Please give me a listing of *who* called while I was in New York. (Subject of verb—*[he]* called)

I do not know *who* the caller may have been. (Complement of "being" verb *been*—the caller may have been *[he]*)

8

Please let me know *who* the winner is. (Complement of "being" verb *is*—the winner is *[he]*)

Who do you think will be appointed to the board? (Omit extra clause *do you think.* Subject of verb phrase—*[he]* will be appointed)

The city council will ratify the appointment of *whoever* is selected. (Subject of verb phrase—*[he]* is selected)

The committee will allow you to select *whoever* you think is qualified. (Omit extra clause *you think.* Subject of verb—*[he]* is qualified)

objective case—"whom" or "whomever"

Whom did Mr. Williams promote to the position of office manager? (Direct object—Mr. Williams did promote *[him]*)

He is a person with *whom* we have done business for over twenty-five years. (Object of preposition—we have done business with *[him]*)

Ask Mr. Robbins *whom* he selected to replace Jerome. (Direct object—he selected *[him]*)

We do not know *whom* to award the contract. (Object of an infinitive—to award *[him]*)

Whom do you think the Savoys will hire as their new manager? (Omit extra clause *do you think.* Direct object—the Savoys will hire *[him]*)

The committee will allow you to select *whomever* you wish. (Direct object—you wish *[him]*)

I'm sure the president will approve *whomever* you choose for the position. (Direct object—you choose *[him]*)

possessive case—"whose"

Whose book is lying here?

We do not know *whose* department will prove to be the most efficient under our new cost-saving plan.

k. Pronouns must agree in gender and number with any nouns or other pronouns they represent.[5]

A *customer* must first register *his* or *her* complaint with an assistant manager.

Both *Ms. Greer* and *Mr. Baty* received *their* orders yesterday.

The *puppy* caught *its* tail in the door.

The *company* will conduct *its* annual inventory next week.

8–8. Relative Pronouns

a. Relative pronouns introduce dependent clauses that refer back (relate) to a noun in the main clause of the sentence. Relative pronoun forms are *who, whom, that,* and *which.*

b. Use *who* and *whom* to refer to a person or persons. For the use of *who,* apply the rules for subjective-case personal pronouns outlined in Section 8–7b. For the use of *whom,* apply the rules for objective-case personal pronouns outlined in Section 8–7c.

subjective case—who

Mr. Vasquez is the applicant *who* was selected for the position. (Refers back to *applicant*) (Subject of verb—*[he]* was selected)

The person *who* served as the seventh president of our college was Ms. Graham. (Refers back to *person*) (Subject of verb—*[he]* served)

Peter is the sales representative *who* I believe will be successful as an editor in the business area. (Refers back to *sales representative*) (Omit extra clause *I believe.*) (Subject of verb—*[he]* will be successful)

Next month our personnel manager, *who* has held this position for over twenty years, will retire. (Refers back to *personnel manager*) (Subject of verb—*[he]* has held)

---

[5]Refer to Section 8–18 for additional information on principles of agreement.

objective case—whom

Mr. Vasquez is the applicant *whom* Ms. Jones selected for the position. (Refers back to *applicant*) (Direct object of verb—Ms. Jones selected *[him]*)

Our new college president, *whom* the board assigned just yesterday, has already called a meeting of campus administrators. (Refers back to *president*) (Direct object of verb—the board assigned *[him]*)

You are a person *whom* I know Ms. Ferraro would be pleased to hire. (Refers back to *person*) (Omit extra clause *I know*) (Object of infinitive—Ms. Ferraro would be pleased to hire *[him]*)

c. **Use *that* or *which* to introduce a dependent clause that refers back to a thing or things in the main clause—any noun that does not represent a person or persons. Careful writers use *that* to introduce restrictive dependent clauses and *which* to introduce nonrestrictive dependent clauses.**

***Restrictive dependent clauses* provide essential ideas that refine the information contained in the main clause; that is, they specify *which one.* *Nonrestrictive dependent clauses* provide extra information that does not alter the substance of the main clause; in other words, the information is not needed to identify *which one.* Nonrestrictive clauses are separated from the main clause with a comma or a pair of commas.**

restrictive dependent clause requiring "that"

Be sure to include on the order form the catalog number of each item *that* you order. (Refers back to *item*) (Specifies only items that are ordered)

The book *that* I have been reading this week must be returned to the library by Friday. (Refers back to *book*) (Specifies which book)

nonrestrictive dependent clause requiring "which"

The Catalog No. 8731 lace-embroidered blouse, *which* you ordered last week, is no longer available. (Refers back to *blouse*) (Clause not needed to identify which blouse—provides extra idea)

Please credit my account for these items, *which* were charged in error to my account. (Refers back to *items*) (Clause not needed to identify which items—provides additional information)

8

8–9. Indefinite Pronouns

a. ***Indefinite pronouns* are pronouns that do not represent a specific person, place, or thing.**

b. **Simple indefinite pronouns include the following words used as subjects or objects:**

each	every
either	neither

c. **Compound indefinite pronouns end with *body, one,* or *thing.***

——body	——one	——thing
anybody	anyone	anything
everybody	everyone	everything
nobody	no one	nothing
somebody	someone	something

d. **Indefinite pronouns used as subjects require singular verbs.**

simple indefinite pronoun as subject

Each of the candidates *has* been given an equal opportunity to address our audience.

Neither of the applicants *is* qualified for the position.

compound indefinite pronoun as subject

Nearly *everybody was* late for the meeting because of the unexpected snow storm.

Everything in these files *is* outdated.

e. **Any other pronouns representing an indefinite pronoun must agree in number and gender with the indefinite pronoun.**

Neither of the winners has claimed *his* or *her* prize.

Would *everyone* please open *his* or *her* book to page 87.

Verbs

8–10. Verbs

a. **Verbs show action or describe a state of being at a certain point in time. Examples of action verbs are *run, swim, talk,* and *write.* Nonaction verbs, those that describe a state of being, include words such as *seem, feel,* and *smell.* The most commonly used nonaction verbs, however, are derived from the verb *be—am, is, are, was, were,* and *been.***

b. **In their infinitive form, verbs are preceded by the preposition *to.***

to go	to be
to demonstrate	to appear
to apply	to taste

c. **Verbs appear alone or in phrases with helpers. The last word in a verb phrase is the main verb. Word groups must contain a verb or a verb phrase to be complete sentences.**

verb in sentence

David *calls* his stockbroker daily.

Please *send* this order to the customer immediately.

Vista Industries *is* one of our best customers.

verb phrase in sentence

We *have received* several payments from this client.

Our company *has been involved* in two lawsuits during the past year.

Our office *is* presently *processing* your order.

How much money *did* you *spend* on this project?

d. **Verbs require varied forms to signify tenses; that is, points in time. The principal forms or parts of a verb used to construct tenses include the present part, the past part, the past participle, and the present participle.**

8-11. Formation of Parts for Regular Verbs

Most verbs, regular verbs, form their parts in the same way: (1) the present part has the infinitive form without the accompanying *to,* (2) the past part adds *ed* to the present form, (3) the past participle uses the past part with at least one verb helper, and (4) the present participle adds *ing* to the present form and uses at least one verb helper.

8

infinitive	*present*	*past*
to ask	ask	asked
to collect	collect	collected
to interview	interview	interviewed

past participle	*present participle*
(have, was) asked	(was, has been) asking
(has, had been) collected	(am, have been) collecting
(were, have been) interviewed	(are, will be) interviewing

sentence examples

We need *to collect* more information for this report. (Infinitive)

Jeff *collects* stamps from countries all over the world. (Present part)

The courier *collected* all our mail for overnight delivery about an hour ago. (Past part)

My assistant *has collected* prospectuses from seven major suppliers of health insurance programs. (Past participle with a helping verb)

Our Research Department *is collecting* more information from consumers. (Present participle with a helping verb)

8–12. Formation of Parts for Irregular Verbs[6]

a. **Many verbs do not form their past part, past participle, and present participle in the usual manner. *All such irregular verb forms are shown in the dictionary; they are listed directly after the present form of the verb.* Any verbs without a listing are regular verbs, and their parts are formed in the regular way described in Section 8–11.**

b. **A number of irregular verbs form their parts in the same way. Most verbs ending in *e* form their past part and past participle by adding *d.* These same verbs form the present participle by dropping the *e* and adding *ing.***

Another group of verbs double the final consonant before adding the regular endings to the past part, past participle, and present participle.

verbs ending in "e"

Infinitive:	to change	to enclose	to complete
Present part:	change	enclose	complete
Past part:	changed	enclosed	completed
Past participle:	(has) changed	(have) enclosed	(have) completed
Present participle:	(is) changing	(are) enclosing	(is) completing

verbs that double the final consonant

Infinitive:	to trim	to stir	to clip
Present part:	trim	stir	clip
Past part:	trimmed	stirred	clipped
Past participle:	(has) trimmed	(has) stirred	(have) clipped
Present participle:	(is) trimming	(are) stirring	(is) clipping

c. **Some irregular verb forms do not follow a particular pattern in forming the past part and the past participle. A list of parts for some such commonly used irregular verbs follows:**

Present Part	*Past Part*	*Past Participle*	*Present Participle*
am	was	been	being
arise	arose	arisen	arising
become	became	become	becoming
begin	began	begun	beginning
bite	bit	bitten	biting
blow	blew	blown	blowing
break	broke	broken	breaking
bring	brought	brought	bringing
burst	burst	burst	bursting
buy	bought	bought	buying
catch	caught	caught	catching

[6]Parts for all irregular verbs are shown in the dictionary directly after the main entry.

8

Present Part	*Past Part*	*Past Participle*	*Present Participle*
choose	chose	chosen	choosing
come	came	come	coming
dig	dug	dug	digging
do	did	done	doing
draw	drew	drawn	drawing
drink	drank	drunk	drinking
drive	drove	driven	driving
eat	ate	eaten	eating
fall	fell	fallen	falling
fight	fought	fought	fighting
fly	flew	flown	flying
forget	forgot	forgotten	forgetting
forgive	forgave	forgiven	forgiving
freeze	froze	frozen	freezing
get	got	got	getting
give	gave	given	giving
go	went	gone	going
grow	grew	grown	growing
hang	hung	hung	hanging
hide	hid	hidden	hiding
know	knew	known	knowing
lay	laid	laid	laying
lead	led	led	leading
leave	left	left	leaving
lend	lent	lent	lending
lie	lay	lain	lying
lose	lost	lost	losing
make	made	made	making
pay	paid	paid	paying
ride	rode	ridden	riding
ring	rang	rung	ringing
rise	rose	risen	rising
run	ran	run	running
see	saw	seen	seeing
set	set	set	setting
shake	shook	shaken	shaking
shrink	shrank	shrunk	shrinking
sing	sang	sung	singing
sink	sank	sunk	sinking
sit	sat	sat	sitting
speak	spoke	spoken	speaking
spring	sprang	sprung	springing
steal	stole	stolen	stealing
strike	struck	struck	striking
swear	swore	sworn	swearing
swim	swam	swum	swimming
take	took	taken	taking
tear	tore	torn	tearing
throw	threw	thrown	throwing
wear	wore	worn	wearing
write	wrote	written	writing

sentence examples

Our holiday sale *begins* this Monday.

We *began* work on this construction project early last June.

Orders from our national television campaign *have begun* flooding our telephone lines.

These stocks *are beginning* to pay substantial dividends.

8–13. Simple Tenses

Verb parts are used to form tenses that place an action or a condition in a time frame. The verb part itself may express tense, or a verb part with helpers (a verb phrase) may be needed to specify the time frame. The most commonly used tenses are the simple tenses—the *present,* the *past,* and the *future.*

a. **The *present tense* is used to indicate an ongoing action or a currently existing condition. Use the present part or a conjugation (changes in spelling to accommodate person) of the present part to form this tense.**

Place an *s* at the end of the present part when it is used with any singular subject except *I* and *you.* For verbs ending in *s, sh, ch, x,* and *z,* add *es* instead of *s.*[7]

8

present tense formations for most verbs

to eat	**to provide**	**to sit**
I eat	I provide	I sit
you eat	you provide	you sit
he eats John eats	he provides John provides	he sits John sits
she eats Mary eats	she provides Mary provides	she sits Mary sits
it eats the cat eats	it provides the company provides	it sits the cat sits
we eat	we provide	we sit
you eat (pl.)	you provide (pl.)	you sit (pl.)
they eat the children eat	they provide the parents provide	they sit the children sit

[7]The verbs *do* and *go* add *es* also; i.e., the singular form of *do* for *he, she,* and *it* is *does.* The corresponding form for *go* is *goes.*

present tense formations for verbs ending in "s," "sh," "ch," "x," and "z"

to wish	**to teach**	**to tax**
I wish	I teach	I tax
you wish	you teach	you tax
he wishes John wishes	he teaches John teaches	he taxes John taxes
she wishes Mary wishes	she teaches Mary teaches	she taxes Mary taxes
it wishes the board wishes	it teaches the program teaches	it taxes the city taxes
we wish	we teach	we tax
you wish (pl.)	you teach (pl.)	you tax (pl.)
they wish the children wish	they teach the schools teach	they tax the states tax

use of present tense

Our purchasing agent *buys* most of his stock from local sources.

I *recognize* the person in this picture.

Our company *establishes* offices in all cities in which it *conducts* business.

Our cleaning crew *waxes* these floors weekly.

He *goes* to the doctor regularly for checkups.

b. **The *past tense* describes a single past action or event. Simply use the past part of a verb to express the past tense.**

The customer *selected* tan carpeting for his new offices.

I *received* these documents last week.

Our purchasing agent *bought* this stock from a local source.

c. **The *future tense* describes expected or anticipated occurrences. To form the future tense, use the present part with the helping verb *will.***

I *will call* you within the next few days to confirm your reservation.

The committee *will review* your proposal by March 1, and Mr. Rosen *will notify* you of the committee's decision by March 8.

Our company *will* not *participate* in the bidding for this contract.

8–14. Perfect Tenses

The perfect tenses—the present, past, and future—use the past participle of the verb along with a helping verb derived from *have.*

a. **The *present perfect tense* describes an action or a condition that began in the past and has continued until the present. This tense is formed by using *has* or *have* with the past participle of the verb.**

Mr. Randolf *has worked* in our Accounting Department since July 1987.

The company *has paid* heavy fines during the past three years for environmental-impact violations.

We *have* already *sent* you three reminders about your past-due account.

b. **The *past perfect tense* describes a past action that occurred before another past action. Use *had* as a helping verb with the past participle of the main verb to form this tense.**

Our client *had signed* this will just three days before he *died.*

We *accepted* this offer only after we *had contacted* three other vendors.

Although we *had paid* for the merchandise, the manufacturer *did* not *ship* it in time for our spring sale.

c. **The *future perfect tense* describes an action that will take place before another future action. Use the helping verbs *will have* with the past participle of the main verb to form this tense.**

By the time you submit the final manuscript, we *will have spent* over $50,000 in fees to free-lance writers.

If allowed to continue, this project at its conclusion *will have cost* United States taxpayers over $3 billion.

8

8–15. Progressive Tenses

The progressive tenses show action in progress during the present, past, and future. Use the present participle of the verb along with a being verb helper—*am, is, are, was, were,* or *be.*

a. **The *present progressive tense* describes an ongoing action during the present time. The being verb helpers *am, is,* and *are* are used with the present participle to form this tense.**

I *am taking* several classes in computer applications this semester.

Our company *is sponsoring* a number of youth programs in the community.

Several of our key employees *are relocating* to our main office in Boston.

b. **The *past progressive tense* relates an ongoing action that occurred in the past. The being verb helpers *was* and *were* with the present participle of a verb are used to form this tense.**

I *was discussing* this problem with the vice president when her secretary interrupted us with an emergency message from the chairman of the board.

Until the end of last year, we *were* still *selling* more copies of the sixth edition than the seventh edition.

c. **The *future progressive tense* forecasts an ongoing future action. To form this tense, use the helping verbs *will* and *be* with the present participle of the verb.**

We *will be staffing* this branch office about one month before construction is completed.

Our auditors *will be reviewing* this company's books for at least another two months.

8–16. Passive Voice Constructions

Unlike other verb constructions, the passive voice does not necessarily identify who does what. Instead, the person or thing performing the action may be cloaked in ambiguity.

In business communications the passive voice is often used to soften the impact of a negative idea or to avoid placing blame for an oversight or error. It is also used simply to provide variety in sentence construction.

To form a passive voice construction, use the past participle of the verb with one of the following being verb helpers: *is, are, was, were, be,* or *been.*

Each order *is entered* into our computer when it arrives at our factory.

Our products *are sold* only through franchised retailers.

Unfortunately, the shipment *was damaged* in transit.

These eviction notices *were mailed* to the tenants on September 1.

The building *will be restored* within the next year.

All the depositors *have been notified* that the insured deposits of Universal Savings *have been assumed* by First Arizona Savings.

8–17. Use of *Lay* and *Lie*

a. **The principal parts of *lie* and *lay* follow:**

Present	*Past*	*Present Participle*	*Past Participle*
lie	lay	lying	lain
lay	laid	laying	laid

b. **Use a form of *lie* when the verb called for is intransitive (does not have a direct object) and a form of *lay* when the verb is transitive (has a direct object).[8] Always use a form of *lay* when the past participle appears with a "being" verb helper *(is, are, was, were, be, been).***

intransitive

The new shopping center *lies* at the foot of the Flintridge Foothills.

He *lay* unconscious for nearly an hour before the doctor arrived.

[8]Use of the verb *lay* with three of its parts—*lay, laid,* and (has, have, or had) *laid*—is often easily identified by substituting a form of the verb *put.* If *put* or one of its forms makes sense, then the use of *lay* or one of its forms is correct. Otherwise, a form of *lie* is more than likely correct.

Our mainframe computer *has lain* idle for nearly six hours.

Your packages *are lying* on the bottom shelf of the cupboard.

transitive

Please *lay* the papers on my desk.

Before leaving the office, she *laid* the file folders in your "in" basket.

We *have* always *laid* these booklets horizontally in their packing boxes.

Retail stores throughout the country *are laying* plans to capture their share of holiday purchases.

always a form of "lay" (being verb + past participle)

These sandbags have *been laid* here because of impending flood damage.

The carpeting for our new building *was laid* yesterday.

8–18. Principles of Agreement

a. The verb of a sentence must agree in person and number with the subject. To identify a subject, omit any prepositional phrase that separates the subject and the verb.

The *legs* of the table *were damaged* in transit. (Omit prepositional phrase *of the table.*)

Our *stock* of ribbons for our IBM and Epson printers *is running* low. (Omit prepositional phrases *of ribbons* and *for our IBM and Epson printers.*)

b. A pronoun that represents the subject must agree in number and gender with the subject.

Mr. Charles was asked to prepare *his* report by the end of this week.

Would *every student* please be sure to submit *his* or *her* class schedule by February 5.

Ellen and *Margaret* were asked to resubmit *their* applications for employment.

The *company* filed for bankruptcy because *it* was unable to meet *its* obligations.

c. Compound subjects joined by *and* generally require the use of a plural verb. When compound subjects are joined by *or* or *nor,* the form of the verb is determined by the part of the subject that is closer to the verb. If one part is plural and the other is singular, place the plural part, where possible, closer to the verb.

compound joined by "and"

My *son and daughter-in-law receive* monthly issues of Business Forecast.

Outgoing *letters and packages leave* our office on a regularly scheduled basis.

Mr. Lopez and his two assistants were requested to attend the board meeting.

compound joined by "or" or "nor"

Neither Sharon nor *John was* available for comment to the press.

Either you or *I am* responsible for writing this section of the report.

Ms. Binder or her *assistants are* reviewing the manuscript.

Candy or *flowers are* typically given on this occasion. (Not: Flowers or *candy is* typically given on this occasion.)

d. **Subjects joined by *and* take singular verbs in only two cases: (1) when the parts separated by *and* constitute a single person or thing and (2) when the compound is preceded by *each, every,* or *many a (an).***

single person or thing

Our *accountant and tax attorney has* prepared all the reports for the Internal Revenue Service.

Her *nurse and companion works* six days a week.

Bacon and eggs is served in our coffee shop until 11 a.m. each day.

Luckily the *horse and carriage was* stolen after the cameraman had shot the scene.

compound preceded by "each," "every," or "many a (an)"

Each apartment and condominium was inspected by our general manager before it was released for rental.

Every man, woman, and child is responsible for carrying his or her belongings during the tour.

Many a student and instructor has requested additional tickets to our Drama Department's production of "Picnic."

8

e. **Indefinite pronouns such as *each, every, everyone, everything, somebody, anybody, either,* and *neither* take singular verbs.**

Each of the books *was* stamped with the company name.

Everyone was pleased with the hotel accommodations.

Everything in these files *needs* to be transferred to microfiche.

Neither of them *was* present at the meeting.

f. **When the word *there* precedes the verb, select the singular or plural verb form on the basis of the number of the noun that follows. If the noun is singular, then use a singular verb; if it is plural, use a plural verb.**

The same rule applies to those words such as *some, all, none, most, a majority, one fourth,* and *part* that indicate portions. When they function as subjects, the number of the nouns that follow govern whether a singular or plural verb is correct.

"there" preceding a singular verb form

There *is* one *person* on the waiting list.

There *appears* to be only one *reason* why we did not receive the contract.

"there" preceding a plural verb form

There *are* three *people* on the reserve list.

There *appear* to be several *reasons* why our bid was not accepted.

portion preceding a singular verb form

Some of the *building has* been infested by mice.

Part of your *order has* been shipped.

One third of our *equipment needs* to be replaced.

portion preceding a plural verb form

All the *materials were* shipped to you yesterday.

Only *one half* of the *packages have* been inspected.

A majority of our *employees receive* extra benefits from our incentive plan.

g. "A number" used as a subject requires a plural verb. "The number" used as a subject requires a singular verb. Keep in mind that descriptive adverbs and adjectives may separate the article *a* or *the* from the word *number.*

"a number" subject, plural verb

Under the circumstances, *a number* of our customers *are* requesting a full refund.

A surprisingly small *number* of our students *have* registered late this semester.

"the number" subject, singular verb

We believe that *the number* of employees selecting the DSE insurance option *has* increased.

The large *number* of responses received from our recent advertising campaign *was* far greater than we had anticipated.

h. To express the subjunctive mood (a situation or condition that is untrue, not yet true, or highly unlikely), use *were* instead of *was* after *if, as if, as though,* or *wish.* The verb *was* is used only if the situation after *if, as if,* or *as though* could be true.

use of "were" instead of "was"

If I *were* you, I would submit another application before the deadline date.

Mr. Greeley took charge *as though* he *were* the owner of the store.

I *wish* I *were* able to answer that question for you.

use of "was"

If Mary *was* here, she did not return the overdue library books.

The customer acted *as though* he *was* irritated with our credit policies.

i. Avoid splitting an infinitive, that is, placing any words between *to* and the verb form.

Unfortunately, I was unable *to follow logically* the speaker's train of thought. (Not: *to logically follow*)

Were you able *to understand fully* the ramifications of this policy change? (Not: *to fully understand*)

j. Collective nouns such as *committee, jury, audience, group, team, class, board, crowd,* and *council* may take either singular or plural verbs, depending upon the situation in which the verb is used. If the individual members of the collective noun are operating as a unit, use a singular verb; if the individual members are acting separately, use a plural verb.

In most cases the use of a plural verb with a collective noun results in an awkward-sounding construction. To avoid such situations, restructure the sentence to use a plural-noun subject.

elements of noun acting as a unit

When an *audience gives* a speaker a standing ovation, you may be sure that he or she has delivered an exceptional address.

Has the *committee* finished its report?

elements of noun acting separately

The *jury were* arguing violently. (Alternative: The jury members were arguing violently.)

The *board have* not yet reached a decision. (Alternative: The board members have not yet reached a decision.)

restructured sentence with plural-noun subject

Unfortunately, the *members* of the council *do* not agree on the purpose of the newly formed committee.

After the game the team *members were seen* arguing with one another on national television.

k. A relative pronoun clause must agree in gender and number with the noun or pronoun it modifies.

Ms. Cohen is a *person* who *is* concerned about maintaining *her* good health.

Our manager is the kind of *man* who *is* always considerate of *his* subordinates.

All the *children* who *attend* this school must maintain *their* grade averages at the "C" level.

Have you read all the *papers* that *were* placed on your desk?

Our committee *meeting,* which *was* scheduled for next Monday, has been canceled.

I. **Those relative pronoun clauses preceded by such phrases as "one of those doctors," "one of those executives," "one of those books," or "one of those secretaries" agree with the plural noun and, therefore, must take a plural verb.**

Mary is one of those business *executives* who *travel* extensively in *their* jobs.

He is one of those *salespersons* who regularly *visit* all *their* customers.

Joshua's Travels is one of those *books* that *have* a tragic ending.

Adjectives

8–19. Adjectives Modify Nouns

Adjectives modify nouns or pronouns. They answer such questions as what kind? how many? which one?

what kind?

damaged merchandise

green lawns

stylish dresses

8

how many?

three insurance salespersons

several years

two dozen pencils

which one?

that chair

those flight attendants

this idea

8–20. Use of the Articles "A" and "An"

Use the article *a* before a word that begins with a consonant sound, a long *u* sound, or an *h* that is pronounced. Use *an* before words that begin with a pronounced vowel sound (except long *u*) or before words that begin with a silent *h*.

use of "a"

a newspaper	a restaurant
a uniform	a union
a history class	a hillside development

use of "an"

an answer	an unusual request
an honest person	an hour

8–21. Adjective Comparison

a. **Adjectives may be used to compare two or more nouns or pronouns. Use the comparative form for comparing two persons or things and the superlative form for comparing three or more.**

b. **Regular one-syllable adjectives ending in *e* add *r* for the comparative and *st* for the superlative. Regular one-syllable adjectives ending in consonants add *er* for the comparative and *est* for the superlative.**

one-syllable adjectives ending in "e"

He has a *fine* set of golf clubs.

He has a *finer* set of golf clubs than I.

He has the *finest* set of golf clubs I have ever seen.

one-syllable adjectives ending in a consonant

This is a *short* letter.

This letter is *shorter* than the last one you dictated.

This is the *shortest* letter I have written today.

c. **Most two-syllable adjectives and all adjectives containing three or more syllables use *more* or *less* and *most* or *least* to form the comparative and superlative. Forms for those two-syllable adjectives that do not follow this pattern are shown in the dictionary after their simple form. These words include *costly, friendly, happy, healthy, merry, lovely, pretty*—all ending in *y*.**

two- and three-syllable adjectives with "more," "most," "less," or "least"

We purchased a *handsome* wallet yesterday.

This wallet is *more handsome* than the one we purchased yesterday.

This is the *most handsome* wallet in the store.

We purchased an *expensive* wallet yesterday.

This wallet is *less expensive* than the one we purchased yesterday.

This is the *least expensive* wallet in the store.

two-syllable adjectives using "er" or "est"

We initiated a *costly* program.

The state's highway program is *costlier* than its conservation program.

Our welfare program is the *costliest* one in the nation.

d. **Irregular forms for adjective comparison appear in the dictionary. They are listed after the simple forms. A list of commonly used irregular adjectives follows:**

simple	*comparative*	*superlative*
good, well	better	best
bad, ill	worse	worst
little	littler, less	littlest, least
many, much	more	most
far	farther, further	farthest, furthest

e. **Use *other* or *else* when comparing one person or object with the other members of the group to which it belongs.**

Our Dallas office earns more revenue than any of our *other* branch offices. (Not *any of our branch offices)*

John is more intelligent than anyone *else* in the class. (Not *anyone in the class*)

f. **Some adjectives cannot be compared in the regular sense because they are absolute. A partial list of such adjectives follows:**

8

finished	perfect	complete
round	dead	straight
unique	full	alive

Absolute adjectives may show comparison by use of the forms "more nearly" or "most nearly."

This water cooler is *full.*

The water cooler in your office is *more nearly full* (not *fuller*) than the one in ours.

The water cooler in the Personnel Office is the *most nearly full* (not *fullest*) one on this floor.

This victim is *dead.*

This victim is *more nearly dead* (not *deader*) than the other one.

This victim is the *most nearly dead* (not *deadest*) one in the emergency room.

8–22. Independent Adjectives[9]

When two or more adjectives appearing before a noun independently modify the noun, separate these adjectives with commas.

[9]See Section 1–8 for a detailed explanation of the use of the comma with independent adjectives.

His *direct, practical* approach to problems created high respect among his staff.

We returned that *boring, poorly written* manuscript to its author.

She handled the problem in a *sure, calm, decisive* manner.

8–23. Adjectives With Linking Verbs

Use adjectives, not adverbs, after linking verbs. Common linking verbs include *feel, look, smell, sound,* and *taste.*

I *feel bad* that you were not elected. (Not *badly*)

This cake *tastes delicious.* (Not *deliciously*)

After the fire the adjoining rooms *smelled terrible.* (Not *terribly*)

8–24. Compound Adjectives[10]

a. **Adjectives containing two or more words that are shown hyphenated in the dictionary are known as *permanent compounds.*[11] These words are always hyphenated when they are used as adjectives.**

Your *up-to-date* files have been very helpful in compiling this data.

My present job is only *part-time,* but I will begin looking for a *full-time* job in September.

As one of the oldest players in the league, Steve doesn't seem to know when he is *well-off.*

b. **When two or more words appearing before a noun function as a single-thought modifier, place hyphens between the words, even though these words do not appear hyphenated in the dictionary. These compound adjectives are *temporary compounds* and are hyphenated only when they appear *before* the noun or pronoun they modify.**

temporary compound adjective appearing before the modified noun

Upon reading your *well-written* report, the committee members agreed to establish a new community center.

Very little of the *high-priced* merchandise was sold during our clearance sale.

Do not exceed the *55-mile-an-hour* speed limit.

You may advertise this opening as a *$30,000-a-year* position.

[10]See Section 2–2 for detailed rules regarding the formation of compound adjectives.

[11]All hyphenations for compound adjectives in this manual are based on those shown in *Webster's Ninth New Collegiate Dictionary* published by Merriam-Webster Inc., 1989 printing.

8

temporary compound adjective following the modified noun

Your report is certainly *well written.*

This merchandise is too *high priced* for our store.

The speed limit on this freeway is *55 miles an hour.*

Our manager's salary is at least *$30,000 a year.*

Adverbs

8–25. Functions and Forms of Adverbs

Adverbs modify verbs, adjectives, or other adverbs. They answer such questions as when? where? why? how? to what degree?

a. **Most adverbs end in *ly*.**

accidentally	daily	finally
carefully	definitely	steadily
cautiously	diligently	usually

8

b. **Some adverbs may either end in *ly* or take the adjective form of the word.[12]**

Please drive *slowly* (or *slow*) on this icy road.

Your order will be processed as *quickly* (or *quick*) as possible.

You may call *directly* (or *direct*) to Chicago on this line.

c. **Other adverbs do not take an *ly* form. Such adverbs include the following:**

again	late	not	there
almost	never	now	very
here	no	soon	well

8–26. Adverb Comparison

a. **One-syllable adverbs and some two-syllable adverbs show comparison by adding *er* or *est*. For comparisons between two items, use *er;* for comparisons among more than two items, use *est.*[13]**

---

[12]Both forms of those adverbs that may end in *ly* or just take the adjective form are shown in the dictionary.

[13]Two-syllable adverbs that show comparison by adding *er* or *est* are considered irregular. Therefore, these forms are shown in the dictionary following the simple form.

comparison of two

You live *closer* to the library than I.

My assistant left *earlier* than I.

comparison of more than two

Of all the students in the study group, you live *closest* to the library.

Who left the *earliest*—Bill, Paul, or Bob?

b. **Most adverbs containing two syllables and all adverbs containing more than two syllables form the comparison by adding *more* or *most* or *less* or *least* to the positive form. Use *more* or *less* in comparing two items and *most* or *least* in comparing more than two items.**

comparison of two

This conveyer belt travels *more slowly* than the one next to it.

Please pack these items *more carefully* than you have done in the past.

This brand of soap is *less widely* used on the East Coast than in the South.

comparison of more than two

Denver has been mentioned *most often* as the likely site for our next convention.

This conference is the *most unusually* conducted one I have ever attended.

This brand of soap is the *least widely* used of all the major brands.

8–27. Adverb Placement

a. **Place adverbs as closely as possible to the words they modify. The misplacement of an adverb can change the meaning of a sentence or result in an awkward-sounding sentence.**

changed meaning

Only Beverly and I were invited to attend the seminar on human relations.

Beverly and I were invited to attend *only* the seminar on human relations.

awkward construction

Our costs have *nearly* risen 20 percent this year. (Awkward)

Our costs have risen *nearly* 20 percent this year. (Correct)

b. **Avoid splitting an infinitive with an adverb; place the adverb after the infinitive.**

We will need *to scrutinize carefully* all applicants for this position.

If you wish *to discuss* this situation *further,* please call me.

8–28. Adverbs vs. Adjectives

Use an adverb after a verb that shows action; use an adjective, however, after a nonaction (or linking) verb.

action verb

You *did well* on your six-month evaluation.

The pedestrian *crossed* the street *cautiously.*

Most of the committee *opposed bitterly* the controversial measure.

Our bowling team *was beaten badly.*

nonaction or linking verb

This room *smells terrible.*

His coffee *tastes bitter.*

I *feel bad* about Mr. Johnson's predicament.

The Sunday evening banquet *was delicious.*

8–29. Double Negatives

Use only one negative word or limiting adverb to express a single idea.

Do *not* release this information to *anybody.* (Not *nobody*)

I did *not* receive *anything* from our insurance agent. (Not *nothing*)

I *can* (not *can't* or *cannot*) *scarcely* believe that our president would make such a foolish statement.

We *were* (not *weren't* or *were not*) *hardly* in the office when Ms. Murch gave us the disappointing news.

He *had* (not *hadn't* or *had not*) *barely* finished the report in time for the board meeting.

Prepositions

8–30. Prepositions as Connectors

a. Prepositions link descriptive words to other words or ideas in a sentence. The most commonly used prepositions are *of* and *for.* Other commonly used prepositions, those listed below, can easily be identified by picturing what an airplane can do to clouds: the airplane can fly ______ the clouds.

above	between	opposite
against	by	outside
among	from	over
around	in	through
at	inside	to
behind	into	under
below	on	with

b. **Prepositions begin a phrase that ends with a noun or pronoun. This phrase is related to another word in the sentence—it describes, limits, or modifies the word in some way by clarifying who, what, when, where, how, why, or to what degree.**

Our staff *of accountants* is available to assist you at any time. (*Of accountants* is related to *staff*—specifies what.)

You may park your car *behind the building.* (*Behind the building* is related to *park*—specifies where.)

8–31. Prepositional Phrases

In determining subject-verb agreement, generally ignore any prepositional phrases that separate the subject and the verb.

One of your brothers *is* waiting in your office. (Omit *of your brothers* to match "One . . . is.")

A large *quantity* of goods *has* been ordered for the sale. (Omit *of goods* to match "quantity . . . has.")

Last Monday our *supply* of paper goods and kitchen utensils *was* destroyed. (Omit *of paper goods and kitchen utensils* to match "supply . . . was.")

8–32. In, Between, or Among?

8

When a preposition has a single object, use *in*. For two separate objects, use *between;* for three or more objects, use *among*.

"in"

There are several discrepancies *in* the auditor's report.

The prosecution noted several discrepancies *in* the witness's testimony.

"between"

Between you and me, I believe our company stock will split within the next several months.

There were several discrepancies *between* the two witnesses' reports.

"among"

Please distribute these supplies *among* the various branch offices.

Among themselves the Board of Directors had consented previously to withdraw that motion.

8–33. Prepositions Used With Certain Words

Certain words require particular prepositions depending upon the meaning to be conveyed. Other words often acquire prepositions incorrectly. A list of commonly used combinations follows:

Agree *on* or *upon* (mutual ideas or considerations—to reach an understanding)
Agree *to* (undertake an action)
Agree *with* (a person or his or her idea)

All *of* (Use *of* when followed by a pronoun; omit *of* when followed by a noun. *All of us . . . . All the people . . . .*)

Angry *about* (a situation or condition)
Angry *at* (things)
Angry *with* (a person or a group of persons)

Both *of* (Use *of* when followed by a pronoun; omit *of* when followed by a noun. *Both of them . . . . Both the managers . . . .*)

Buy *from* (Not *off* or *off of*)

Comply or compliance *with* (Not *to*)

Conform *to* (to act in accordance with prevailing standards)
Conform *with* (to be similar or in agreement)

Convenient *to* (a location)
Convenient *for* (a person)

Correspond *with* (a person—by writing)
Correspond *to* (a thing)

Discrepancy *in* (one thing)
Discrepancy *between* (two things)
Discrepancy *among* (three or more things)

Different *from* (Not *than*)

From (a person) (Not *off* a person)

Help (Not *help from*)

Identical *with* (Not *to*)

Inside (Not *inside of*)

Off (Not *off of; off* a thing)

Opposite (Not *opposite to* or *opposite of*)

Outside (Not *outside of*)

Plan *to* (Not *plan on*)

Retroactive *to* (Not *retroactive from*)

Take *off* (a thing)
Take *from* (a person)

Conjunctions

Conjunctions join words or groups of words within a sentence. While some conjunctions join equal ideas, others join contrasting ideas or introduce dependent clauses.

8–34. Coordinating Conjunctions

a. **The most commonly occurring coordinating conjunctions—*and, but, or,* and *nor*—are used to join like or equal ideas within a sentence. These ideas may be words, phrases, or clauses.**

words

Please place copies of the *proposal* and *contract* in each client's file.

You may obtain additional information from *Mr. Phelps, Ms. Dow,* or *me.*

phrases

Please post these notices *on all campus bulletin boards* and *in student gathering places throughout the campus.*

Ms. Ross has agreed to *edit the manuscript* and *follow it through all the production stages.*

clauses

If you accept our offer, *we will sign a guarantee of completion by May 1* and *you will be protected against any losses beyond this date.*

Our advertising funds for this year have been depleted, but *we are interested in considering your proposal for our next year's budget.*

b. **Because coordinating conjunctions join equal ideas, the ideas they join must be expressed in the same way; that is, they must have *parallel structure.* Parallel structure requires that the connected ideas have the same format. For example, if the first idea begins with a noun or pronoun, so must any others. If the first idea begins with an infinitive, then all others must begin with an infinitive. Be sure to match each idea—gerund with gerund, verb with verb, prepositional phrase with prepositional phrase, etc.**

8

parallel structure with gerunds

You may obtain your free trial subscription by *calling* or *writing* our main office.

We would appreciate your *paying* this bill as soon as possible and *sending* us a copy of the receipt issued at the time of payment.

parallel structure with verb phrases (past participles)

The contractor has already *leveled* the construction site and *poured* the foundation.

As you requested, we have *notified* our delinquent customers of their status, *requested* immediate payment of all overdue amounts, and *halted* any charge orders in progress.

parallel structure with clauses (subject and verb)

As soon as we receive your credit application, *we will* check your credit rating and *our Credit Department will* contact you.

Our *local chamber of commerce has endorsed* this proposal, but other *chambers of commerce* in the county *are opposed* to it.

8–35. Conjunctions Used in Pairs

a. **Use *either . . . or* for positive statements; use *neither . . . nor* for negative statements. The same grammatical construction should be used after each part.**

positive statements, "either . . . or"

Either Ms. Saunders *or* Mr. Ramirez will inspect the property.

You may specify *either* black *or* brown on your order.

negative statements, "neither . . . nor"

Neither a Toyota *nor* a Datsun is available for rental this week.

I could not believe that *neither* Larry *nor* Debbie would accept the assignment.

b. **Use the same grammatical construction after each part of the conjunctive pair *not only . . . but also.***

Our company manufactures *not only* furniture *but also* major appliances. (Not: Our company *not only* manufactures furniture *but also* major appliances.)

8

Our company *not only* manufactures and services major appliances *but also* services small appliances.

c. **In comparisons use *as . . . as* for positive ideas and *so . . . as* for negative ideas.**

positive ideas, "as . . . as"

Our Model 874 clock radio has become *as* popular *as* our Model 923.

I believe that her understudy is *as* talented *as* Ms. Saito.

negative ideas, "so . . . as"

Our Model 874 radio is not *so* popular *as* our Model 923.

Avocados are not *so* expensive *as* they were last year.

8–36. Subordinate Conjunctions

Subordinate conjunctions may be used to introduce dependent clauses. A partial listing of subordinate conjunctions follows:

if	because	while
as	since	before
when	although	after

a. **When a subordinate conjunction with its corresponding clause introduces a sentence, place a comma after the introductory clause.**

If you wish any additional information, Mr. Johnson will be pleased to supply it.

Before you sign these contracts, you should speak with some of this company's former clients.

b. **When a subordinate conjunction with its corresponding clause follows a main clause, separate the two clauses with a comma only if the subordinate conjunction introduces a nonrestrictive idea.**

no comma separating clauses

We will ship your merchandise *when we receive your authorization.*

You may wish to verify this information *before you make any further payments.*

comma separating clauses—nonrestrictive idea

Mr. Johnson would be pleased to supply you with any additional information, *if you need it.*

My clients have agreed to settle this matter out of court, *although I advised them against doing so.*

8–37. As vs. Like

8

As **is a conjunction and is used when the following construction is a clause (a word group containing a subject and a verb).** ***Like*** **is a preposition and is used when the following construction is a prepositional phrase (a phrase ending with a noun or pronoun).**

"as" with a clause

They did not package the order *as* (not *like*) *he expected they would.*

As (not *like*) *you indicated in your letter,* we cannot expect to make a profit during our first year of operation.

"like" with a prepositional phrase

We need more qualified agents *like you.*

Please order another desk *like the one* you have in your office.

CHAPTER 9

Spelling, Proofreading, and Editing

Spelling, Proofreading, and Editing Solution Finder

Spelling

9–1. Words Commonly Misspelled in Business Writing

a. Some frequently used words in business writing are often misspelled because they are mispronounced, contain double-letter combinations, or have silent letters. Since these words appear repeatedly in letters, memorandums, and reports, anyone involved with the preparation of such documents should become conversant with their spellings.

commonly misspelled words

absence
accommodate
acknowledgment
acquire
adequate
advantageous
advertisement
advisable
allotted
among
analysis
analyze
appointment
argument
assistance
attorney
awkward
bankruptcy
becoming
beginning
beneficial
benefit
budget
bureau
business
calendar
canceled
catalog
clientele
column
commission
committee
competition
competitor
congratulate
conscientious
conscious
consecutively
consistent
convenient
correspondence
courteous
creditor
currency
decision
deductible
defendant
deferred
definitely
dependent
describe
desirable
development
dissatisfied
division
efficient
embarrass
emphasis
emphasize
employee
endorsement
envelope
equipped
especially
evidently
excellent
exempt
exorbitant
extraordinary
familiar
feasible
fiscal
foreign
forty
fourth
genuine
government
grammar
grateful
handicapped
harass
height
independent
interest
interrupt
itinerary
judgment
knowledgeable
laboratory
library
license
maintenance
manageable
manufacturer
mileage
miscellaneous
mortgage
necessary
nevertheless
nineteenth
ninety
ninth
noticeable
occasionally
occurred
offered
omission
omitted
opposite
ordinarily
paid
pamphlet
permanent
permitted
pertinent
physician
possession
postpaid
practical
prevalent
privilege
procedure
professor
profited
prominent
quantitative
quantity
questionnaire
receipt
receive
recognize
recommendation
regarding
remittance
restaurant
schedule
separate
serviceable
severely
similar
sincerely
succeed
sufficient
superintendent
supervisor
tenant
thank you
therefore
thorough
though
through
truly
undoubtedly
unnecessarily
usable
usage
using
valuable
volume
weekday

b. Some common words used in business writing are misspelled because they are confused with other words. Combinations such as *affect—effect, loose—lose, pole—poll, realty—reality, their—their,* and others are covered in Chapter 7.

9–2. General Rules to Improve Spelling

a. For one-syllable words ending with a single consonant that is preceded by a single vowel, repeat the consonant before adding the suffix *y* (bag + y = baggy). Also repeat the consonant when adding a suffix beginning with a vowel (bag + age = baggage). Exceptions to this rule are many words ending in *s* and all words ending in *w, x,* and *y.*

final consonant doubled

clam	clammy	skin	skinny	run	runny
stop	stopped	trim	trimmed	ship	shipped
big	bigger	sit	sitting	slip	slippage

exceptions

"s"		"w"		"x"		"y"	
bus	buses	sow	sowing	tax	taxes	pay	payable
yes	yeses	tow	towing	box	boxed	say	saying
gas	gases	snow	snowy	wax	waxy	buy	buyer

9

b. Do not repeat the final consonant for those one-syllable words that add a suffix beginning with a consonant (ship + ment = shipment).

sad	sadness	bad	badly	sin	sinful
glad	gladly	star	stardom	hat	hatless

c. For multisyllable words ending with a consonant preceded by a single vowel *(prefer),* repeat the final consonant *(r)* before adding a suffix beginning with a vowel *(ed)* if the resulting word places the accent on the final syllable of the root word (*-fer* in *preferred*). If, however, the resulting word (e.g., *preference*) places the accent on the first syllable of the root word *(pref-),* do not repeat the final consonant *(r)* before adding the suffix *(ence).* There are exceptions to this rule.

accent on final syllable of root word, final consonant repeated

occurred	occur + r + ed
transferred	transfer + r + ed
beginning	begin + n + ing
unforgettable	un + forget + t + able
referring	refer + r + ing
preferred	prefer + r + ed

accent on first syllable of root word, final consonant not repeated

canceled	cancel + ed
profitable	profit + able
credited	credit + ed
benefited	benefit + ed
reference	refer + ence
preferable	prefer + able

exceptions

programmed handicapped formatted

d. The prefix *fore-*, which means "before," is used to precede whole words to form another word (fore + thought = forethought); the prefix *for-*, on the other hand, is generally used with letter combinations that by themselves are not separate words (for + tunate = fortunate).

prefix "fore-"

forego	fore + go
foreclose	fore + close
foreground	fore + ground
foresight	fore + sight

prefix "for-"

forceps	for + ceps
forfeit	for + feit
formative	for + mative
formerly	for + merly

exceptions

forgive forget forsake forswear

e. For words ending with a silent *e*, generally drop the *e* before adding a suffix that begins with a vowel.

silent "e" dropped

desire	desirable	approve	approval
file	filing	sense	sensible
finance	financial	execute	executive

exceptions

dye	dyeing	mile	mileage
acre	acreage	Europe	European

f. Retain the silent *e* when adding suffixes beginning with *a* or *o* to words ending in *ce* and *ge*.

9

silent "e" retained

notice	noticeable	manage	manageable
service	serviceable	knowledge	knowledgeable
replace	replaceable	advantage	advantageous
enforce	enforceable	courage	courageous

exception

mortgage mortgagor

g. For words ending with a silent *e*, generally retain the *e* when adding a suffix that begins with a consonant.

silent "e" retained

manage	management	achieve	achievement
sure	surely	precise	precisely
sincere	sincerely	nine	ninety
whole	wholesome	home	homeless

exceptions

nine	ninth	true	truly
judge	judgment	acknowledge	acknowledgment
wise	wisdom	whole	wholly
argue	argument	gentle	gently

h. For words ending with *y* preceded by a consonant, generally change the *y* to *i* before adding any suffix except one beginning with *i*.

final "y" changed to "i"

penny	pennies	easy	easiest
likely	likelihood	twenty	twentieth
cloudy	cloudiness	vary	variable
carry	carried	ordinary	ordinarily

final "y" retained before suffix beginning with "i"

fly	flying	lobby	lobbyist
try	trying	thirty	thirtyish

exception

shy shyly

i. When adding any suffix, retain the final *y* in words if it is preceded by a vowel.

final "y" retained

money	moneyed	display	displaying
employ	employable	pay	payment
convey	conveyer	okay	okayed

exceptions

pay	paid	day	daily
lay	laid	say	said

j. Place *i* before *e* except after *c* or when the combination is pronounced like the *a* in "neighbor" or "weigh."

"ie" combination

believe	relief	niece	chief
thief	achieve	yield	piece

"ei" combination after "c"

receive	receipt	ceiling	perceive

"ei" combination when sounded like "a"

weight	freight	sleigh	vein

exceptions

either	neither	leisure	weird
financier	species		

k. For words ending with the syllable pronounced "seed," only one word is spelled *sede,* three words are spelled *ceed,* and the rest are spelled *cede.*

word ending in "sede"

supersede

words ending in "ceed"

exceed	proceed	succeed

words ending in "cede"

accede	precede	concede
intercede	recede	secede

9–3. Use of the Dictionary to Locate Correct Spellings

a. Use a recognized up-to-date collegiate, desk, or unabridged dictionary to locate any spellings of words you do not know or about which you are unsure. The dictionary used for all spellings in this manual is the 1989 printing of *Webster's Ninth New Collegiate Dictionary* published by Merriam-Webster Inc.

b. When the dictionary offers two spellings for a word in the same entry, use the *first* spelling.

judgment not *judgement*

canceled not *cancelled*

c. When verifying the spelling of words, be sure to match the word with its correct counterpart in the dictionary. For example, if the word is used as a noun in the sentence, then check to make sure you are comparing it with the noun spelling of this word in the dictionary. As an illustration of differences in spellings, note that *under way* used as a verb is two words but *underway* as an adjective is one. Similar situations occur with many other words.

mark down (verb)	markdown (noun)
set up (verb)	setup (noun)
double-space (verb)	double space (noun)

9

d. The spellings of irregular plural nouns and irregular verb forms appear in the dictionary directly after the root word in the entry. Therefore, when in doubt about the formation of these words, consult your dictionary for their spellings.

irregular plural nouns

secretary	secretaries	tomato	tomatoes
half	halves	child	children
analysis	analyses	alumnus	alumni

irregular verb forms

bring	brought	brought
sing	sang	sung
run	ran	run
lie	lay	lain
see	saw	seen

e. The spellings of irregular adjective and adverb comparisons appear in the dictionary directly after the root word in the entry. Check your dictionary to verify these spellings. (See Sections 8–21 and 8–26 for rules on adjective and adverb comparisons.)

irregular adjective comparison

costly	costlier	costliest
good	better	best

irregular adverb comparison

early	earlier	earliest
far	farther	farthest

f. Acquaint yourself with the various letter combinations that represent sounds in the written English language so that you can easily locate the spellings of unfamiliar words in the dictionary. Both consonants and vowels can have different letter combinations that represent the same sound. The chart below presents just a few of the sounds and combinations with which you should become familiar.

Sound	*Letter Combinations to Represent the Sound*
ā	*a*lienate, *ai*de, g*au*ge, st*ea*k, f*ei*g n, w*eigh*t
ak	*ac*tuary, *acc*olade, *ack*nowledgment, *acq*uiesce, *aq*ueduct
ar	*ae*rosol, *air*borne, *ar*eas, *arr*ogant
as	*as*piration, *asc*ending, *ass*ertive
aw	f*a*ther, *au*dacity, fr*augh*t, *aw*esome, *o*stracize, *ough*t
ē	*e*dict, *ea*sement, d*ee*m, rec*ei*pt, p*eo*ple, f*i*asco, p*ie*ce
er	simil*ar*, *er*adicate, *ear*nings, *err*oneous, f*ir*mly, w*or*risome, t*our*nament, *ur*banization
f	*f*elony, e*ff*icient, *ph*onetic, rou*gh*age
g	*g*rimace, *gh*astly, *gu*ardian
h	*h*azardous, *wh*olly
ī	*ai*sle, h*eigh*t, *i*dentify, t*ie*d, th*igh*, h*y*draulic
j	ju*dg*ment, *g*ermane, exa*gg*eration, *j*eopardize
k	*c*oincide, a*cc*ountant, *ch*emotherapy, *k*ilometer, *q*uandary
m	*m*iraculous, pa*lm*istry
n	*gn*aw, *kn*otty, *mn*emonic, *n*arrative, *pn*eumonia
ō	b*eau*, *o*dor, fl*oa*t, d*oe*skin, p*ou*ltry, d*ough*nut, sn*ow*
oi, oy	sp*oi*l, ann*oy*ance
oo	n*eu*tral, fl*ew*, ad*ieu*, t*o*mb, l*oo*se, l*ou*ver, thr*ough*, n*u*trition, tr*ue*, s*ui*t
ow	ann*ou*nce, fl*ow*er
r	*r*etrieve, *rh*ythm, *wr*est.
s	*c*ertainty, *s*alable, *ps*ychologist, *sc*intillate
sh	ma*ch*inery, espe*ci*ally, *s*urely, con*sc*ience, *sch*nauzer, nau*se*ous, *sh*rewd, preci*si*on, percu*ss*ion, substan*ti*al
t	*pt*omaine, *t*ranslate
ū	be*au*tiful, f*eu*d, sk*ew*ed, *u*niform, f*ue*l, *yu*letide
w	ch*oi*r, q*u*arterly, *w*asteful, *wh*imsical

9

Proofreading

Look for ↓

9–4. Procedures for Proofreading Documents

Proofreading is the process of checking one document against another to ensure that it conforms with the original in all respects. Use these guidelines to proofread a document:

a. If you have prepared the document using a computerized word processing program, you should complete a spell check (if this feature is available) before printing the document and/or beginning the proofreading process.

b. Check for consistency of style throughout the document before actually beginning to read the text.

   (1) Assess the appropriateness of margins (top, bottom, left, and right), line spacing (between paragraphs, with main and text headings, with letter closing lines, etc.), and general appearance.

   (2) Inspect to ensure that the document contains no widow or orphan lines (single lines of a paragraph at the top or bottom of a page).

c. Read the text initially for content.

   (1) Does the material make sense?

   (2) Are there any missing words?

   (3) Are any words or groups of words repeated?

9

d. Read the text again for accuracy. Check it carefully against the original copy.

   (1) Are any letters transposed or omitted? Are all words spelled correctly? Have any words, sentences, or paragraphs been omitted?

   (2) When proofreading names and unfamiliar words or terminology, check each spelling meticulously letter by letter.

   (3) Double-check all figures carefully with the original source. For long numbers verify the number of digits and then compare the digits in groups of three.

   If the numbers are in a column with a total, the easiest method of proofreading is to use a calculator to check the total in the original document and then check the same total in the document being proofread.

e. When proofreading hard copy, use the pen-and-forefinger technique to maintain attention and keep the eyes focused on the line being proofread. To use this technique, hold the pen in the hand with which you will be making corrections and place the copy to be proofread on that side. Place the original on the opposite side and use the forefinger of that hand to follow along as you compare the two copies.

f. When proofreading hard copy, use the standardized revision marks shown in Section 9–5 and also on the inside back cover to show your corrections.

9–5. Standardized Revision Marks to Show Corrections

a. Standardized revision marks (also called *proofreaders' marks*) are used to show corrections in handwritten, typewritten, computer-generated, or printed copy. These symbols are used so that anyone who reads the document will interpret the corrections in the same way. Use the following marks and symbols to make changes in words or word groups:

Instruction	*Example*
Omit or delete stroke.	. . . occassion. . . .
Omit or delete stroke.	. . . policy, and send us. . . .
Omit or delete word(s).	. . . a ~~postal~~ money order for $50.
Change word(s).	Because ~~In view of the fact that~~ you have. . . .
Insert word(s).	. . . your latest income tax form. . . .
Restore word(s) crossed out.	. . . our ~~furniture~~ warehouse in Toledo.
Insert a space.	Inaddition, you will be. . . .
Close up space.	You can, never the less, receive. . . .
Join to word.	. . . in our micro computer laboratory.
Make lowercase.	. . . of the Association. . . .
Use all lowercase letters.	. . . in the UNITED STATES OF AMERICA.
Capitalize letter.	. . . to the Retailers association.
Use all capitals.	. . . from the Wall Street Journal.
Insert comma or semicolon.	. . . now therefore you. . . .
Insert period or colon.	. . . follows pen, ink, and paper
Insert apostrophe or quotation marks.	. . . its a good deal?
Spell out word or number.	. . . 3 stores on Fifth Ave. in. . . .
Transpose letters.	. . . and all thier profits.
Hyphenate word(s).	. . . up to date records. . . .
Underscore word(s).	We <u>cannot</u> overemphasize the. . . .

b. Use the following symbols to move words or word groups.

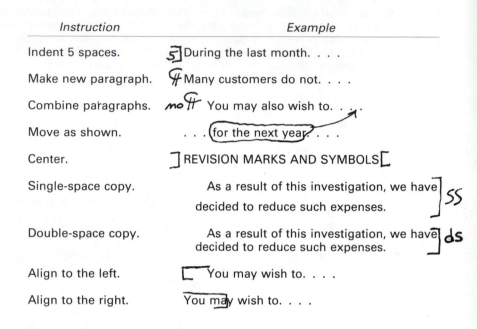

Instruction	*Example*
Indent 5 spaces.	5] During the last month. . . .
Make new paragraph.	¶ Many customers do not. . . .
Combine paragraphs.	no ¶ You may also wish to. . . .
Move as shown.	. . . (for the next year) . . .
Center.	] REVISION MARKS AND SYMBOLS [
Single-space copy.	As a result of this investigation, we have decided to reduce such expenses.] ss
Double-space copy.	As a result of this investigation, we have decided to reduce such expenses.] ds
Align to the left.	[You may wish to. . . .
Align to the right.	You may wish to. . . .

Editing

9

9–6. Preparing to Edit

a. The proofreading process involves the comparison of one document with another to assess the correctness of the prepared copy. Editing, on the other hand, is a more challenging process since editors do not have "correct" copies upon which they may rely to determine if the copy they are reading has been prepared properly. Editors themselves are responsible for determining the accuracy and appropriateness of all language and format applications.

b. Assemble all the materials you will need to edit a document:

(1) An up-to-date (printed within the last three years) collegiate, desk, or unabridged dictionary, e.g., *Webster's Ninth New Collegiate Dictionary*

(2) An up-to-date (published within the last three years) reference manual, e.g., *How 6: A Handbook for Office Workers, Sixth Edition*

(3) An up-to-date (published within the last five years) thesaurus, e.g., *Roget's II: The New Thesaurus*

(4) Reference sources from which the document was created; e.g., rough drafts, authorization letters, file copies, meeting notes, etc.

(5) Any other published references that may relate to the document; e.g., mailing lists, telephone directories, zip code directories, maps, encyclopedias, books, magazines, newspapers, etc.

9–7. Editing the Document

a. Because the editor does not just "check" a document against another source, you will probably need to read the material several times. As an editor you must evaluate the overall effectiveness of a document in terms of its attaining the goal for which it was written. Therefore, you will wish to read the material critically with several criteria in mind:

(1) Are there any omissions in ideas or content? All important ideas should be included in the document as well as any information to substantiate the ideas. Check to make sure the document is complete in every respect.

(2) Is the document well organized so that the reader can easily follow the ideas as they are presented? Coherent writing results in clarity and allows the reader to understand easily the purpose and contents of the document. The editor needs to make sure that ideas are placed in logical order and that each sentence flows smoothly and lucidly from the previous sentence.

(3) Is the document correct in every way—content, format, grammar, spelling, punctuation, capitalization, and number expression? Be sure to check the accuracy of all the data. In addition, make sure that all the conventions of correct language usage have been observed and that the document has been formatted appropriately.

(4) Is the content easily understood? Examine the document to ensure that the ideas are presented vividly and with ample illustrations so that the reader can picture concretely what the writer had in mind.

(5) Have all the ideas been expressed in as few words as possible? Look at each sentence to make sure that it does not contain superfluous wording. Evaluate sentences and paragraphs to see if they contribute to achieving the overall purpose of the document. Any excess words, sentences, or paragraphs should be deleted.

(6) Are all abbreviations, number expressions, and other format considerations handled in the same way? Check for inconsistencies in these areas and in the contents of the document.

(7) Are the tone and language appropriate for accomplishing the purpose of the document? Check to make sure that letters are written in a friendly and courteous manner. Reports, on the other hand, should have a more formal tone. Match the formality of tone and language with the purpose of the document.

b. Use revision marks and symbols to indicate changes made during the editing process. These marks and symbols are explained and illustrated in Section 9–5 and on the inside back cover.

CHAPTER 10

Address Format and Forms of Address

Address Format and Forms of Address Solution Finder

General Address Format

10–1. General Address Format

a. **Use combinations of the following to address general business correspondence: full name with appropriate courtesy title, professional title, company name, street address, city, state, and zip code (5 digits or 9 digits, depending upon availability of 9-digit code). Use the same format for both the inside address and the envelope, unless the company uses the envelope format recommended by the U.S. Postal Service described in Section 11–27.**

addressed to individual

Ms. Elizabeth Bennett
2879 Balboa Boulevard, Apt. 2
San Clemente, CA 92672-2036

Dear Ms. Bennett:

addressed to individual within company

Mr. Jay V. Berger, Manager
Policy Issue Department
General Insurance Company of America
341 Prospect Avenue
Hartford, Connecticut 06105-1702

Dear Mr. Berger:

addressed to company

F. M. Tarbell Company
2740 Troy Avenue, S.W.
Indianapolis, IN 46241-6054

Attention: Mr. William F. Schlossinger, Manager, Personnel Department

Gentlemen:

b. **An address may have a maximum of six lines and a minimum of two lines.**

minimum two-line address

Phillips Foods, Inc.
Morristown, NJ 07960-4968

maximum six-line address

Ms. Stephanie R. Whitaker
Chief Operations Manager
Quality Control Department
Neware Aluminum Accessories
3618 Chelwood Boulevard, N.E.
Albuquerque, NM 87111-8549

Names and Titles

10–2. Courtesy Titles

a. **Abbreviate the courtesy titles *Mr.* and *Mrs.* when they are used with the names of individuals. The courtesy title *Ms.* ends with a period, although it is not an abbreviation. Always spell out the courtesy title *Miss.***

Mr. Stanley Hutchinson

Ms. Frances Cates

Mrs. Charlene Carnachan

Miss Natalie Granados

b. **When the name of an individual does not signify whether the person is a man or a woman, omit the courtesy title or use *Mr.* When addressing a woman, use the courtesy title *Ms.* unless *Miss* or *Mrs.* is specified by the addressee.**

name does not signify gender

Lynn Sebatian *or* Mr. Lynn Sebatian

T. R. Najjar *or* Mr. T. R. Najjar

Chris V. Stauber *or* Mr. Chris V. Stauber

woman does not indicate a title preference

Ms. Elizabeth Rankin

Ms. Ellen Togo

c. **The courtesy title *Master* is used for addressing young boys (boys too young to be called *Mister*).**

Master William J. Clark

d. **The abbreviated courtesy title *Esq.* is sometimes used after the surname. In such cases no courtesy title precedes the name.**

Murray T. Silverstein, *Esq.*

e. **Female correspondents who have a courtesy title preference other than *Ms.* should indicate this preference in the signature lines of their correspondence by enclosing the preferred title in parentheses before their names. Female correspondents who have names that do not indicate gender may also wish to indicate a courtesy title preference by enclosing it in parentheses before their names in a signature line.**

female with courtesy title preference other than "Ms."

(Mrs.) Nancy Willett

(Miss) Karen L. Butler

female whose name does not indicate gender

(Ms.) J. T. Robinson

(Ms.) Lonnie Abrams

(Mrs.) Chris Dobrian

10–3. Professional Titles

a. Except for *Dr.* and long professional titles consisting of more than one word, write out and capitalize all professional titles when they precede the names of individuals. *Professor, Dean, The Reverend, Governor, Senator, Colonel, Lieutenant,* and *The Honorable* are examples of titles that are capitalized and written in full.

"Doctor" abbreviated

Dr. Allen Wiedmeyer

professional title written out

Professor Marly Bergerud

long professional title abbreviated

Lt. Col. Ret. Maurice P. Wiener (Lieutenant Colonel Retired)

b. In addressing business correspondence or completing signature lines, capitalize and write out professional titles that follow an individual's name.

single-line address format

Mr. Ray Johnson, *Dean*

Ms. Patricia A. Wilson, *Vice President*

two-line address format

Ms. Margaret M. Fielding
Plant Superintendent

Mr. Michael T. Huggins, Jr.
Assistant Vice President

single-line signature format

Jean Loucks, *Dean*

(Mrs.) Joyce Moore, *President*

William A. Murillo, *Manager*

two-line signature format

John S. Minasian
Plant Superintendent

(Ms.) Orolyn L. Ruenz
Vice President of Operations

(Mrs.) Brenda Browning
Collections Manager

c. **Capitalize professional titles *not* appearing in address format or signature lines only when they precede and are used directly with an individual's name. Do not capitalize titles following an individual's name, except in the case of high-ranking government officials (President of the United States, Vice President of the United States, Cabinet members, members of Congress, and governors).**

title preceding name

President Lloyd W. Bartholome will deliver the main address.

title following name

Lloyd W. Bartholome, *president* of A & P Enterprises, will deliver the main address.

title of high-ranking government official

The Honorable Scot Ober, *Senator* from Michigan, has agreed to deliver the main address.

d. **Only one professional courtesy title with the same meaning should appear with a single name. Use *Dr.* or *M.D.*, but not both titles, with the same name.**

titles with the same meaning

Dr. James V. Glaser

James V. Glaser, *M.D.*

10

titles with different meanings

Dr. Sue Rigby, *Professor*

e. **Do not capitalize professional titles that substitute for individuals' names except in the case of high-ranking government officials.**

title substituted for name

The *general* scheduled a staff meeting for Thursday afternoon.

title of high-ranking government official

Did the *Governor* appear for the press conference?

10–4. Company Names

Spell out company names in full unless the company itself uses abbreviations in its official name. *Inc.* and *Ltd.* usually appear in abbreviated form.

company name written in full

Pacific Mutual Life Insurance Company

Richter and Sons

Watson Corporation

company name containing abbreviation

Consolidated Factors, *Ltd.*

McKnight, Fisher *&* Donovan

International Computer *Corp.*

Places

10–5. Buildings and Units

Capitalize the names of buildings and units therein. In address formats place the unit after the building name, but separate the two with a comma. If an address contains a unit without a building name, place the unit after the street address. Separate the street address and the unit with a comma. Use figure form for all unit numbers.

building name with unit

Tishman Building, Suite 103

California State Capitol, Office 243F

Medical Arts Center, Suites 680–681

Greenwich Apartments, Unit 3

unit without building name

140 Willow Street, Suite 103

18564 Clark Street, Apt. 4

9830 Grand Oaks Avenue, Unit 22

10–6. Street Addresses

a. **Use figures to express house or building numbers. Only the house or building number *one* is written in word form.**

house or building number "one"

One Lakeview Terrace

house or building number in figures

8 Burbank Lane

210 Third Avenue, Apt. 303

b. **Spell out compass directions that appear within a street address. Compass points following the street address are preceded by a comma and abbreviated.**

compass point within street address

1864 *East* 37 Street

compass point following street address

180 Central Avenue, *S.W.*

4210 Broxten Street, *N.E.,* Apt. 23

c. **All numbered street names *ten* and below are written in words (using ordinal numbers—*first, second, third,* etc.) Numbered street names above *ten,* however, are written in figures. Use cardinal numbers (*11, 12, 13,* etc.) when a compass point appears between the house and street numbers; use ordinal numbers (*11th, 12th, 13th,* etc.) when no such compass point is present.**

numbered street name "ten" or below

1183 *Fifth* Avenue   983 West *First* Street

numbered street name above "ten"—with compass point

980 North *81* Street   3624 West *59* Place

numbered street name above "ten"—without compass point

2036 *48th* Street   11843 *123rd* Street

d. **Spell out street designations such as *Boulevard, Avenue, Street, Place, Drive,* and *Lane.* Only the street designation *Boulevard (Blvd.)* may be abbreviated with exceptionally long street names.**

street designation spelled out

18394 Lankershim *Boulevard*

street designation abbreviated

9263 North Coldwater Canyon *Blvd.*

e. **Spell out where possible mailing designations such as *Rural Route* or *Post Office Box* that are used in the place of street addresses. Abbreviate the mailing designation only with long addresses.**

postal designation spelled out

Post Office Box 207

postal designation abbreviated

P.O. Box 1269, Terminal Annex

f. **Apartment, suite, and unit numbers are expressed in figures and are generally included on the same line as the building name. In addresses**

without building names, these numbers appear on the same line with the street address. The term *Apartment* may be abbreviated when it appears on the same line as the street address.

With long street addresses, apartment numbers may be placed on the following line. The term *Apartment* in these cases is spelled out.

apartment, suite, or unit number with building

Richmond Medical Plaza, *Suite 540*

unit number with street address

6176 Arroyo Road, *Unit 2*

apartment number with street address

3964 West 81 Street, *Apt. 3*

no specific designation with street address

16932 Wilshire Boulevard, *C-110*

apartment number on line following street address

8564 Kensington Street, S.W.
Apartment 230

10–7. City, State, and Zip Code

a. **Spell out in full the names of cities.**

Saint Louis New York Fort Worth Los Angeles

b. **Use the two-letter post office designation for state names or spell out in full the state name. Select either mode based upon (1) the degree of formality of the correspondence or (2) the one that provides better balance for setting up the entire address. Should both be equally suitable, use the two-letter postal designation. Use the same form for both the inside address and the envelope address unless the company chooses to use the U.S. Postal Service recommendations for addressing envelopes described in Section 11–26.**

10

state two-letter zip code designation

Ms. Jessica Morton
108 Academy Avenue
Boston, MA 02188-6593

state name written in full

Mr. William R. Stephenson
257 American Legion Highway
Boston, Massachusetts 02131-4365

c. **Zip codes are typed a single space after the state.**

Atlanta, GA 30331-8732 or Atlanta, Georgia 30331

Forms of Address

10–8. Personal and General Professional Titles

The following table lists the proper forms of address, salutation, and complimentary close for correspondence addressed to a general individual, two or more individuals, certain professionals, and a company.

Addressee	*Address on Letter and Envelope*	*Salutation and Complimentary Close*
Man	Mr. (full name) (local address) 00000	Dear Mr. (surname): Sincerely,
Married Woman	Mrs. (husband's first name, last name) (local address) 00000	Dear Mrs. (surname): Sincerely,
	or	
	*Mrs. or Ms. (wife's first name, last name) (local address) 00000	Dear Mrs. or Ms. (surname): Sincerely,
Single Woman	Miss or Ms. (full name) (local address) 00000	Dear Miss or Ms. (surname): Sincerely,
Woman, Marital Status Unknown	Ms. (full name) (local address) 00000	Dear Ms. (surname): Sincerely,
Widow	Mrs. (husband's first name, last name) (local address) 00000	Dear Mrs. (surname): Sincerely,
	or	
	Mrs. or Ms. (wife's first name, last name) (local address) 00000	Dear Mrs. or Ms. (surname): Sincerely,
Two or More Men	Mr. (full name) and Mr. (full name) (local address) 00000	Dear Mr. (surname) and Mr. (surname): Dear Messrs. (surname) and (surname): Gentlemen: Sincerely,
Two or More Women	Mrs. (full name) and Mrs. (full name) (local address) 00000	Dear Mrs. (surname) and Mrs. (surname): Dear Mesdames (surname) and (surname): Mesdames: Sincerely,
	or	
	Miss (full name) and Mrs. (full name) (local address) 00000	Dear Miss (surname) and Mrs. (surname): Sincerely,
	or	

*This form is also used for a woman who is separated or divorced from her husband.

10

Addressee	Address on Letter and Envelope	Salutation and Complimentary Close
	Ms. (full name) and Ms. (full name) (local address) 00000	Dear Ms. (surname) and Ms. (surname): Dear Mses. (surname) and (surname): Sincerely,
One Woman and One Man	Ms. (full name) and Mr. (full name) (local address) 00000	Dear Ms. (surname) and Mr. (surname): Sincerely,
Married Couple	Mr. and Mrs. (husband's full name) (local address) 00000	Dear Mr. and Mrs. (surname): Sincerely,
Professional Married Couple	(title) (full name of husband) (title) (full name of wife) (local address) 00000	Dear (title) and (title) (surname): Dear (plural of title and surname if both husband and wife have same title): Sincerely,
President of a College or University (Doctor)	Dr. (full name), President (name of institution) (local address) 00000	Dear Dr. (surname): Sincerely,
Dean of a School or College	Dean (full name) School of (name) (name of institution) (local address) 00000	Dear Dean (surname): Sincerely,
	or	
	†Dr. or Mr. (full name) Dean of (title) (name of institution) (local address) 00000	Dear Dr. or Mr. (surname): Sincerely,
Professor	Professor (full name) (name of department) (name of institution) (local address) 00000	Dear Professor (surname): Sincerely,
	or	
	Dr. (full name), Professor (name of department) (name of institution) (local address) 00000	Dear Dr. (surname): Sincerely,
	or	
	†Dr. or Mr. (full name) Assistant Professor (name of department) (name of institution) (local address) 00000	Dear Dr. or Mr. (surname): Sincerely,
Physician	(full name), M.D. (local address) 00000	Dear Dr. (surname): Sincerely,

†When the addressee is a woman, substitute *Miss, Mrs.,* or *Ms.* for *Mr.*

Addressee	Address on Letter and Envelope	Salutation and Complimentary Close
Lawyer	†Mr. (full name) Attorney at Law (local address) 00000	Dear Mr. (surname): Sincerely,
Service Personnel	(full rank, full name, and abbreviation of service designation) (Retired is added if applicable.) (title and organization) (local address) 00000	Dear (rank) (surname): Sincerely,
Company or Corporation, Men	(full name of organization) (local address) 00000	Gentlemen: Sincerely,
Company or Corporation, Men and Women	(full name of organization) (local address) 00000	Gentlemen: or Ladies and Gentlemen: Sincerely,
Company or Corporation, Women	(full name of organization) (local address) 00000	Ladies: Sincerely,

†When the addressee is a woman, substitute *Miss, Mrs.,* or *Ms.* for *Mr.*

10–9. Government Officials

The following table shows the proper forms of address, salutation, and complimentary close for specific government officials. When the addressee is a woman, substitute one of the following for the salutation shown:

Madam for *Mr.* before formal terms such as *President, Vice President, Chairman, Secretary, Ambassador,* and *Minister.*

Ms., Miss, or *Mrs.* for *Mr.* before the name of a member of the House of Representatives, a senator-elect, a representative-elect, or a lesser government official.

10

Addressee	Address on Letter and Envelope	Salutation and Complimentary Close
The President	The President The White House Washington, DC 20500	Dear Mr. President: Respectfully,
*Former President	Honorable (full name) Former President of the United States (local address) 00000	Dear Mr. (surname): Sincerely,
Wife of the President	Mrs. (full name) The White House Washington, DC 20500	Dear Mrs. (surname): Sincerely,

*This form of address may be adapted to address other former high-ranking government officials.

Addressee	Address on Letter and Envelope	Salutation and Complimentary Close
Assistant to the President	Honorable (full name) Assistant to the President The White House Washington, DC 20500	Dear Mr. (surname): Sincerely,
The Vice President	The Vice President United States Senate Washington, DC 20510 or The Honorable (full name) Vice President of the United States Washington, DC 20501	Dear Mr. Vice President: Sincerely,
The Chief Justice	The Chief Justice of the United States The Supreme Court of the United States Washington, DC 20543	Dear Mr. Chief Justice: Sincerely,
Associate Justice	Mr. Justice (surname) The Supreme Court of the United States Washington, DC 20543	Dear Mr. Justice: Sincerely,
United States Senator	Honorable (full name) United States Senate Washington, DC 20510 or Honorable (full name) United States Senator (local address) 00000	Dear Senator (surname): Sincerely,
United States Representative	Honorable (full name) House of Representatives Washington, DC 20515 or Honorable (full name) Member, United States House of Representatives (local address) 00000	Dear Mr. (surname): Sincerely,
Cabinet Members	Honorable (full name) Secretary of (name of department) Washington, DC 00000	Dear Mr. Secretary: Sincerely,
	or Honorable (full name) Postmaster General Washington, DC 20260	Dear Mr. Postmaster General: Sincerely,
	or Honorable (full name) Attorney General Washington, DC 20530	Dear Mr. Attorney General: Sincerely,

10

Addressee	*Address on Letter and Envelope*	*Salutation and Complimentary Close*
Deputy Secretaries, Assistants, or Under Secretaries	Honorable (full name) Deputy Secretary of (name of department) Washington, DC 00000	Dear Mr. (surname): Sincerely,
	or	
	Honorable (full name) Assistant Secretary of (name of department) Washington, DC 00000	
	or	
	Honorable (full name) Under Secretary of (name of department) Washington, DC 00000	
Head of Independent Offices and Agencies	Honorable (full name) Comptroller General of the United States General Accounting Office Washington, DC 20548	Dear Mr. (surname): Sincerely,
	or	
	Honorable (full name) Chairman, (name of commission) Washington, DC 00000	Dear Mr. Chairman: Sincerely,
	or	
	Honorable (full name) Director, Bureau of the Budget Washington, DC 20503	Dear Mr. (surname): Sincerely,
American Ambassador	Honorable (full name) American Ambassador (City), (Country)	Sir: (formal) Dear Mr. Ambassador: (informal) Very truly yours, (formal) Sincerely, (informal)
American Consul General or American Consul	Mr. (full name) American Consul General (or American Consul) (City), (Country)	Dear Mr. (surname): Sincerely,
Foreign Ambassador in the United States	His Excellency (full name) Ambassador of (country) (local address) 00000	Excellency: (formal) Dear Mr. Ambassador: (informal) Very truly yours, (formal) Sincerely, (informal)
Governor of State	Honorable (full name) Governor of (name of state) (City), (State) 00000	Dear Governor (surname): Sincerely,
Lieutenant Governor	Honorable (full name) Lieutenant Governor of (name of state) (City), (State) 00000	Dear Mr. (surname): Sincerely,

Addressee	*Address on Letter and Envelope*	*Salutation and Complimentary Close*
State Senator	Honorable (full name) (name of state) State Senate (City), (State) 00000	Dear Senator (surname): Sincerely,
State Representative, Assemblyman, or Delegate	Honorable (full name) (name of state) House of Representatives (or State Assembly or House of Delegates) (City), (State) 00000	Dear Mr. (surname): Sincerely,
Mayor	Honorable (full name) Mayor of (name of city) (City), (State) 00000	Dear Mayor (surname): Sincerely,
President of a Board of Commissioners	Honorable (full name) President, Board of Commissioners of (name of city) (City), (State) 00000	Dear Mr. (surname): Sincerely,
Judge	Honorable (full name) (name of court) (local address) 00000	Dear Judge (surname): Sincerely,

10-10. Religious Dignitaries

The following table shows the proper forms of address, salutation, and complimentary close for specific religious dignitaries:

Addressee	*Address on Letter and Envelope*	*Salutation and Complimentary Close*
Catholic Clergy	His Eminence (given name) Cardinal (surname) Archbishop of (diocese) (local address) 00000	Your Eminence: (formal) Dear Cardinal (surname): (informal) Sincerely,
	or	
	The Most Reverend (full name) Archbishop of (diocese) (local address) 00000	Your Excellency: (formal) Dear Archbishop (surname): (informal) Sincerely,
	or	
	The Most Reverend (full name) Bishop of (city) (local address) 00000	Your Excellency: (formal) Dear Bishop (surname): (informal) Sincerely,
	or	
	The Right Reverend Monsignor (full name) (local address) 00000	Right Reverend Monsignor: (formal) Dear Monsignor (surname): (informal) Sincerely,
	or	

10

Addressee	Address on Letter and Envelope	Salutation and Complimentary Close
	The Very Reverend Monsignor (full name) (local address) 00000	Very Reverend Monsignor: (formal) Dear Monsignor (surname): (informal) Sincerely,
	or	
	The Reverend (full name) (add initials of order, if any) (local address) 00000	Reverend Sir: (formal) Dear Father (surname): (informal) Sincerely,
	Mother (full name) (initials of order, if used) Superior (name of convent) (local address) 00000	Dear Mother (full name): Sincerely,
	or	
	Sister (full name) (initials of order, if used) (name of convent) (local address) 00000	Dear Sister (full name): Sincerely,
Jewish Clergy	Rabbi (full name) (local address) 00000	Dear Rabbi (surname): Sincerely,
Protestant Clergy	The Right Reverend (full name) Bishop of (name) (local address) 00000	Right Reverend Sir: (formal) Dear Bishop (surname): (informal) Sincerely,
	or	
	The Very Reverend (full name) Dean of (name of church) (local address) 00000	Very Reverend Sir: (formal) Dear Dean (surname): (informal) Sincerely,
	or	
	The Reverend (full name) Bishop of (name) (local address) 00000	Reverend Sir: (formal) Dear Bishop (surname): (informal) Sincerely,
	or	
	The Reverend (full name) (title), (name of church) (local address) 00000	Dear Reverend (surname): Dear Mr. (surname): Sincerely,
Chaplains	Chaplain (full name) (full rank, service designation) (post office address of organization and station) (local address) 00000	Dear Chaplain (surname): Sincerely,
Lay Clergy	Deacon (full name) (name of church) (local address) 00000	Dear Deacon (surname): Sincerely,

10

Addressee	Address on Letter and Envelope	Salutation and Complimentary Close
	Brother [or Sister] (full name) (name of church) (local address) 00000	Dear Brother [or Sister] (surname): Sincerely,

10–11. Undetermined Individual or Group

Although addressing correspondence to an undefined or undetermined individual or group should generally be avoided, circumstances sometimes provide no other alternative. In these cases the letter contains no inside address. The phrase *To Whom It May Concern:* replaces the standard salutation, and the complimentary close is either *Sincerely yours,* or *Yours very truly,* . . . .

10

CHAPTER 11

Business Letters and Memorandums

Business Letters and Memorandums Solution Finder

Letter Styles[1]

11–1. Full Block

The full block letter style is the most efficient letter style because all parts and all lines begin at the left margin.

full block letter

Gibraltar Insurance Company of America

916 New Britain Avenue
Hartford, Connecticut 06106-2845
Telephone: (203) 743-1200

June 16, 1991

Lynch & Marten Insurance Agency
16320 San Fernando Mission Boulevard
Sepulveda, California 91343-2471

1 blank line →

Gentlemen

1 blank line →

SUBJECT: CLAIM NO. AT 6509, INSURED THOMAS A. GLASCO

1 blank line →

The claim of your client, Mr. Thomas A. Glasco, for $450 to replace the golf clubs that were stolen from him in Las Vegas is covered under his homeowner's policy, No. 19362084.

To process Mr. Glasco's claim, we must have a copy of the police report filed at the time of the theft. Please contact the police agency handling the theft report and have them forward us a copy addressed to my attention.

As soon as we receive the necessary information, Mr. Glasco's check will be sent to your office.

Sincerely yours

1 blank line →

GIBRALTAR INSURANCE COMPANY OF AMERICA

3 blank lines →

(Mrs.) Marian R. Marsh, Claims Adjuster

1 blank line →

fd

1 blank line →

cc: Mr. Thomas A. Glasco

11

[1] All letters appearing in this chapter have been designed by the authors for illustrative purposes. They are not reproductions of actual letters.

11–2. Modified Block

a. The modified block letter style with blocked paragraphs is the most popular letter style used in business. All lines except the return address (if used), the date, and the closing lines begin at the left margin.

modified block letter with blocked paragraphs

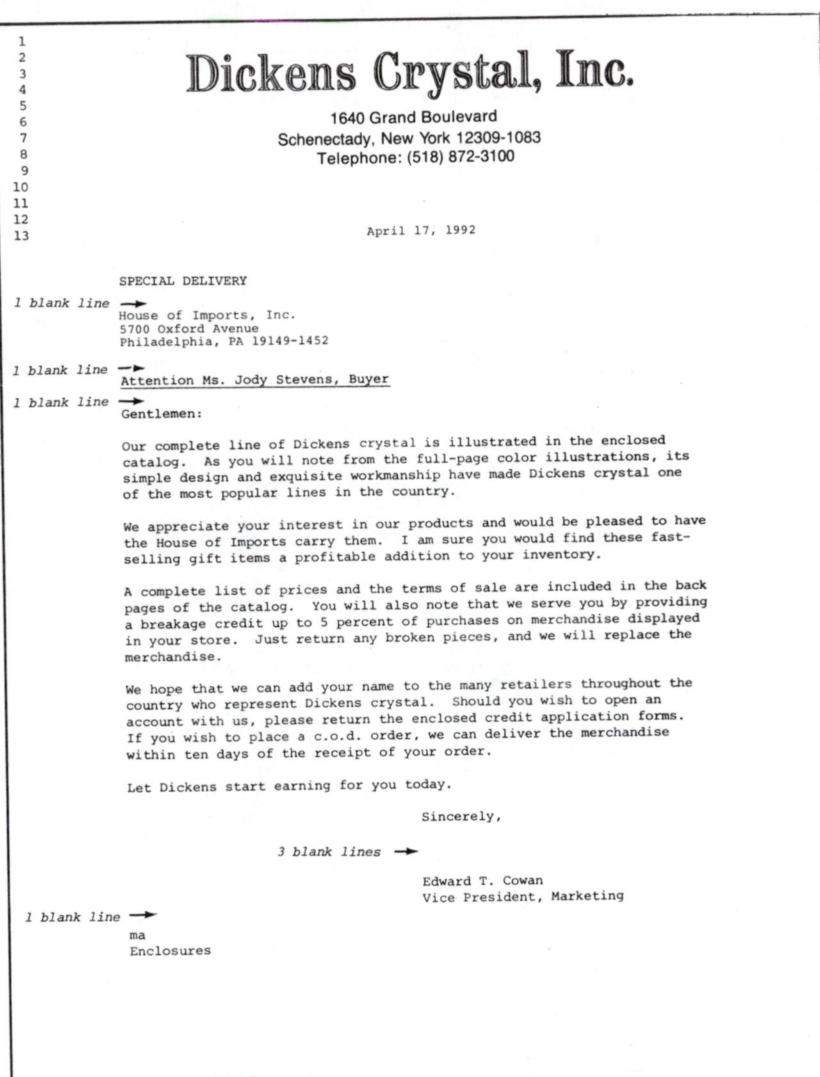

Dickens Crystal, Inc.

1640 Grand Boulevard
Schenectady, New York 12309-1083
Telephone: (518) 872-3100

April 17, 1992

SPECIAL DELIVERY

1 blank line →

House of Imports, Inc.
5700 Oxford Avenue
Philadelphia, PA 19149-1452

1 blank line →

Attention Ms. Jody Stevens, Buyer

1 blank line →

Gentlemen:

Our complete line of Dickens crystal is illustrated in the enclosed catalog. As you will note from the full-page color illustrations, its simple design and exquisite workmanship have made Dickens crystal one of the most popular lines in the country.

We appreciate your interest in our products and would be pleased to have the House of Imports carry them. I am sure you would find these fast-selling gift items a profitable addition to your inventory.

A complete list of prices and the terms of sale are included in the back pages of the catalog. You will also note that we serve you by providing a breakage credit up to 5 percent of purchases on merchandise displayed in your store. Just return any broken pieces, and we will replace the merchandise.

We hope that we can add your name to the many retailers throughout the country who represent Dickens crystal. Should you wish to open an account with us, please return the enclosed credit application forms. If you wish to place a c.o.d. order, we can deliver the merchandise within ten days of the receipt of your order.

Let Dickens start earning for you today.

Sincerely,

3 blank lines →

Edward T. Cowan
Vice President, Marketing

1 blank line →

ma
Enclosures

b. The modified block letter style with indented paragraphs is also used frequently. All lines except the first line of each paragraph, the return address (if used), the date, and the closing lines begin at the left margin.

modified block letter with indented paragraphs

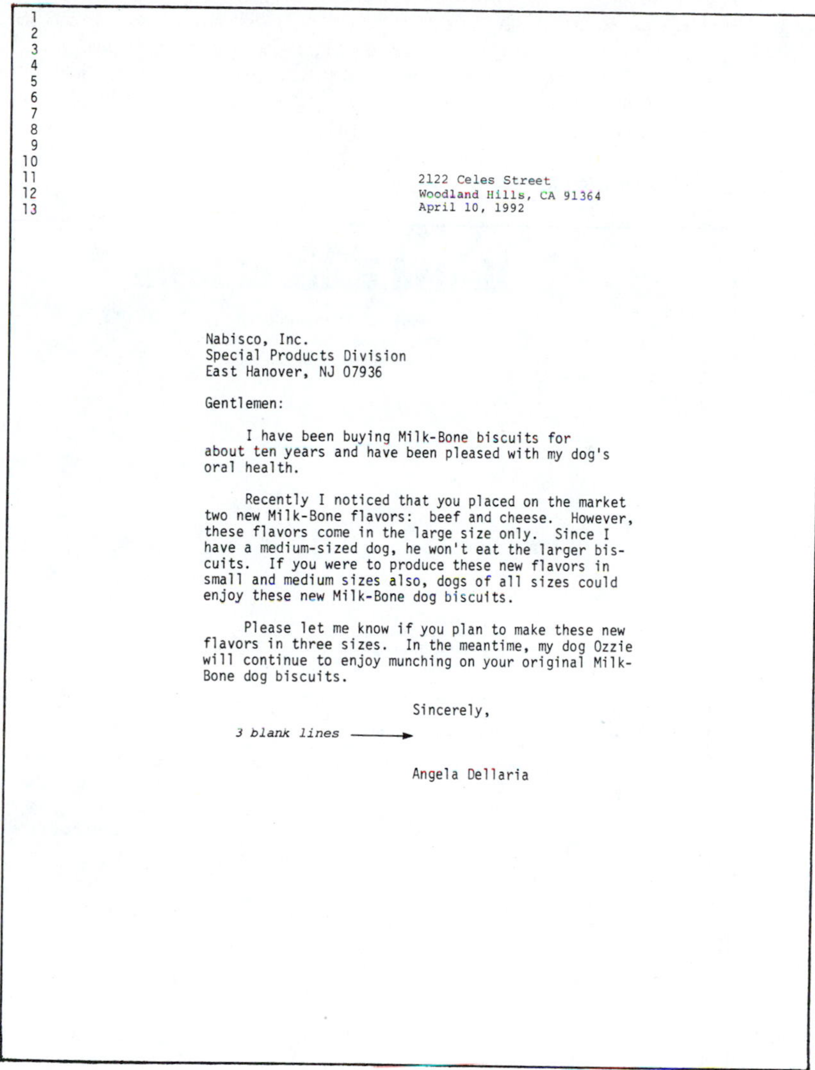

2122 Celes Street
Woodland Hills, CA 91364
April 10, 1992

Nabisco, Inc.
Special Products Division
East Hanover, NJ 07936

Gentlemen:

I have been buying Milk-Bone biscuits for about ten years and have been pleased with my dog's oral health.

Recently I noticed that you placed on the market two new Milk-Bone flavors: beef and cheese. However, these flavors come in the large size only. Since I have a medium-sized dog, he won't eat the larger biscuits. If you were to produce these new flavors in small and medium sizes also, dogs of all sizes could enjoy these new Milk-Bone dog biscuits.

Please let me know if you plan to make these new flavors in three sizes. In the meantime, my dog Ozzie will continue to enjoy munching on your original Milk-Bone dog biscuits.

Sincerely,

3 blank lines →

Angela Dellaria

11–3. Social Business

The social business letter style is used for social business correspondence. In this informal format the inside address is placed after the closing lines. The salutation may be followed by a comma instead of a colon, and the typed signature line is optional. Paragraphs are either indented or blocked. Reference initials, enclosure notations, and copy notations are usually omitted on the original, but these parts may be included below the inside address on the file copy or on the copies for distribution. Leave a double space after the inside address and single-space on all copies except the original the notations that are to be included.

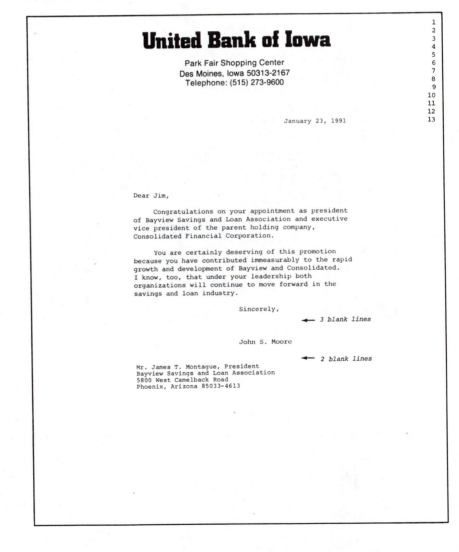

social business letter

United Bank of Iowa

Park Fair Shopping Center
Des Moines, Iowa 50313-2167
Telephone: (515) 273-9600

January 23, 1991

Dear Jim,

Congratulations on your appointment as president of Bayview Savings and Loan Association and executive vice president of the parent holding company, Consolidated Financial Corporation.

You are certainly deserving of this promotion because you have contributed immeasurably to the rapid growth and development of Bayview and Consolidated. I know, too, that under your leadership both organizations will continue to move forward in the savings and loan industry.

Sincerely,

← *3 blank lines*

John S. Moore

← *2 blank lines*

Mr. James T. Montague, President
Bayview Savings and Loan Association
5800 West Camelback Road
Phoenix, Arizona 85033-4613

11–4. Simplified

The simplified letter style was introduced by the Administrative Management Society. All parts of the letter begin at the left margin. In this style a subject line typed in all capital letters replaces the salutation. Two blank lines are left before and after the subject line. No complimentary close is used in the simplified letter style. Instead, the signature line is typed on the fifth line below the last line of the message. Use all capital letters and a single line for the signature line.

simplified letter

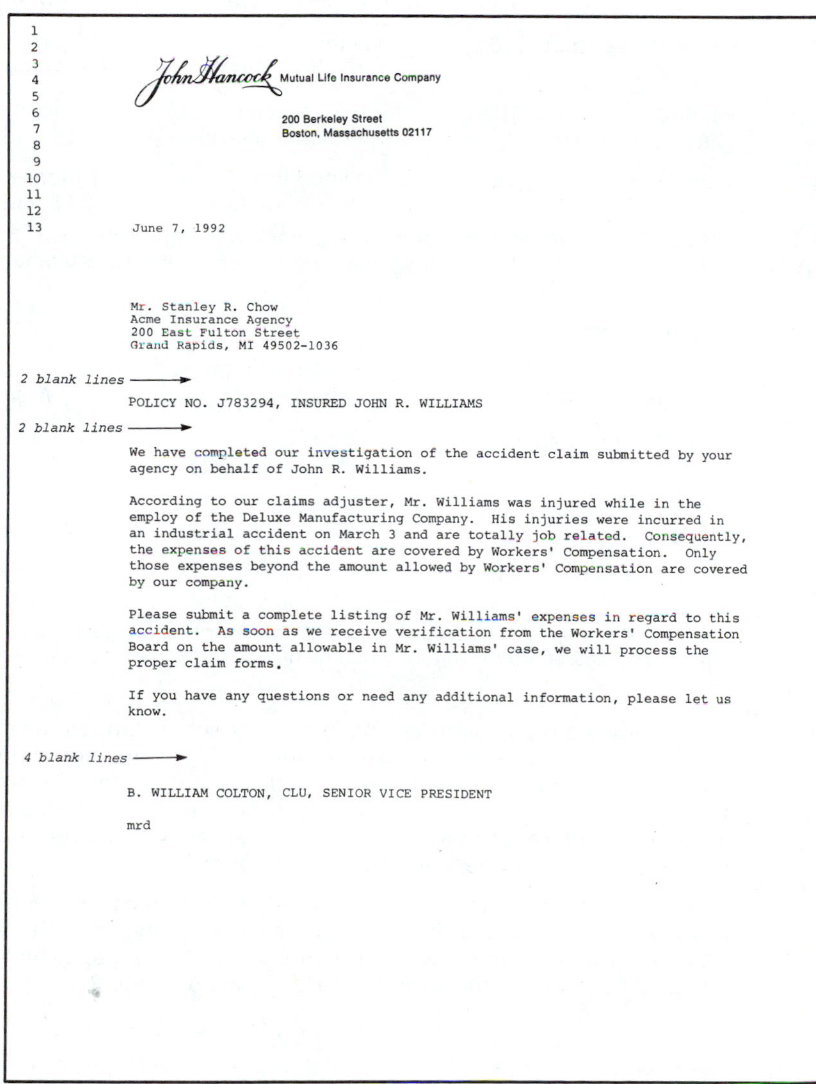

John Hancock Mutual Life Insurance Company

200 Berkeley Street
Boston, Massachusetts 02117

June 7, 1992

Mr. Stanley R. Chow
Acme Insurance Agency
200 East Fulton Street
Grand Rapids, MI 49502-1036

2 blank lines →

POLICY NO. J783294, INSURED JOHN R. WILLIAMS

2 blank lines →

We have completed our investigation of the accident claim submitted by your agency on behalf of John R. Williams.

According to our claims adjuster, Mr. Williams was injured while in the employ of the Deluxe Manufacturing Company. His injuries were incurred in an industrial accident on March 3 and are totally job related. Consequently, the expenses of this accident are covered by Workers' Compensation. Only those expenses beyond the amount allowed by Workers' Compensation are covered by our company.

Please submit a complete listing of Mr. Williams' expenses in regard to this accident. As soon as we receive verification from the Workers' Compensation Board on the amount allowable in Mr. Williams' case, we will process the proper claim forms.

If you have any questions or need any additional information, please let us know.

4 blank lines →

B. WILLIAM COLTON, CLU, SENIOR VICE PRESIDENT

mrd

Letter Format and Placement of Major Parts

11–5. Margins[2]

a. Select line lengths according to the number of words in the letter and the type pitch used to prepare the letter. The following table may be used as a guideline for preparing short, medium, and long letters in 10- or 12-pitch type on typewriters or computer-based equipment.

10-pitch type

Letter Length	*Line Length*	*Margins*
Short (fewer than 100 words)	4½-inch line (45 characters)	2 inch— 21 and 65–70*
Medium (between 100 and 200 words)	5½-inch line (55 characters)	1½-inch— 16 and 70–75*
Long (over 200 words)	6½-inch line (65 characters)	1 inch— 11 and 75–80*

*The extra five spaces allow for the margin-bell warning on standard typewriters. Disregard this figure when using computer-based equipment.

12-pitch type

Letter Length	*Approximate Line Length*	*Margins*
Short (fewer than 100 words)	4-inch line (48 characters)	2¼ inch— 27 and 76–81*
Medium (between 100 and 200 words)	5-inch line (60 characters)	1¾ inch— 22 and 81–86*
Long (over 200 words)	6-inch line (72 characters)	1¼ inch— 16 and 87–92*

*The extra five spaces allow for the margin-bell warning on standard typewriters. Disregard this figure when using computer-based equipment.

11

b. To simplify typing procedures and letter setup on a standard or electronic typewriter, use a letter placement guide to prepare correspondence. Although the lines in the following guide do not conform exactly to all the margins and line lengths specified in Section 11–5a, they provide an easy-to-use reference that will result in an attractively placed letter. Margins in any case will be held to a ¼-inch variation.

Place the guide directly behind the original. The lines on the guide will assist you in setting margins, placing the date rapidly, and calculating the letter length. Make your own guide on 8½- by 11-inch paper by following the specifications on the sample guide shown on page 263.

[2]See Chapter 13—Sections 13–1, 13–2, and 13–3—for detailed procedures to format letters on computer-based equipment.

letter placement guide

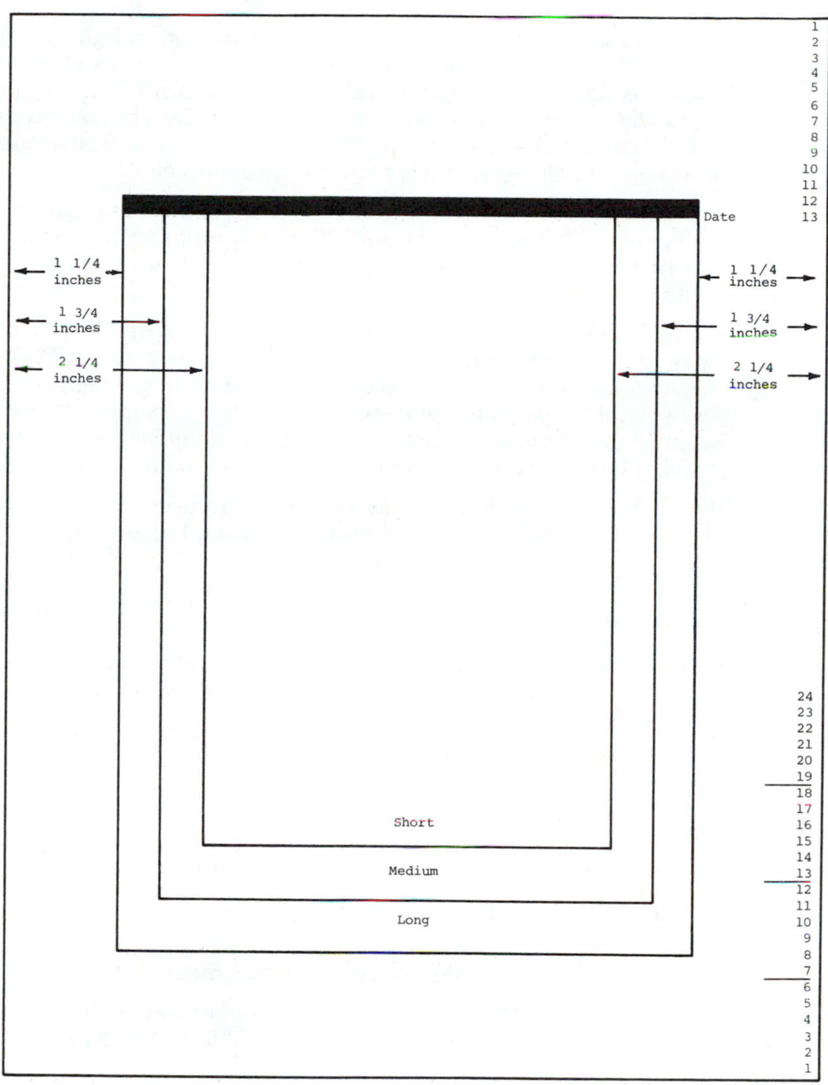

The heavy horizontal line at the top of the guide signifies the location of the date for standard-depth letterhead stationery. Should the letterhead drop farther, place the date a double space below the last line of the letterhead.

The outermost group of lines represents the parameters of a long letter (more than 200 words); the middle group of lines represents the parameters of a medium-length letter (100 to 200 words); and the innermost group of lines represents the parameters of a short letter (fewer than 100 words).

Estimate the length of your letter, and set the left margin at the proper corresponding vertical line on your placement guide. For electronic typewriters using automatic carrier return (word wrap), set the right margin at the appropriate corresponding vertical line. On standard typewriters, though, set the right margin five spaces to the right of the appropriate vertical line to allow for the typewriter warning bell.

To regulate the vertical placement of the letter, adjust the number of blank line spaces between the date and the inside address. See Section 11–9c for information regarding the range of allowable blank lines for each letter length.

The numbers at the bottom right edge of the placement guide indicate the number of standard typewritten lines remaining on an 11-inch page. These numbers may be used to assist in determining whether the closing lines should be expanded or condensed so that a balanced placement can be achieved. The line indicators will also be useful for two-page letters by showing the remaining number of lines on the page.

The letter placement guide may be altered to accommodate other than standard-sized stationery and standard-spacing typewriters.

11–6. Return Address

a. **No return address is needed for business letters prepared on paper containing a complete company letterhead. When plain bond paper or letterhead paper without a mailing address is used, a return address must be included. The return address in the modified block letter style is illustrated in Section 11–2b.**

b. **On plain paper begin the return address so that the last line is 2 inches (line 12 on standard typewriters and printers) from the top edge of the paper. The following table may be used to determine return address placement:**

11

Return Address Placement

Number of Lines in Address	*Typing Line for First Line of Address*
2	11
3	10
4	9
5	8

In the full block and simplified letter styles, all lines begin at the left margin. In the modified block or social business styles, the return address may (1) begin at the center of the page, (2) begin five spaces to the left of the page center, (3) have the longest line back-spaced (pivoted) from the right margin to determine the placement, or (4) have each line centered.

return address in full block or simplified letter style without letterhead

University Village
538 Hale Street
Boise, Idaho 83706
June 11, 1992

return address in modified block or social business letter style without letterhead

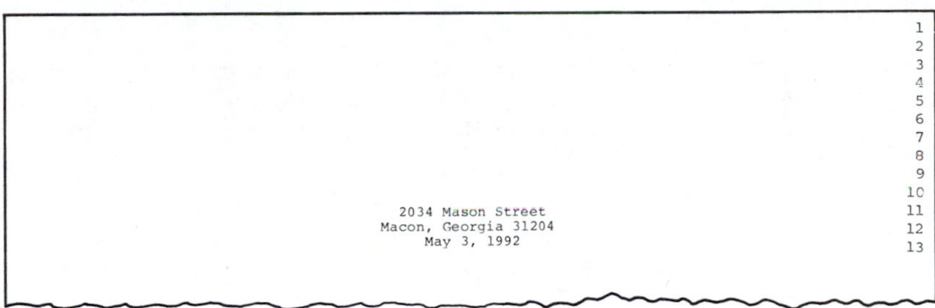
2034 Mason Street
Macon, Georgia 31204
May 3, 1992

c. On letterhead paper without a mailing address, begin the return address a double space below the last line in the letterhead or end it 2 inches (line 12 on standard typewriters and printers using standard line formats) below the top edge of the paper. Select the procedure that places the return address in the lower position.

return address begun a double space below letterhead—full block or simplified letter

Committee for the Reelection of the Governor
A Nonprofit Organization

Endorsed by:

9978 Access Road
Minneapolis, MN 55431-3642
September 27, 1992

return address ending 2 inches from top edge of paper—modified block or social business letter

Continental Floors

A Subsidiary of Meredith Corporation

1728 North King Street
Honolulu, HI 96819-5912
March 10, 1992

11–7. Date

a. **On letterhead paper with a mailing address, place the date a double space below the last line in the letterhead or allocate a 2-inch margin from the top edge of the paper (line 13). Select the procedure that places the date in the lower position.**

In full block or simplified letters, place the date at the left margin. In modified block and social business letters, the date may be centered, begun at the center of the paper, or back-spaced (pivoted) from the right margin.

date placed a double space below letterhead—full block letter

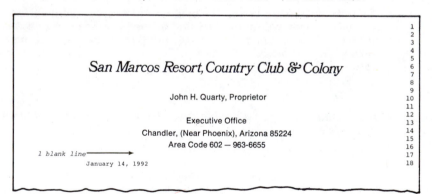

San Marcos Resort, Country Club & Colony

John H. Quarty, Proprietor

Executive Office
Chandler, (Near Phoenix), Arizona 85224
Area Code 602 — 963-6655

1 blank line →

January 14, 1992

date placed 2 inches below top edge of paper—modified block or social business letter

Los Angeles Pierce College

6201 Winnetka Avenue
Woodland Hills, California 91364
Telephone: (213) 347-0551

May 8, 1992

b. In letters requiring return addresses, place the date on the line directly below the last line of the return address. A date used with the return address in a complete letter is illustrated in Section 11–2b.

date with return address

Southern California Edison Company

1776 North Palm Canyon Drive
Palm Springs, California 92662-1032
August 8, 1991

11–8. Addressee and Mailing Notations

a. Addressee notations such as *Personal* and *Confidential* are typed in all capital letters either (1) a double space below and even with the date or (2) a double space above the inside address.

even with date

November 12, 1992

1 blank line →

PERSONAL

at least 2 blank lines →

Ms. Jane L. Quinn
Arco Mortgage Company
Post Office Box 38
Tulsa, OK 74102

double space above inside address

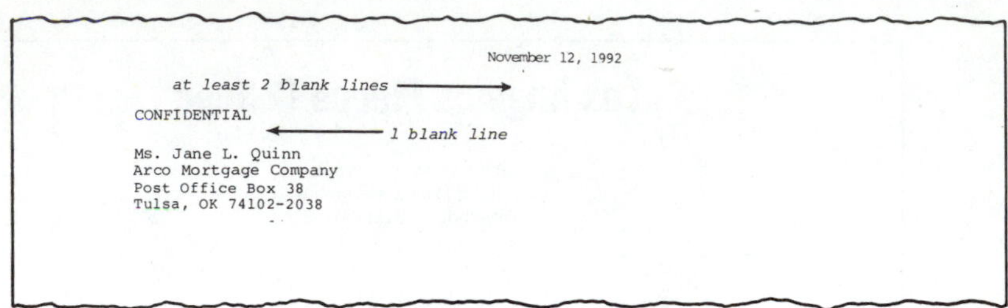

November 12, 1992

at least 2 blank lines →

CONFIDENTIAL

← *1 blank line*

Ms. Jane L. Quinn
Arco Mortgage Company
Post Office Box 38
Tulsa, OK 74102-2038

b. **Mailing notations such as *Special Delivery, Registered Mail,* and *Certified Mail* are typed in all capital letters (1) a double space below and even with the date, (2) a double space above the inside address, or (3) a single or double space below the reference initials or enclosure notation, whichever appears last. A mailing notation is illustrated in a complete letter in Section 11–2a.**

even with date

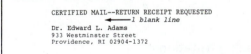

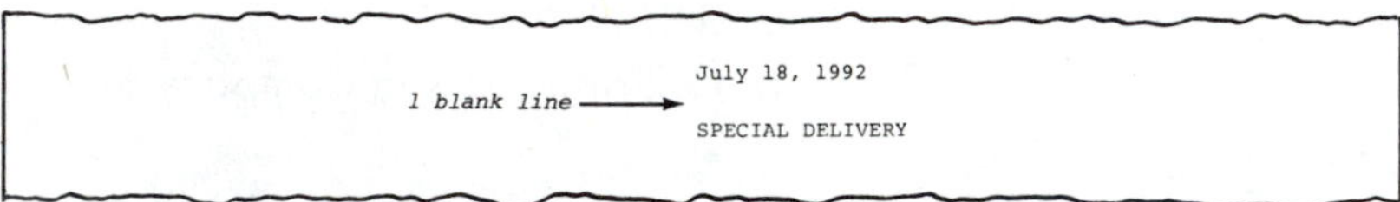

July 18, 1992

1 blank line →

SPECIAL DELIVERY

double space above inside address

CERTIFIED MAIL--RETURN RECEIPT REQUESTED
← *1 blank line*
Dr. Edward L. Adams
933 Westminster Street
Providence, RI 02904-1372

after reference initials or enclosure notation

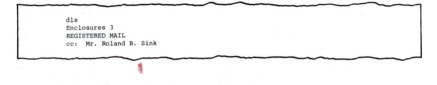

dls
Enclosures 3
REGISTERED MAIL
cc: Mr. Roland B. Sink

c. **If an addressee notation and mailing notation appear in the same letter, place the addressee notation on the third line above the inside address and the mailing notation on the line directly below. Both notations are typed in all capital letters. Leave *at least* two blank lines between the date and the addressee notation.**

addressee and mailing notation in same letter

```
February 11, 1992
              ←— at least 2 blank lines
CONFIDENTIAL
SPECIAL DELIVERY
              ←— 1 blank line
Mr. Frank D. Parsons
Vice President, Sales
Western Foundry, Inc.
3210 West Polk Street
Chicago, IL 60612-6427
```

11–9. Inside Address

a. **The inside address contains some or all of the following: courtesy title, full name, professional title, department name, company name, street or mailing address, city, state, and zip code. Single-space and begin at the left margin those parts necessary to direct the letter to the addressee.**

The courtesy title and full name are placed on the first line. The professional title and department name have no specific line designations; they are to be placed so that they balance with the remaining parts of the inside address. The street or mailing address appears on a separate line. Place the city, state, and zip code together on another separate line.

arrangement of an inside address

Ms. Margaret A. Williamson
Manager, Accounting Department
Eastern Savings and Loan Association
6750 East Independence Boulevard
Charlotte, North Carolina 28212-7610

Mr. Allen Davis, Manager
Personnel Department
Eastern Federal Bank
3452 West Sixth Street
Charlotte, NC 28212-4310

b. **Abbreviate only the courtesy titles *Mr., Mrs.,* and *Dr.* The courtesy title *Ms.* is not an abbreviation; its only form is *Ms.***

Spell out all street designations such as *Street, Avenue,* and *Boulevard. Boulevard* may be abbreviated, however, with exceptionally long street names. Spell out the state name or use the two-letter post office abbreviation, whichever form achieves balance with the remaining lines.

Each inside address may contain from a minimum of two lines to a maximum of six lines.

two-line inside address

Holiday Inn
Cedar Rapids, IA 52406

six-line inside address

Mr. M. J. Fujimoto
Airline Training Specialist
Division of Personnel Instruction
TransAmerica-Continental Airlines
12700 East Funston Street
Wichita, Kansas 67207-3402

c. **In the modified block, full block, and simplified letter styles, the inside address usually follows the date. The number of blank lines between the date and the inside address is determined by the length of the letter.**

For letters prepared on computer-based equipment, refer to Sections 13–1d, 13–2d, and 13–3e. For letters prepared on standard or electronic typewriters, use the following table to determine the number of blank lines between the date and the inside address for 8½- by 11-inch paper.

The following guide takes into consideration ordinary business letters—those without mailing notations, addressee notations, attention lines, subject lines, and postscripts. Letters containing these supplementary parts should be readjusted (in line length and/or lines between date and inside address) to accommodate these parts.

Letter Formatting Guide

Approximate Number of Words in Body of Letter	*Spaces in Line Length*		*Blank Lines Between Date and Inside Address*	
	Elite	*Pica*	*Elite*	*Pica*
Under 100	48	45	8–12	8–12
100–200	60	55	2–8	2–8
Over 200	72	65	2–3	2–3

inside address in modified block letter

Lawndale Pharmaceutical Company
5170 Medina Road
Akron, Ohio 44321-2843
Telephone: (216) 382-4955

March 10, 1992

Dr. Roy C. Trever
560 Yale Drive
Austin, TX 76015-4613

d. In the social business letter, the inside address is placed after the closing lines. If the typed signature line is omitted, leave five or six blank lines after the complimentary close before beginning the inside address. If a typed signature line is included, leave two blank lines after the typed signature before beginning the inside address.

social business letter without typed signature

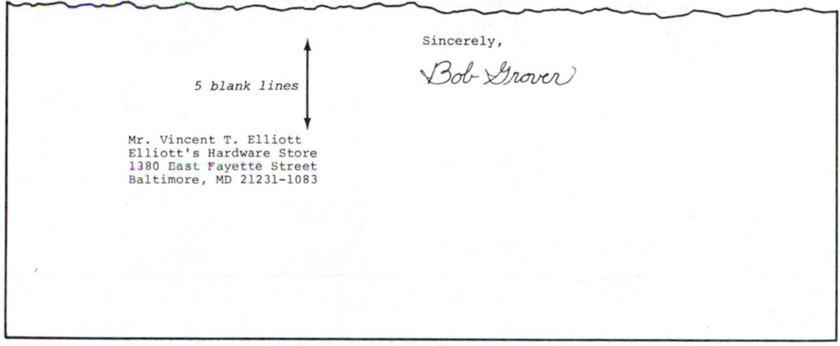

social business letter with typed signature

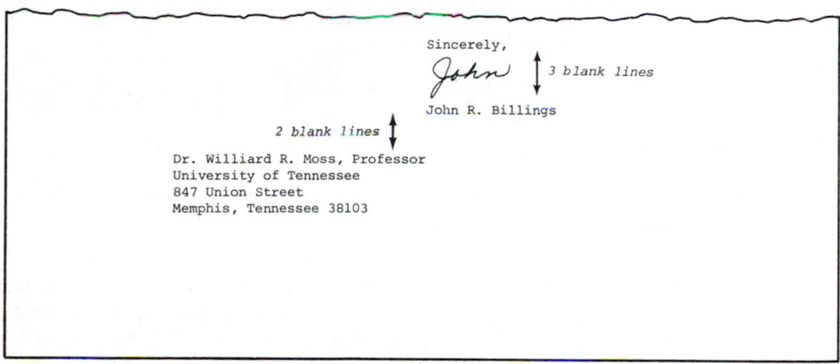

Sincerely,
John
3 blank lines
John R. Billings
2 blank lines
Dr. Williard R. Moss, Professor
University of Tennessee
847 Union Street
Memphis, Tennessee 38103

11

11–10. Attention Line

a. The attention line is used for directing correspondence to an individual or department within a company while still officially addressing the letter to the organization. In the modified block style, the attention line is placed at the left margin, centered, or indented to align with the paragraphs in the letter.

Place the attention line a double space below the last line of the inside address. Use all capital letters or a combination of initial capital letters and lowercase letters underlined. The word *attention* is typed with or without a colon following it. An attention line is illustrated in a complete letter in Section 11–2a.

attention line at left margin

```
Prescott Industries, Inc.
5450 North 37 Street
Tampa, Florida 33610-7230
                    ←——— 1 blank line
ATTENTION:  DR. JAMES MANOS
```

attention line centered

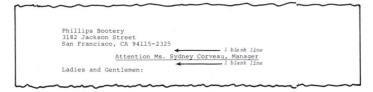

```
Phillips Bootery
3182 Jackson Street
San Francisco, CA 94115-2325
                        ←——— 1 blank line
          Attention Ms. Sydney Corveau, Manager
                        ←——— 1 blank line
Ladies and Gentlemen:
```

attention line aligned with paragraph indentions

```
Freestone Rubber Company
1200 North Clybourn Avenue
Chicago, Illinois 60610-1392
                        ←——— 1 blank line
     Attention:  Personnel Director
                        ←——— 1 blank line
Gentlemen:
                        ←——— 1 blank line
     As accounts supervisor for a major industrial firm in the
greater Detroit area for the past seven years, I have had an
opportunity to handle transactions involving wholesalers through-
out the country.  That is why I am applying . . . .
```

11

b. In the full block letter style, the attention line is placed at the left margin a double space below the last line of the inside address. Use all capital letters or a combination of initial capital letters and lowercase letters underlined. The word *attention* may or may not be followed by a colon.

```
SST Products, Inc.
840 30th Street
Boulder, CO 8030-4162
                    ←——— 1 blank line
ATTENTION ADJUSTMENT DEPARTMENT
```

c. In the simplified letter style, the attention line is included in the inside address and is placed directly below the organization's name. Treat the attention line as you would any other line in the inside address. The word *Attention* may or may not be followed by a colon. Some companies that use the modified or full block letter styles also prefer to handle the attention line in this manner and use the same format for the envelope address.

attention line included in inside address

```
Valley Manufacturing Company
Attention:  Ms. Karen Long, Manager
18692 Sierra Bonita Boulevard
San Bernardino, California 91783-5201
```

11–11. Salutation[3]

a. **Type the salutation a double space below the last line of the inside address or the attention line, if used. Omit the salutation in the simplified letter style. Begin the salutation at the left margin for all other letter styles. In letters addressed to individuals, use one of the following salutations, depending upon the degree of formality desired. Use a colon after the salutation if mixed punctuation is used; use no punctuation mark if open punctuation is used.**

informal salutation

Dear Fred: Dear Connie:

standard business letter salutation to a single addressee

Dear Mr. Hampton: Dear Miss Baker:
Dear Ms. Harris: Dear Mrs. Chin:

standard business letter salutation to two men

Dear Mr. Hampton and Mr. Cranston:

or

Dear Messrs. Hampton and Cranston:

or

Gentlemen:

standard business letter salutation to two women—courtesy title "Ms."

Dear Ms. Reed and Ms. Johnson:

or

Dear Mses. Reed and Johnson:

standard business letter salutation to two women—courtesy title "Miss"

Dear Miss Frazier and Miss Goodlad:

or

Dear Misses Frazier and Goodlad:

[3]See Sections 10–8, 10–9, and 10–10 for proper use of formal titles, salutations, and complimentary closes.

11

standard business letter salutation to two women—courtesy title "Mrs."

Dear Mrs. Koonce and Mrs. O'Donnell:

or

Dear Mesdames Koonce and O'Donnell:

or

Mesdames:

standard business letter salutation to two persons with different courtesy titles

Dear Ms. Knott and Mr. Wade:

Dear Ms. Gallagher and Mrs. Moreno:

standard salutations to persons with professional titles

Dear Dr. Parsons:

Dear Professor Bredow:

Dear Colonel Jones:

formal salutations for certain government officials and religious dignitaries

Sir:

Excellency:

Reverend Sir:

Your Eminence:

b. If the gender of an addressee is unknown, use the courtesy title *Mr.* or the full name of the person without a courtesy title. Use the courtesy title *Ms.* for a woman unless another title is specified by the addressee.

courtesy title "Mr."

Mr. Orolyn Ruenz (Dear Mr. Ruenz:)

Mr. Chris Meister (Dear Mr. Meister:)

Mr. J. T. Weyenberg (Dear Mr. Weyenberg:)

full name without courtesy title

Orolyn Ruenz (Dear Orolyn Ruenz:)

Chris Meister (Dear Chris Meister:)

J. T. Weyenberg (Dear J. T. Weyenberg:)

courtesy title for a woman

Ms. Sharon Reember (Dear Ms. Reember:)

Ms. Laura Nguyen (Dear Ms. Nguyen:)

c. **In correspondence addressed to companies, associations, or other groups, use one of the following salutations:**

salutations for groups composed of men and women

Gentlemen: (most common)

Ladies and Gentlemen:

Gentlemen and Ladies:

salutation for groups composed entirely of men

Gentlemen:

salutations for groups composed entirely of women

Mesdames:

Ladies:

d. **Letters addressed to a firm but directed to the attention of an individual within the company receive the salutation used to open a letter to a group: *Gentlemen, Ladies and Gentlemen, Gentlemen and Ladies, Mesdames,* or *Ladies.***

```
Grand Avenue Merchants Association
2834 Central Avenue, N.W.
Albuquerque, New Mexico 87105-1742
                                   ←—— 1 blank line
ATTENTION MR. CORDAY WESTPHAL, PRESIDENT
                                   ←—— 1 blank line
Ladies and Gentlemen:
```

e. **Letters to an undetermined individual or group of individuals should generally be avoided. When used, such letters contain no inside address and use *To Whom It May Concern:* as the salutation.**

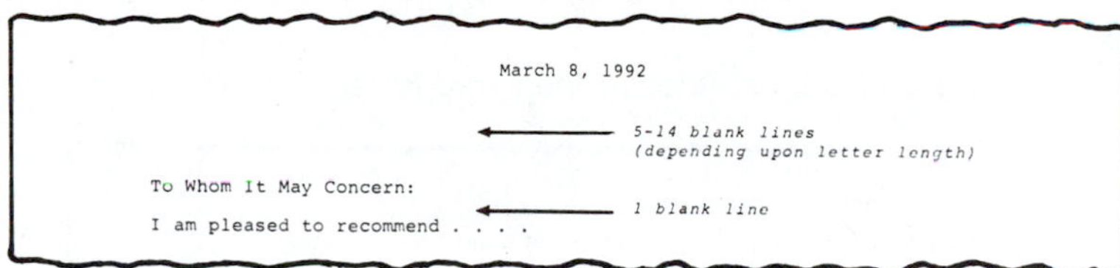

```
                         March 8, 1992

                   ←—— 5-14 blank lines
                       (depending upon letter length)
To Whom It May Concern:
                   ←—— 1 blank line
I am pleased to recommend . . . .
```


11–12. Subject Line

a. **In the modified block style, begin the subject line at the left margin, center it, or align it with the paragraph indentions. Place it a double space below the salutation. The word *subject* may or may not precede the line. If it is used, it is followed by a colon.**

Type the subject line in (1) all capital letters or (2) initial capital letters and lowercase letters underlined. If an attention line appears in the same letter, use the same format for both lines.

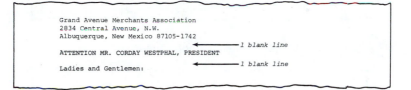

subject line at left margin

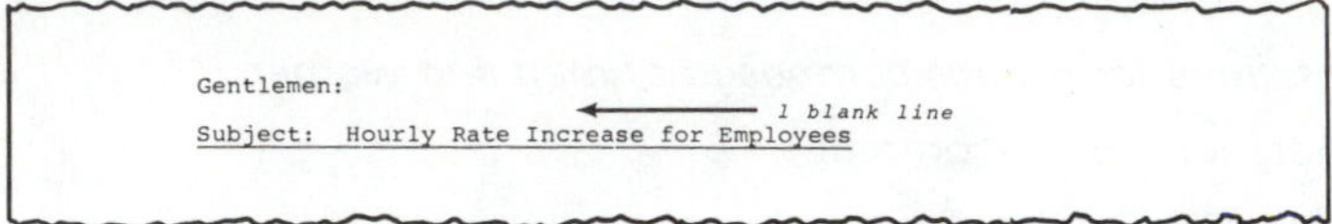

Gentlemen:
← 1 blank line
Subject: Hourly Rate Increase for Employees

two-line subject with book title

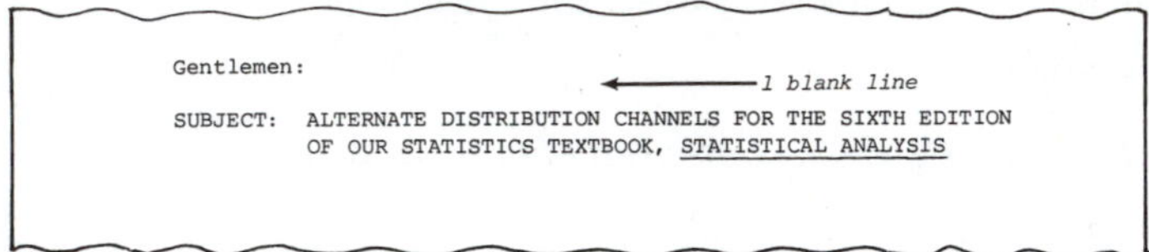

Gentlemen:
← 1 blank line
SUBJECT: ALTERNATE DISTRIBUTION CHANNELS FOR THE SIXTH EDITION
OF OUR STATISTICS TEXTBOOK, STATISTICAL ANALYSIS

subject line centered

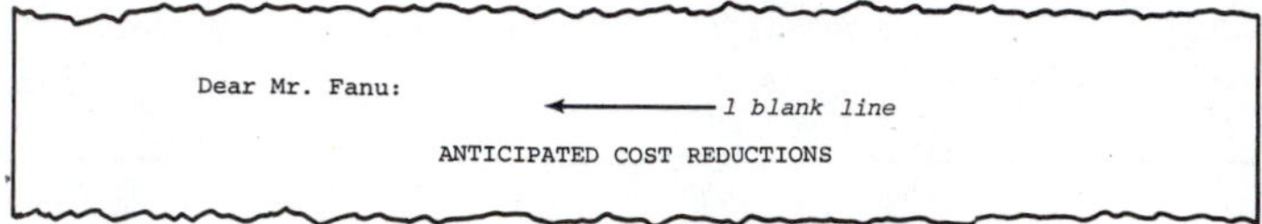

Dear Mr. Fanu:
← 1 blank line
ANTICIPATED COST REDUCTIONS

subject line aligned with paragraph indention

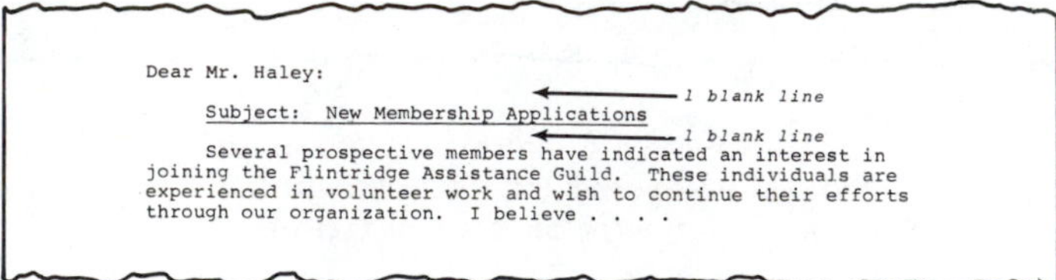

Dear Mr. Haley:
← 1 blank line
Subject: New Membership Applications
← 1 blank line
Several prospective members have indicated an interest in joining the Flintridge Assistance Guild. These individuals are experienced in volunteer work and wish to continue their efforts through our organization. I believe . . . .

11

attention and subject lines in the same letter

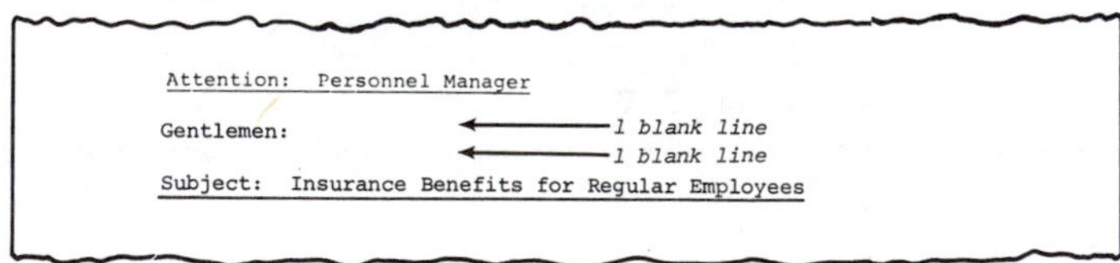

Attention: Personnel Manager
← 1 blank line
Gentlemen:
← 1 blank line
Subject: Insurance Benefits for Regular Employees

b. **In the full block style, begin the subject line at the left margin a double space below the salutation. The word *Subject:* may or may not precede the line.**

Type the subject line in (1) all capital letters or (2) initial capital letters and lowercase letters underlined. If an attention line appears in the same

letter, select the same format for both lines. The subject line is illustrated in a full block letter in Section 11–1.

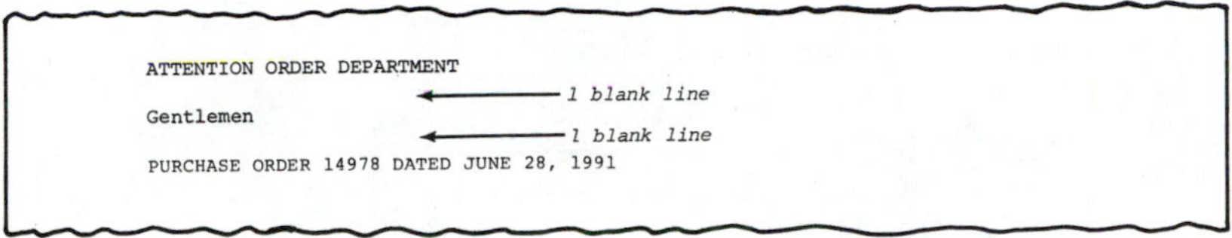
ATTENTION ORDER DEPARTMENT

1 blank line

Gentlemen

1 blank line

PURCHASE ORDER 14978 DATED JUNE 28, 1991

c. The subject line replaces the salutation in the simplified style. Begin the subject line at the left margin a triple space below the inside address. Type it in all capital letters without the term *Subject:*. Triple-space between the subject line and the first line of the body of the letter.

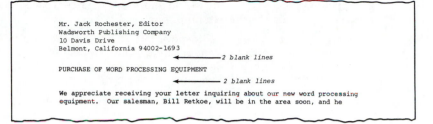

Mr. Jack Rochester, Editor
Wadsworth Publishing Company
10 Davis Drive
Belmont, California 94002-1693

2 blank lines

PURCHASE OF WORD PROCESSING EQUIPMENT

2 blank lines

We appreciate receiving your letter inquiring about our new word processing equipment. Our salesman, Bill Retkoe, will be in the area soon, and he

d. Insurance and financial institutions, attorneys, and government offices often use the reference *Re:* or *In re:* in place of the word *Subject:* at the beginning of the subject line.

IN RE: TOLBERT VS. FEINBERG

Re: Policy 489-6342, Insured Michael T. Block

e. When initiating or replying to correspondence that has a special policy number, order number, or other such reference, include this information in a subject line (as illustrated in Section 11–11a-d) or in a specific reference below and aligned with the date.

If references are not printed on the letterhead, use designations such as *When replying, refer to:, File No.:, In reply to:, Re:, Your reference:, Refer to:,* etc. These notations are typed in initial capital and lowercase letters; they are placed a double space below the date or a double space below an addressee or a mailing notation appearing below the date (if used).

below date

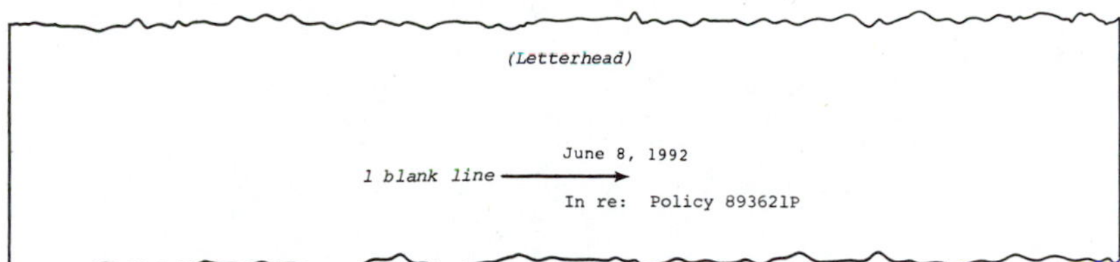
(Letterhead)

June 8, 1992

1 blank line

In re: Policy 893621P

below addressee or mailing notation

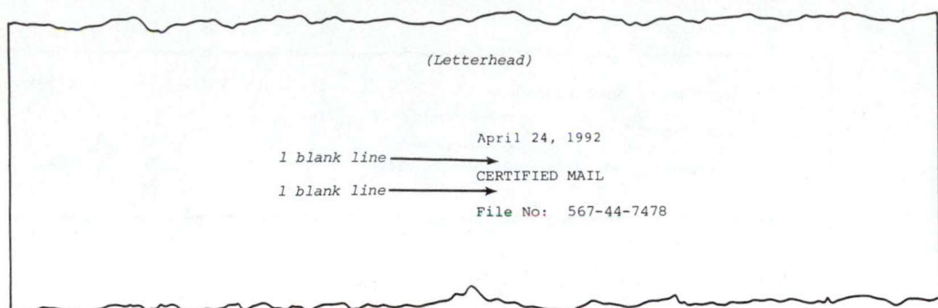

(Letterhead)

April 24, 1992
1 blank line →
CERTIFIED MAIL
1 blank line →
File No: 567-44-7478

f. **Some companies prefer to place the subject line above the salutation. In such cases begin the subject line a double space below the inside address. If an attention line follows the inside address, then begin the subject line a double space below the attention line.**

Type the subject line in (1) all capital letters or (2) initial capital letters and lowercase letters underlined. The caption *Subject, Re,* or *In re* precedes the content and is followed by a colon. If an attention line appears in the same letter, use the same format for both lines.

Double-space after the subject line to begin the salutation.

subject line above salutation

Great Midwestern Bank
4430 Greenbriar Street
Iowa City, IA 52247-0321
← *1 blank line*
Subject: Account 183-573245, John R. Hagle
← *1 blank line*
Gentlemen:

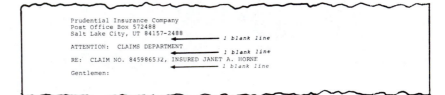

subject line above salutation (with attention line)

Prudential Insurance Company
Post Office Box 572488
Salt Lake City, UT 84157-2488
← *1 blank line*
ATTENTION: CLAIMS DEPARTMENT
← *1 blank line*
RE: CLAIM NO. 845986532, INSURED JANET A. HORNE
← *1 blank line*
Gentlemen:

11–13. Body of the Letter

a. **For the majority of business letters, single-space paragraphs within the body of the letter and double-space between each paragraph. For the modified block style with blocked paragraphs, the full block style, and the simplified style, begin each paragraph at the left margin. For the modified block style with indented paragraphs, indent the first line of each paragraph from five to ten typewritten spaces. Paragraphs may be either indented or blocked in the social business letter style.**

body of letter with blocked paragraphs

```
Dear Mr. Bedrosian:
                        ←———— 1 blank line
Your Zippo portable sound system arrived yesterday, along with your
explanation of the needed repairs.
                        ←———— 1 blank line
As you suggested, the station tuning mechanism has been replaced
under the terms of the warranty.  In examining your system, how-
ever, our service representative noticed that the speaker had been
damaged from an apparent jarring or dropping.  The installation
cost (parts and labor) for a new speaker would be $54.98.
```

body of letter with indented paragraphs

```
Dear Mrs. Russell:
                        ←———— 1 blank line
     We enjoyed the presentation on color coordination that you
gave to Dr. Satterwait's office management class last Saturday.
Thank you for sharing your valuable ideas with us.
                        ←———— 1 blank line
     The class especially appreciated the material you gave us on
the Wilson color wheel.  Everyone agreed that this information will
certainly be helpful in making wardrobe selections for the office
and coordinating colors in the office environment.
```

b. The body of letters consisting of one or two short paragraphs may be double spaced using the modified block style with indented paragraphs or the social business style with indented paragraphs.

short, one-paragraph letter

Connecticut Life Insurance Company

916 New Britain Avenue Hartford, Connecticut 06106
Telephone: (203) 761-8211

July 7, 1992

Aaron, Aaron, & Cohen
Attorneys at Law
9324 Wilshire Boulevard
Beverly Hills, CA 90212-1870

Gentlemen:

Our copy of the Bixby contract arrived today.

Thank you for forwarding it so promptly.

Sincerely yours,

Frances T. Archer
General Counsel

rn

11

short, two-paragraph letter

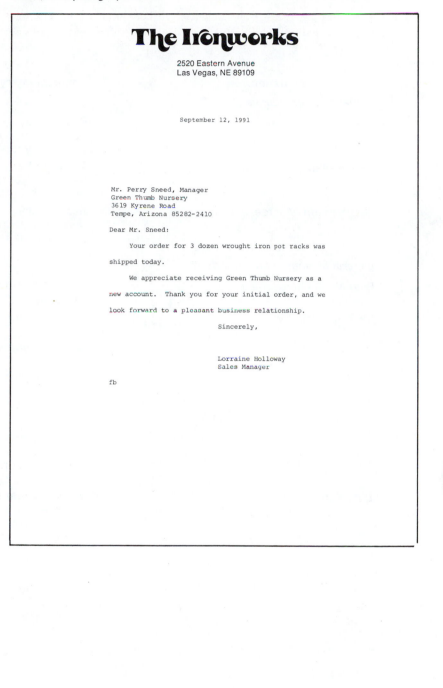

The Ironworks

2520 Eastern Avenue
Las Vegas, NE 89109

September 12, 1991

Mr. Perry Sneed, Manager
Green Thumb Nursery
3619 Kyrene Road
Tempe, Arizona 85282-2410

Dear Mr. Sneed:

Your order for 3 dozen wrought iron pot racks was shipped today.

We appreciate receiving Green Thumb Nursery as a new account. Thank you for your initial order, and we look forward to a pleasant business relationship.

Sincerely,

Lorraine Holloway
Sales Manager

fb

11–14. Complimentary Close

a. **The complimentary close selected to conclude a business letter must conform to the formality of the salutation. Sample salutations as well as suitable complimentary closes are listed here.**

Salutation	Complimentary Close
formal correspondence	
Dear Mr. President	Respectfully Very truly yours Sincerely yours
His Excellency	Respectfully Very truly yours Sincerely yours
Dear Senator Monroe	Respectfully Very truly yours Sincerely yours
general business correspondence	
Dear Mr. Siebert	Sincerely yours Sincerely
Dear Ms. Mendoza	Sincerely yours Sincerely
Dear Dr. Wilson	Sincerely yours Sincerely
Gentlemen	Sincerely yours Sincerely
informal business correspondence	
Dear Bill	Sincerely yours Sincerely Cordially yours Cordially
Dear Karen	Sincerely yours Sincerely Cordially yours Cordially

b. **In the modified block styles and the social business style, the complimentary close is placed a double space below the last line of the body. Begin the closing (1) at the page center, (2) five spaces to the left of the page center, or (3) aligned with the longest closing line that has been back-spaced (pivoted) from the right margin.**

complimentary close begun at page center

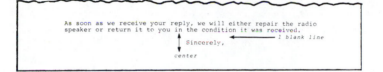

As soon as we receive your reply, we will either repair the radio speaker or return it to you in the condition it was received.

Sincerely,

1 blank line

center

complimentary close begun five spaces to the left of page center

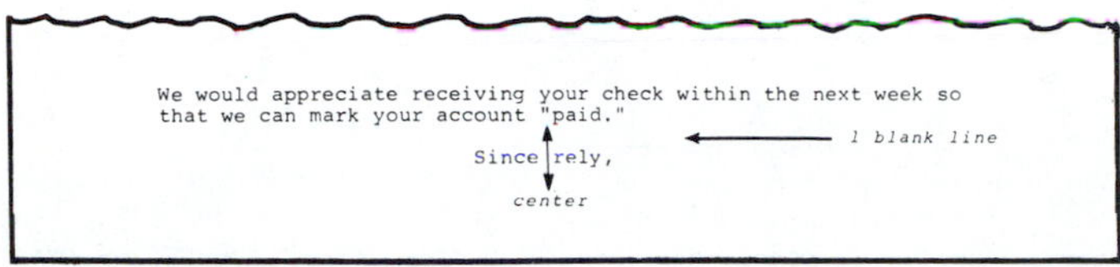

We would appreciate receiving your check within the next week so that we can mark your account "paid."

Sincerely,

1 blank line

center

complimentary close aligned with longest closing line back-spaced (pivoted) from right margin

Don't delay; act now to receive a copy of Your Banking Future--while the supply lasts. Just sign the enclosed postcard and drop it in the mail today.

1 blank line

Sincerely yours,

1 blank line

BRADSTREET TRAINING INSTITUTE

3 blank lines

Morgan Riley, Director

c. In the full block letter style, the complimentary close is placed at the left margin a double space below the last line of the body.

11

May I please have an opportunity to review my qualifications with you? Just call me at 349-8211, and I will be pleased to come to your office for an interview.

1 blank line

Sincerely yours,

d. No complimentary close is used in the simplified letter style.

11–15. Signature Block

a. **Some business firms include the name of the company in the signature block. In such cases the name of the company is placed in all capital letters a double space below the complimentary close. The first letter of the company name is aligned with the first letter of the complimentary close.**

Company signature lines may be used in all letter formats except the social and simplified letter styles. Use of the company name in the signature block is illustrated in a full block letter in Section 11–1.

modified block letter

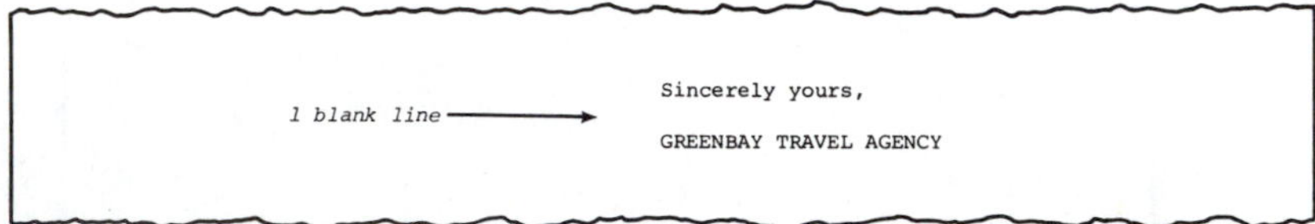

full block letter

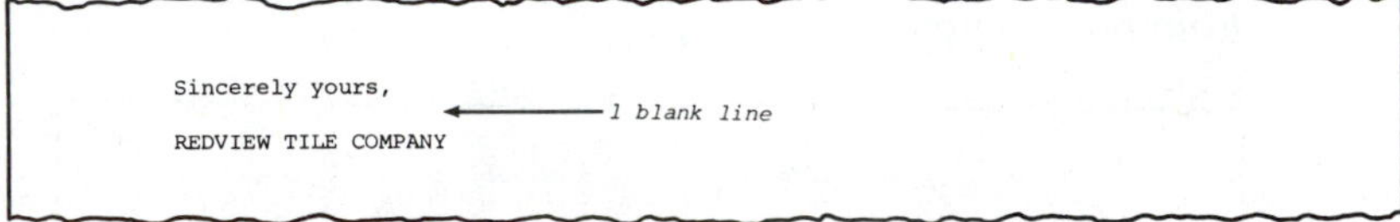

b. **In the modified and full block letter styles, begin typing the writer's signature line or lines on the fourth line below the last typed line, which will be either the complimentary close or the company name. Align the first letter of the individual's name with the first letter of the complimentary close and/or the company name.**

full block letter

Sincerely,
3 blank lines
John R. Gregg
Vice President

11

modified block letter

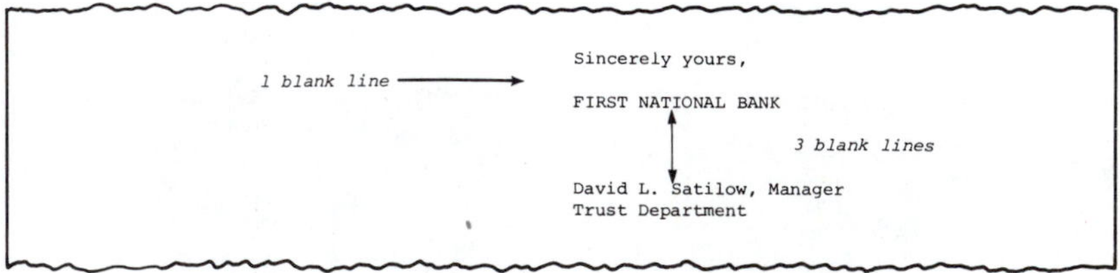

Sincerely yours,
1 blank line
FIRST NATIONAL BANK
3 blank lines
David L. Satilow, Manager
Trust Department

c. **Place combinations of names, titles, and organizational sectors so that the contents of the signature lines appear balanced. The name and title may appear on the same line or on separate lines, depending upon the length of each item. Use commas to separate categories within the same line, but do not use commas to conclude any of the signature lines.**

single-line signature line

Phillip Ashton, President

Susan R. Mayfield, M.D.

two-line signature line

Margaret T. Washington
Manager, Credit Department

John S. Ross, Supervisor
Data Processing Department

Horace F. Tavelman
Accounts and Sales Representative

three-line signature line

Roberta Casselman, Ed.D.
Curriculum Consultant
Division of Secondary Education

d. **Signature lines containing the names of men are not preceded by the courtesy title *Mr.* Signature lines containing the names of women are preceded by a courtesy title if the writer prefers to make the distinction of *Ms., Mrs.,* or *Miss.* The title is usually placed in parentheses, but it may appear without them.**

signature lines containing name of man

George R. Bezowski
Regional Manager

signature lines containing name of woman

Mary R. Stevens
Regional Manager

or

(Ms.) Mary R. Stevens Regional Manager	Ms. Mary R. Stevens Regional Manager
(Miss) Mary R. Stevens Regional Manager	Miss Mary R. Stevens Regional Manager
(Mrs.) Mary R. Stevens Regional Manager	Mrs. Mary R. Stevens Regional Manager

11

e. **Correspondence that is signed by a person other than the one whose name appears in the typed signature line usually shows the initials of the person signing the letter.**

Sincerely yours,

Wallace C. Murietta (lc)

Wallace C. Murietta

f. **In the simplified letter style, the entire signature line is typed in all capital letters on a single line. It begins at the left margin on the fifth line below the last line of the message.**

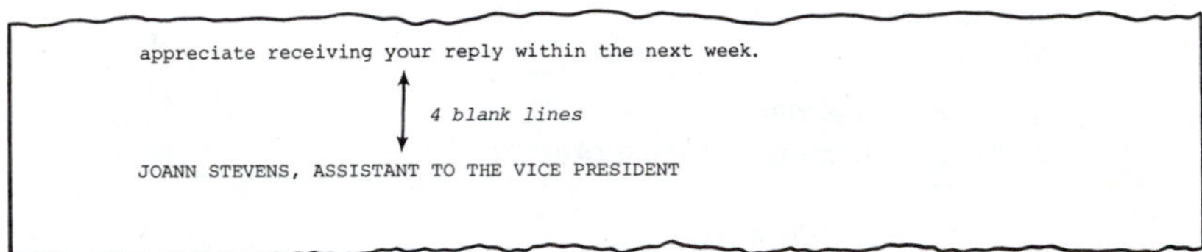
appreciate receiving your reply within the next week.

JOANN STEVENS, ASSISTANT TO THE VICE PRESIDENT

g. **In the social business style, the typed signature line may be omitted. If it is included, only the individual's name, not title, is written.**

typed signature line omitted

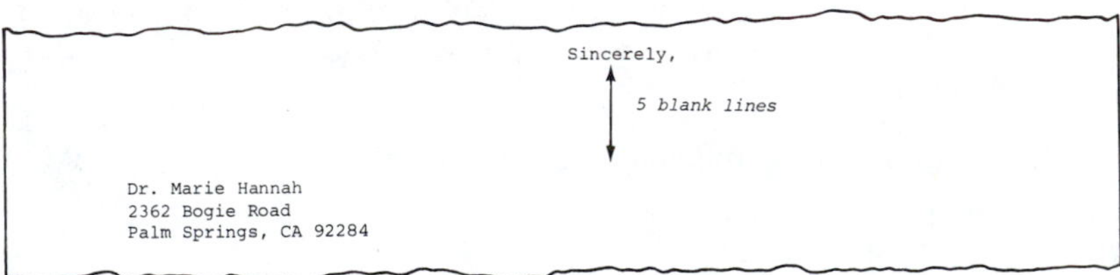
Sincerely,

Dr. Marie Hannah
2362 Bogie Road
Palm Springs, CA 92284

11

typed signature line included

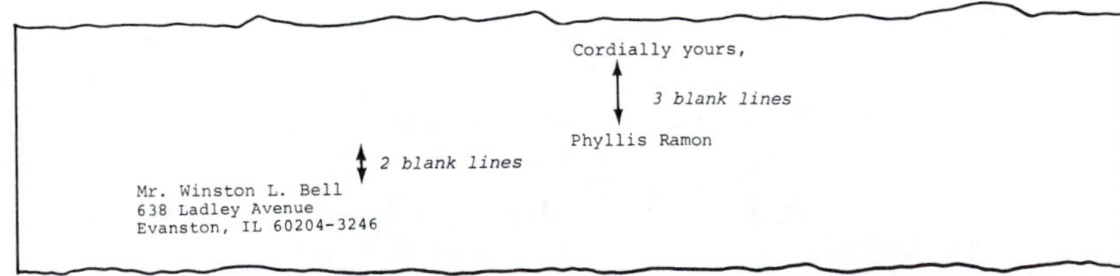
Cordially yours,

Phyllis Ramon

Mr. Winston L. Bell
638 Ladley Avenue
Evanston, IL 60204-3246

11–16. Reference Initials

a. **Except in the social business style, reference initials are used to show who typed the letter. The typist's initials are placed in lowercase letters at the left margin a double space below the last line in the signature block.**

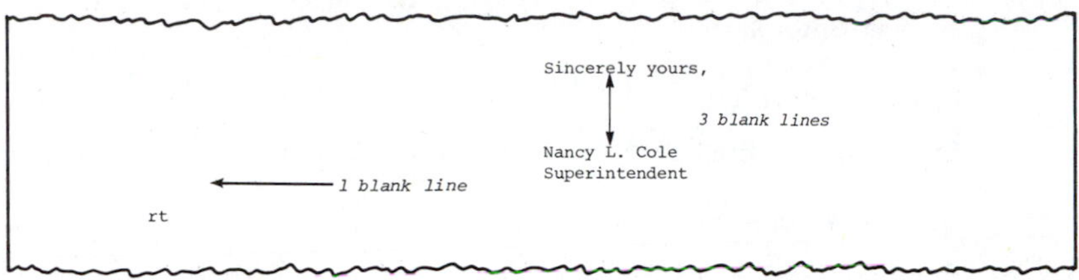

Sincerely yours,
3 blank lines
Nancy L. Cole
Superintendent
1 blank line
rt

b. **The initials of both the writer and the typist *may* be included in the reference notation. When the person whose name appears in the signature lines is the one who wrote the letter, his or her initials appear in capital letters before the typist's initials. The initials are separated by a colon or a diagonal line.**

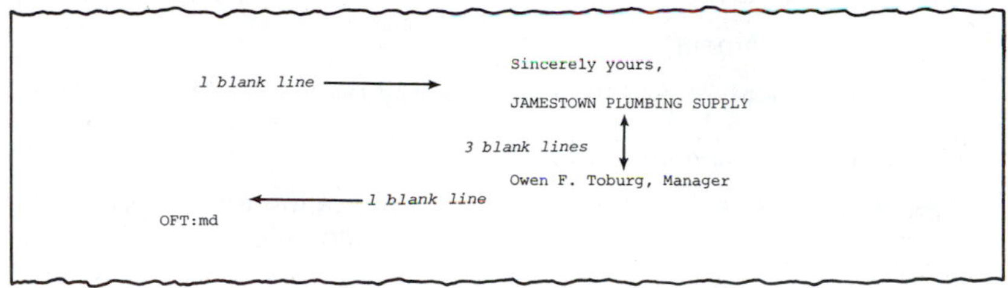

Sincerely yours,
1 blank line
JAMESTOWN PLUMBING SUPPLY
3 blank lines
Owen F. Toburg, Manager
1 blank line
OFT:md

c. **When correspondence is written by a person other than the one whose name appears in the signature lines, the writer's name or capitalized initials precede the initials of the typist. Separate the name or initials of the dictator from the typist's initials by a colon or a diagonal line.**

11

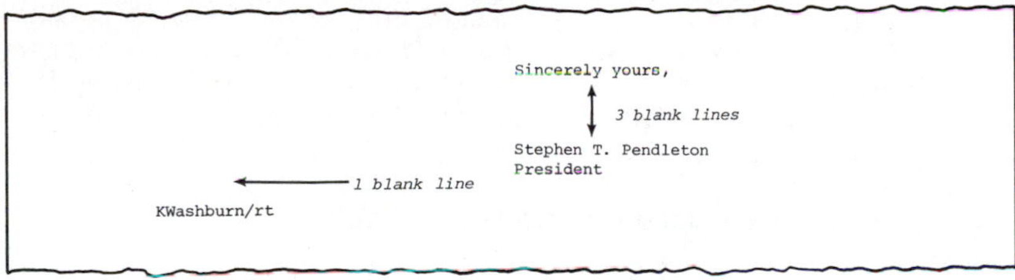

Sincerely yours,
3 blank lines
Stephen T. Pendleton
President
1 blank line
KWashburn/rt

11–17. Enclosure or Attachment Notations

a. **If any enclosures are included with the letter, an enclosure notation is placed on the second line (or next line to conserve space) below the reference initials. Begin the enclosure notation at the left margin. If more than one enclosure is included, be sure to list the enclosures or the number with the enclosure notation. Following are some examples of enclosure notations:**

one enclosure

Enclosure   Enclosure: Wilson Contract   Enc.

more than one enclosure

Enclosures: Check for $20
            Copy of Invoice 1362   2 Enclosures

Enclosures 3   Enc. 2

b. **When an enclosure is attached to the letter, the word *Attachment* or its abbreviation may be used in place of the enclosure notation. If more than one item is attached, be sure to include a listing or the number with the attachment notation.**

one attachment

Attachment   Attachment: Survey results   Att.

more than one attachment

Attachments 2   Attachments: Application for admission
                              Student information form

Att. 2   3 Attachments

11–18. Copy Notations

11

a. **When copies of correspondence are directed to individuals other than the addressee, note the distribution at the bottom of the letter. The copy notation is placed on the second line (or next line to conserve space) following the enclosure notation, if used. Otherwise, it appears a single or double space below the reference initials. However, if a mailing notation follows the reference initials or enclosure notation, the copy notation is placed below it.**

copy notation following reference initials

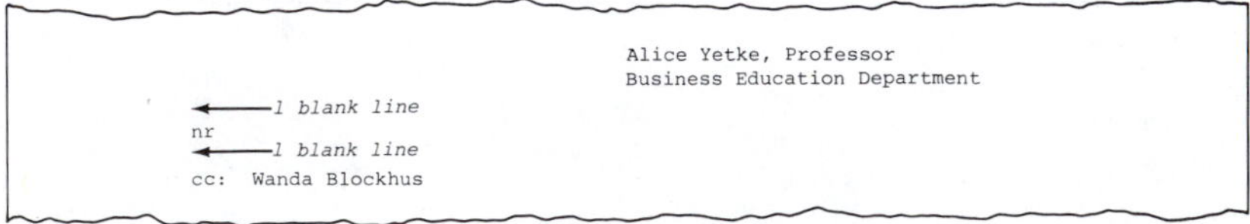
Alice Yetke, Professor
Business Education Department

←1 blank line
nr
←1 blank line
cc: Wanda Blockhus

copy notation with additional notations

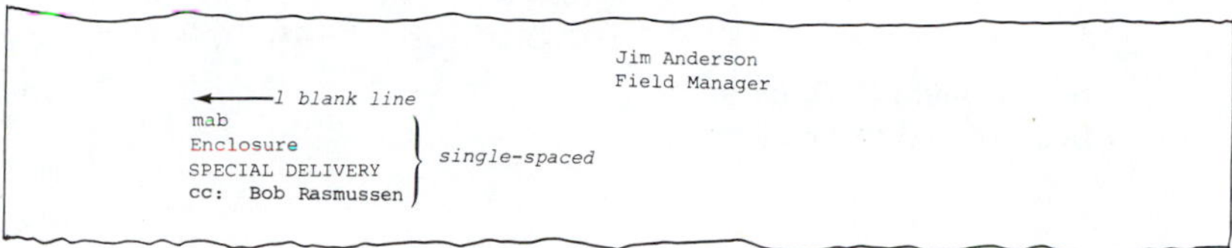
Jim Anderson
Field Manager

←1 blank line
mab
Enclosure
SPECIAL DELIVERY
cc: Bob Rasmussen

} single-spaced

b. **Copies of correspondence are prepared with a photocopier—or in rare cases with carbon paper. The traditional "cc" notation represents the terms *courtesy copy* or *carbon copy,* so this notation is appropriate for copies produced by either method.**

Copy notations may include a combination of the courtesy title, name, position, department, company, and complete address of an individual. Following are some examples of appropriate copy notations:

cc: Mr. John R. Robinson
1865 Rinaldi Street
Oklahoma City, OK 73103

CC: Francis P. Olsen, President, Wilson Corporation

cc Alice Morley, Credit Clerk

CC Gene Rupe

Some companies prefer to note copies made on a photocopier in the following ways:

copy: Ms. Janice Welch

copies: Bill Acevedo
Donna Mellert

c: Sales Department Staff

C: Mrs. Phuong Nguyen

copy to Mr. Bill Hughes, Manager, Hillsdale Paper Corporation

pc: Vernon R. Milliken, M.D.

c. **If copies are directed to more than one individual, list the individuals according to rank. If the individuals are equal in rank or ranking is unimportant, alphabetize the list. The list may be prepared either vertically or horizontally.**

11

ranked list

cc: R. F. Gillham, President
T. L. McMillan, Vice President
F. S. Brotherton, General Manager

alphabetized list

cc Marcus L. Brendero, Anne S. Langville, David M. Silverman

d. **If sending a copy of the letter to other individuals is unnecessary or inappropriate for an addressee to know, use a blind copy notation. The blind copy notation appears only on copies of the letter, not on the original.**

The blind copy notation may be placed (1) on the seventh line from the top of the page at the left margin or (2) where the regular copy notation normally appears. Examples of blind copy notations follow:

bcc: David P. Dauwalder
bcc Ms. Marty Hayes

11–19. Postscripts

A postscript may be used to emphasize an idea or add an idea that was unintentionally omitted from the body of the letter. The postscript appears in last position; it may be typed or handwritten with or without the abbreviation *P.S.*

For typewritten postscripts leave a blank line between the previous letter part and the postscript. If a postscript introduced by *P.S.* is longer than one line, indent any subsequent lines to align with the first word of the message.

with abbreviation "P.S."

cr

Enclosure ← *1 blank line*

P.S. Don't miss the opportunity to order Living World Today.
Remember that this offer ends October 31!

cr
Enc. 2
P.S. Don't miss the opportunity to order Living World Today. Remember that this offer ends October 31!

11

without abbreviation "P.S."

JNT/rpn
cc: Ellen Anderson, Kathleene Basil, Sylvia Cohen ← *1 blank line*

Don't miss the opportunity to order Living World Today. Remember that this offer ends October 31!

↕ *at least 6 blank lines*

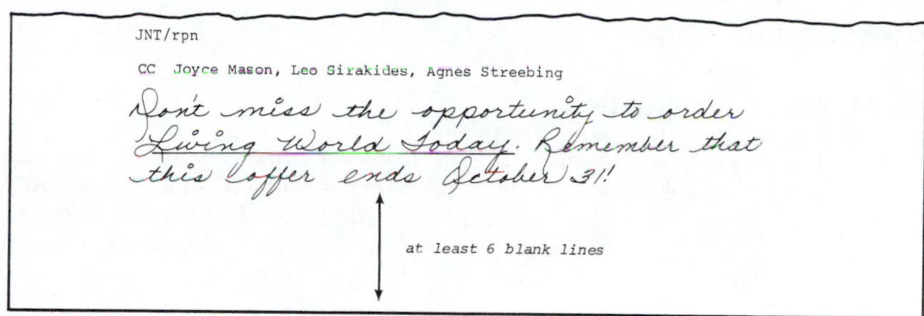
JNT/rpn

CC Joyce Mason, Leo Sirakides, Agnes Streebing

Don't miss the opportunity to order Living World Today. Remember that this offer ends October 31!

11–20. Second-Page Headings

a. **Type headings for second and succeeding pages on plain paper. Allow a 1-inch top margin, and use the same side margins that appear on the first page. These continuation-page headings include the name of the addressee, the page number, and the date. Either a horizontal or vertical format may be used.**

horizontal format

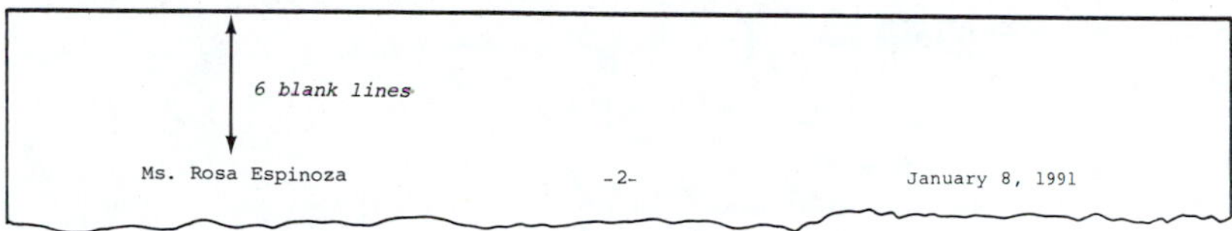

Ms. Rosa Espinoza -2- January 8, 1991

vertical format

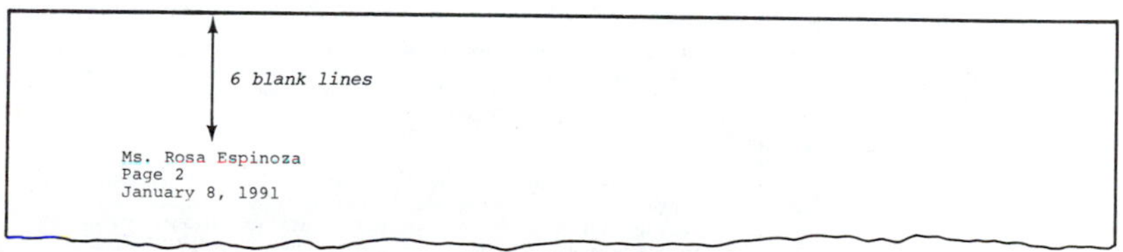

Ms. Rosa Espinoza
Page 2
January 8, 1991

b. **Before resuming the message, space down three lines from the last line of the heading. Two blank lines should separate the heading and the continuation of the message.**

c. **If a page does not end at the conclusion of a paragraph, include *at least* two lines of any new paragraph begun at the bottom of the page. Do not divide the last word on the page. Likewise, carry forward to the next page *at least* two lines from a paragraph begun on the previous page. Leave at least six, but no more than nine, blank lines at the bottom of each page—except, of course, for the last one.**

d. **The closing lines of a business letter should not be isolated on a continuation page. At least two lines of the message must precede the complimentary close or signature lines (when no complimentary close is used).**

Punctuation Style

11–21. Mixed Punctuation

The most popular punctuation style for business letters is mixed punctuation. In this format a colon follows the salutation and a comma appears after the complimentary close. No other closing punctuation marks are used except those concluding an abbreviation or ones appearing within the body of the letter.

Dickens Crystal, Inc.

1640 Grand Boulevard
Schenectady, New York 12309-1083
Telephone: (518) 872-3100

April 17, 1992

House of Imports, Inc.
5700 Oxford Avenue
Philadelphia, PA 19149-3476

Attention Ms. Jody Stevens, Buyer

Gentlemen:

Our complete line of Dickens crystal is illustrated in the enclosed catalog. As you will note from the full-page color illustrations, its simple design and exquisite workmanship have made Dickens crystal one of the most popular lines in the country.

We appreciate your interest in our products and would be pleased to have the House of Imports carry them. I am sure you would find these fast-selling gift items a profitable addition to your inventory.

A complete list of prices and the terms of sale are included in the back pages of the catalog. You will also note that we serve you by providing a breakage credit up to 5 percent of purchases on merchandise displayed in your store. Just return any broken pieces, and we will replace the merchandise.

We hope that we can add your name to the many retailers throughout the country who represent Dickens crystal. Should you wish to open an account with us, please return the enclosed credit application forms. If you wish to place a c.o.d. order, we can deliver the merchandise within ten days of the receipt of your order.

Let Dickens start earning for you today.

Sincerely,

Edward T. Cowan
Vice President, Marketing

ma
Enclosures

11

11–22. Open Punctuation

Writers of business letters sometimes use open punctuation. No closing punctuation marks except those concluding an abbreviation appear after the letter parts. The only other ending punctuation marks are ones used within the body of the letter.

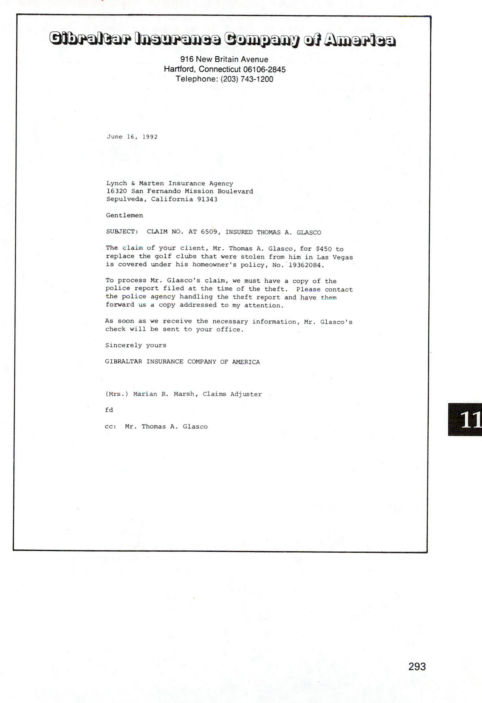

Gibraltar Insurance Company of America

916 New Britain Avenue
Hartford, Connecticut 06106-2845
Telephone: (203) 743-1200

June 16, 1992

Lynch & Marten Insurance Agency
16320 San Fernando Mission Boulevard
Sepulveda, California 91343

Gentlemen

SUBJECT: CLAIM NO. AT 6509, INSURED THOMAS A. GLASCO

The claim of your client, Mr. Thomas A. Glasco, for $450 to replace the golf clubs that were stolen from him in Las Vegas is covered under his homeowner's policy, No. 19362084.

To process Mr. Glasco's claim, we must have a copy of the police report filed at the time of the theft. Please contact the police agency handling the theft report and have them forward us a copy addressed to my attention.

As soon as we receive the necessary information, Mr. Glasco's check will be sent to your office.

Sincerely yours

GIBRALTAR INSURANCE COMPANY OF AMERICA

(Mrs.) Marian R. Marsh, Claims Adjuster

fd

cc: Mr. Thomas A. Glasco

11

Addressing Envelopes

11–23. Return Address

a. The return address is usually printed in the upper left corner of the envelope. In large companies the initiator's initials or name and location are typed above the company name and return address. This practice facilitates routing the letter to the sender in case of nondelivery by the post office.

b. On an envelope without a printed return address, type the return address in the upper left corner. Single-space the typewritten lines and include (1) the name of the individual; (2) the title of the individual, if applicable; (3) the company name, if applicable; (4) the mailing address; and (5) the city, state, and zip code. Begin typing on the third line from the top of the envelope and on the fourth space from the left edge.

2 blank lines
John R. Stevens
460 Old Dorsett Road
Hazelwood, MO 63043
3 blank spaces

11–24. Mailing Address

a. Single-space the mailing address, using at least two lines. The last line of the address should contain the city, state, and zip code. If the envelope is used to mail correspondence, type the address exactly as it appears in the inside address.

b. On legal-sized envelopes, No. 10 envelopes (4⅛ by 9½ inches), space down to line 12 (for 5- and 6-line addresses) or line 13 (for 3- and 4-line addresses). Begin typing the address 4¼ inches from the left edge.

Simplify addressing legal-sized envelopes by setting a tab at the horizontal center of an 8½- by 11-inch sheet of paper (at 51 for 12-pitch type or 43 for 10-pitch type). This practice places most addresses attractively on the envelope (4¼ inches from the left edge) while at the same time providing the starting point for the date and closing lines in the modified block letter style.

No. 10 envelope

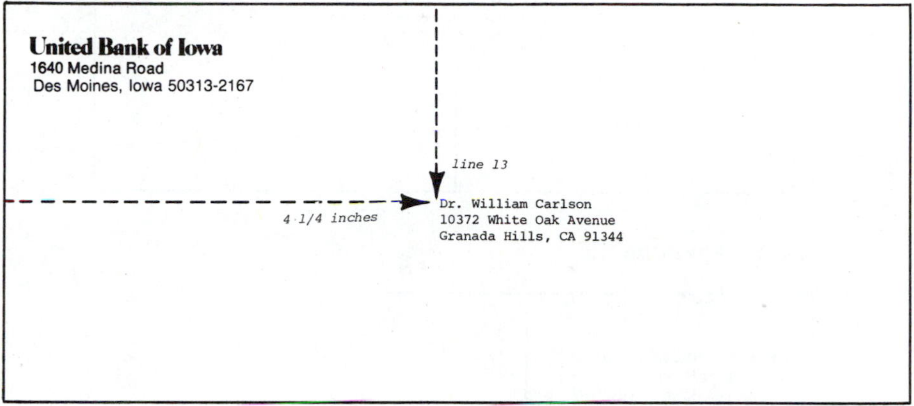

c. **On letter-sized envelopes, No. 6¾ envelopes (3⅝ by 6½ inches), space down to line 11 (for 5- and 6-line addresses) or line 12 (for 3- and 4-line addresses). Begin typing the mailing address 2½ to 3 inches from the left edge, depending upon the line length of the mailing address.**

No. 6¾ envelope

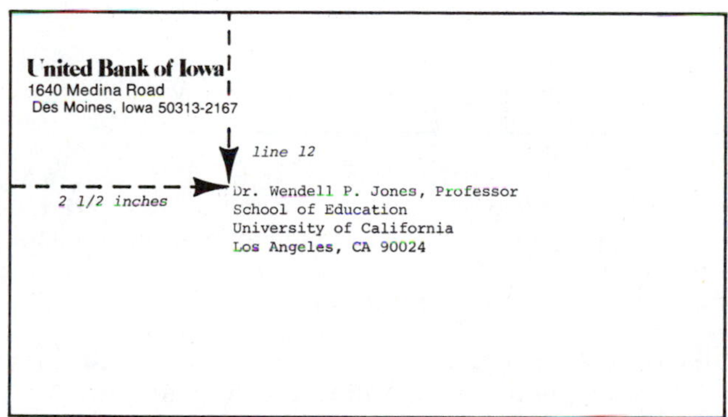

d. **No. 7 (3⅞ by 7½ inches) and No. 5⅛ (4⅝ by 5¹⁵⁄₁₆ inches) envelopes are used less frequently than the standard No. 10 and No. 6¾ envelopes. On No. 7 envelopes space down to line 12; on No. 5⅛ envelopes space down to line 13. Begin typing the mailing address ½ to 1 inch left of the envelope center, depending upon the length of the address lines.**

11

No. 7 envelope

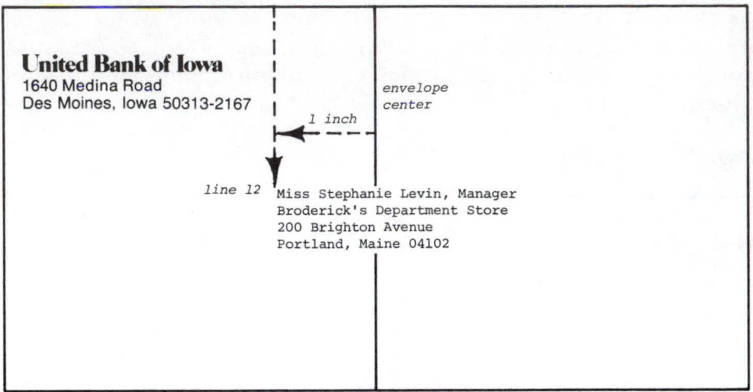

No. 5⅛ envelope

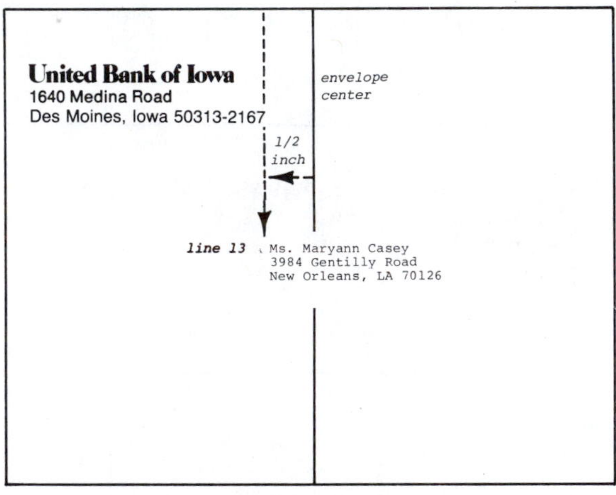

11

e. **Letter-sized manila envelopes (9 by 12 inches or 10 by 12 inches) may have the address typed directly on the envelope or have a label with the address affixed to the envelope. In either case, position the envelope so that the flap and opening are on the right side. Place the first line of the mailing address 4½ inches (for 9- by 12-inch envelopes) or 5 inches (for 10- by 12-inch envelopes) from the top edge and 4½ to 5 inches from the left edge, depending upon the length of the address lines.**

letter-sized manila envelope

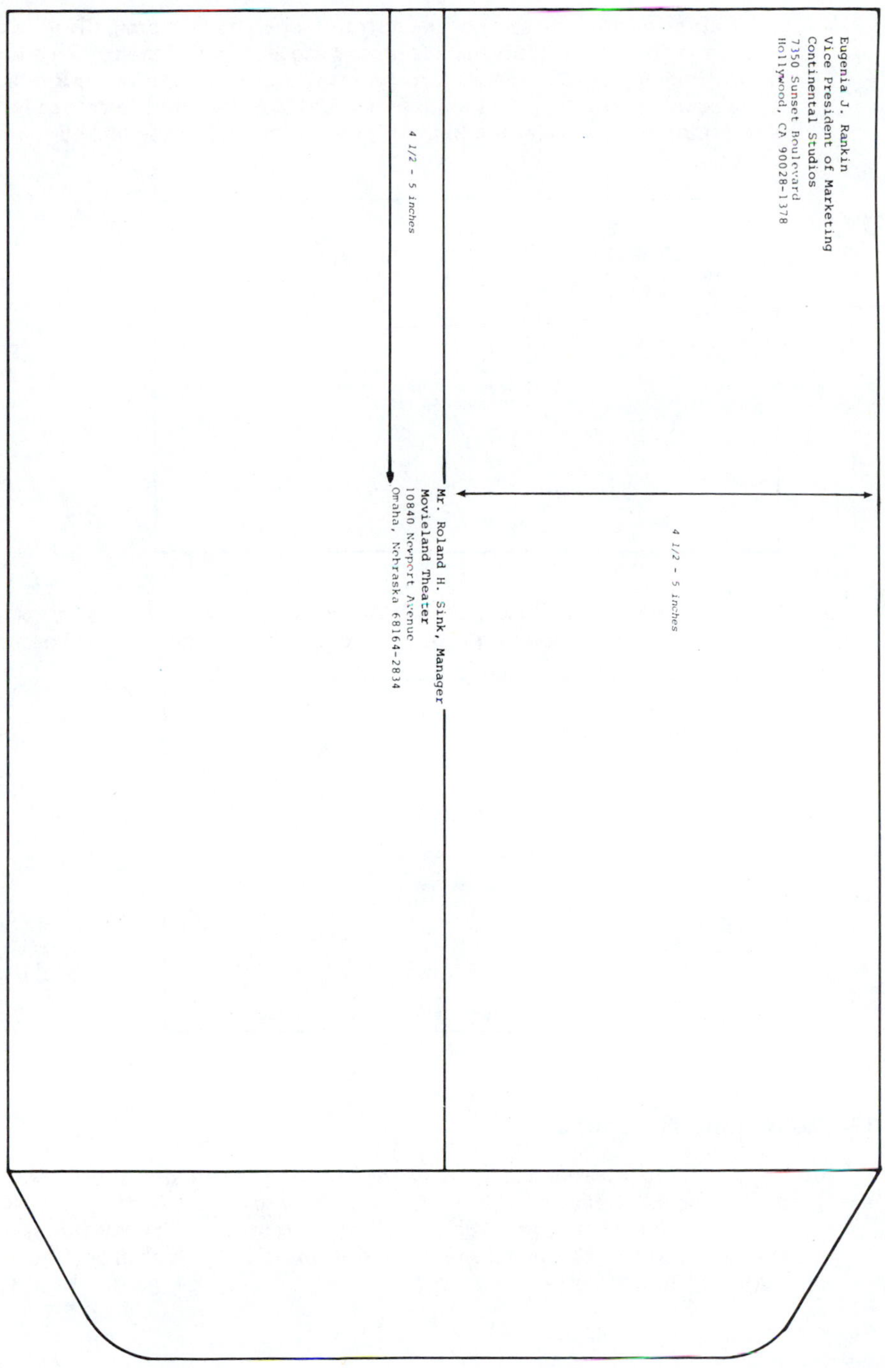

11–25. Addressee Notations

a. **Type an attention line or a special notation such as *Personal, Confidential,* or *Please Forward* a double space below the last line of the return address or 1½ inches (line 9 for standard typewriters) from the top edge of the envelope, whichever position is lower. Use capital and lowercase letters and underline the notation. Begin typing ½ inch from the left edge of the envelope.**

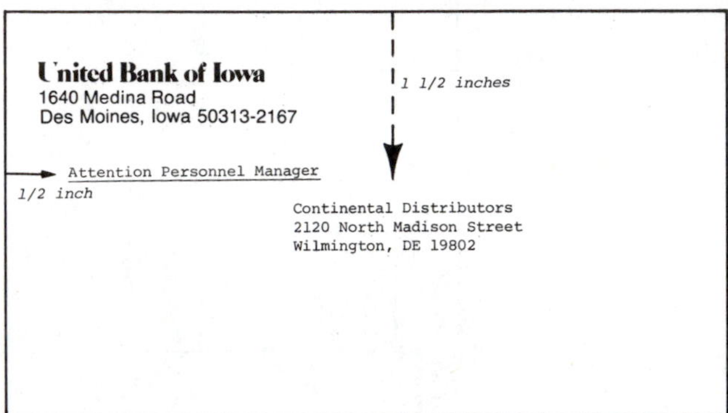

b. **If an attention line is included with the mailing address instead of placed on a separate line, position it directly below the organizational name.**

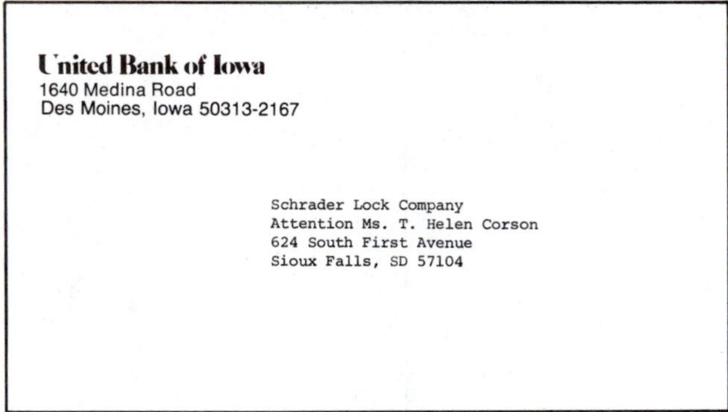

11

11–26. Mailing Notations

a. **Type mailing notations such as *Airmail* (for foreign destinations), *Express Mail, Special Delivery, Certified Mail,* or *Registered Mail* in all capital letters below the stamp, 1½ inches (line 9 for standard typewriters) from the top edge of the envelope. End the notation ½ inch from the right edge of the envelope.**

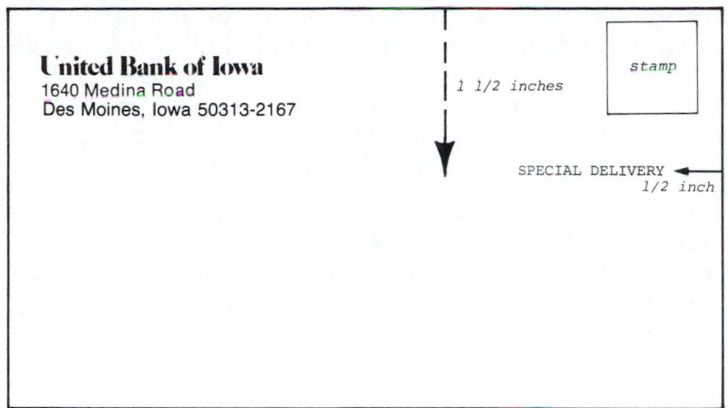

b. **If an addressee and a mailing notation are on the same envelope, type both in all capital letters. The addressee notation appears a double space below the last line of the return address or 1½ inches (line 9 for standard typewriters) from the top edge of the envelope, whichever position is lower. Begin this notation ½ inch from the left envelope edge. Mailing notations are placed below the stamp, 1½ inches (line 9 for standard typewriters) from the top edge of the envelope. They end ½ inch from the right edge.**

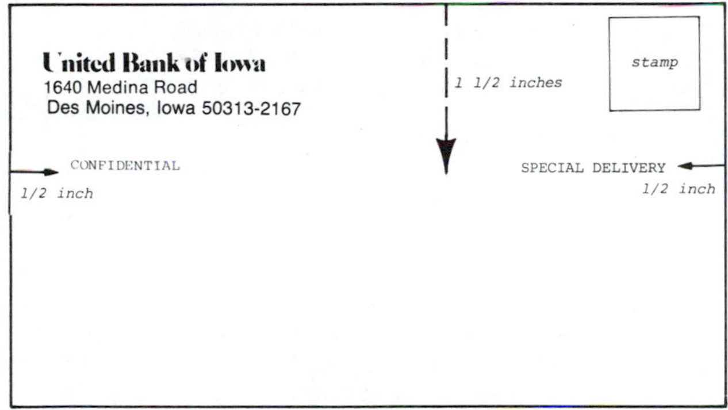

11

11–27. Addressing Envelopes for Optical Character Recognition (OCR)

In 1972 the U.S. Postal Service introduced a format for faster handling of mail addressed by plates or computerized equipment (Customer Services Publication 59). This publication was updated in 1975. In a 1974 publication (Customer Services Notice 23-B) and again in a 1977 publication (Customer Services Publication 62), the U.S. Postal Service recommended that a similar addressing format be used for all other mail.

For general business correspondence most companies still prefer the formality of using the same form of address for both the inside address and the envelope. This format is described in Sections 11–24 through 11–26.

If a company follows the U.S. Postal Service recommendations, however, use the following guidelines for addressing all mail. These guidelines are based on the information given in *A Guide to Business Mail Preparation* (August 1988) issued by the U.S. Postal Service and *A Teacher's Guide to Addressing for Success* (1989) published by Marketing and Communications, Louisville Division, U.S. Postal Service.

a. Addresses should be placed at least 1 inch from the left and right edges of the envelope. The bottom of the last line must be at least $\frac{5}{8}$ of an inch, but no more than $2\frac{3}{4}$ inches, from the bottom edge of the envelope. Keep the lower right half of the envelope free of extraneous printing or symbols, and be careful not to type the address at a slant. The following illustration shows the margin limitations recommended by the U.S. Postal Service.[4]

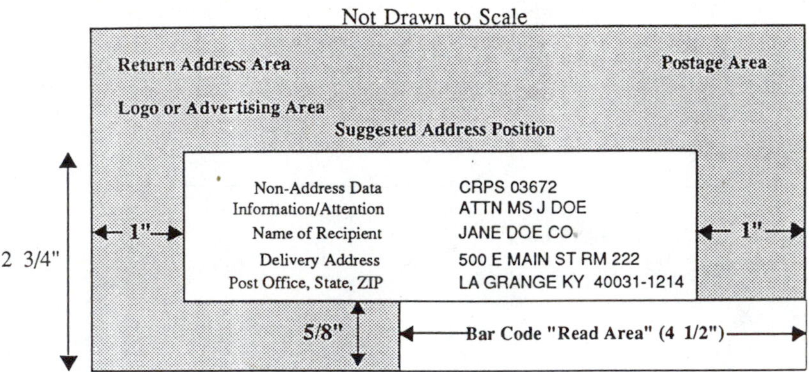

11

b. Use block-style type or print (no italic, script, artistic, foreign-type, or certain dot matrix [in which dots do not touch] styles). The address area on all mail materials should be blocked, with all lines having uniform margins. Typed addresses in all capital letters without punctuation are preferred, but they are required only when the vertical line spacing contains eight lines per inch. Consequently, combinations of capital and lowercase letters may be used for mail addressed on standard typewriters.

c. The bottom line of the address should include the city, state, and zip code in that sequence. Use the two-letter state abbreviation separated from the zip code by one or two spaces. When addressing foreign mail, use the country name as the last line of the address block.

---

[4]Taken from *A Teacher's Guide to Addressing for Success,* Marketing & Communications, Louisville Division, United States Postal Service, p. 4, 1989. These materials are being distributed to colleges, business and secretarial schools, and high schools by the United States Postal Service, Director of Marketing & Communications, P.O. Box 31600, Louisville, Kentucky 40231-9996.

last line of domestic address

DALLAS TX 75201-2310

CY OF INDUSTRY CA 90014-1326

concluding lines of foreign address

WIESBADEN
GERMANY

d. The delivery point for the mail, whether it is a street address or a box number, must be shown on the second line from the bottom, directly above the city, state, and zip code. When apartment numbers, suite numbers, room numbers, etc., are used, they should be placed immediately after the street address on the same line.

When mail is addressed to a box number, place the box number first and then the station name, both on the same line.

street address

8325 W HALBY ST APT 27
DENVER CO 80202-3210

box number with station name

PO BOX 3302 JEFFERSON STN
DETROIT MI 48214-3302

e. Attention lines or other information may be shown on any line of the address block above the second line from the bottom. The attention line is usually placed on the line following the organizational name.

attention line

GENERAL MANUFACTURING COMPANY
ATTEN MR EDWARD R KING
PO BOX 3302 JEFFERSON STN
DETROIT MI 48214-3302

other information

MR H JENKINS MGR
ACCOUNTING DEPT
ABC CORP RM 809
3515 INDUSTRIAL PKY
CLEVELAND OH 44135-3473

f. Account numbers, subscription numbers, presort codes, etc., may be located within the address block. Such numbers are placed immediately above the addressee's name.

973-81269346
MS ROBERTA W FRANK
8325 W HALBY ST APT 27
DENVER, CO 80202-3210

g. The following common address abbreviations may be used for addressing correspondence in conjunction with the U.S. Postal Service recommendations:

Apartment	APT	Post Office	PO
Attention	ATTEN	Ridge	RDG
Avenue	AVE	River	RV
Boulevard	BLVD	Road	RD
East	E	Room	RM
Expressway	EXPY	Route	RT
Heights	HTS	Rural	R
Hospital	HOSP	Rural Route	RR
Institute	INST	Shore	SH
Junction	JCT	South	S
Lake	LK	Square	SQ
Lakes	LKS	Station	STA
Lane	LN	Street	ST
Meadows	MDWS	Terrace	TER
North	N	Turnpike	TPKE
Palms	PLMS	Union	UN
Park	PK	View	VW
Parkway	PKY	Village	VLG
Plaza	PLZ	West	W

envelope prepared according to postal service recommendations

M. D. Riverton

CONFIDENTIAL

CERTIFIED MAIL--RETURN RECEIPT REQUESTED

DR ALICE T MILLS
SUPVR BUS ED DEPT
CALIF STATE DEPT OF EDUC
51 CAPITOL MALL RM 2142
SACRAMENTO CA 95814

acceptable envelope address format for OCR

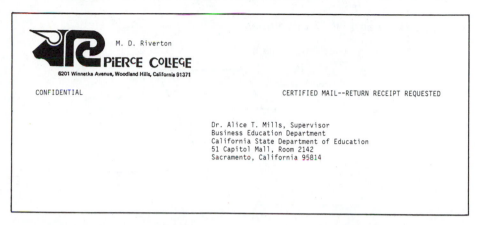

M. D. Riverton
PIERCE COLLEGE
6201 Winnetka Avenue, Woodland Hills, California 91371

CONFIDENTIAL

CERTIFIED MAIL--RETURN RECEIPT REQUESTED

Dr. Alice T. Mills, Supervisor
Business Education Department
California State Department of Education
51 Capitol Mall, Room 2142
Sacramento, California 95814

11–28. Zip + 4

a. For the faster and more economical processing of mail, the U.S. Postal Service has assigned four additional digits to the present zip code of mailing addresses. This series of four digits is separated from the original zip code with a hyphen.

Northridge, CA 91325-*6213*	Boise, Idaho 83702-*4819*
Jackson, MS 39203-*1073*	Reno, Nevada 89503-*2103*

b. The use of Zip + 4 is optional. Its use on individual mail pieces does not ensure that the item will reach its destination in a shorter time period, but the U.S. Postal Service hopes to reduce its operating costs by encouraging the public to use the nine-digit code. Reduced rates, however, for the use of Zip + 4 can be obtained by bulk mailers.

c. While zip codes may be located through a directory published by the U.S. Postal Service, the additional four digits result in producing too many codes to be published in volumes for public distribution. Zip + 4 National State Directory Computer Tapes are available for computerized mailers. Zip + 4 codes will be provided free of charge by the U.S. Postal Service to institutions and businesses that do not have access to large-scale computers. Lists from these institutions and businesses will be updated once for each customer, but the U.S. Postal Service may grant exceptions.

Folding and Inserting Correspondence

11–29. No. 10 and No. 7 Envelopes

a. **Fold up one third of the page.**

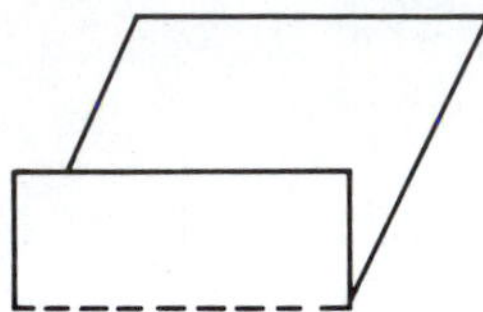

b. **Fold down the upper third of the page so that the top edge is approximately ⅓ inch above the first fold.**

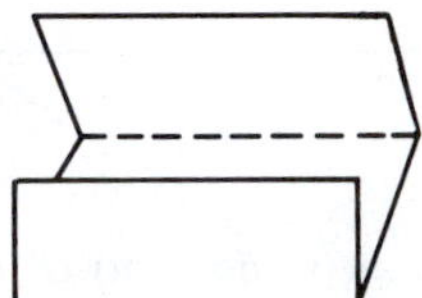

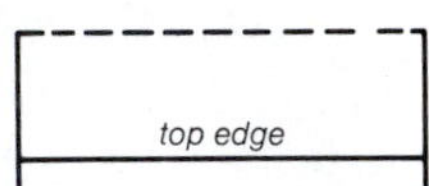

c. **Insert the page so that the top edge is near the top edge of the envelope.**

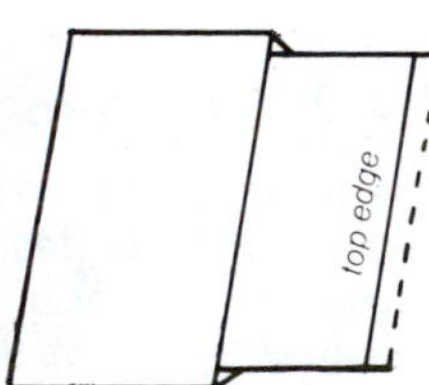

11–30. No. 6¾ Envelopes

11

a. **Fold up one half of the page so that the bottom edge is approximately ⅓ inch below the top edge.**

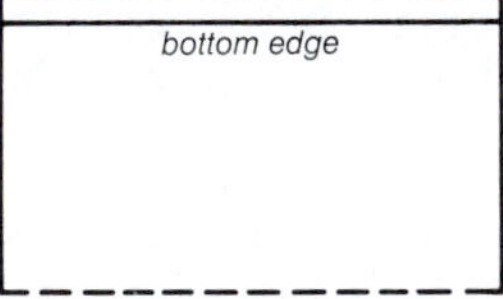

b. **From the right side fold over one third of the page.**

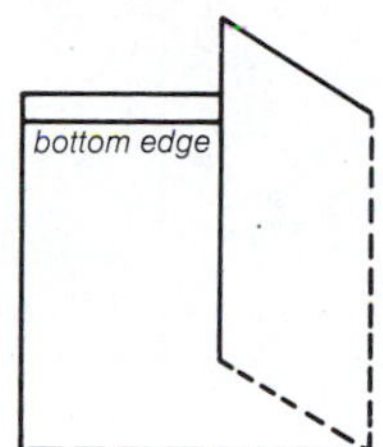

c. **Fold over the second third of the page so that the left edge is approximately ⅓ inch from the right fold.**

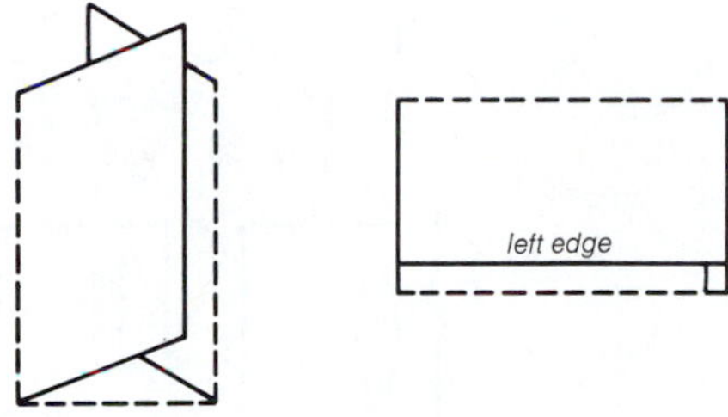

d. **Insert the page so that the left edge is near the top edge of the envelope.**

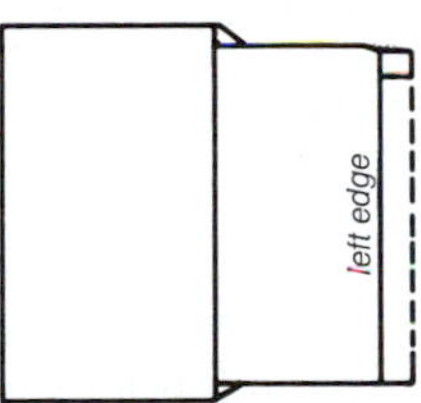

11–31. Window Envelopes

a. **Fold up one third of the letter.**

b. Turn the folded letter face down.

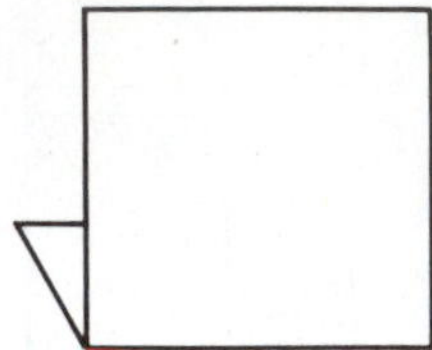

c. Fold down the upper third of the letter so that the top edge meets the first fold.

d. Insert the letter so that the address appears in the window of the envelope.

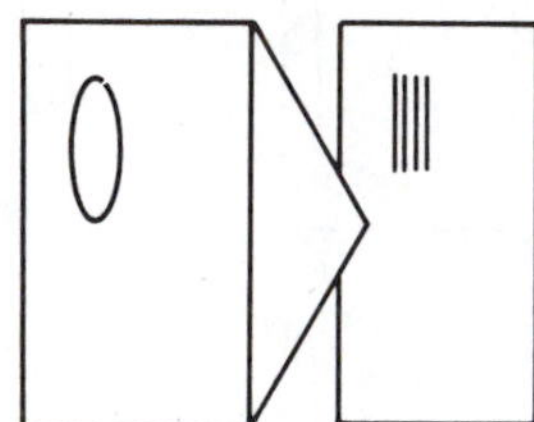

Memorandums

11–32. Usage

Letters generally involve the transmission of written messages sent outside an organization. Written messages sent within the organization, however, more often take the form of a memorandum. Memorandums comprise the major medium for internal written communication.

11–33. Preparation

a. Procedures for preparing memorandums vary widely from office to office, but there are a few general guidelines. Most organizations have prepared forms for typing memorandums. These forms contain printed headings for directing the message to the addressee, designating the source of the message, indicating the date written, and identifying the subject content. Although the arrangement and design may vary, these basic elements are found in most printed memorandum forms.

printed memorandum forms

Northridge Manufacturing Company

To:

From:

Date:

Subject:

MattelToys Memo

MAT—3497-B

TO: **DATE:**

FROM: **REFERENCE:**

SUBJECT:

GENERAL MOTORS ACCEPTANCE CORPORATION

INTRAORGANIZATION LETTERS ONLY

TO ADDRESS

FROM ADDRESS

SUBJECT DATE

b. Some companies do not have standardized forms for typing memorandums. In these cases use the following procedures for typing the memorandum on plain paper or paper containing the company letterhead:

(1) A memorandum is usually prepared on 8½- by 11-inch paper. For short memorandums, however, a half sheet (8½ by 5½ inches) may be used.

(2) On 8½- by 11-inch paper, begin the preliminary lines 2.17 inches (line 13) from the top edge of the paper. For memorandums prepared on half sheets, begin the preliminary lines 1.17 inches (line 7) from the top edge of the paper.

(3) Type in all capital letters and double-space the headings *DATE:*, *TO:*, *FROM:*, and *SUBJECT:* at the left margin. Align the information following the headings two spaces after the colon in the *SUBJECT:* heading. Any other headings the company may wish to use should be placed on the same lines as the *DATE:*, *TO:*, or *FROM:* headings and begin after the information for those headings.

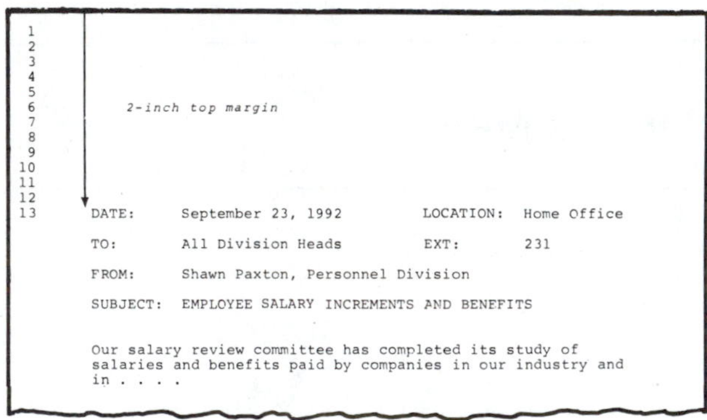

2-inch top margin

DATE: September 23, 1992 LOCATION: Home Office

TO: All Division Heads EXT: 231

FROM: Shawn Paxton, Personnel Division

SUBJECT: EMPLOYEE SALARY INCREMENTS AND BENEFITS

Our salary review committee has completed its study of salaries and benefits paid by companies in our industry and in . . . .

c. Use a 6-inch typing line for the body of 8½-by 11-inch memorandums and a 3.5-inch typing line for half sheets. Triple-space after the subject line, and begin typing the body of the memorandum at the left margin. Single-space the message, but double-space between paragraphs. For short, one-paragraph memorandums, the body may be double spaced.

The following table indicates margin settings for memorandums prepared in 10- and 12-pitch type:[5]

Type Style	*Full-Sheet Margin Settings*	*Half-Sheet Margin Settings*
10 pitch	14 and 73	11 and 45
12 pitch	16 and 87	13 and 54

[5]See Section 13-1 for margin settings on computer-based equipment.

memorandum on company letterhead

Northridge Manufacturing Company
6201 Winnetka Avenue Woodland Hills, California 91364
Telephone: (213) 347-0551

April 24, 1992

TO: All Employees

FROM: Donna Anderson, President

SUBJECT: GROUP HEALTH INSURANCE

As you know, Stanley Hutchinson, your employee representative, proposed to the Board of Directors last January that we consider adopting an employee group health insurance plan. He pointed out the many medical expenses incurred by our employees throughout the year and the benefits a group health insurance policy would have in helping meet some of the medical expenses resulting from sickness and injuries.

After careful study of several group health insurance policies, the board concluded that the group policy proposed by the Edgewater Insurance Company would give the most comprehensive medical coverage for its cost. As a result, the board voted unanimously to adopt this policy at no cost to the employees, effective June 1.

Attached is a brochure that explains in detail the health-care services covered by the Edgewater policy. If you have any questions, please call Don Curry at Ext. 7351. He will be glad to assist you.

rm

d. When a memorandum contains more than one page, the heading for the second and succeeding pages should have a 1-inch top margin. Show the name of the person to whom the memorandum is addressed, the page number, and the date. This information may be arranged vertically at the left margin or be placed on a single line with the name beginning at the left margin, the page number centered, and the date back-spaced (pivoted) from the right margin. Triple-space after the heading before continuing the body of the memorandum.

vertical second-page heading

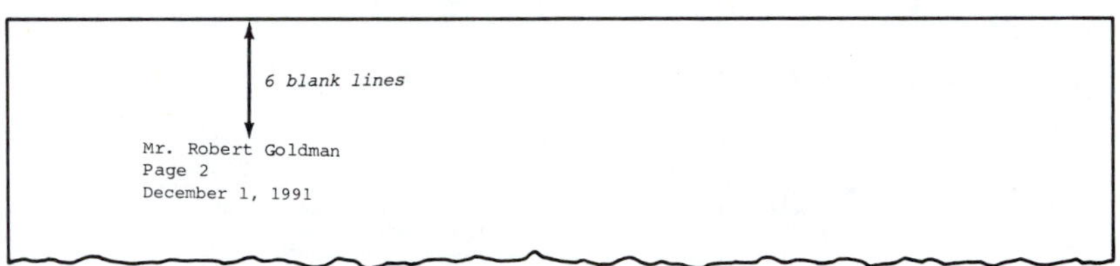

horizontal second-page heading

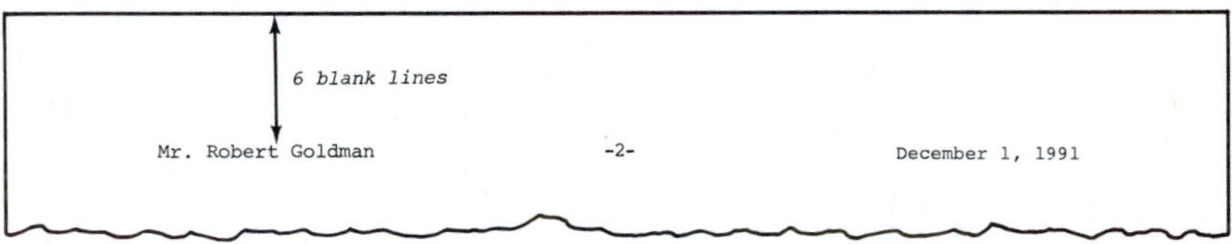

6 blank lines
Mr. Robert Goldman
-2-
December 1, 1991

CHAPTER 12

Reports, Manuscripts, and Minutes

Reports, Manuscripts, and Minutes Solution Finder

Reports and Manuscripts

12–1. General Format

All reports and manuscripts contain a title page and the contents of the report. Other parts may be added depending upon the length, complexity, and formality of the document. The parts of a report or manuscript include the following:

Title page
Letter of transmittal
Summary
Table of contents
List of tables (and/or list of illustrations)
Contents of the report
Endnotes (if applicable)
Bibliography
Appendix (or Appendixes)

a. Reports and manuscripts may be prepared with *either* 1.25-inch left and right margins *or* 1-inch left and right margins, depending upon the preference of the originator. If the report or manuscript is to be bound, allow an additional .25 inch for the left margin.

b. Section openers with main headings require 2-inch top margins. These pages are included in the page count, but the page number is usually not printed on the page. If it is, it is centered on the line directly above a 1-inch bottom margin, with at least one blank line separating it from the last line of text.

section opener with 2-inch top margin

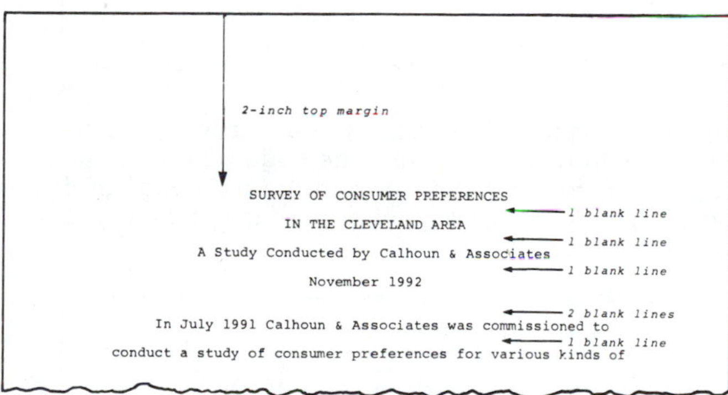

SURVEY OF CONSUMER PREFERENCES

IN THE CLEVELAND AREA

A Study Conducted by Calhoun & Associates

November 1992

In July 1991 Calhoun & Associates was commissioned to
conduct a study of consumer preferences for various kinds of

section opener without page number

in our industry have been experiencing a steady market decline
in this area for the past three years even though economic

1- to 2-inch bottom margin

section opener with page number—1-inch bottom margin

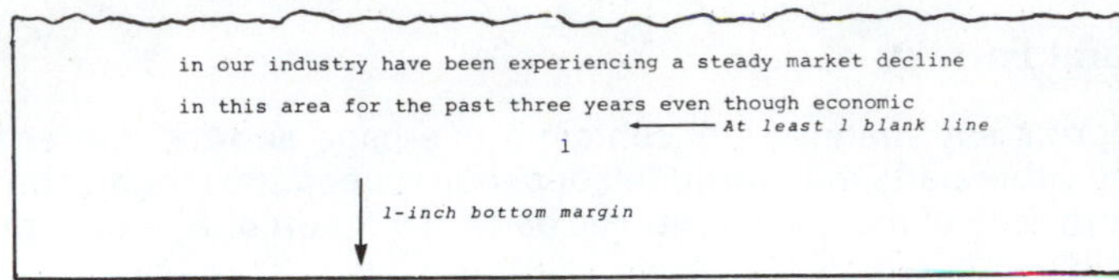

An alternative method permits the page numbers for section openers to be centered on the line directly above a .5-inch bottom margin, with at least two blank lines separating the page number from the last line of text.

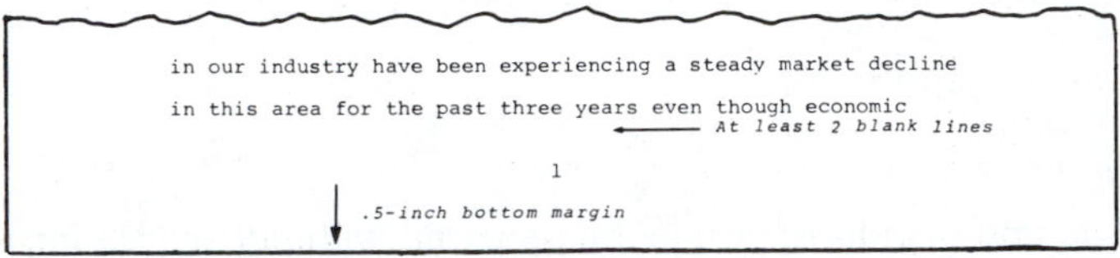

c. Use a 1-inch top margin for all pages except those with main headings. The page number begins the page and is aligned with the right margin. One or preferably two blank lines separate the page number and the first line of text (line 9 or 10 for standard line spacing).

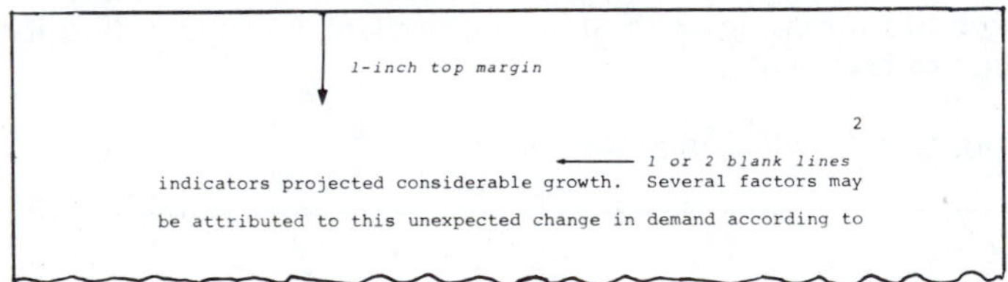

An alternative acceptable format permits a .5-inch top margin on all pages except those with main headings. The page number is placed one line below the top margin and .5 inch from the right edge of the page. Two blank lines separate the page number from the first line of text (line 7 for standard line spacing).

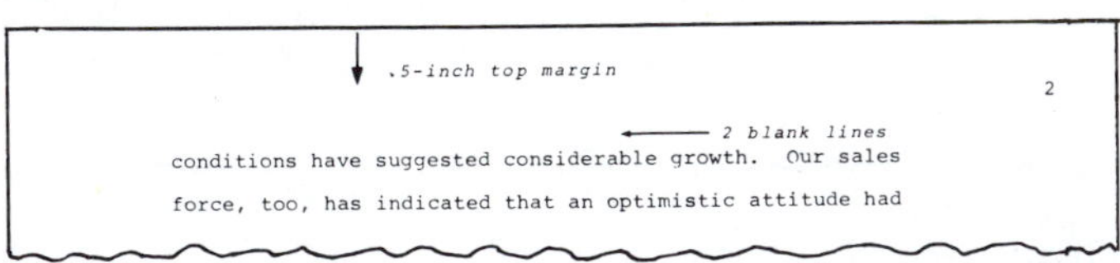

d. Conclude report or manuscript text 1 to 2 inches from the bottom edge of the page, ensuring that at least two lines (one full line and at least one word on a second line) of a paragraph appear at the bottom or top of any page. A single line that belongs to a paragraph may not be isolated at the top or bottom of a different page.

e. Use a manuscript typing guide for setting up reports and manuscripts.[1] Commercially prepared guides made of manila tag that indicate the remaining number of lines on a page are available. Usually these guides are larger than the standard-sized paper so that the remaining number of lines is readily visible.

f. When commercially prepared typing guides are not available, use an 8½-by 11-inch sheet of paper to design your own. Draw heavy black lines to represent the left and right margins as well as the top and bottom margins. Allow 1-inch top and bottom margins and either 1-inch or 1.25-inch left and right margins, unless the manuscript or report is to be bound at the left; then allow an additional .25 inch for the left margin.

   Draw a heavy black horizontal line 2 inches from the top edge (to signify the location of main headings) and a vertical line directly between the left and right margins (to aid in centering). At the right edge of the paper, number the lines of the last four inches of paper. Separate each inch with a 1-inch horizontal line as illustrated in the example on page 316 (to assist in gauging the end of the paper and in setting up footnotes). Finally, if you choose to use the alternative method for page numbering, type .25-inch lines where the top and bottom page numbers are to be located.

[1]See Sections 13–5 and 13–6 for preparing reports and manuscripts on computer-based equipment.

manuscript typing guide

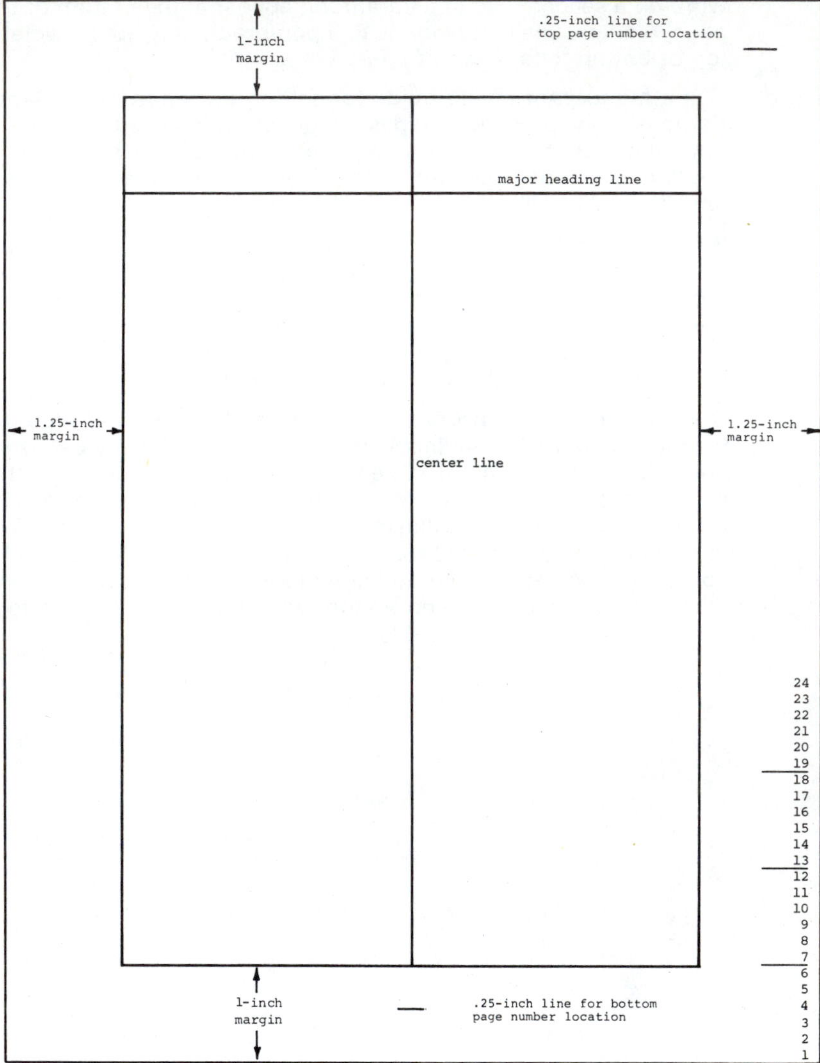

12–2. Title Page

a. The title page will generally contain (1) the name or title of the report or manuscript, (2) the name and title of the person and/or the name of the group or organization for whom it was written, (3) the name and title of the person and/or the name of the group who wrote it, and (4) the date it was submitted. The contents of a title page are not restricted to these items.

b. The title page should have 2-inch top and bottom margins. All lines on the title page should be centered.

The title of the report or manuscript appears in all capital letters and begins on the line directly below the 2-inch top margin (line 13 for standard line spacing). Single-space any titles containing more than one line.

Space equally between the top and bottom margins all other parts following the title. Although the title page is counted in the pagination, do not number the page. An illustration of a title page appears below.

title page

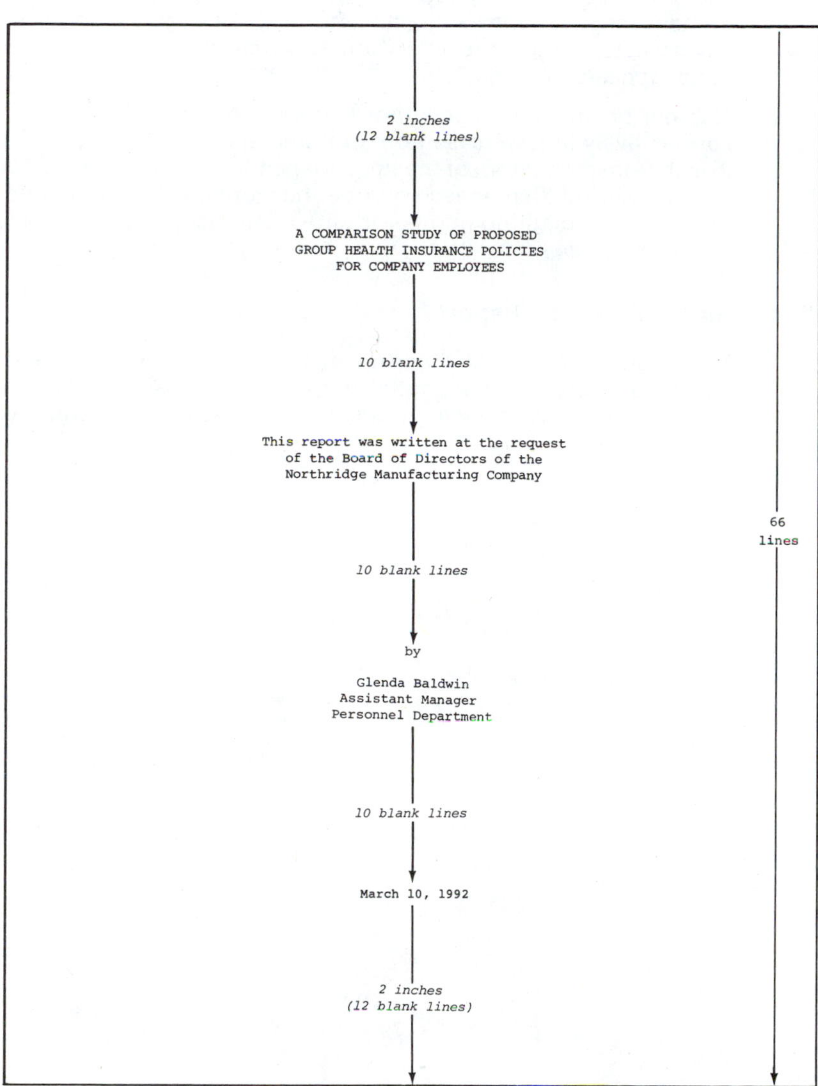
A COMPARISON STUDY OF PROPOSED
GROUP HEALTH INSURANCE POLICIES
FOR COMPANY EMPLOYEES

This report was written at the request
of the Board of Directors of the
Northridge Manufacturing Company

by

Glenda Baldwin
Assistant Manager
Personnel Department

March 10, 1992

12

12–3. Letter of Transmittal

a. The letter of transmittal, if used, introduces the reader to the report or manuscript. Although the content of the transmittal letter will depend upon the complexity and scope of the report or manuscript, it should basically tell the reader (1) what the topic is, (2) why the report was written, (3) how the report was compiled (method of research), (4) who worked on it or helped with its development, and (5) what major findings or conclusions resulted (if a synopsis or summary page is not included).

b. The letter of transmittal should be friendly and concise, usually concluding with the writer showing appreciation for the opportunity to do the report or manuscript. It appears directly after the title page and may be typed in any acceptable business letter format. An illustration of a letter of transmittal appears on page 000.

c. Number preliminary pages (those preceding the contents of the report) consecutively in lowercase Roman numerals (*i, ii, iii, iv, v,* etc.) 1 inch or .5 inch from the bottom of the page, depending upon the page numbering format selected. Center each number horizontally. Count the title page as page *i* even though no number is shown on that page; number the letter of transmittal *ii.*

12–4. Summary of the Report

Long reports—especially those not including a letter of transmittal or those including a letter of transmittal without a synopsis—usually require a summary. Use the following guidelines to prepare the summary.

letter of transmittal

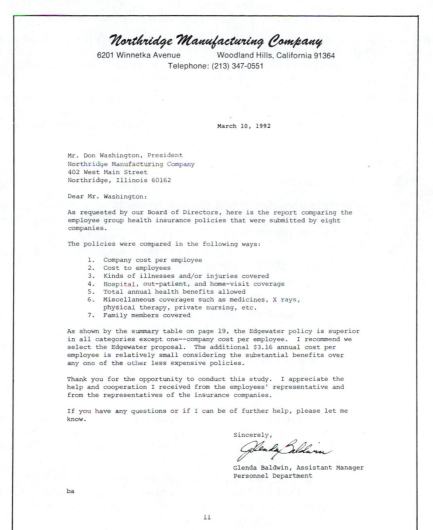

Northridge Manufacturing Company
6201 Winnetka Avenue Woodland Hills, California 91364
Telephone: (213) 347-0551

March 10, 1992

Mr. Don Washington, President
Northridge Manufacturing Company
402 West Main Street
Northridge, Illinois 60162

Dear Mr. Washington:

As requested by our Board of Directors, here is the report comparing the employee group health insurance policies that were submitted by eight companies.

The policies were compared in the following ways:

1. Company cost per employee
2. Cost to employees
3. Kinds of illnesses and/or injuries covered
4. Hospital, out-patient, and home-visit coverage
5. Total annual health benefits allowed
6. Miscellaneous coverages such as medicines, X rays, physical therapy, private nursing, etc.
7. Family members covered

As shown by the summary table on page 19, the Edgewater policy is superior in all categories except one--company cost per employee. I recommend we select the Edgewater proposal. The additional $3.16 annual cost per employee is relatively small considering the substantial benefits over any one of the other less expensive policies.

Thank you for the opportunity to conduct this study. I appreciate the help and cooperation I received from the employees' representative and from the representatives of the insurance companies.

If you have any questions or if I can be of further help, please let me know.

Sincerely,

Glenda Baldwin

Glenda Baldwin, Assistant Manager
Personnel Department

ba

ii

12

a. Allow a 2-inch top margin. Center the main heading *SUMMARY* in all capital letters on the line directly following the top margin (line 13 for standard line spacing). Triple-space after the main heading.

b. Double-space the text of the summary; indent each paragraph 5 spaces. Begin with stating the purpose of the report. Briefly describe the procedures used in preparing the report, and conclude with a concise presentation of the conclusions and recommendations.

c. Number the summary page or pages with lowercase Roman numerals centered at the bottom of the page. Allow a 1-inch or .5-inch bottom margin, depending upon the numbering format selected for the document.

12–5. Table of Contents

The content and format of a table of contents vary with the length and complexity of the report or manuscript, but the following guidelines may be used for its preparation:

(1) Allow a 2-inch top margin. Center the main heading *TABLE OF CONTENTS* or *CONTENTS* in all capital letters on the line directly following the top margin (line 13 for standard line spacing).

(2) Type the word *Page* a triple space below the table of contents heading; back-space (pivot) it from the right margin.

(3) Type in all capital letters and double-space the listing for the preliminary sections of the report (e.g., letter of transmittal, summary, list of tables, list of interviews). Begin a double space below *Page* and at the left margin. Although it is counted and paginated with a lowercase Roman numeral, the table of contents is not included in this listing.

(4) Begin the major division heading of the report (e.g., *Chapter, Section, Unit,* or *Topic*) at the left margin. The major division heading may either appear on the same line as *Page* or be typed a double space below the preliminary parts.

(5) Beginning at the left margin, type the major sections of the report in all capital letters. Those sections of lesser degree should be indented, typed in capital and lowercase letters, and placed in the same sequence as they appear in the report.

12

(6) Major sections of a report may be numbered by using uppercase Roman numerals. Type the longest numeral at the left margin, and indent the shorter numerals so the periods following the numerals are aligned.

(7) Use leaders (a line of alternating periods and spaces) to assist the reader in locating the page number of a particular section, and align vertically the leaders for each section or subsection of the report. Although all major headings must have corresponding page numbers, the assignment of page numbers to subheadings appearing in the table of contents is optional. An example of a table of contents appears on page 321.

table of contents

TABLE OF CONTENTS

iii

12–6. List of Tables or List of Illustrations

a. When a report or manuscript contains several tables, include as a helpful reference to the reader a list of tables after the table of contents. The format for the list of tables follows:

(1) Center the heading *LIST OF TABLES* in all capital letters on the line following a 2-inch top margin (line 13 for standard line spacing).

(2) Triple-space after the *LIST OF TABLES* heading. Type the word *Table* at the left margin, and type the word *Page* back-spaced (pivoted) from the right margin.

(3) Indent three spaces from the left margin, and type the number of each table followed by two spaces and its title in all capital letters. Single-space each title; double-space between titles.

(4) Use leaders (a line of alternating periods and spaces) to assist the reader in locating the page number of a particular table. Number the list of tables at the bottom of the page with a lowercase Roman numeral.

list of tables

LIST OF TABLES

Table		Page
1	A COMPARISON OF THE ANNUAL COST PER EMPLOYEE OF HEALTH INSURANCE POLICIES SUBMITTED BY EIGHT COMPANIES	8
2	EMPLOYEE CLAIMS SUBMITTED OVER A TEN-YEAR PERIOD BY THREE COMPANIES OF EQUAL SIZE	14
3	ESTIMATED COST OF HEALTH EXPENSES PER EMPLOYEE OVER A TEN-YEAR PERIOD WITHOUT HEALTH INSURANCE	17
4	A COMPARISON OF THE COST OF GROUP INSURANCE VS. INDIVIDUAL HEALTH POLICIES	25

b. A list of illustrations may be used for a report that contains figures or a combination of tables and figures. For one that contains only figures, use the same format described in the previous section for a list of tables. Change the title to *LIST OF ILLUSTRATIONS* and the subtitle *Table* to *Figure.* Use the following procedures to format a list of illustrations that contains both tables and figures:

12 (1) Center the heading *LIST OF ILLUSTRATIONS* in all capital letters on the line following a 2-inch top margin (line 13 for standard line spacing).

(2) Triple-space after the *LIST OF ILLUSTRATIONS* heading, and center the subheading A. Tables in capital and lowercase letters underlined. Double-space after the subheading, and type *Table* at the left margin and *Page* back-spaced (pivoted) from the right margin. Double-space before beginning the listing.

(3) Indent three spaces from the left margin, and type the number of each table followed by two spaces and its title in all capital letters. Use leaders (a line of alternating periods and spaces) to assist the reader in locating the page number. Single-space each title; double-space between titles; and triple-space after the last title.

(4) Center and underline the subheading B. Figures; type it in capital and lowercase letters. Double-space after the subheading, and type *Figure* at the left margin and *Page* back-spaced (pivoted) from the right margin. Double-space before beginning the listing.

(5) Indent three spaces from the left margin, and type the number of each figure followed by two spaces and its title in all capital letters. Use leaders to assist the reader in locating the page number. Single-space each title; double-space between titles.

(6) Number the list of illustrations at the bottom of the page with a lowercase Roman numeral.

list of illustrations

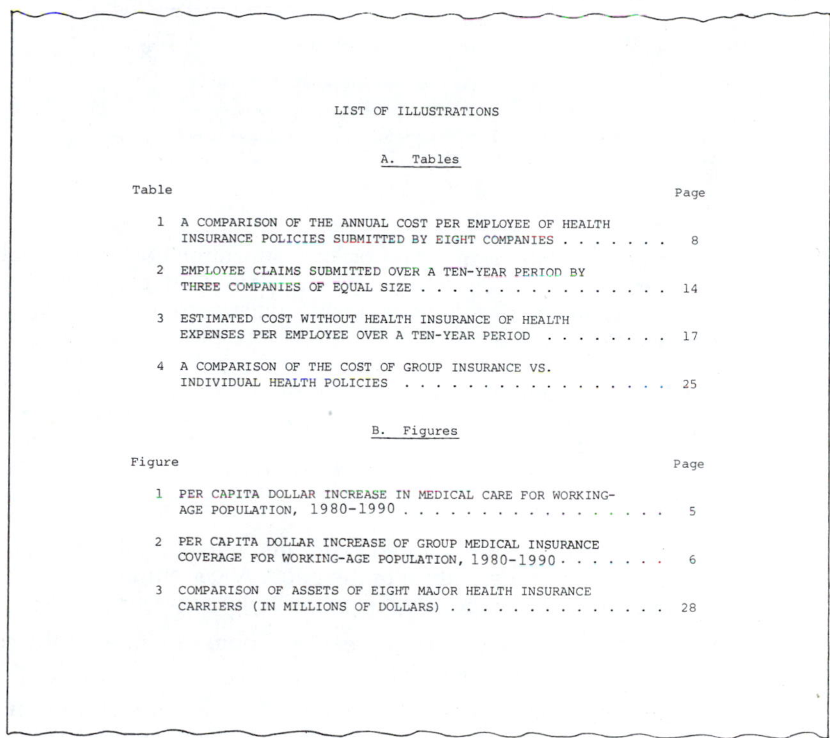

LIST OF ILLUSTRATIONS

A. Tables

Table | Page

1 A COMPARISON OF THE ANNUAL COST PER EMPLOYEE OF HEALTH INSURANCE POLICIES SUBMITTED BY EIGHT COMPANIES 8

2 EMPLOYEE CLAIMS SUBMITTED OVER A TEN-YEAR PERIOD BY THREE COMPANIES OF EQUAL SIZE 14

3 ESTIMATED COST WITHOUT HEALTH INSURANCE OF HEALTH EXPENSES PER EMPLOYEE OVER A TEN-YEAR PERIOD 17

4 A COMPARISON OF THE COST OF GROUP INSURANCE VS. INDIVIDUAL HEALTH POLICIES 25

B. Figures

Figure | Page

1 PER CAPITA DOLLAR INCREASE IN MEDICAL CARE FOR WORKING-AGE POPULATION, 1980-1990 5

2 PER CAPITA DOLLAR INCREASE OF GROUP MEDICAL INSURANCE COVERAGE FOR WORKING-AGE POPULATION, 1980-1990 6

3 COMPARISON OF ASSETS OF EIGHT MAJOR HEALTH INSURANCE CARRIERS (IN MILLIONS OF DOLLARS) 28

12–7. Preparing the Body of the Report or Manuscript

a. Allow a 2-inch top margin on pages that begin the body of the report or major sections of the report body. Begin all main headings on the line following the 2-inch top margin (line 13 for standard line spacing). Center the heading in all capital letters; double-space multiple-line main headings. Triple-space after the main heading if it is not followed by a secondary heading.

b. Secondary headings are often used to explain or elaborate on a main heading. These headings begin a double space below the main heading and are typed in capital and lowercase letters. All lines are centered, and multiple lines are double-spaced. Triple-space after the secondary heading.

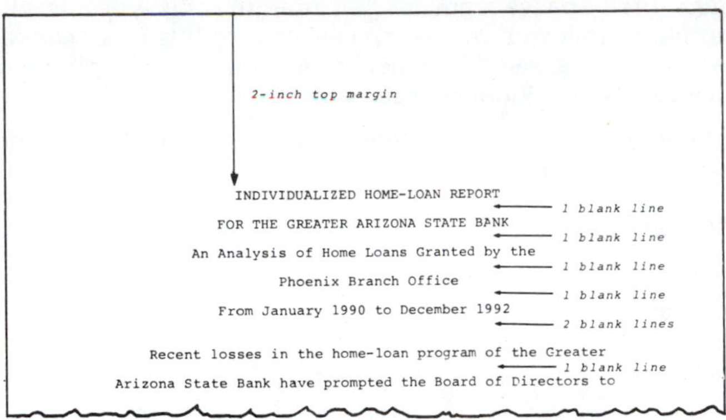

2-inch top margin
INDIVIDUALIZED HOME-LOAN REPORT
1 blank line
FOR THE GREATER ARIZONA STATE BANK
1 blank line
An Analysis of Home Loans Granted by the
1 blank line
Phoenix Branch Office
1 blank line
From January 1990 to December 1992
2 blank lines
Recent losses in the home-loan program of the Greater
1 blank line
Arizona State Bank have prompted the Board of Directors to

c. Double-space the body of the report or manuscript. Each paragraph should be indented five spaces to offset it clearly from the previous one. If page and paragraph endings do not coincide, be sure to place at least two lines of a new paragraph at the end of a page and carry over at least the same (one complete line and a minimum of one word on a second line) from a previous paragraph to a new page. In other words, do not permit widow and orphan lines—adjust page endings so that single lines from a paragraph are not at the top or bottom of a page. Example pages from the body of a report appear on pages 325 and 326.

d. Number each page as follows:

(1) For pages with first-degree headings, either omit the page number or center it at the bottom of the page. Allow either a 1-inch or .5-inch bottom margin, depending upon the page-numbering system selected.

(2) For pages without first-degree headings, use one of the following page-numbering formats:

(a) Type the page number one line below a 1-inch top margin and even with the right margin. Leave one or two blank lines before continuing with the text.

(b) Type the page number one line below a .5-inch top margin and .5 inch from the right edge of the paper.

body of report

SECTION I

INTRODUCTION

The following report provides a comparison of the employees' health and major medical insurance programs submitted by eight major insurance companies.

Purpose of the Report

Last January Norman Rittgers, one of the employee representatives for our company, requested that company-sponsored health insurance be considered by the Board of Directors as a supplement to our wage and salary schedule. As a result, the board directed the Personnel Department to (1) contact insurance companies for the purpose of determining what health insurance policies were available and (2) compare the coverages for the purpose of determining which policy would best meet our employees' health insurance needs for the least cost.

Scope of the Report

The scope of this investigation was limited to an analysis of the written proposals and copies of policies submitted by the participating insurance companies. Of the 28 insurance companies contacted, the majority provided only verbal explanations as to what the estimated coverage and cost of a group health and major medical insurance program would be for our employees. Only eight of these companies submitted written documents for our consideration. Proposals and policies from these companies were evaluated according to the following criteria:

body of report, continued

2

Company cost per employee
Cost to employee
Kinds of illnesses and/or injuries covered
Hospital, out-patient, and home-visit coverages
Exclusions
Deductibles and dollar amounts of coverage

An explanation of the factors considered in each of these criteria is provided in the ensuing sections.

Company Cost Per Employee

Each health insurance package was analyzed to determine the cost per employee to the company. This analysis took into consideration such variables as discounts for insuring over a minimum number of employees and savings accruing from making payments on a monthly basis rather than on a quarterly basis.

Cost to Employees

None of the health insurance packages considered in this report included any direct cost to the employees. Some of the policies did, however, provide options whereby individual employees could increase the amount of coverage at their own expense.

Kinds of Illnesses and/or Injuries Covered

Although all the health insurance packages studied in this report covered most of the common types of illnesses and injuries, there were differences in specific coverages. The most common differences appeared in coverages for illnesses resulting in operations, and these differences were analyzed in making the final recommendation.

12–8. Text Headings

a. Text headings of different degrees signal content in a report or manuscript and contribute to its readability. A common classification of text headings includes first-, second-, and third-degree headings. An explanation of how each degree heading should be formatted follows and is repeated in the context of its corresponding illustration.

(1) **First-degree headings.** Center a first-degree heading, and capitalize the first letter of each main word. The heading may or may not be underlined. Triple-space before a first-degree heading, and double-space after it.

(2) **Second-degree headings.** Begin the second-degree heading at the left margin. Capitalize the first letter of each main word, and underline the heading. Triple-space before a second-degree heading, and double-space after it.

(3) **Third-degree headings.** The third-degree heading begins a paragraph, so it is indented from the left margin the same number of spaces as any other paragraph. Capitalize only the first word and any proper nouns. Underline the heading and conclude it with a period. Double-space before a third-degree heading, and begin typing the paragraph text directly after the heading.

first-degree heading

```
that main headings and secondary headings introduce the
report or a main section of the report.

             Format for a First-Degree Heading
     A first-degree text heading, also referred to as a
"centered heading," is centered and typed in capital and
lowercase letters with or without a continuous underline.
Triple-space before a first-degree heading and double-space
after it.
```

second-degree heading

```
Triple-space before a first-degree heading and double-space
after it.

Format for a Second-Degree Heading
     A second-degree heading is often called a "margin
heading" because it begins at the left margin.  Use capital
and lowercase letters with a continuous underline.  Triple-
space before a second-degree heading and double-space after
it.
```

third-degree heading

```
space before a second-degree heading and double-space after
it.
     Format for a third-degree heading.  Because the third-
degree heading is part of the paragraph that follows, it is
also referred to as a "paragraph heading."  Only the first
word and proper nouns in the heading are capitalized.
     The third-degree heading is underlined and followed by
a period.  Double-space before a third-degree heading, and
begin typing the paragraph on the same line directly after
the heading.
```

b. Text headings indicate divisions of a topic or subtopic; therefore, if a first-, second-, or third-degree heading is used, it must be followed by at least one or more matching headings. For example, if you use one first-degree heading in the report or manuscript, you must use at least one other first-degree heading in the same document.

c. All text headings should be separated by at least two lines of text, regardless of their place in the heading hierarchy. In other words, a lesser-degree heading may not follow another heading without any intervening text.

d. Text headings must be used in ascending order of degree from first degree to third degree, *but* the first-degree heading may be omitted if only one or two levels of headings are required in a report. The following table illustrates what heading levels may be used depending upon the number of levels or divisions required.

Number of Text Headings Required	*Levels of Text Headings to Be Used*
3	First-degree heading Second-degree heading Third-degree heading
2	First-degree heading Second-degree heading or Second-degree heading Third-degree heading
1	First-degree heading or Second-degree heading

12

12–9. Listings

a. Both vertical and horizontal listings are often used in letters, memorandums, reports, and manuscripts. Whether to use a horizontal listing or a vertical listing depends upon (1) the number of items in the listing, (2) the number of words contained in each item, and (3) the degree of emphasis the writer wishes to assign to the listing.

Vertical listings are more emphatic than horizontal listings. They may be numbered or unnumbered. Lengthy and complex listings are more readily understood in the vertical format.

Horizontal listings are less emphatic. They are generally used with short listings that are few in number. Each item in a horizontal listing is preceded by an arabic number or a lowercase letter enclosed in parentheses.

b. *Numbered vertical listings* are numbered in consecutive order with arabic numerals. In all business letters, memorandums, reports, and manuscripts, use the following format for listing numbered items vertically:

(1) Introduce a vertical listing with a complete thought.

(2) Indent the listing five spaces from both the left and right margins. In business letters and memorandums, vertical listings *may* assume the left and right margins of the main text.

(3) Number each item; space twice after the period.

(4) Double-space before the first item, between items, and after the last item in the listing.

(5) Single-space items that are more than one line. Begin the second and any succeeding lines directly under the first word, not the number, of the item.

(6) Capitalize the first word in each listed item.

(7) Use a period after each item *only* in listings containing complete sentences.

numbered vertical listing, complete sentences

```
     When explaining our investment program to new clients,

use the following procedures:
                                  <------- 1 blank line
     1.  Introduce yourself to the clients, and be sure
         you solicit the correct pronunciation of their
         names.
                                  <------- 1 blank line
     2.  Begin sessions by using the clients' surnames
         with a courtesy title.
                                  <------- 1 blank line
     3.  Enter into a discussion that discloses their
         leisure activities and interests.
                                  <------- 1 blank line
     4.  Move into a discussion about their future and
         plans for financing it.
                                  <------- 1 blank line
     5.  Relate financial planning . . . .
                                  <------- 1 blank line
```

12

c. *Unnumbered vertical listings* are similar in most respects to numbered vertical listings. Use the following format for listing unnumbered items vertically:

(1) Introduce a vertical listing with a complete thought.

(2) Indent the listing five spaces from both the left and right margins.

(3) Double-space before the first item, between items, and after the last item in the listing. Single-space items that are more than one line.

(4) Capitalize the first word in each listed item.

(5) Use a period after each item *only* in listings containing complete sentences.

unnumbered vertical listing, complete sentences

```
     All managers are required to use the following procedures

for closing the store:
                                   ←——— 1 blank line
     Place all receipts in the vault.
                                   ←——— 1 blank line
     Ensure that all other employees except the security
     guard have left the premises.
                                   ←——— 1 blank line
     Check to make sure that all customer entrances have
     been locked and bolted.
                                   ←——— 1 blank line
     Engage the alarm system.
                                   ←——— 1 blank line
     Lock the employee entrance upon leaving.
                                   ←——— 1 blank line
```

unnumbered vertical listing—words or phrases

```
     This position requires that the employee be qualified to

perform the following duties:
                                   ←——— 1 blank line
     Greet clients and other office visitors
                                   ←——— 1 blank line
     Answer the telephone and direct incoming calls to
     the appropriate person
                                   ←——— 1 blank line
     Schedule appointments for attorneys in the office
     and inform them of their scheduled appointments
                                   ←——— 1 blank line
     Assist the legal secretaries when time permits
                                   ←——— 1 blank line
```

12

```
        In our new offices all work stations will be equipped

    with the following computers and peripherals or their

    equivalents:
                                            ←—— 1 blank line
        IBM PS2 computer, Model 70
                                            ←—— 1 blank line
        IBM extended keyboard
                                            ←—— 1 blank line
        IBM VGA color monitor
                                            ←—— 1 blank line
        IBM Proprinter III XL
                                            ←—— 1 blank line
```

Unnumbered vertical listings consisting of words or phrases that are typed on single lines *may be* single-spaced, although a double space still appears before and after the listing. Such a listing is shown below and in the report page illustrated on page 326.

```
        In our new offices all work stations will be equipped

    with the following computers and peripherals or their

    equivalents:                            ←—— 1 blank line

        IBM PS2 computer, Model 70
        IBM extended keyboard
        IBM VGA color monitor
        IBM Proprinter III XL               ←—— 1 blank line
```

d. Horizontal listings may be part of a sentence, or they may be introduced by a complete thought. Whenever a horizontal listing contains three or more items, the items are separated by commas or semicolons. Use commas to separate words or phrases; use semicolons to separate complete thoughts or items that contain internal commas.

The following formats are used for listing items horizontally:

(1) Use a colon to introduce the list only when it is preceded by a complete thought.

(2) Capitalize the first word of each item only if it is a proper noun.

(3) Identify the listed items by enclosing either lowercase letters or numbers in parentheses before each item. Do not conclude a line with a letter or number enclosed in parentheses; at least one word of the item must appear after the letter or numeral.

12

horizontal listing—items separated by commas

```
    as requested.  Each team will consist of (a) a manager, (b) a

    scientist, (c) an engineer, (d) an administrative assistant,

    and (e) a secretary.  The team will function under the super-
```

horizontal listing—items separated by semicolons

```
on Tuesday, June 10.  While I am in New York, would you
please take care of the following items:  (1) complete the
negotiations with Office Maintenance Services for an addi-
tional one-year contract; (2) respond to and follow through
on the inquiry from Medco Financial Services regarding our
medical software line; and (3) contact reviewers to test and
evaluate our newly developed line of software for dental
offices.
```

12–10. Methods of Citing Sources

When either direct quotations or other information needs to be cited in a report or manuscript, any one of a number of methods may be used. The most common ones include footnotes, bibliographical notes, endnotes, the MLA (Modern Language Association) style of notation, and the APA (American Psychological Association) style of notation.

a. Footnotes[2]

Indicate the presence of a footnote by typing a superior (slightly raised) figure after the reference material to be documented. Place the footnote itself at the bottom of the page on which the reference notation appears.

(1) Set off the footnotes from the rest of the page by typing a 1.5-inch line at the left margin, at least a single space after the last line of text on the page. Use the underline key, and double-space after typing this line.

(2) Indent five spaces, and number each footnote consecutively by typing a superior (slightly raised) figure at the beginning of the footnote.

(3) Single-space each footnote, but double-space between footnotes.

(4) Type the name of the author, if any, in a first-name, last-name sequence.

(5) Provide the complete title of the cited reference. Place the titles of magazine articles, sections of books, and newspaper columns in quotation marks. Underline or italicize the titles of books, pamphlets, magazines, and newspapers.

---

[2]The formats suggested here for footnotes and endnotes (except for noted deviations) are based on the traditional format alternatives contained in *The Chicago Manual of Style,* 13th ed. (Chicago and London: The University of Chicago Press, 1982), 399–420, 485–510.

(6) Include next the publishing information. Enclose in parentheses the geographical location of the publisher followed by a colon, the name of the publisher, and the date of publication. Eliminate the state name from the geographical location when the city is commonly known; otherwise, use the standard state abbreviation with the city name.

(7) Follow the complete title of magazines and newspapers with the date of publication.

(8) Conclude footnotes with the page location of the cited material.

(9) Separate the parts of a footnote with commas.

book, one author

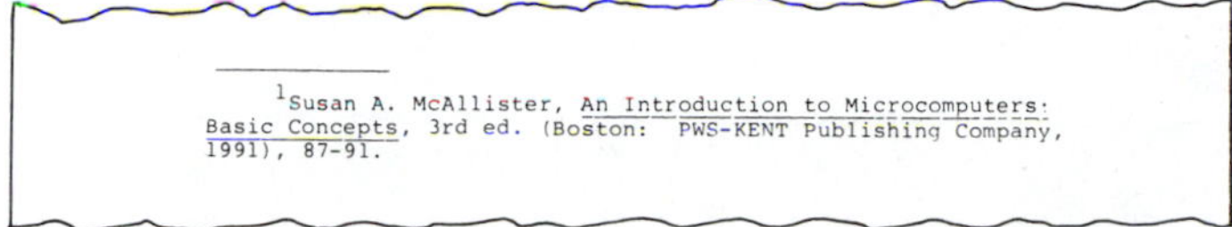

[1]Susan A. McAllister, An Introduction to Microcomputers: Basic Concepts, 3rd ed. (Boston: PWS-KENT Publishing Company, 1991), 87-91.

book, two authors

[2]E. Bryant Phillips and Andrea Kessler, Principles of Management, 2nd ed. (New York: John Wiley & Sons, Inc., 1990), 108.

book, more than two authors

[3]Patricia Whitman, David Kane, James E. Wellington, and Ida Mason, Human Relations in the Office (New York: McGraw-Hill Book Company, 1989), 208-214.

paperback book

[4]Mark T. Mathews, Managerial Psychology in a Global Economy (Chicago: University of Chicago Press, 1990), 105.

article in a professional journal with volume number

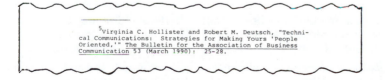

[5]Virginia C. Hollister and Robert M. Deutsch, "Technical Communications: Strategies for Making Yours 'People Oriented,'" The Bulletin for the Association of Business Communication 53 (March 1990): 25-28.

magazine article with author

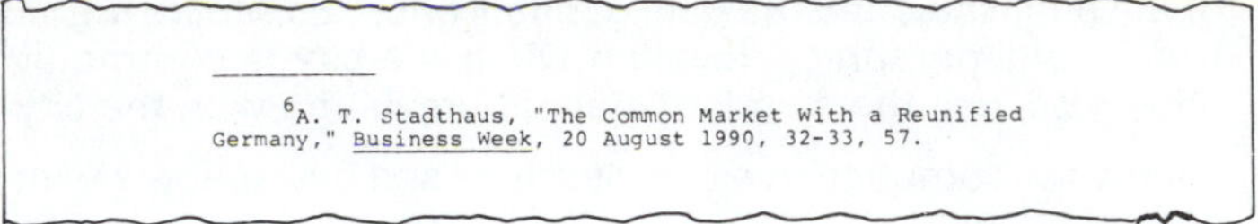

[6]A. T. Stadthaus, "The Common Market With a Reunified Germany," Business Week, 20 August 1990, 32-33, 57.

magazine article without author

[7]"The Declining Dollar in Our International Economy," Changing Times, December 1989, 40-42.

newspaper article with author

[8]Richard A. Donnelly, "Commodities Corner," Los Angeles Times, 10 November 1990, San Fernando Valley edition, sec. D, p. 6, cols. 3-4.

government publication

[9]Statistical Abstract of the United States, U.S. Bureau of the Census (Washington, D.C.: U.S. Government Printing Office, 1992), 256.

unsigned encyclopedia article

12

[10]"Adams, John," The New Encyclopaedia Britannica, 15th ed. (Chicago: Encyclopaedia Britannica, Inc., 1989) 1:83-84.

Once a reference has been cited, a shortened form may be used when the same reference is shown again. These shortened forms—*Ibid., loc. cit.,* and *op. cit.*—are explained and illustrated in the following discussion.

Ibid. is used when the reference cited is identical to the one in the preceding footnote. If the reference source is the same but the page numbers differ, use *Ibid.* with appended page numbers.

Ibid.—identical reference

[3]Patricia Whitman, David Kane, James E. Wellington, and Ida Mason, Human Relations in the Office (New York: McGraw-Hill Book Company, 1989), 208-214.

[4]Ibid.

Ibid.—same reference but different page number(s)

[5]Mark T. Mathews, Managerial Psychology in a Global Economy (Chicago: University of Chicago Press, 1990), 105.

[6]Ibid., 134.

The notation *loc. cit.* means "in the place cited." It is used when the reference and the same page numbers have been previously cited but intervening citations have occurred.[3] Begin the citation with the last name of the author. For two authors separate the last names with *and;* for more than two authors, merely add *et al.* after the last name of the first author. Conclude the citation with *loc. cit.*

loc. cit.

[3]Patricia Whitman, David Kane, James E. Wellington, and Ida Mason, Human Relations in the Office (New York: McGraw-Hill Book Company, 1989), pp. 208-214.

[4]Ibid.

[5]Mark T. Mathews, Managerial Psychology in a Global Economy (Chicago: University of Chicago Press, 1990), p. 105.

[6]Ibid., pp. 134-135.

[7]Whitman et al., loc. cit.

12

The notation *op. cit.* (meaning "in the work cited") also refers to a previously cited reference, but different page numbers are being referenced and intervening references have occurred.[4] Begin the citation with the last name of the author. For two authors separate the last names with *and;* for more than two authors, merely add *et al.* after the last name of the first author. Conclude the citation with *op cit.* and the new page number(s).

[3]*The Chicago Manual of Style* recommends the use of shortened titles in place of the term *loc. cit.* Ibid., 489.

[4]*The Chicago Manual of Style* recommends the use of shortened titles in place of the term *op. cit.* Ibid.

op. cit.

[5]Mark T. Mathews, Managerial Psychology in a Global Economy (Chicago: University of Chicago Press, 1990), p. 105.

[6]Ibid., pp. 134-135.

[7]E. Bryant Phillips and Andrea Kessler, Principles of Management, 2nd ed. (New York: John Wiley & Sons, Inc., 1990), p. 108.

[8]Mathews, op. cit., p. 147.

b. Bibliographical notes

References to the bibliography may be used as alternatives to formal footnotes. The reference to the bibliography is shown in parentheses at the end of the cited material by referring first to the number of the reference in the bibliography followed by a colon and the page number(s) of the source. The complete source appears in the bibliography following the body of the paper (see Section 12–12).

bibliographical note

. . . Income has risen 16 percent during the last fiscal period. To offset this increased income, however, expenses have risen 21 percent over the same period. (6:10-11)

c. Endnotes

Another alternative to footnotes is endnotes. Endnotes are placed on a separate page at the end of the body of the report or at the end of each chapter in a long report. Use the following format for showing endnotes:

(1) Allow a 2-inch top margin. Type the heading *NOTES* in all capital letters centered directly below the top margin (line 13 for standard line spacing.)

(2) Triple-space after the heading. Single-space each note, but double-space between notes.

(3) Indent the first line of each note five spaces. Number the notes consecutively using Arabic numerals followed by a period and two spaces.

(4) Use the same format for endnotes as shown for footnotes in Section 12–10a. Number the page at the bottom, or omit (but count) the page number—select whichever style was used for the beginning pages of other major sections in the body of the report.

(5) Use a .5- or 1-inch top margin for any second and succeeding pages, depending upon the page numbering format selected. Be sure to follow the same format used for the body of the report.

endnotes page

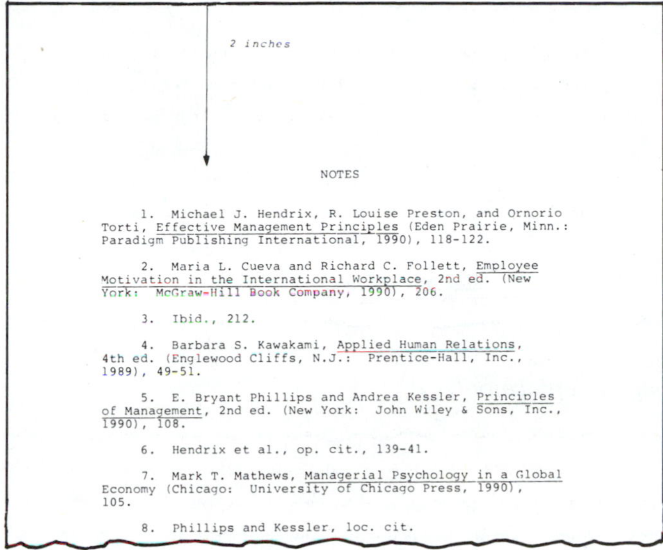

2 inches

NOTES

1. Michael J. Hendrix, R. Louise Preston, and Ornorio Torti, Effective Management Principles (Eden Prairie, Minn.: Paradigm Publishing International, 1990), 118-122.

2. Maria L. Cueva and Richard C. Follett, Employee Motivation in the International Workplace, 2nd ed. (New York: McGraw-Hill Book Company, 1990), 206.

3. Ibid., 212.

4. Barbara S. Kawakami, Applied Human Relations, 4th ed. (Englewood Cliffs, N.J.: Prentice-Hall, Inc., 1989), 49-51.

5. E. Bryant Phillips and Andrea Kessler, Principles of Management, 2nd ed. (New York: John Wiley & Sons, Inc., 1990), 108.

6. Hendrix et al., op. cit., 139-41.

7. Mark T. Mathews, Managerial Psychology in a Global Economy (Chicago: University of Chicago Press, 1990), 105.

8. Phillips and Kessler, loc. cit.

d. MLA referencing style[5]

Another method for citing sources is the MLA (Modern Language Association) style. In this style a short description of the source and the pertinent page number(s) appear in parentheses after the information to be cited. The main purpose of the parenthetical reference is to point the reader to a specific work in the Works Cited—the bibliography.

Common practice for citing the reference to a source is to include the last name of the author or authors. If the work has more than three authors, use only the first author's last name followed by *et al.* with no intervening punctuation, e.g., Greenburg et al. If a work has no author listed, begin the citation with the title of the work or a shortened version of the title, e.g., Employment Trends in Manufacturing.

Follow the author or title reference with relevant page number(s), and place the citation in parentheses directly after the referenced material. Examples of such references would be (Greenburg et al. 113) and (Employment Trends in Manufacturing 65-67).

If the author(s) or source is named in the context of the text, include only the page number(s) in the citation.

A full description of all cited sources is given in the Works Cited, the MLA version of a bibliography.

12

[5]For a complete discussion of the preparation of reports and manuscripts according to the MLA style, consult Joseph Gibaldi and Walter S. Achtert, *MLA Handbook for Writers of Research Papers,* 3rd ed. (New York: The Modern Language Association of America, 1988).

MLA referencing style

According to recent surveys, investment in personal computers continues to be a major investment item for United States corporations. Advancements in technology have forced corporations to update continually with hopes of obtaining a competitive edge. (McAllister and Doyle 32). Between now and 1995 corporations will spend between $20 billion and $25 billion on personal computers and their peripherals (U.S. News and International Report 114).

MLA page reference only

According to McAllister and Doyle (32), investment in personal computers continues to be a major investment item for United States corporations. Advancements in technology have forced corporations to update continually with hopes of obtaining a competitive edge. Between now and 1995, as reported in U.S. News and International Report, corporations will spend between $20 billion and $25 billion on personal computers and their peripherals (114).

e. APA referencing style[6]

Another method for citing sources is the APA (American Psychological Association) style. In this style a short description of the source, the year of publication, and the pertinent page number(s) appear in parentheses after the information to be cited. Each of these items is separated by a comma. The main purpose of the parenthetical reference is to point the reader to a specific work in the reference list—the bibliography.

Common practice for citing the reference to a source is to begin the citation with the last name of the author. If a source has two authors, cite both authors' last names each time the source is referenced. For sources with three to six authors, cite each author's last name in the first reference; additional references require only the first author's last name followed by *et al.* Join the names in a multiple-author citation with an ampersand (&) instead of the word *and* when they appear in parentheses or in the reference list, e.g., (Hendrix, Preston & Torti, 1990, pp. 110–113).

[6]For a complete discussion of the preparation of reports and manuscripts according to the APA style, consult *Publication Manual of the American Psychological Association,* 3rd ed. (Washington, D.C.: American Psychological Association, 1984).

If a work has no author listed, begin the citation with the first two or three words of the entry in the reference list—usually the title of the work. Use quotation marks around titles of articles or chapters; underline the names of books or magazines, e.g., (Employment Trends, 1989, pp. 65–67).

Follow the author or title reference with the date of publication and any relevant page number(s). Additional examples of such references would be (Greenburg et al., 1989, p. 113) and ("Marketing Aspects," 1989, pp. 87–88).

If the author(s) or source is named in the context of the text, include only the date of publication and any applicable page numbers in the citation.

A full description of all cited sources is given in the reference list, the APA version of a bibliography.

APA referencing style

According to recent surveys, investment in personal computers continues to be a major investment item for United States corporations. Advancements in technology have forced corporations to update continually with hopes of obtaining a competitive edge. (McAllister & Doyle, 1990, p. 32). Between now and 1995 corporations will spend between $20 billion and $25 billion on personal computers and their peripherals (U.S. News, 1990, p. 114).

APA year and page reference only

According to McAllister and Doyle (1990, p. 32), investment in personal computers continues to be a major investment item for United States corporations. Advancements in technology have forced corporations to update continually with hopes of obtaining a competitive edge. Between now and 1995, as reported in U.S. News and International Report, corporations will spend between $20 billion and $25 billion on personal computers and their peripherals (1990, p. 114).

12–11. Illustrations

Visuals in the form of tables, pie charts, bar charts, or line charts may be used to illustrate data in a report. Where possible, a table or chart should appear on the same page as the narrative describing it. If there is insufficient space on the same page for the table or chart and its explanation, then the illustration should be placed on the following page. A statement such as "As shown in Table 3 on page 9, . . ." must be used in the narrative to direct the reader to the illustration. The type of illustration used will vary according to the kind of data presented; suggestions for preparing each type of illustration are provided here.

a. Tables

As shown in the illustration on page 341, either open tables or ruled tables may be used to arrange data in an orderly fashion by employing a system of headings and columns to present information. Although the length, style, and number of columns will vary according to the type of data presented, use the following general procedures to set up tables:

(1) Leave two blank lines before and after a table if it does not appear on a separate page. (Some authorities prefer three blank lines before and after the table; be consistent in the use of whichever of the two formats you choose.)

(2) If more than one table appears in the report, number each table consecutively with Arabic numerals. Center *Table* and its corresponding number over the proposed position of the table.

(3) Double-space, and then center under the table number the title of the table; use all capital letters. If a secondary title is needed, center and use capital and lowercase letters for this subtitle, placing it a double-space below the main title. Triple-space after the final line of either the main title or the subtitle.

(4) Determine the longest line in each column; take into consideration the column headings and the column entries. Also determine the amount of space or number of spaces to be left between the longest line of each column. Center the entire table between the left and right margins of the report or manuscript.

(5) Type columnar headings in capital and lowercase letters and underline the last line of the heading. Double-space after the last line in the columnar headings.

(6) For typewritten copy center headings and tabular columns horizontally using either the back-space or arithmetic method of horizontal centering. On word processing equipment use setup lines or specialized functions to center tabular headings and columns horizontally. Set tab stops appropriate for the method of entry used and type the table.

(7) A table appearing on a separate page should be centered vertically as well as horizontally.

an open table

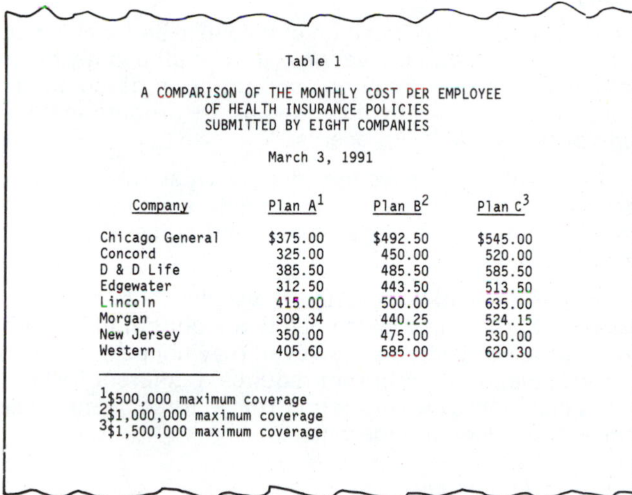

Table 1

A COMPARISON OF THE MONTHLY COST PER EMPLOYEE
OF HEALTH INSURANCE POLICIES
SUBMITTED BY EIGHT COMPANIES

March 3, 1991

Company	Plan A[1]	Plan B[2]	Plan C[3]
Chicago General	$375.00	$492.50	$545.00
Concord	325.00	450.00	520.00
D & D Life	385.50	485.50	585.50
Edgewater	312.50	443.50	513.50
Lincoln	415.00	500.00	635.00
Morgan	309.34	440.25	524.15
New Jersey	350.00	475.00	530.00
Western	405.60	585.00	620.30

[1]$500,000 maximum coverage
[2]$1,000,000 maximum coverage
[3]$1,500,000 maximum coverage

a ruled table

Table 1

A COMPARISON OF THE MONTHLY COST PER EMPLOYEE
OF HEALTH INSURANCE POLICIES
SUBMITTED BY EIGHT COMPANIES

March 3, 1991

Company	Plan A[1]	Plan B[2]	Plan C[3]
Chicago General	$375.00	$492.50	$545.00
Concord	325.00	450.00	520.00
D & D Life	385.50	485.50	585.50
Edgewater	312.50	443.50	513.50
Lincoln	415.00	500.00	635.00
Morgan	309.34	440.25	524.15
New Jersey	350.00	475.00	530.00
Western	405.60	585.00	620.30

[1]$500,000 maximum coverage
[2]$1,000,000 maximum coverage
[3]$1,500,000 maximum coverage

12

b. Pie charts

Pie charts are used to illustrate the parts of a whole when that whole represents 100 percent of something. They may be prepared manually or with a computer graphics program. To achieve maximum clarity in this type of visual, do not exceed seven or eight segments in the illustration. Notice how the example pie charts shown on pages 342 and 343 follow the guidelines outlined below.

(1) Begin the illustration approximately three blank spaces below the last line of type.

(2) Starting at the 12 o'clock position of the circle and moving clockwise, slice the pie in appropriate wedges, showing the largest wedge first. The remaining wedges may or may not be in descending order of size, but the size of each wedge should be proportional to the percentage of the whole it represents.

(3) If possible, within each wedge identify what it represents and its corresponding percentage. If the wedges are too small, place this information outside the circle and extend a line (if possible) to the appropriate wedge.

(4) Numbers and titles of pie charts are usually centered in capital and lowercase letters a triple space below the bottom of the chart. Computerized graphic programs, however, may not permit this format. In those cases where the program requires a different format, use the format dictated by the program. Leave three blank lines before resuming the typewritten narrative.

pie chart prepared manually

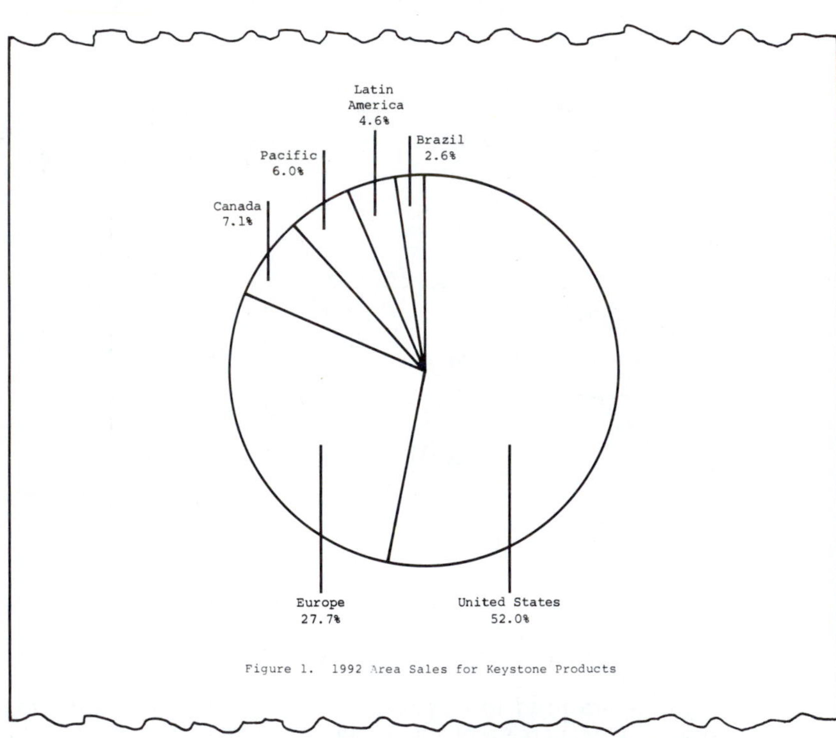

Figure 1. 1992 Area Sales for Keystone Products

pie chart prepared with computerized graphics program[7]

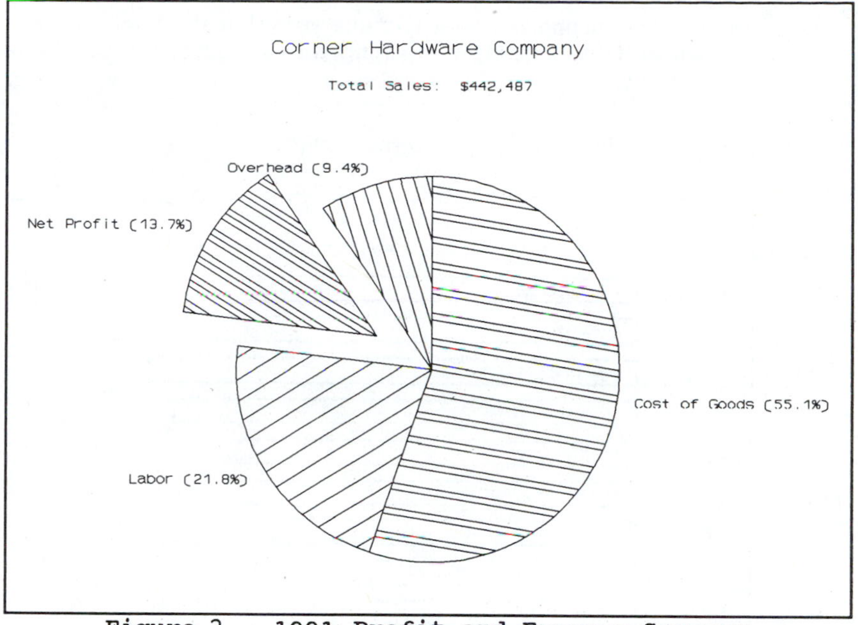

Figure 2. 1991 Profit and Expense Summary

c. Bar charts

Bar charts are used to compare quantities within a class or over a time period. They may be illustrated either horizontally or vertically, as shown in Figures 3, 4, 5, and 6 on pages 344 through 347. Bar charts may be prepared either manually or with computer graphic programs. Use the following procedures for constructing bar graphs:

(1) Leave three blank lines before and after a bar chart when it interrupts the narrative.

(2) Bar charts require both a vertical axis and a horizontal axis. One axis represents the quantity and the other represents the varying items in the class or the time period over which the quantities are measured.

(3) In constructing horizontal bar charts, the horizontal axis is used to represent the different quantities for each variable or time period; the vertical axis represents the variable or time period. Each axis must be labeled clearly.

(4) For vertical bar charts use the vertical axis to represent the different amounts for each variable or time period; use the horizontal axis to

[7]This graphic was prepared with Lotus 1-2-3 and imported into WordPerfect. It was printed on a LaserJet Series II printer.

represent the variables or time periods. Be sure to label both axes clearly.

(5) In constructing bar charts, make sure that the bars are of uniform width. If the bars are not touching, they should be placed equidistantly in the chart.

a horizontal bar chart prepared manually

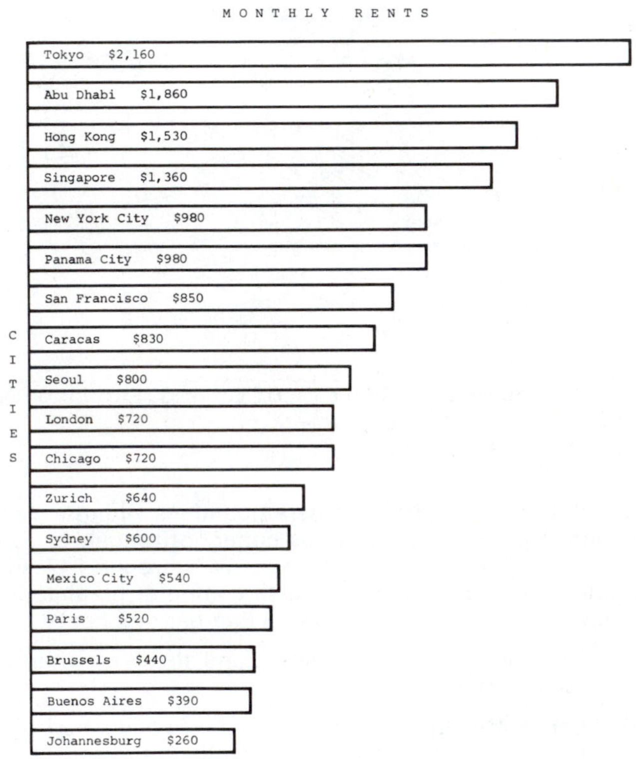

MONTHLY RENTS

CITIES

Tokyo $2,160

Abu Dhabi $1,860

Hong Kong $1,530

Singapore $1,360

New York City $980

Panama City $980

San Francisco $850

Caracas $830

Seoul $800

London $720

Chicago $720

Zurich $640

Sydney $600

Mexico City $540

Paris $520

Brussels $440

Buenos Aires $390

Johannesburg $260

Figure 3. Monthly Rents for Medium-Priced, One-Bedroom Unfurnished Apartments in Major Cities--1991

Source: Union Bank of Switzerland

a vertical bar chart prepared manually

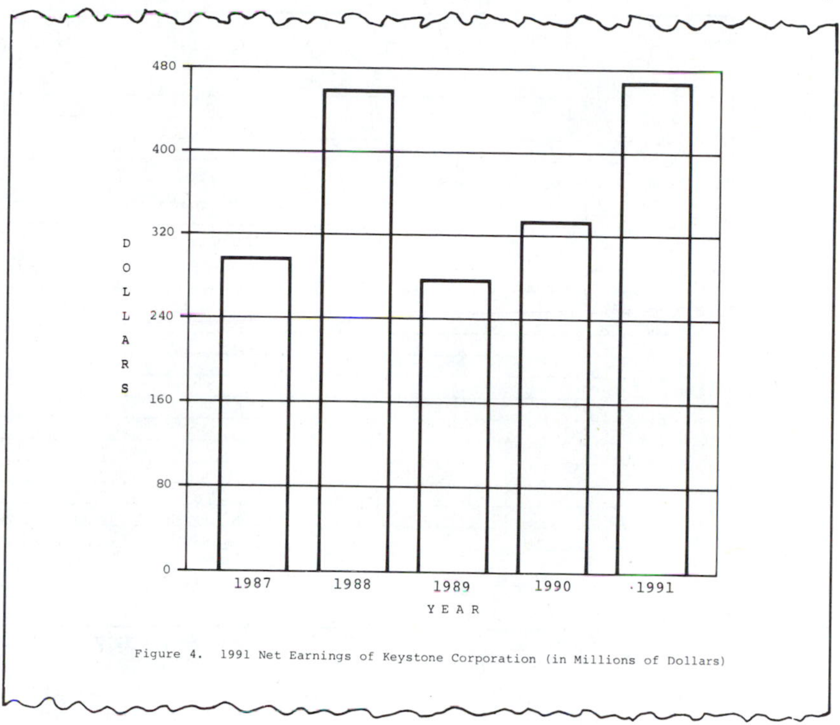

Figure 4. 1991 Net Earnings of Keystone Corporation (in Millions of Dollars)

(6) Numbers and titles of bar charts are centered a triple space below the last line of the chart. Capitalize the main words in the title. Computerized graphic programs, however, may not permit this format. In those cases where the program requires a different format, use the format dictated by the program.

d. Line charts

Line charts are used to illustrate movement or trends over a time period. They may also be used to compare two or more sets of data over a time period. As with pie and bar charts, these graphics may be prepared manually or with computer graphics programs. Study Figures 7 and 8 on pages 347 and 348 to see how the following guidelines were used to construct these line charts:

(1) Leave three blank lines before and after a line chart that interrupts text.

(2) At the left of the line chart, use a straight vertical line to portray the quantity scale. The bottom of the scale represents the lowest quantity, and the top of the scale represents the largest quantity. At the bottom

a vertical bar chart prepared with a computer graphics program[8]

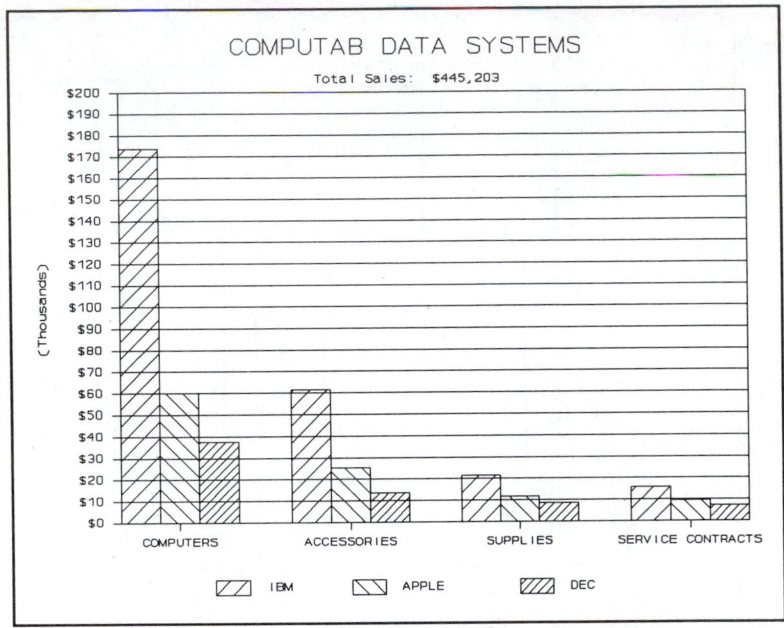

Figure 5. May 1990 Sales Summary

of the vertical line, place at right angles a horizontal line that extends to the right side of the line chart. This horizontal line represents the time periods encompassed by the chart. Each quantity and time period should be marked equidistantly on its respective scale.

(3) Quantities should be plotted above the time period indicated, and these quantities should be connected with a line. When two or more factors are plotted on the same graph, a different color or line style must be used for each set of data.

(4) Numbers and titles of line charts are centered a triple space below the last line contained in the chart, and all main words in the title are capitalized. Computerized graphic programs, however, may not permit this format. In those cases where the program requires a different format, use the format dictated by the program.

12

[8]This graphic was prepared with Lotus 1-2-3 and imported into WordPerfect. It was printed on a LaserJet Series II printer.

a stacked bar chart prepared with a computer graphics program[9]

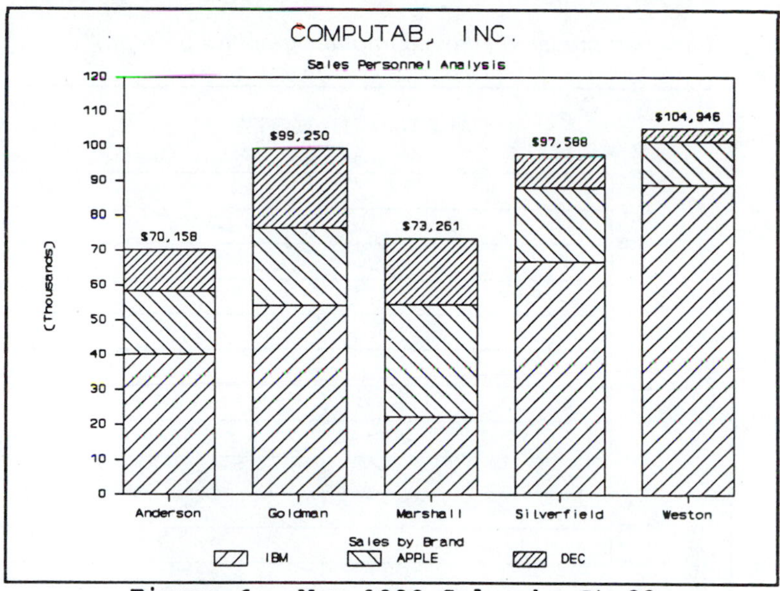

Figure 6. May 1990 Sales by Staff

a line chart prepared manually

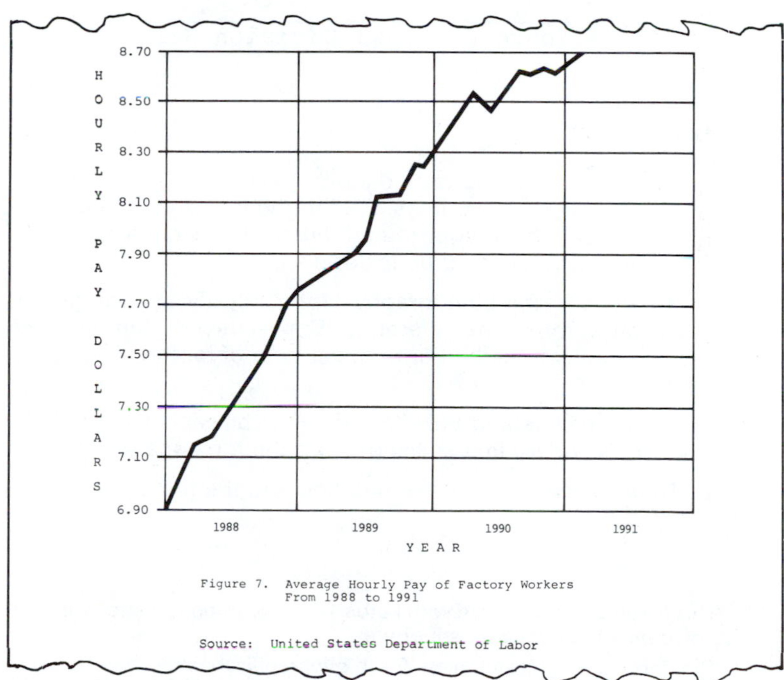

Figure 7. Average Hourly Pay of Factory Workers From 1988 to 1991

Source: United States Department of Labor

---

[9]This graphic was prepared with Lotus 1-2-3 and imported into WordPerfect. It was printed on a LaserJet Series II printer.

a line chart prepared with a computer graphics program[10]

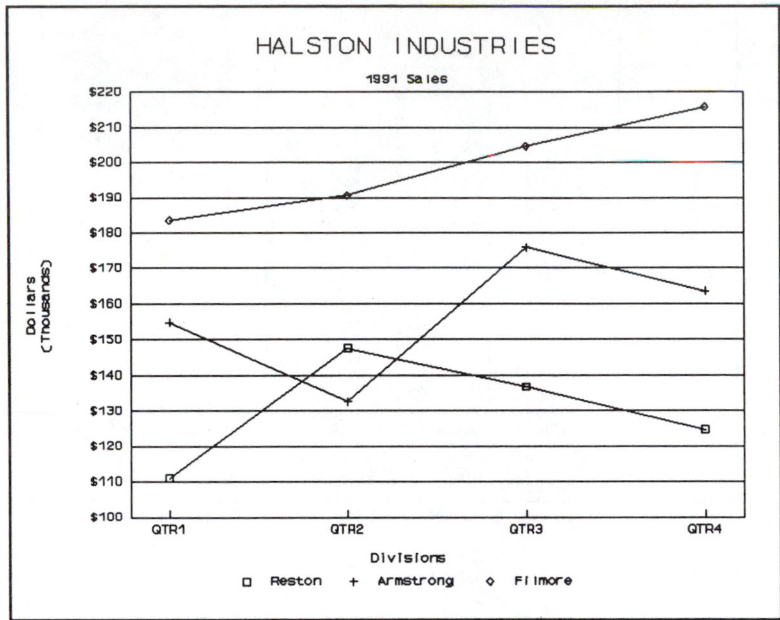

Figure 8. 1991 Division Sales

12–12. Bibliography[11]

a. The bibliography follows immediately after the body of the report or manuscript and contains all sources cited in the text. Any source material that is not cited but that has contributed directly to the development of a report or manuscript should also be included.

b. List the items in the bibliography alphabetically by authors' last names or the first entry of the reference. Consecutively number each item in the bibliography if the bibliographical form of footnoting is used (Section 12–10b).

12

(1) Center the heading *BIBLIOGRAPHY* in all capital letters 2 inches (line 13 for standard line spacing) from the top edge of the page.

(2) Triple-space between the heading and the first reference.

---

[10]This graphic was prepared with Lotus 1-2-3 and imported into WordPerfect. It was printed on a LaserJet Series II printer.

[11]The formats suggested here for bibliographical references (except for noted deviations) are based on the traditional format alternatives contained in *The Chicago Manual of Style,* 13th ed. (Chicago and London: The University of Chicago Press, 1982), 399–483.

(3) Single-space each reference and double-space between references. If a reference requires more than one line, indent the second and succeeding lines five spaces.

(4) If an author has more than one reference listed, type a five-space underline in place of his or her name, starting with the second reference.

(5) When the author is unknown, alphabetize the reference by title.

(6) End the references for magazine, journal, or other such source articles with page references.

unsigned encyclopedia article

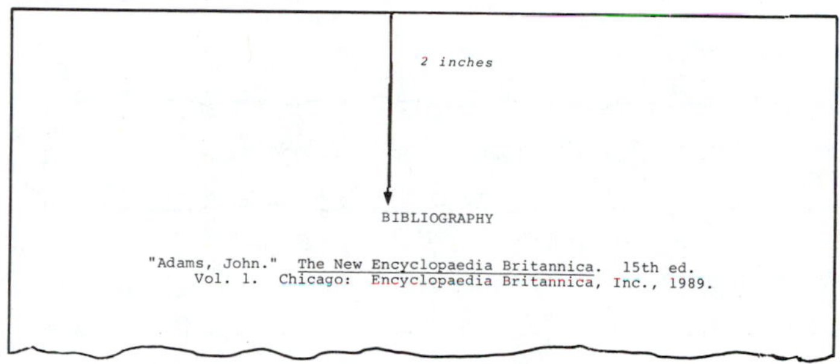

"Adams, John." The New Encyclopaedia Britannica. 15th ed. Vol. 1. Chicago: Encyclopaedia Britannica, Inc., 1989.

newspaper column with author

Doran, Lawrence J. "Computer File." Los Angeles Times, 17 May 1990.

magazine article with author

Drew, Richard. "Multinational Corporations in the International Marketplace." Business Week, 17 August 1991, 78-80.

magazine article without author

"Electronic Games Still the No. 1 Toy." Consumer Reports, March 1990, 47-51.

article in a professional journal with volume number

Hollister, Virginia C., and Robert M. Deutsch. "Technical Communications: Strategies for Making Yours 'People Oriented.'" The Bulletin for the Association of Business Communication 53 (March 1990): 25-28.

signed encyclopedia article

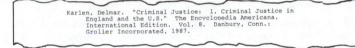

Karlen, Delmar. "Criminal Justice: 1. Criminal Justice in England and the U.S." The Encyclopedia Americana. International Edition. Vol. 8. Danbury, Conn.: Grolier Incorporated, 1987.

paperback book

Larson, Harold G. Managerial Psychology. 5th ed. Chicago: University of Chicago Press, 1991.

book, one author

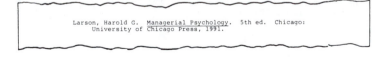

Morrison, Alice T. Microcomputers: Introductory Concepts and Applications. 2nd ed. Boston: PWS-KENT Publishing Company, 1991.

book, same author

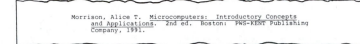

_____. Microcomputers: Business and Accounting Spreadsheet Applications. Boston: PWS-KENT Publishing Company, 1990.

book, two authors

Patterson, L. David, and Kathryn Lim. Principles of Real Estate. 3rd ed. New York: John Wiley & Sons, Inc., 1989.

book, three or more authors

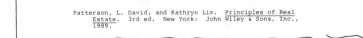

Rodriguez, Rose P., Charles T. Bove, and Saad Najjar. Fundamentals of Accounting. 2nd ed. Pittsfield, Mass.: The Financial Press, 1989.

government publication

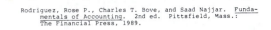

Statistical Abstract of the United States. U.S. Bureau of the Census. Washington, D.C.: U.S. Government Printing Office, 1991.

c. Reports prepared according to the MLA (Modern Language Association) style title the bibliography Works Cited.[12] References are listed alphabetically as in any other bibliography. Specific formats follow:

(1) Place the title Works Cited 1 inch from the top edge of the page; number the page in the upper right corner, .5 inch from the top edge and pivoted (back-spaced) from the right margin.

(2) Double-space after the heading, and double-space within and between the entries. Begin each entry at the left margin, but indent any subsequent lines 5 spaces from the left margin.

Works Cited—MLA bibliographical style

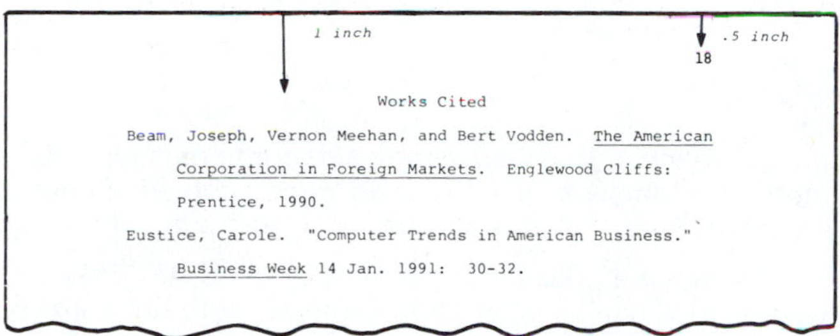

Works Cited

Beam, Joseph, Vernon Meehan, and Bert Vodden. The American Corporation in Foreign Markets. Englewood Cliffs: Prentice, 1990.

Eustice, Carole. "Computer Trends in American Business." Business Week 14 Jan. 1991: 30-32.

d. Reports prepared according to the APA (American Psychological Association) style refer to the bibliography as a *reference list.*[13] References are listed alphabetically as in any other bibliography. Specific formats follow:

(1) Begin the reference list on a new page, and place the title References 1.5 inches from the top edge of the page (use 1.5-inch top, bottom, left, and right margins). Number all pages of the reference list in the upper right corner, 1 inch from the top edge and pivoted (back-spaced) from the right margin. Place a shortened version of the title of the report a double space above the page number, pivoted from the right margin.

(2) Double-space after the heading, and double-space within and between the entries. Begin each entry at the left margin, but indent any subsequent lines 3 spaces from the left margin.

12

[12]For a complete discussion of arrangements and formats for the Works Cited according to the MLA style, consult the *MLA Handbook for Writers of Research Papers.* Gibaldi and Achtert, op. cit., 86–202.

[13]For a complete discussion of arrangements and formats for the reference list according to the APA style, consult the *Publication Manual of the American Psychological Association. Publication Manual,* op. cit., 111–156.

reference list—APA bibliographical style

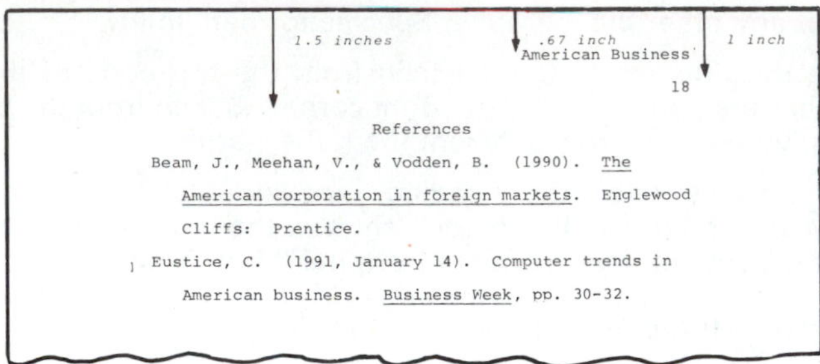

References

Beam, J., Meehan, V., & Vodden, B. (1990). The American corporation in foreign markets. Englewood Cliffs: Prentice.

Eustice, C. (1991, January 14). Computer trends in American business. Business Week, pp. 30-32.

12–13. Appendix

a. The appendix follows the bibliography and contains supportive material. This material may include such items as letters, copies of questionnaires, maps, contracts, lists, tables, and other documents not shown elsewhere.

b. The appendix may be preceded by a page entitled *APPENDIX* or *APPENDIXES* (typed in all capital letters and centered both horizontally and vertically). The introductory page may also include a list of the items contained in the appendix. In this case (1) both the title and the listing are centered vertically or (2) the title is placed 2 inches from the top edge of the page with the listing beginning a triple space thereafter. The material should be numbered with alphabetic letters if more than one item appears in the appendix.

introductory appendix page

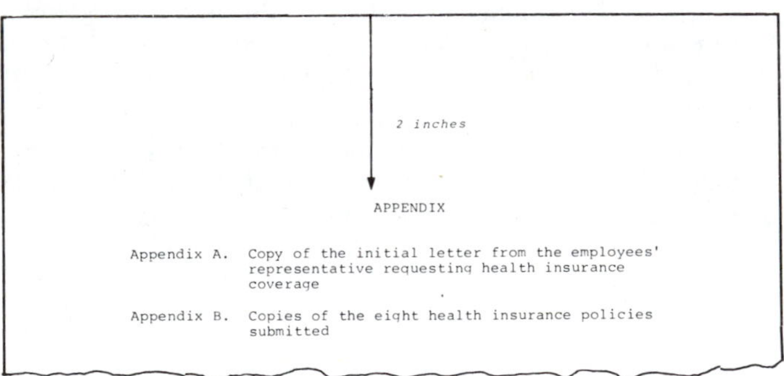

APPENDIX

Appendix A. Copy of the initial letter from the employees' representative requesting health insurance coverage

Appendix B. Copies of the eight health insurance policies submitted

12

Meeting Minutes

12–14. Purpose and Contents

Minutes are compiled to provide a written record of announcements, reports, significant discussions, and decisions that have taken place during a meeting. Although the degree of formality and extent of coverage may vary, the specific information contained in meeting minutes usually includes the following:

(1) Name of group and meeting

(2) Date, place, time meeting called to order, and time of adjournment

(3) Names of persons present (if applicable, names of persons absent)

(4) Disposition of any previous minutes

(5) Announcements

(6) Summaries of reports

(7) Motions presented and actions taken on motions

(8) Summaries of significant discussions

(9) Name and signature of person compiling minutes

12–15. Organization and Format of Formal Minutes

a. Use 8½- by 11-inch white bond paper, and set the typewriter or computer margins for a 6-inch line. Begin typing and center the name of the group and/or meeting in all capital letters on the line following a 2-inch top margin (line 13 for standard line spacing). Double-space down; then center in capital and lowercase letters the date and scheduled time of the meeting. The place where the meeting was held appears another double space below the time and date. This information, too, is centered in capital and lowercase letters. See page 255 for an illustration of the heading format for meeting minutes.

b. A listing of those persons attending the meeting follows the preliminary information. This listing is typed a triple space below the meeting place. Begin the listing with a phrase such as *Members Present:*, *Managers Present:*, or *Persons Present:*. Then list horizontally or vertically the names of the individuals present at the meeting in the order of their importance or in alphabetical order.

In addition to showing the members or persons in attendance, those regular members absent from a meeting may be noted. In this case a separate listing appears a double space below the listing of members present. It is usually preceded by *Members Absent:*, *Persons Absent:*, or another such designation. Examples of vertical attendance listings appear on page 255.

c. The initial paragraph of the meeting minutes appears a triple space below the attendance listing or listings. It generally begins with a statement giving the exact time the meeting was called to order and by whom. This statement is usually followed by a discussion of the dispensation of any previous minutes.

d. If there were any announcements, these are listed after the opening paragraph. Use a side heading to introduce the announcements, allowing two blank lines above the heading and one blank line below it. Then number and list each announcement made. If only one announcement occurred, show it in paragraph form without a number.

e. Most meeting agendas are organized according to old business and new business. These two categories may be used for topic headings (use side headings) in presenting the motions and discussions that have taken place during short meetings. For lengthy meetings, however, readers can more easily locate information in the minutes if the topic headings describe concretely the subject matter discussed, reported, or voted upon.

f. Reports presented at a meeting should be noted and in some cases summarized. The amount of information provided in the minutes will depend upon their purpose, formality, and use. Include with the reference to the report contents the name of the person giving the report as well as its disposition.

g. The exact wording of motions must be given in the meeting minutes. Persons making and seconding the motions may be named in the motion statement. Include a brief summary of the discussion for each motion. Finally, indicate whether the motion was passed, defeated, or tabled. The number of yeses, noes, and abstentions for each motion should be recorded.

h. If the meeting is not concluded with a motion for adjournment, the secretary preparing the minutes should indicate the time the meeting was adjourned and by whom. This information is placed in the concluding paragraph of the meeting minutes.

i. The typed signature of the person preparing the minutes usually appears on the fourth line below the concluding paragraph. It may be typed at the left margin or begun at the page center. The preparer's signature is placed directly above the typed signature line.

   The complimentary closing *Respectfully submitted* may precede the signature line. In this case the entire signature block simulates the signature block of a business letter. Place *Respectfully submitted,* a double space below the concluding paragraph, and leave three blank lines for the written signature before typing the preparer's name.

   This style of signature block may also begin at the left margin or page center.

   The major components of formal meeting minutes are illustrated in the following example on pages 355 to 358.

formal meeting minutes

STATE MUTUAL LIFE INSURANCE COMPANY
MINUTES, MONTHLY MEETING OF HOME OFFICE DEPARTMENT MANAGERS

April 11, 1991, 2 p.m.

Room 625, State Mutual Building

Officers Present: Louise Brannon, Agency Accounting
Robert Childress, Legal
Anthony Coletta, Claims
Phillip Horowitz, Personnel
Vern Knudsen, Vice President, Operations
Gaylord Martin, Policy Issue
Robert Miles, Actuarial
Wayne Nugent, Data Processing
Doris Penrose, Investments
George Ross, Treasurer
Dwayne Schramm, Central Records
Fred Wyatt, Finance

Officers Absent: Neil Tsutsui, Group Insurance
Diane Zimmerman, Public Relations

The meeting was called to order at 2:05 p.m. by Vern Knudsen. Minutes from the previous meeting held on March 14, 1991, were read and approved.

Announcements

1. Effective June 1 Anthony Coletta will assume the position of administrative assistant to the vice president of operations. This new position has been created because of the increased workload within the last three years in the home office. John Davis, the present assistant manager of the Claims Department, will assume the role of manager on June 1.

2. Two new State Mutual agencies will be opened on July 1. The Chadwick Agency (located in Fort Worth, Texas) will become Agency No. 137, and Graff & Phelps (located in Salem, Oregon) will become Agency No. 138. Marian Rosetti in Agency Accounting will coordinate the opening of these agencies.

3. The employees' cafeteria will be closed from May 16 through May 25 for renovation. It will be enlarged to accommodate 100 more people. This renovation should help to ease the overcrowded conditions we are now experiencing. Barring any unforeseen circumstances, the cafeteria will reopen on May 26. All department managers are requested to inform their staffs of this temporary shutdown.

formal meeting minutes (continued)

2

Financial Report for Period Ending March 31, 1991

George Ross distributed copies of the financial report for the first quarter of 1991. He pointed out that overall life insurance sales had increased nearly 8 percent over the same period for last year. The greatest increase in sales had taken place in the Southwest, mainly in New Mexico, Nevada, and Arizona. Sharp declines, however, were noticeable in the Eastern Seaboard area; namely, in states such as Connecticut, Rhode Island, and Massachusetts. These kinds of regional differences have not been so apparent in previous years.

Claims for the period from January 1 to March 31, 1991, increased 6 percent over the same period for last year. This rise has been assessed to be within the statistical projection based on sales and volume presently carried by the company.

Income from other sources has risen 4 percent over the last comparable period. Operational expenses during the first quarter have increased 12 percent, mainly because of rising prices due to inflationary factors. Net operations income, consequently, for this period has decreased 0.5 percent over the same period for last year.

Progress Report, Central Records Microfilm Conversion

Dwayne Schramm reported that a committee had been formed of representatives from those departments that use or store records in the Central Filing Department. These representatives met to discuss which records could be placed on microfilm and which ones should be retained in their present form. Those records referred to frequently and those that are current (within the last year) will be retained in their original form. The committee also decided that records dated prior to May 31, 1990, needed to be analyzed individually to determine which ones should be microfilmed.

Each department was given a list of records presently maintained by the Central Filing Department. Departmental representatives were asked to survey their respective departments to determine which of the listed records were used. The representative is to note those records used, the purpose and frequency of their use, and by whom they are used. On the basis of this information, individual decisions will be made by subcommittees to determine the precise time line for microfilming each kind of stored data.

Microfilm readers must be purchased, and the cost of these readers is $738 each. Viewers may be placed in individual departments or centralized in the Central Filing Department. Capital investment in equipment would be reduced considerably by centralizing the viewers in the Central Filing Department; however, additional time would be lost by persons using the equipment if the viewers were isolated there.

Louise Brannon moved that a microfilm viewer be placed in those departments that frequently use microfilm records and have the space in which to place the viewer. Viewers should also be placed in the Central Filing Department for those departments that do not need direct access to them. The motion was seconded by Robert Miles.

formal meeting minutes (continued)

In the discussion that followed, most of the department managers agreed that too much time would be lost in traveling to and from the Central Filing Department if viewers were placed exclusively in that area. It was pointed out, however, by other managers that the additional cost associated with purchasing viewers for individual departments would be an excessive capital outlay. Also, the premium space required for each viewer is not always available. The motion was passed 8-2-0.

Revision of Employee Dress Code

Phillip Horowitz reported that a number of employees are concerned about our present dress code. They believe the present code reflects last decade's styles and has not been updated to incorporate new fashion trends. Basically, these employees feel that smartly styled, well-pressed jeans should be permissible attire for women employees.

At present the only pants allowed for women employees are pantsuits with matching jackets. These employees maintain that pantsuits are no longer stylish and are sold in few stores. Jeans with coordinating tops have replaced the traditional pantsuit they argue, and therefore the present dress policy should be revised.

The department managers expressed concern over revising the dress standards to include jeans. Many indicated that jeans are not appropriate in an office situation because they are too casual. Also, it would be difficult to control their condition, i.e., fadedness and wrinkled appearance.

Gaylord Martin moved that the present dress policy be retained and that jeans not be allowed as acceptable attire for women employees. Doris Penrose seconded the motion. The motion was passed 10-0-0.

Employment Freeze on Office Personnel

Phillip Horowitz reported that in February the company established a Word Processing Group to assist all departments with their written communications. Eight clerical employees plus a supervisor were hired to staff this group, which was placed under the direction of the Data Processing Department.

At the time the group was established, it was decided that the new positions created would be offset by the natural attrition of clerical persons within the company. In the cases where this natural attrition has occurred, the departments losing the positions have indicated that their function is being impaired. Phillip Horowitz recommended that this body appoint a committee to study the problem and determine if and where clerical positions may be eliminated or consolidated.

Wayne Nugent moved that a five-person committee be formed to study the work flow generated to the Word Processing Group and the effect of this delegation on the workloads in all affected departments. The committee is to be charged with making recommendations regarding the staff size

12

formal meeting minutes (continued)

4

of the Word Processing Group and the staff size of clerical employees in other departments. The motion was seconded by Fred Wyatt. It was passed 7-2-1.

Vern Knudsen appointed the following persons to the committee: Louise Brannon, Phillip Horowitz, Gaylord Martin, Neil Tsutsui, and Fred Wyatt.

The meeting was adjourned at 4:15 p.m. by Vern Knudsen. The next meeting of the department managers is scheduled for May 10 at 2 p.m. in Conference Room 621-A.

Respectfully submitted,

Chris Weiser, Secretary

kc

12–16. Organization and Format of Informal Minutes

The organization and format of informal minutes may vary. The only essential requisite is that the minutes provide an adequate record of the information needed by the group or organization and that this information be presented in an easy-to-understand fashion.

informal meeting minutes[14]

OFFICE ADMINISTRATION ADVISORY COMMITTEE
LOS ANGELES PIERCE COLLEGE
TUESDAY, APRIL 4, 1989
2 - 4 P.M., BUSINESS 3216

M I N U T E S

ACTIVITY/DISCUSSION	ISSUES RELATIVE/INFORMATION	RESOLUTION
Survey of Classrooms and Laboratories	Familiarization with the equipment presently being used.	Information only.
Language Skills	It was explained that the department has five (5) courses that meet requirements for the certificate programs. An additional course is required by the State for students completing the A.A. degree program. The committee emphasized the importance of language skills and how those skills relate to productive use of a computer.	Information only.
Equipment Training: Hardware Issues	The committee discussed the philosophy of acquiring IBM computers, clones, Apples, or a combination of vendors' models and equipment.	**MSP** to purchase IBM computers with hard disks. **MSP** to seek additional funding to acquire Macintosh computers.
	A discussion about printer usage in business indicated that laser printers are in heavy demand. While dot-matrix printers are appropriate for rough-draft copies, all final work is produced on laser printers. In addition, laser printers are required to produce output formatted with desktop publishing software.	**MSP** to acquire laser printers and fonts so that more sophisticated software can be taught; e.g., desktop publishing systems.
	The committee felt that students should understand the use of modems, facsimiles, and other telecommunicating equipment.	**MSP** that a modem and facsimile machine be purchased and incorporated into our courses.
Equipment Training: Software Issues	Several companies have changed to Microsoft Word software.	**MSP** that a course in Microsoft Word be implemented.
	A discussion was held concerning the philosophy of upgrading software versions in the business community.	Recommendation: Upgrade software as soon as possible.

[14]Format developed by K. Basil and Associates.

12

informal meeting minutes (continued)

Office Administration Advisory Committee
MINUTES - April 4, 1989
Page 2

	Knowing more than one software program enhances the students' job opportunities. For example, it is an advantage to the student if he or she has been trained in at least one word processing program, as well as a program in spreadsheet and/or data base.	Recommendation: Students should be exposed to graphics software.
Review of Legal Secretarial Program	The legal secretarial program was presented with an emphasis on the internship program, which is applicable to not only the legal major but also all the other majors in the Office Administration Department. Advisory committee members were invited to participate in the program by providing the on-site location for a student's internship.	Information only.
Job-Related Issues:	Entry-level salaries vary from location to location and from specialization to specialization. Students should be trained to be flexible in their expectations and to study the overall package that an employer offers. In our geographical area entry-level salaries range from $1,300 to $1,600 a month.	Information only.
	Shorthand continues to be a viable skill to seek promotion to the executive secretarial or administrative assistant level. Few employers ask for shorthand skill for an entry-level position, however.	Information only.
Recommendations for Future Meetings	Survey technology, software, and business trends by utilizing a questionnaire sent to advisory committee members prior to the meeting date.	Information only.

Submitted by: Kathy Basil, Professor
Office Administration Department

12

CHAPTER 13

Document Formats and Terminology in the Automated Office

Document Formats and Terminology in the Automated Office Solution Finder

Document Formats

Entries are listed in alphabetical order.

Document Formats

The unique features of computerized word processing programs enable business communicators to prepare documents more easily and efficiently. Because these programs are so diverse in their handling of format features, we can no longer rely on applying standard typewritten formats for margin settings. Other features of these programs too—such as word-wrap, automatic margin tops and bottoms, automatic line-ending hyphenation prompts, and pitch choices—require our looking at document formats specifically from a word processing perspective.

13–1. Single-Page Business Letters Prepared With 10-Pitch Print[1]

a. Set right-margin justification to "off."

b. For 8½- by 11-inch letterhead stationery, set a 2-inch top margin (12 standard blank lines) and a 1-inch bottom margin (6 standard blank lines).

c. Determine the left and right margins *OR* writing line length for your letter, depending upon the method used by your word processing program. Vary the margins or line length according to whether you are preparing short, medium, or long letters. Generally, letters are classified according to the number of words in the letter.

When preparing letters in 10-pitch print, keep in mind that there are 85 spaces across the page of a standard 8½- by 11-inch sheet of paper. Therefore, any margin or line-length settings must be centered within the 85 spaces to balance the letter horizontally.

Refer to Table 1 if your program uses margin settings. Margin settings are typically displayed in *inches* or *columns.* Programs using *inches* set the margins to reflect the amount of blank space from the left and right edges of the paper (e.g., 1.5″ and 1.5″). Those programs using *columns* set margins in one of two ways: (1) the left and right margin settings indicate the number of blank columns from the left and right edges of the paper (e.g., 15 and 15) or (2) the left and right margin settings indicate the column number from the left edge of the paper (e.g., 16 and 70).

Table 1
Margin Settings for One-Page Business Letters Printed in 10 Pitch

Letter Length	*Number of Words*	*Margin Settings in Inches*	*Margin Settings in Columns*
Short	Up to 100	2″ – 2″	20 – 20 or 21 – 65
Medium	100 – 200	1.5″ – 1.5″	15 – 15 or 16 – 70
Long	200 +	1″ – 1″	10 – 10 or 11 – 75

[1]See Chapter 11 for placement and format of letter and memorandum parts.

13

If your program uses ruler or format lines, refer to Table 2 to determine the line length and corresponding print or page offset for achieving even left and right margins. Settings are shown for both *inches* and *columns;* select the configuration your program uses.

Table 2
Ruler or Format Line Settings for One-Page Business Letters Printed in 10 Pitch

Letter Length	*Number of Words*	*Line Length*	*Blank Space(s) in Left Margin*	*Blank Space(s) in Right Margin*
Short	Up to 100	4.5 inches or 45 spaces	2 in. or 20 spaces	2 in. or 20 spaces
Medium	100–200	5.5 inches or 55 spaces	1.5 in. or 15 spaces	1.5 in. or 15 spaces
Long	200 +	6.5 inches or 65 spaces	1 in. or 10 spaces	1 in. or 10 spaces

d. Balance the letter vertically by regulating the number of lines between the date and the inside address. Use the following procedures to achieve this balance *after* the entire letter has been typed:

(1) Upon typing the *last* line of the letter (*usually* reference initials or an enclosure notation), press the ENTER/RETURN key until the page-break line or signal is reached.

(2) Count the number of returns (blank lines) from the last line of the letter until the page break; then count the number of returns (blank lines) between the date and the inside address. Total the two line counts, and divide this total by two. Disregard any fraction.

(3) Use deletion or insertion commands to ensure that the number of blank lines between the *date and the inside address* EQUALS the result obtained in Step (2) above. However, do not leave fewer than 2 or more than 12 blank lines between the date and the inside address. The letter will then be balanced vertically on the page.

See the examples of short, medium, and long letters prepared in 10-pitch print on pages 365, 366, and 367.

e. If your printer is set up for single-sheet feeding, prepare an envelope on the second page of the document. To address a standard No. 10 envelope that contains a printed return address, follow the procedures outlined here:

(1) Place your cursor at the beginning of page 2. *If possible,* change your page length or page format to accommodate the envelope length—4.13 inches or 25 lines.

(2) If your program uses *margin* settings, use one of the following—depending upon the margin configuration of your program:

4.3 inches and 1 inch or
Column 43 and Column 10 or
Column 43 and Column 75

(3) If your program uses *ruler or format lines,* retain the line set for the letter but change the page or print offset to 4.3 inches or Column 43,

short letter printed in 10 pitch

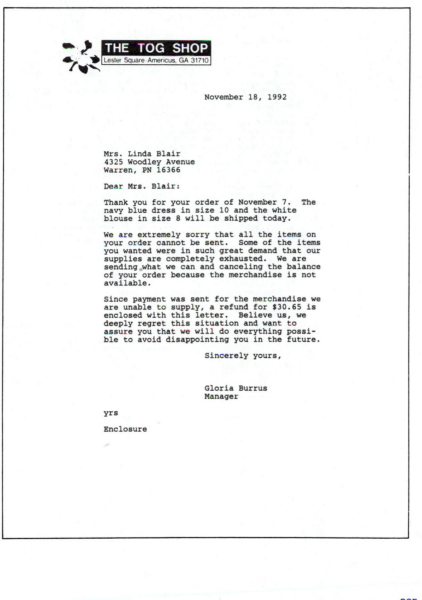

November 18, 1992

Mrs. Linda Blair
4325 Woodley Avenue
Warren, PN 16366

Dear Mrs. Blair:

Thank you for your order of November 7. The navy blue dress in size 10 and the white blouse in size 8 will be shipped today.

We are extremely sorry that all the items on your order cannot be sent. Some of the items you wanted were in such great demand that our supplies are completely exhausted. We are sending what we can and canceling the balance of your order because the merchandise is not available.

Since payment was sent for the merchandise we are unable to supply, a refund for $30.65 is enclosed with this letter. Believe us, we deeply regret this situation and want to assure you that we will do everything possi-ble to avoid disappointing you in the future.

Sincerely yours,

Gloria Burrus
Manager

yrs

Enclosure

medium letter printed in 10 pitch

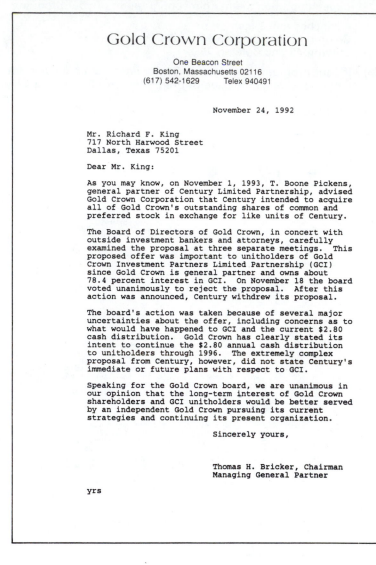

Gold Crown Corporation

One Beacon Street
Boston, Massachusetts 02116
(617) 542-1629 Telex 940491

November 24, 1992

Mr. Richard F. King
717 North Harwood Street
Dallas, Texas 75201

Dear Mr. King:

As you may know, on November 1, 1993, T. Boone Pickens, general partner of Century Limited Partnership, advised Gold Crown Corporation that Century intended to acquire all of Gold Crown's outstanding shares of common and preferred stock in exchange for like units of Century.

The Board of Directors of Gold Crown, in concert with outside investment bankers and attorneys, carefully examined the proposal at three separate meetings. This proposed offer was important to unitholders of Gold Crown Investment Partners Limited Partnership (GCI) since Gold Crown is general partner and owns about 78.4 percent interest in GCI. On November 18 the board voted unanimously to reject the proposal. After this action was announced, Century withdrew its proposal.

The board's action was taken because of several major uncertainties about the offer, including concerns as to what would have happened to GCI and the current $2.80 cash distribution. Gold Crown has clearly stated its intent to continue the $2.80 annual cash distribution to unitholders through 1996. The extremely complex proposal from Century, however, did not state Century's immediate or future plans with respect to GCI.

Speaking for the Gold Crown board, we are unanimous in our opinion that the long-term interest of Gold Crown shareholders and GCI unitholders would be better served by an independent Gold Crown pursuing its current strategies and continuing its present organization.

Sincerely yours,

Thomas H. Bricker, Chairman
Managing General Partner

yrs

one-page long letter printed in 10 pitch

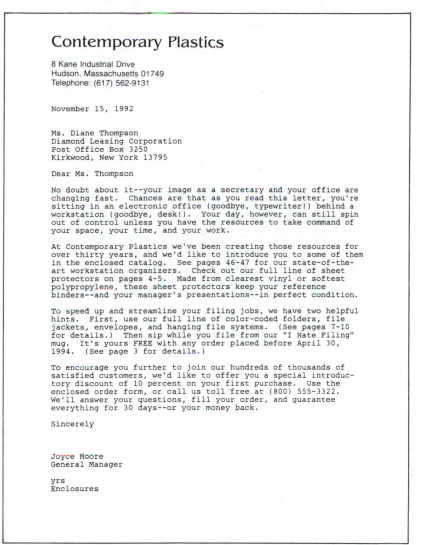

Contemporary Plastics

8 Kane Industrial Drive
Hudson, Massachusetts 01749
Telephone: (617) 562-9131

November 15, 1992

Ms. Diane Thompson
Diamond Leasing Corporation
Post Office Box 3250
Kirkwood, New York 13795

Dear Ms. Thompson

No doubt about it--your image as a secretary and your office are changing fast. Chances are that as you read this letter, you're sitting in an electronic office (goodbye, typewriter!) behind a workstation (goodbye, desk!). Your day, however, can still spin out of control unless you have the resources to take command of your space, your time, and your work.

At Contemporary Plastics we've been creating those resources for over thirty years, and we'd like to introduce you to some of them in the enclosed catalog. See pages 46-47 for our state-of-the-art workstation organizers. Check out our full line of sheet protectors on pages 4-5. Made from clearest vinyl or softest polypropylene, these sheet protectors keep your reference binders--and your manager's presentations--in perfect condition.

To speed up and streamline your filing jobs, we have two helpful hints. First, use our full line of color-coded folders, file jackets, envelopes, and hanging file systems. (See pages 7-10 for details.) Then sip while you file from our "I Hate Filing" mug. It's yours FREE with any order placed before April 30, 1994. (See page 3 for details.)

To encourage you further to join our hundreds of thousands of satisfied customers, we'd like to offer you a special introductory discount of 10 percent on your first purchase. Use the enclosed order form, or call us toll free at (800) 555-3322. We'll answer your questions, fill your order, and guarantee everything for 30 days--or your money back.

Sincerely

Joyce Moore
General Manager

yrs
Enclosures

depending upon your program configuration. For those programs that use ruler or format lines but do not permit variances in page or print offset within the same document (e.g., MultiMate), extend the format line for short and medium letters to 65 (6.5 inches). Set a tab at the following *inch* or *column* location to begin each line of the envelope address:

	Inch	*Column*
Short letter	2.3 in.	23
Medium letter	2.8 in.	28
Long letter	3.3 in.	33

(4) Use the copy command to copy the inside address of the letter to line 1 of the second page. The top margin of 2 inches (12 lines) set for the letter will position the address correctly on the envelope. Copy the inside address to the left margin—except for programs that use a format line and do not permit a change in the print or page offset. For programs that do not permit the print offset change, copy the inside address to one of the tab settings specified in Item (3).

13–2. Single-Page Business Letters Prepared With 12-Pitch Print

a. Set right-margin justification to "off."

b. For 8½- by 11-inch letterhead stationery, set a 2-inch top margin (12 standard blank lines) and a 1-inch bottom margin (6 standard blank lines).

c. Determine the left and right margins OR the writing line length for your letter, depending upon the method used by your word processing program. Vary the margins or line length according to whether you are preparing short, medium, or long letters. Generally, letters are classified according to the number of words in the body of the letter.

When preparing letters in 12-pitch print, keep in mind that there are 102 spaces across the page of a standard 8½- by 11-inch sheet of paper. Therefore, any margin or line-length settings must be centered within the 102 spaces to balance the letter horizontally.

Refer to Table 3, page 369, if your program uses margin settings. Margin settings are typically displayed in *inches* or *columns.* Programs using *inches* set the margins to reflect the amount of blank space from the left and right edges of the paper (e.g., 1.75" and 1.75"). Those programs using *columns* set margins in one of two ways: (1) the left and right margin settings indicate the number of blank columns from the left and right edges of the paper (e.g., 21 and 21) or (2) the left and right margin settings indicate the column number from the left edge of the paper (e.g., 22 and 81).

If your program uses ruler or format lines, refer to Table 4, page 369, to determine the line length and corresponding print or page offset for achieving even left and right margins. Settings are shown for both *inches* and *columns;* select the configuration your program uses.

Table 3
Margin Settings for One-Page Business Letters Printed in 12 Pitch

Letter Length	*Number of Words*	*Margin Settings in Inches*	*Margin Settings in Columns*
Short	Up to 100	2.25" – 2.25"	27 – 27 or 28 – 75
Medium	100 – 200	1.75" – 1.75"	21 – 21 or 22 – 81
Long	200 +	1.25" – 1.25"	15 – 15 or 16 – 87

Table 4
Ruler or Format Line Settings for One-Page Business Letters Printed in 12 Pitch

Letter Length	*Number of Words*	*Line Length*	*Blank Space(s) in Left Margin*	*Blank Space(s) in Right Margin*
Short	Up to 100	4 inches or 48 spaces	2.25 in. or 27 spaces	2.25 in. or 27 spaces
Medium	100–200	5 inches or 60 spaces	1.75 in. or 21 spaces	1.75 in. or 21 spaces
Long	200 +	6 inches or 72 spaces	1.25 in. or 15 spaces	1.25 in. or 15 spaces

d. Balance the letter vertically by regulating the number of lines between the date and the inside address. Use the following procedures to achieve this balance *after* the entire letter has been typed:

(1) Upon typing the *last* line of the letter (*usually* reference initials or an enclosure notation), press the ENTER/RETURN key until the page-break line or signal is reached.

(2) Count the number of returns (blank lines) from the last line of the letter until the page break; then count the number of returns (blank lines) between the date and the inside address. Total the two line counts, and divide this total by two. Disregard any fraction.

(3) Use deletion or insertion commands to ensure that the number of blank lines between the *date and the inside address* EQUALS the result obtained in Step (2) above. However, do not leave fewer than

13

2 or more than 12 blank lines between the date and the inside address. The letter will then be balanced vertically on the page.

See the examples of short, medium, and long letters prepared in 12-pitch print on pages 370, 371, and 372.

e. If your printer is set up for single-sheet feeding, prepare an envelope on the second page of the document. To address a standard No. 10 envelope that contains a printed return address, follow the procedures outlined here:

(1) Place your cursor at the beginning of page 2. *If possible,* change your page length or format to accommodate the envelope length—4.13 inches or 25 lines.

short letter printed in 12 pitch

THE TOG SHOP
Lester Square Americus, GA 31710

November 18, 1992

Mrs. Linda Blair
4325 Woodley Avenue
Warren, PN 16366

Dear Mrs. Blair:

Thank you for your order of November 7. The navy blue dress in size 10 and the white blouse in size 8 will be shipped today.

We are extremely sorry that all the items on your order cannot be sent. Some of the items you wanted were in such great demand that our supplies are completely exhausted. We are sending what we can and canceling the balance of your order because the merchandise is not available.

Since payment was sent for the merchandise we are unable to supply, a refund for $30.65 is enclosed with this letter. Believe us, we deeply regret this situation and want to assure you that we will do everything possible to avoid disappointing you in the future.

Sincerely yours,

Gloria Burrus
Manager

yrs

Enclosure

13

medium letter printed in 12 pitch

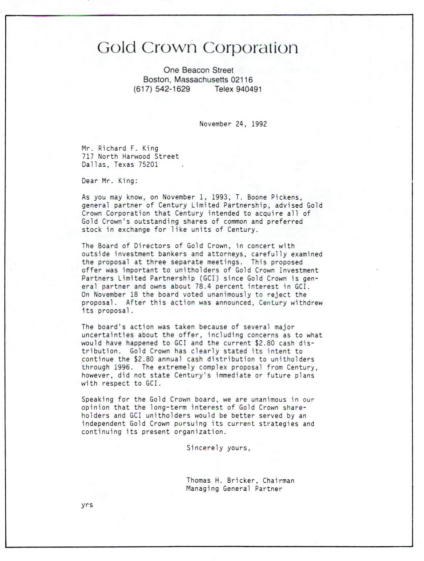

Gold Crown Corporation

One Beacon Street
Boston, Massachusetts 02116
(617) 542-1629 Telex 940491

November 24, 1992

Mr. Richard F. King
717 North Harwood Street
Dallas, Texas 75201

Dear Mr. King:

As you may know, on November 1, 1993, T. Boone Pickens, general partner of Century Limited Partnership, advised Gold Crown Corporation that Century intended to acquire all of Gold Crown's outstanding shares of common and preferred stock in exchange for like units of Century.

The Board of Directors of Gold Crown, in concert with outside investment bankers and attorneys, carefully examined the proposal at three separate meetings. This proposed offer was important to unitholders of Gold Crown Investment Partners Limited Partnership (GCI) since Gold Crown is general partner and owns about 78.4 percent interest in GCI. On November 18 the board voted unanimously to reject the proposal. After this action was announced, Century withdrew its proposal.

The board's action was taken because of several major uncertainties about the offer, including concerns as to what would have happened to GCI and the current $2.80 cash distribution. Gold Crown has clearly stated its intent to continue the $2.80 annual cash distribution to unitholders through 1996. The extremely complex proposal from Century, however, did not state Century's immediate or future plans with respect to GCI.

Speaking for the Gold Crown board, we are unanimous in our opinion that the long-term interest of Gold Crown shareholders and GCI unitholders would be better served by an independent Gold Crown pursuing its current strategies and continuing its present organization.

Sincerely yours,

Thomas H. Bricker, Chairman
Managing General Partner

yrs

one-page long letter printed in 12 pitch

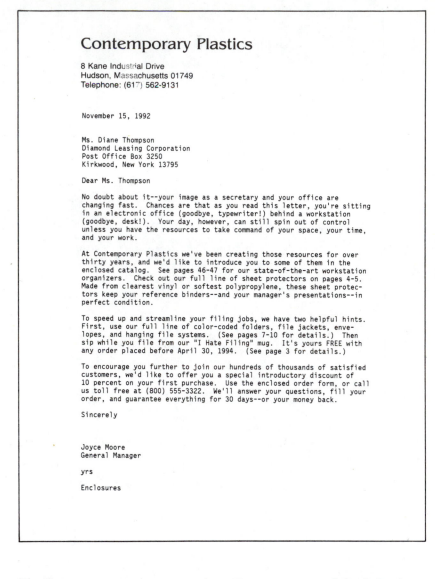

Contemporary Plastics

8 Kane Industrial Drive
Hudson, Massachusetts 01749
Telephone: (617) 562-9131

November 15, 1992

Ms. Diane Thompson
Diamond Leasing Corporation
Post Office Box 3250
Kirkwood, New York 13795

Dear Ms. Thompson

No doubt about it--your image as a secretary and your office are changing fast. Chances are that as you read this letter, you're sitting in an electronic office (goodbye, typewriter!) behind a workstation (goodbye, desk!). Your day, however, can still spin out of control unless you have the resources to take command of your space, your time, and your work.

At Contemporary Plastics we've been creating those resources for over thirty years, and we'd like to introduce you to some of them in the enclosed catalog. See pages 46-47 for our state-of-the-art workstation organizers. Check out our full line of sheet protectors on pages 4-5. Made from clearest vinyl or softest polypropylene, these sheet protectors keep your reference binders--and your manager's presentations--in perfect condition.

To speed up and streamline your filing jobs, we have two helpful hints. First, use our full line of color-coded folders, file jackets, envelopes, and hanging file systems. (See pages 7-10 for details.) Then sip while you file from our "I Hate Filing" mug. It's yours FREE with any order placed before April 30, 1994. (See page 3 for details.)

To encourage you further to join our hundreds of thousands of satisfied customers, we'd like to offer you a special introductory discount of 10 percent on your first purchase. Use the enclosed order form, or call us toll free at (800) 555-3322. We'll answer your questions, fill your order, and guarantee everything for 30 days--or your money back.

Sincerely

Joyce Moore
General Manager

yrs

Enclosures

13

(2) If your program uses *margin* settings, use one of the following—depending upon the margin configuration of your program:

4.25 inches and 1.25 inches or
Column 51 and Column 15 or
Column 51 and Column 87

(3) If your program uses *ruler or format lines,* retain the line set for the letter but change the page or print offset to 4.25 inches or Column

51, depending upon your program configuration. For those programs that use ruler or format lines but do not permit variances in page or print offset within the same document (e.g., MultiMate), extend the format line for short and medium letters to 72 (6 inches). Set a tab at the following *inch* or *column* locations to begin each line of the envelope address:

	Inch	*Column*
Short letter	2.0 in.	24
Medium letter	2.5 in.	30
Long letter	3.0 in.	36

(4) Use the copy command to copy the inside address of the letter to line 1 of the second page. The top margin of 2 inches (12 lines) set for the letter will position the address correctly on the envelope. Copy the inside address to the left margin—except for programs that use a format line and do not permit a change in the print or page offset. For programs that do not permit the print offset change, copy the inside address to one of the tab settings specified in Item (3).

13–3. Multiple-Page Business Letters Prepared With 10- or 12-Pitch Print

a. Set right-margin justification to "off."

b. For standard 8½- by 11-inch letterhead stationery, set a 1-inch top margin (6 blank lines). Enter 6 additional blank lines before typing the date so that when the document is printed, the first page will have a 2-inch top margin and the date will appear on line 13.

c. Set a bottom margin of 1 inch, 6 blank lines.

d. Determine the left and right margins OR writing line length for your letter, depending upon the method used by your word processing program. Vary the margins or line length according to whether you will print the document in 10 or 12 pitch.

When preparing letters in 10-pitch print, keep in mind that there are 85 spaces across the page of a standard 8½- by 11-inch sheet of paper. Therefore, any line length or margin settings must be centered within the 85 spaces. The same concept is true for letters prepared in 12 pitch except that the 8½-inch page contains 102 spaces.

Use Table 5, page 374, to select the appropriate *margin* OR *ruler or format line* settings for your word processing program. Keep in mind that the figures shown in the column labeled *Space(s) in Left Margin* are equivalent to the figures used for a page or print offset in those programs that use this command with a ruler or format line. Settings are shown for both *inches* and *columns;* select the configuration your program uses.

13

Table 5
Margin and Line-Length Settings for Multiple-Page Business Letters Printed in 10 and 12 Pitch

Letter Length	*Pitch*	*Margin Settings*	*Line-Length Settings*	*Space(s) in Left Margin*	*Space(s) in Right Margin*
Long	10	1″ – 1″ or 10 – 10 or 11 – 75	6.5 inches or 65 spaces	1″ or 10	1″ or 10
Long	12	1.25″ – 1.25″ or 15 – 15 or 16 – 87	6 inches or 72 spaces	1.25″ or 15	1.25″ or 15

e. Place from 2 to 3 blank lines between the date and the inside address.

f. Use a multiple-page heading for the second and succeeding pages. Begin this heading at the left margin on the first regular typing line of the second page, and repeat the heading on the first regular typing line of all succeeding pages. Select either of the two succeeding formats, and follow the heading with a triple space.

vertical format

Mr. Todd Wenzel (Name of addressee)
Page 2 (Actual page number)
January 18, 1993 (Date of letter)
(Triple space)

horizontal format

Mr. Todd Wenzel -2- January 18, 1993
(Triple space)

g. If your printer is set up for single-sheet feeding, prepare an envelope on the page directly following the last page of the document. To address a standard No. 10 envelope that contains a printed return address, follow the procedures outlined here:

(1) Place your cursor at the beginning of the new page. *If possible,* change your page length or page format to accommodate the envelope length—4.13 inches or 25 lines.

(2) If your program uses *margin* settings, set the margins as follows, depending upon your program configuration:

13

	Inches	Columns
10 pitch	4.3″ – 1″	43 – 10 or 43 – 75
12 pitch	4.25″ – 1.25″	51 – 15 or 51 – 87

(3) If your program uses *ruler or format lines,* retain the line set for the letter but change the page or print offset to 4.3 inches for 10-pitch print or 4.25 inches for 12-pitch print (Column 43 for 10-pitch print or Column 51 for 12-pitch print). For those programs that use ruler or format lines but do not permit variances in page or print offset within the same document (e.g., MultiMate), set a tab at 3.3 inches (Column 33) for 10-pitch print and 3 inches (Column 36) for 12-pitch print.

(4) Space down 1 inch (6 vertical lines) so that your cursor is at the beginning of the seventh typing line. Copy the inside address of the letter to the left margin—except for programs that use a format line and do not permit a change in the print or page offset. For programs that do not permit the print offset change, copy the inside address to one of the tab settings specified in Item (3).

13–4. Memorandums Prepared With 10- or 12-Pitch Print

a. Set right-margin justification to "off."

b. Set 1-inch (6 lines) top and bottom margins.

c. Determine the left and right margins or the writing line length for your memorandum, depending upon the method used by your word processing program. Vary the margins or line length according to whether you will print the document in 10 or 12 pitch.

When preparing memos in 10-pitch print, keep in mind that there are 85 spaces across the page of a standard 8½- by 11-inch sheet of paper. Therefore, any line length or margin settings must be centered within the 85 spaces to give the memo a balanced look from the horizontal perspective. The same concept is true for memos prepared in 12 pitch except that the 8½-inch page contains 102 spaces.

Use Table 6, page 376, to select the appropriate settings for your word processing program. Keep in mind that the figures shown in the column labeled *Space(s) in Left Margin* are equivalent to the figures used for a page or print offset in those programs that use this command with a ruler or format line.

Table 6
Margin and Line-Length Settings for Memorandums Printed in 10 and 12 Pitch

Format	*Pitch*	*Margin Settings*	*Line-Length Settings*	*Space(s) in Left Margin*	*Space(s) in Right Margin*
Memo	10	1.3″ – 1.2″ or 13 – 12 or 14 – 73	6 inches or 60 spaces	1.3″ or 13	1.2″ or 12
Memo	12	1.25″ – 1.25″ or 15 – 15 or 16 – 87	6 inches or 72 spaces	1.25″ or 15	1.25″ or 15

d. For standard 8½- by 11-inch printed memorandum forms, use a line-space measurement ruler to locate the fill-in positions for the preliminary *To:, From:, Date:,* and *Subject:* lines. Place an asterisk (*) where each typed part is to appear. For programs that do not register the line count in the top margin, be sure to consider these lines in deciding the placement of the asterisks.

   Store this document format. When a memo needs to be prepared, copy the format into your document. Use the Search or Find function to replace the asterisks with the specific information pertaining to the current document.

e. To prepare memorandums on plain 8½- by 11-inch paper, space down 1 inch (6 lines), unless you use a typewritten letterhead. The first line of the preliminary lines should appear on line 13 of the printed document, 2.17 inches from the top edge of the paper. An example of a memorandum prepared in 12-pitch print on plain paper with a word processing program appears on page 377.

f. Triple-space after the subject line, and begin typing the body of the memorandum. Single-space the memorandum and double-space between paragraphs. Use block paragraphs.

g. For memorandums containing more than one page, use the same multiple-page headings described for letters in Section 13–3f.

13–5. Manuscripts Prepared With 10-Pitch Print[2]

a. Set right-margin justification to "off."

b. Determine the left and right margins or the writing line length for your report or manuscript, depending upon the method used by your word

[2]See Chapter 12 for complete information on the preparation of reports and manuscripts.

processing program. Vary the margins or line length according to whether you wish to use 1-inch or 1.25-inch left and right margins. Allow an additional .25-inch left margin for left-bound manuscripts.

When preparing manuscripts in 10-pitch print, keep in mind that there are 85 spaces across the page of a standard 8½- by 11-inch sheet of paper. Therefore, any margin or line-length settings must be centered within the 85 spaces to give the manuscript a balanced look from the horizontal perspective.

memorandum prepared on plain paper

L O S   A N G E L E S   P I E R C E   C O L L E G E

Interoffice Memorandum

To: All Accounting Instructors

From: Lyn Clark

Date: September 9, 1992

Subject: ANNOUNCEMENT TO ALL ACCOUNTING STUDENTS

Do you know which microcomputer software program was <u>the top-seller for June</u>? According to last month's issue of a leading microcomputing periodical,

L O T U S   1 - 2 - 3

was the No. 1 microcomputer software program purchased by business, government, and industrial organizations.

OA 85A--which uses Lotus and an IBM Personal Computer to teach spreadsheet construction, design, and applications--has openings for any of your accounting students who are interested in gaining a competitive edge in the job market. Knowledge of Lotus in many cases provides "the foot in the door" for both part-time and full-time jobs.

The first eight-week module (1 1/2 units) for the fall semester is scheduled on Mondays, Wednesdays, and Fridays at 10 a.m. with an additional two hours of laboratory to be arranged in the Computer Center. If interested, students may continue during the fall semester with the second eight-week module (1 1/2 units), which deals with constructing spreadsheets from data bases and designing graphics from spreadsheets.

I would appreciate very much your announcing to your classes the openings in OA 85A. Attached are several fliers that publicize the course. Please have interested students see me for an Add Card in Business 3 between 10 a.m. and 11 a.m. or in my office, Business 2B, after 11 a.m.

yrs

Attachments

Use Table 7 to select the appropriate settings for your word processing program. Keep in mind that the figures shown in the column labeled *Space(s) in Left Margin* are equivalent to the figures used for a page or print offset in those programs that use this command with a ruler or format line.

Table 7
Margin and Line-Length Settings for Manuscripts and Reports Printed in 10 Pitch

Inches in Margins	*Pitch*	*Margin Settings*	*Line-Length Settings*	*Space(s) in Left Margin*	*Space(s) in Right Margin*
1.00	10	1″ – 1″ or 10 – 10 or 11 – 75	6.5 inches or 65 spaces	1″ or 10	1″ or 10
1.25	10	1.3″ – 1.2″ or 13 – 12 or 14 – 73	6 inches or 60 spaces	1.3″ or 13	1.2″ or 12

c. Allow 1 inch (6 lines) for the top and bottom margins. Space down, however, a sufficient number of lines to allow for a 2-inch top margin on the opening pages of major sections of the report or manuscript. Begin second and succeeding pages on the first typing line of the page. The preset top margin should be set so that the *page number* begins on the line directly below the 1-inch top margin.

d. Omit the page numbers on section openers. Use header and/or page numbering commands to number the second and remaining pages of a section. Page numbers appear on the line directly following the 1-inch top margin (line 7) and are aligned with the right margin. They are separated from the text by one or two blank lines.

13–6. Manuscripts Prepared With 12-Pitch Print

13

a. Set right-margin justification to "off."

b. Determine the left and right margins or the writing line length for your report or manuscript, depending upon the method used by your word processing program. Vary the margins or line length according to whether you wish to use 1-inch or 1.25-inch left and right margins. Allow an additional .25-inch left margin for left-bound manuscripts.

When preparing manuscripts in 12-pitch print, keep in mind that there are 102 spaces across the page of a standard 8½- by 11-inch sheet of paper. Therefore, any margin or line-length settings must be centered within the 102 spaces to give the manuscript a balanced look from the horizontal perspective.

Use Table 8 to select the appropriate settings for your word processing program. Keep in mind that the figures shown in the column labeled *Space(s) in Left Margin* are equivalent to the figures used for a page or print offset in those programs that use this command with a ruler or format line.

Table 8
Margin and Line-Length Settings for Manuscripts and Reports Printed in 12 Pitch

Inches in Margins	*Pitch*	*Margin Settings*	*Line-Length Settings*	*Space(s) in Left Margin*	*Space(s) in Right Margin*
1.00	12	1″ – 1″ or 12 – 12 or 13 – 90	6.5 inches or 78 spaces	1″ or 12	1″ or 12
1.25	12	1.25″ – 1.25″ or 15 – 15 or 16 – 87	6 inches or 72 spaces	1.25″ or 15	1.25″ or 15

c. Allow 1 inch (6 lines) for the top and bottom margins. Space down, however, a sufficient number of lines to allow for a 2-inch top margin on the opening pages of major sections of the report or manuscript. Begin second and succeeding pages on the first typing line of the page. The preset top margin should be set so that the *page number* begins on the line directly below the 1-inch top margin.

d. Omit the page numbers on section openers. Use header and/or page numbering commands to number the second and remaining pages of a section. Page numbers appear on the line directly following the 1-inch top margin (line 7) and are aligned with the right margin. They are separated from the text by one or two blank lines.

Terminology

13–7. Computer Words and Phrases Used in the Automated Office

Access
To open and look into a computer file.

Access time
Refers to how long the computer takes to locate (retrieve) a piece of data in its storage system.

Acoustic coupler
A special type of modem that allows a standard telephone headset to be attached to a computer terminal for the transmission of data over telephone lines from one computer to another or from one terminal to another.

Address
That portion of a computer instruction that references the location within the computer of the data to be processed.

American Standard Code for Information Interchange (ASCII)
A seven-bit code widely used in data communications.

Applications software
Computer programs developed for a specific purpose such as word processing, graphics, spreadsheets, data base management, accounting, telecommunications, etc.

Archiving
The process of transferring data from operating diskettes or on-line computer storage to permanent storage diskettes or tape.

Assembler language
A symbolic programming language that uses symbols and abbreviations to represent the function to be performed.

Asynchronous transmissions
The transmission of a single character at a time preceded by a start bit and followed by a stop bit.

Auxiliary storage
Storage by using usually either magnetic tapes or disks to supplement the working storage of the computer.

BASIC
A programming language now commonly used on personal and small business computers.

Batch
A collection of data that can be processed during one operation.

Baud
A unit of measure used to describe data transmission speeds through communication lines.

Binary numbering system
A numbering system with a base of 2 that uses either 0 or 1 to represent values.

Bit
A binary digit (either 0 or 1).

Boilerplate
A series of standardized paragraphs that can be arranged in any specified order as needed to produce a document.

Boot
The process of loading the operating system program into the computer enabling it to accept and run applications software. A *cold boot* loads the operating system from the computer "off" position. A *warm boot* removes all the data in the random access memory and reloads the operating system while the computer is on. The warm boot is achieved by depressing simultaneously a specific key combination on the keyboard—usually the Control, Alternate, and Delete keys.

Buffer
The area within a computer or printer memory into which information is read and held until the data are recorded or printed.

Byte
A group of eight bits used as a measure of the storage capacity of computers, e.g., 32K = 32,000 bytes of data that can be stored in memory. One byte may be equated to a single letter or space.

Cathode ray tube (CRT)
A television-like screen used with a computer or word processor for displaying data.

Central processing unit (CPU)
Components of computer and word processing systems that cause processing to occur by controlling the input and output functions.

Character printer
A printer that prints like a typewriter, one character at a time. (cf. line printer)

Chip
A tiny electronic component that enables computers to process and store data.

COBOL
A common business-oriented computer language.

Communicating computer or word processor
A computer or word processor that is connected through a modem to other computers and/or word processors so that data may be exchanged between or among the terminals.

Compatible
The ability of one computer to accept and process data from another computer without conversion or code modification.

CP/M (Controlled Program/Monitor)
An operating system for microcomputers.

Cursor
A highlighted mark on a display screen that shows where the next character will appear.

Daisy wheel
A circular print wheel used in computer printers.

Data base
A collection of interrelated data that may be accessed in a nonsequential manner.

Data Processing (DP)
The process of employing computers to store, manipulate, and report on data used by an organization.

Dedicated
A piece of computer equipment used for only one type of work, such as word processing.

Default
A setting in a computer, printer, or program that is automatically implemented if no other choice is designated.

Desktop publishing
Combines a laser printer with a microcomputer and software application programs to create documents that appear as if they have been professionally printed. Desktop publishing permits the use of graphics and a variety of fonts to achieve print quality.

Disk or diskette
A magnetic storage device on which information can be stored. Disks may be either "floppy" or "hard." "Hard" disks have considerably more storage capacity than "floppy" disks.

Documentation
A set of instructions that enables an operator to run a computer or program.

DOS (Disk Operating System)
Currently the most widely used operating system for microcomputers.

Dot matrix
A type of computer printer that employs closely spaced dots to form a printed character. (cf. letter-quality printer)

Dual-density disk
A magnetic storage disk that has twice the storage capacity of a standard disk (single-density disk) of the same size.

Dual pitch
Capacity to print two type sizes, usually 10 pitch and 12 pitch.

Electronic mail
The transmission of computer-generated documents from one point to another through the use of telephone lines, satellite, microwaves, or direct cable.

Ergonomics
The science of designing office systems to meet the needs of the human body.

Execute
A command on a computer to carry out an instruction, perform an operation, or run a program.

Facsimile
A device used to scan printed pages—including tables, charts, diagrams, photographs, and other graphic data—and transmit copies of these pages electronically.

Fiber optics
A technology that uses hair-like glass fibers to enable telecommunications systems to transmit data at high rates of speed.

Field
A defined group or block of data.

File
A named location within a computer disk or diskette in which data can be placed and stored.

Flowchart
A diagram that graphically illustrates the sequential steps involved in solving a problem.

Font
A typestyle that can be used to print data.

Format
The organized layout or appearance of data, usually when the data is printed on paper.

FORTRAN
A computer language designed primarily for use by mathematicians, scientists, and engineers.

Global search
A computer search throughout an entire document for words, characters, or other data that might need to be changed.

Graphics
Information that is entered into a computer and formatted as graphs or charts. These graphs may be displayed on the screen or printed on paper.

Hard copy
A document printed on paper that has been transferred from the document displayed on a CRT screen or a file stored on a computer disk.

Hard disk
A magnetic storage device that has a large data storage capacity. Many microcomputers have a permanently installed hard disk that can hold from 20 to 100 megabytes (20,000,000 to 100,000,000 bytes) of data.

Hardware
A term used to describe the actual equipment, in contrast to the programs, used in the computing process. (cf. software)

Impact printer
A printer that operates by striking a printing device against a ribbon and paper.

Information processing
The movement of words, symbols, or numbers from the origination of an idea to its destination.

Input
Data entered into a computer for processing.

Interface
The process that connects one component of the computer or word processor with another or connects one computer with another.

Justification
Distributing letters, numbers, symbols, and spaces within lines of text so that the right margin ends evenly.

K
A term used to describe the storage capacity of computer memory and storage devices. One *K* equals 1,024 bytes of memory. Thus, 256K of memory would equal a memory capacity of 262,144 bytes; and a 360K disk could store up to 368,640 bytes.

Keyboarding
Using a keyboard to enter data into a computer.

Laser printer
A high-speed, high-quality nonimpact printer that employs a narrow beam of electromagnetic light to enable it to print over 20,000 lines per minute.

Letter-quality printer
A printer that produces typewriter-quality print. (cf. dot matrix)

Line printer
A computer printer that prints one entire line at a time. (cf. character printer)

Loop
A sequence of instructions that is repeated continuously.

Mag
Shortened form of the word *magnetic.* "Mag card" and "mag tape" are commonly used to refer to these magnetic devices.

Medium
The material on which information is recorded; e.g., magnetic tape, cards, or disks.

Megabyte
A term used to describe the storage capacity of computer memory and storage devices. One megabyte equals 1,024,000 bytes of memory or storage capacity.

Memory
That part of the computer that holds information for use.

Memory, programmable read only (PROM)
ROM chips whose memory can be programmed before they are set into the computer and become a fixed part of the system. Data in PROM memory is retained after the computer is turned off.

Memory, random access (RAM)
RAM is temporary memory within the computer and is used primarily for loading programs from disk or tape or holding data until it is stored to disk. Data in RAM memory is lost when the computer is turned off.

Memory, read only (ROM)
Permanent programs are stored in ROM, and these programs may not be altered. They are the ones that instruct the computer what to do when the power is turned on and how to do various jobs like loading application programs from disk or tape. ROM will not lose its information when the power is turned off.

Menu
A listing on the screen of possible actions an operator may take to perform tasks on a computer.

Merge
A word processing function that allows the data in two prefiled locations to be combined—usually during the printing process.

Modem
A device attached to computer or word processing terminals that allows the transmission of data between terminals over telephone wires by converting digital signals to analog signals at one end and reconverting the analog signals back to digital signals at the other end.

Monitor
A television-like screen that connects to a computer and displays data. The monitor is also referred to as the "CRT screen."

Mouse
A small hand-held device that moves the cursor on the screen by rotating the device around the computer table. Files may be opened or closed and menus may be displayed on the screen by pressing a button on the mouse.

Network
A group of computers and/or word processors connected into a planned system to enable the transmission of data among the members of the system.

OCR (Optical character recognition)
Data read into a computer by scanning a document electronically.

Operating system
An integrated collection of service routines for supervising the sequencing and processing of programs by a computer. Operating systems may perform debugging, input-output, machine accounting, compilation, and storage-assignment tasks. Computers will perform no functions until an operating system has been loaded.

OS2
A computer operating system that permits multitasking, that is, working on two separate programs simultaneously.

Peripheral
Equipment such as printers, monitors, and modems that work in conjunction with the computer but are not part of the computer itself.

Processing
Changes the input in a computer undergoes that result in the final product.

Program
A set of instructions designed to provide a computer solution to a problem by directing the computer to carry out a desired sequence of operations.

Programming
Writing instructions to direct a computer to perform a desired process.

Protocol
A set of conventions for the electronic transmission of data including modes, speed, character length, and code.

Reprographics
The duplication of hard copy usually by employing a computer peripheral such as a high-speed film or photocopier.

Scrolling
The process of moving text up or down on a CRT screen.

Search and Replace
A word processing command that directs a computer to locate a piece of information wherever it occurs in a document and replace it with another piece of information.

Software
Programs written to direct the operations of a computer or word processor. (cf. hardware)

Split screen
The ability of some software programs to display two or more documents on the screen simultaneously.

Spreadsheet
A computer program similar to an accounting worksheet that displays columns and rows in the form of cells on the screen. When the values in the cells are changed, the result is automatically calculated throughout the worksheet.

Stand-alone system
A computer or word processing work station that is independent or can function by itself without being connected to a mainframe computer.

Terminal
A configuration connected to the computer for the purpose of entering and retrieving data. The most common computer terminal consists of a CRT screen and a keyboard.

User friendly
The degree to which the operations of a computer or software program are made relatively easy to learn through the use of menus, function keys, software, and documentation.

Turtle graphics
A method of drawing on a CRT screen by using a drawing cursor called a *turtle* to produce geometric shapes.

Windows
Divisions on a CRT screen that enable an operator to view parts of a document or different documents simultaneously. Windows are created on a CRT screen through software programs.

Word processing
The use of computerized equipment and software programs to keyboard, edit, produce, and store business documents.

CHAPTER 14

Conventional Mail Services

Conventional Mail Services Solution Finder

United States Postal Service Domestic Mail Classes and Services

There are a number of domestic mail classes. Each varies in (1) the type, weight, and size of the matter that may be sent; (2) the cost of mailing; and (3) the priority in which the mail will be delivered.

The U.S. Postal Service limits single-piece mailings to 70 pounds and 108 inches, combined length and girth. To determine the combined length and girth of a parcel, use the following procedures:

(1) Measure the length of the longest side.

(2) Measure the distance around the parcel at its thickest part.

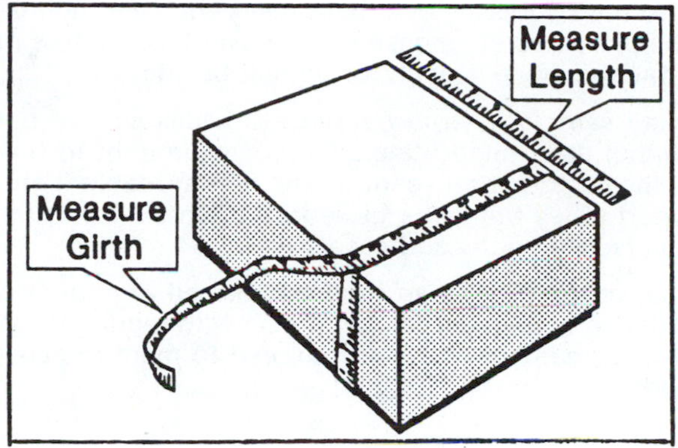

(3) Add the two measurements. The result may not exceed 108 inches.

A brief description of the domestic mail classes and services offered by the U.S. Postal Service follows:

14–1. Express Mail Service

Express mail service receives the highest priority handling in terms of destination arrival time. It is a high-speed intercity delivery system geared to the special needs of business and industry for the fast transfer of letters, documents, or merchandise. All domestic shipments sent by express mail are insured against loss or damage at no extra charge, subject to the limitations of coverage listed in the *Domestic Mail Manual.*[1] For an extra charge return receipts are available.

Postage varies by weight and type of service selected, but flat rates for shipments weighing ½ pound or less have been established for all express

[1]The information given here on domestic mail classes and services is based on the *Domestic Mail Manual,* Effective June 17, 1990, U.S. Postal Service, Issue 35 (Washington, D.C.: U.S. Postal Service, 1990). Copies of the *Domestic Mail Manual* are available on a subscription basis through the Superintendent of Documents, U.S. Government Printing Office, Washington, D.C. 20402-9371 [Tel: (202) 783-3238].

mail services. The maximum weight for domestic express mail is 70 pounds; the combined length and girth permitted is 108 inches. Types of express mail services include, but are not limited to, the following:

a. *Express mail next-day or second-day service* is available to all five-digit zip codes. Express mail next-day service is provided in major cities throughout the United States, and each city has its list of other cities to which it guarantees this service. Express mail second-day service is available for shipments received up to 5 p.m. or to service areas not eligible for same-day service.

   Express mail may be sent post office to post office or post office to addressee. This means that mail brought in by the local cut-off time or deposited in an express mail collection box by the posted time will be delivered to its destination city by its guaranteed day. The mailing will be delivered to the addressee by 3 p.m. (weekends and holidays included), or it can be picked up at its destination post office by 10 a.m. of the next business day the office is open for regular business.

b. *Express mail same-day airport service* provides service between major airports within the United States. Items are brought to the airport mail facility by the customer and sent on the first available flight to the destination airport. They are to be picked up upon arrival at the destination airport mail facility by the addressee.

c. *Express mail custom-designed service* is offered 24 hours a day, 365 days a year, under an agreement for customers with regularly scheduled shipments. Each agreement is custom tailored to meet the customer's individual needs.

14–2. First-Class Mail

The following examples are always considered first-class mail if the weight is 11 ounces or less:

(1) Handwritten and typewritten messages, including identical copies, but excluding computer material

(2) Bills and statements of account

(3) Notebooks or account books containing handwritten or typewritten entries

(4) Postcards and postal cards

(5) Canceled and uncanceled checks

(6) Printed forms filled out in writing

(7) Printed price lists with written or typed changes

(8) Business-reply mail

(9) Matter having the characteristics of actual or personal correspondence

(10) Any other type of mail weighing 11 ounces or less sent as first class at the option of the mailer

All first-class mail pieces must be at least 0.007 inch thick. First-class mail pieces that are ¼ inch or less in thickness are nonmailable unless they are (1) rectangularly shaped, (2) at least 3½ inches high, (3) and at least 5 inches long.

A surcharge is assessed on each piece of first-class mail weighing one ounce or less if it exceeds any one of the following criteria: (1) a height of 6⅛ inches, (2) a length of 11½ inches, (3) a thickness of ¼ inch. In addition, the surcharge is assessed if the length divided by the height is less than 1.3 or more than 2.5.

For oversized materials (larger than legal-sized envelopes), use the white envelopes with a green diamond border available for purchase at the post office. This border automatically indicates that these materials are to be sent first class.

a. *Priority mail* is first-class mail weighing over 11 ounces. The rate schedule is determined by weight and zone, but the delivery time is faster than for fourth-class mail. Priority mail receives two- to three-day delivery nationwide and overnight service to designated cities. The maximum weight for priority mail is 70 pounds, and its dimensions are limited to 108 inches in combined length and girth, the maximum standard set for mailings handled by the U.S. Postal Service.

b. *Business-reply mail* is a first-class mail service supplied to mailers who want to encourage responses by paying the postage. Mailers guarantee they will pay the postage plus a fee for all replies returned to them. Anyone wishing to use this service must obtain a permit from the U.S. Postal Service and prepare the replies to conform to a specified format.

c. *Mailgram service* provides next-business-day delivery for messages to addresses in the United States except for parts of Alaska. By taking directly or telephoning a message to a Western Union office, the sender can ensure delivery with the next business day's mail. The message is transmitted electronically to a post office near its destination from where it is placed in a special envelope and delivered with regular mail.

14–3. Second-Class Mail

Second-class mail is used by newspaper and magazine publishers to mail publications at a special bulk rate. A publisher mails at the second-class rate on the basis of an authorization obtained from the post office.

Publications must be issued at least four times annually to qualify for the special bulk rate. They must be reproduced by a printing process, have a known office of publication, and cannot be designed primarily for advertising purposes. Second-class publications must generally have a list of paid subscribers or requesters.

14–4. Third-Class Mail

Third-class mail consists of circulars, booklets, catalogs, and other printed materials such as form letters (printed or computer generated), newsletters, or proofs. It also includes merchandise, farm and factory products, photographs, keys, identification devices, and printed drawings.

Except for keys and identification devices, third-class mailings must meet the same minimum size requirements specified for first-class mail (Section

14–2). There are no maximum size requirements for single-piece mailings; bulk mailings must conform to specified size limitations.

Each piece of third-class mail is limited in weight to fewer than 16 ounces. The same material weighing 16 ounces or more is classified as fourth-class, or parcel post, mail. If a piece of third-class mail is computed at a higher rate than any fourth-class rate for which the mailing and matter could qualify except for weight, then the lower fourth-class rate is applied.

Third-class mail may be sent at a single-piece rate or at a bulk rate. Additionally, certain nonprofit organizations qualify for a special third-class bulk postage rate. Keys and identification devices may be mailed for still another rate.

14–5. Fourth-Class Mail (Parcel Post)

Fourth-class mail is generally called "parcel post" and includes such items as merchandise, bound printed matter, books, films, manuscripts, and library materials. The minimum weight for fourth-class mail is 16 ounces per item; mail under this weight is usually sent at third-class rates. Maximum weight and size restrictions are 70 pounds and 108 inches combined length and girth. Postage rates for this class are determined by the weight of the parcel and the distance from its point of origin to its destination.

a. A *bulk-rate fourth-class mail* is available for (1) mailings of 300 or more pieces or (2) mailings of at least a 2,000-pound total weight with individual pieces having identical weights. The parcels need not contain identical contents or be the same size.

b. A *special fourth-class rate* may be used for mailing books, certain kinds of films, printed music, printed test materials, sound recordings, manuscripts, educational reference charts, and medical information. Items mailed at this *special fourth-class rate* may weigh less than 16 ounces. Books containing advertising for merchandise, telephone directories, corporation reports, house organs, and periodicals do not qualify for this special rate.

   All items mailed with the *special fourth-class rate* should be marked as such. In addition, a description of the item should be included, such as "Books," "Sound Recordings," "Films," etc.

c. *Library rate* is used for certain kinds of materials that are loaned to, exchanged between, mailed to, or mailed by schools, colleges, libraries, museums, and similar kinds of nonprofit organizations. Materials include books, printed music, academic theses, sound recordings, etc. All items must be marked "Library Rate."

d. Securely bound advertising, promotional, directory, or educational material may be sent at a special *bound printed matter rate.* Material may not have the nature of personal correspondence and cannot be a book.

14–6. Mixed Classes

A first-class letter may be attached to or enclosed in a parcel sent by a lower class. If the letter is attached to the parcel, each item should have separate postage. If the letter is enclosed in the package, "First-Class Mail

Enclosed" should be marked on the outside of the parcel, along with the correct postage affixed for both items.

14–7. Special Delivery

This special service is used to hasten the delivery of a mailed item. It provides for delivery, even on Sundays and holidays, during prescribed hours that extend beyond the hours for delivery of ordinary mail. The purchase of special delivery does not always mean the article will be delivered by messenger. Special delivery may be delivered by a regular carrier if it is available before the carrier departs for morning deliveries. Although sending an item special delivery virtually ensures delivery on the day received at that post office, it does not necessarily speed up the transportation time to that point from its origin.

This service is available to all customers served by city carriers and to other customers within a one-mile delivery radius of the delivery post office. All classes of mail may be sent special delivery for an additional fee.

14–8. Special Handling

A special handling service is provided for preferential handling in the dispatch and transportation of third- and fourth-class mail. A special handling fee must be paid on parcels that take special care, such as baby chicks, baby alligators, packaged bees, etc.

14–9. Insured Mail

a. *Registered mail* is the safest way to send valuables through the mail. This service may be used only for first-class mail, priority mail, or c.o.d. parcels with prepaid postage at the first-class mail rate. Except for c.o.d. parcels, each mailing may be insured for its full value up to $25,000; c.o.d. service is limited, however, to items valued at a maximum of $500. Registered mail may not be deposited in collection boxes since a receipt must be issued at the point of mailing.

   This service is offered for the protection of negotiable instruments, jewelry, and other items of value. The registry fees, in addition to first-class mail or priority-mail postage, are scaled according to the declared value of the mail. For an additional fee a mailer can obtain a return receipt and/or restrict to whom the mail is delivered.

b. *Insured mail* consists of third- and fourth-class mail items insured for protection against loss or damage. This service is also available for any third- and fourth-class mail items that are mailed at first-class mail or priority-mail rates.

   Insured mail has a maximum indemnity of $500. A receipt is given to the mailer at the time of mailing, and a signature is required upon delivery. You may obtain a return receipt and/or request restricted delivery for an additional fee.

c. *C.o.d. (collect on delivery)* may be used for first-, third-, and fourth-class mail. When the mail is delivered, the addressee pays the amount due for the contents. The addressee may also be required to pay the postage and the c.o.d. fee, depending upon the prior agreement between the sender and receiver.

The c.o.d. fee includes insurance against loss, damage, or failure to receive the amount collected from the addressee. The maximum amount that can be collected for one item is $500. The goods shipped must have been ordered by the addressee, and the sender agrees to pay any return postage unless specified differently on the mail.

Senders of c.o.d. mail may (1) request restricted delivery, (2) alter the charges or direct delivery to a different address, or (3) register first-class mail.

d. *Postal money orders* provide for sending money through the mail safely. If they are lost or stolen, they can be replaced. Domestic money orders up to $700 may be purchased and redeemed at any post office.

14–10. Proof of Mailing and Delivery

The U.S. Postal Service provides ways in which proof may be obtained that an item has been mailed or received. These optional services are available to any mailer.

a. *Certified mail* is used for first-class and priority-mail items that have no money value since there is no insurance feature with this service. Certified mail provides for a record of delivery to be maintained by the post office from which the item was delivered. The carrier delivering certified mail obtains a signature from the addressee on a receipt form that is kept for two years. In this way the sender can prove that items were received by the addressee. Proof of delivery may be obtained at a later time during the two-year period following delivery.

Return receipts showing to whom, when, and where items were delivered may be obtained for an additional charge for mail that is registered, insured, certified, or sent c.o.d. During the two-year period after delivery, proof of delivery may be obtained from the post office from which the items were delivered.

Certified mail may be deposited in a collection box if the mailer has attached a "Certified" sticker and the appropriate postage and fees.

b. A *certificate of mailing* for any item may be obtained from the sender's post office. Unlike certified mail, however, the post office does not keep any record of the certificate issued or of the delivery of the item. It only provides proof that the item was mailed.

U.S. Postal Service International Classes and Services

Because the regulations regarding international mailings vary according to country, the information presented here provides only general guidelines for international mailings through the United States Postal Service.

For details regarding a specific country, consult the main post office serving your area or the *International Mail Manual (IMM).*[2]

14–11. Classes of International Mail[3]

Classes of international mail may be separated into three categories. *LC mail,* derived from the French words *Lettres and Cartes* (letters and cards), consists of letters, letter packages, aerogrammes, and postcards. *AO mail,* derived from the French expression *Autres Objets* (other articles), includes regular printed matter, books, sheet music, matter for the blind, small packets, and publishers' periodicals. The third category, *CP mail,* is an abbreviation for *Colis Postaux,* the French version of *parcel post.*

a. ***Letters and letter packages.*** Mail items containing current correspondence, handwritten or typewritten, must be sent as *letters* or *letter packages.* Merchandise or other articles may also be mailed at letter postage rates as long as they are allowed by the destination country. Letters and letter packages may be sent at either air rates or surface rates, and the weight limit to all countries for this class is 4 pounds.

b. ***Postcards.*** Postcards and postal cards consist of single cards sent without an envelope or wrapper. They may be sent at either air or surface rates. Folded (double) cards must be mailed in envelopes at the letter postage rate.

c. ***Aerogrammes.*** Aerogrammes are air letter sheets that are folded into the form of an envelope and sealed with tape or stickers. Enclosures are not permitted in this class of mail.

d. ***Printed matter.*** Printed matter refers to paper on which words, letters, characters, figures, and/or images not resembling a bill or statement of account or correspondence have been reproduced by a process other than handwriting or typewriting. Included in this classification are publishers' periodicals, books, sheet music, and other regular printed matter. Items not permitted under this classification include articles of stationery, postage stamps, framed photographs or certificates, photographic negatives or slides, films, microfilm or microfiche, punched paper tapes or ADP cards, and playing cards. Weight limits to various countries vary, depending upon the contents and country of destination. Printed matter may be sent at either air or surface rates.

e. ***M-Bag mail.*** Printed matter in quantities of 15 pounds or more may, under certain circumstances, be enclosed in mail sacks addressed directly to a single addressee. The combined weight of the sack and its contents may not exceed 66 pounds. M-Bag mail may be sent at either air or surface rates.

---

[2]Copies of the *International Mail Manual* are available on a subscription basis through the Superintendent of Documents, U.S. Government Printing Office, Washington, D.C. 20402-9371 [Tel: (202) 783-3238].

[3]Information presented here has been derived from *International Postal Rates and Fees,* From April 17, 1988, U.S. Postal Service, Publication 51 (Washington, D.C.: U.S. Government Printing Office, 1988), 1–12. For full details consult your local post office or the *International Mail Manual.*

f. ***Matter for the blind.*** Weight limit for this class is 15 pounds, and the surface rate is free. Consult your local post office for matter eligible for this class and for air rates.

g. ***Small packets.*** Small items of merchandise, commercial samples, or documents that do not resemble current or personal correspondence may be sent by this class. The postage rates are lower than those for letter packages or parcel post, and the weight limit for most countries is 4 pounds. Small packets may be sent at either air or surface rates.

h. ***Parcel post.*** Packages of merchandise or any other articles that are not required to be mailed as letters or letter packages may be sent as parcel post. Any written communication resembling current or personal correspondence is not permitted. Parcel post offers insurance protection against loss. The maximum weight limit per package depends upon the destination country, but this limit is usually either 22 or 44 pounds. International parcel post resembles domestic zone-rated fourth-class mail.

i. ***Express mail international service.*** Express mail international service (EMS) offers reliable high-speed mail service to a number of countries. In addition to the regular service, there are options tailored for specific business needs. EMS includes merchandise and document reconstruction insurance at no extra charge. The weight limit is generally 33 or 44 pounds, depending upon the country of destination. Unlike domestic express mail, there is no service guarantee for international express mail.

j. ***International priority airmail service.*** International priority airmail service is intended to meet the demand by business mailers for an international service that is faster than regular mail, but mailers must meet specific minimum volume and sortation requirements. This service is available for all LC (letters, cards, and letter packages) and AO (other articles) classes and to all countries except Canada.

k. ***International surface air lift.*** International surface air lift (ISAL) provides expedited dispatch and transportation for all types of printed matter. Mailing costs are lower than airmail while the service is faster than that provided by surface mail. ISAL shipments are brought by the customer to a designated U.S. airport mail facility from which they are sent by air to their foreign destination. Upon arrival the shipments are placed into the surface mail system for delivery to the addressee.

l. ***INTELPOST service.*** International electronic post service, INTELPOST, offers same- or next-day delivery of facsimile documents from post offices in major cities to addresses in Canada, Europe, South America, and the Near and Far East. Any item that can be photocopied can be sent in minutes. It can be picked up by the addressee within an hour, delivered by special delivery the same day (depending on time differences around the world), or delivered by regular mail the next day.

14–12. Special Services for International Mail[4]

a. ***Registered mail.*** Registered mail arranges for the secure handling of mail and provides an indemnity of $24.60 (up to $1,000 in Canada). This service is available only for letter-class mail, small packets, and all printed matter to all countries except Cambodia and North Korea.

b. ***Insurance.*** Insurance offers indemnity for loss of or damage to items sent as parcel post. Insurance is not available for letter-class mail, small packets, or printed matter. The maximum indemnity is $500, but only certain countries are eligible for this service and the maximum limits vary according to country.

c. ***Return receipt.*** Return receipt provides the mailer evidence of delivery of registered or insured mail. Return receipts must be purchased at the time of mailing.

d. ***Restricted delivery.*** Restricted delivery limits who may receive an item. This service is available to many countries for registered mail. Details of the service, however, are governed by the internal legislation of the destination country.

e. ***Special delivery.*** Special delivery provides for faster delivery of letter-class mail, small packets, and printed matter at the post office serving the addressee, according to the special delivery regulations of the destination country. This service is not available for items sent as parcel post. Special delivery is available to most countries.

f. ***Special handling.*** Special handling provides for preferential handling to the extent practical in dispatch and transportation from the office of mailing to the U.S. office of dispatch. This service does not offer preferential dispatch from the U.S. or special treatment in the destination country. Special handling is available only for parcel post, printed matter, matter for the blind, and small packets sent at surface rates. The purchase of this service is at the sender's option except when sending honey bees to Canada.

g. ***COD.*** Collect on delivery mail (COD) is not available for international items.

h. ***Certified mail.*** Certified mail is not available for international mail items.

United Parcel Service

14–13. United Parcel Service

United Parcel Service (commonly called UPS) is a commercial company that is widely used throughout the United States to deliver small packages.

[4]Information presented here has been derived from *International Postal Rates and Fees,* From April 17, 1988, U.S. Postal Service, Publication 51 (Washington, D.C.: U.S. Government Printing Office, 1988), 1–12. For full details consult your local post office or the *International Mail Manual,* which is available on a subscription basis through the Superintendent of Documents, U.S. Government Printing Office, Washington, D.C. 20402-9371 [Tel: (202) 783-3238].

United Parcel also provides this service internationally. Domestic packages may be sent by truck or air, and customers may either take their packages to their local UPS office or have UPS pick up the packages at their home or place of business for a small extra charge. Packages sent by UPS may not weigh over 70 pounds or be over 108 inches in length, with a combined length and girth limitation of 130 inches. All packages are automatically insured for up to $100.

Private Courier Services

14–14. Private Courier Services

A number of private courier services specialize in expediting the delivery of letters and packages throughout the United States. These companies offer a variety of services, but the majority specialize in overnight delivery of letters and small packages to major cities throughout the country. Consult the yellow pages of your local telephone directory to determine which private courier services have offices in your area.

Facsimile (Fax)

14–15. Facsimile (Fax)

Facsimile transmission of typewritten, handwritten, and computer-generated documents; charts, graphs, and diagrams; photographs; and other kinds of hard copy has become an everyday occurrence. It is the most popular method of electronic document transmission used by modern businesses today.

Businesses or stations using facsimiles (faxes) require a fax telephone line and a modem to which they connect their fax machine. The fax machine scans any hard copy, and the modem converts the scanned images to analog signals that are transmitted over telephone lines to a receiving fax machine. Here the signals are reconverted to images and a replica of the hard copy is produced at the receiving station, often thousands of miles from the sending source. Fax machines are capable of both sending and receiving documents to and from locations locally or around the world.

Costs include the purchase of a facsimile and modem, installation and monthly service charges for a telephone line, and regular local and long-distance telephone rates for on-line transmission. Simple documents are sent and received in just a matter of minutes.

This high-speed, low-cost method of document transmission is also available to the general public through the U.S. Postal Service, stationery stores, and various businesses in major cities throughout the United States.

Western Union Message Services

Western Union specializes in regular domestic money transfers, credit card money transfers, Mexican money transfers, international money transfers, and several other pay or transfer plans. These services enable cash transfers between distant locations to take place rapidly.

Western Union also provides domestic and international electronic messaging services for business use (e.g., OfficeAccess, EasyLink FAX, EasyLink Telex, EasyLink International, to name just a few) in addition to several conventional messaging services: telegrams, Mailgrams, and cablegrams.[5]

14–16. Telegrams

a. Although telegram message volume has declined over the past few years, telegrams are still used by individuals and businesses to deliver high-impact or social communications. Telegram service is provided through Western Union's computerized message-switching network, its central telephone bureaus, and its Spanish-language telephone center.

b. *Regular telegrams* may be sent around the clock for telephone or physical delivery within the 48 contiguous states. Physical delivery (usually within four hours) is provided by approximately 2,600 independent agents.

   Regular telegrams may also be sent to Alaska, Hawaii, Puerto Rico, the Virgin Islands, Canada, and Mexico.

   There is a base charge for up to 15 words, which does not include the recipient's address or telephone number and the sender's name and title. Additional charges are assessed in 10-word increments up to 35 words with new rates applying for 50, 75, 100, 115, and over 115 words.

c. *Overnight telegrams* are priced lower than regular telegrams. Delivery is guaranteed the following day. Rates are determined by the same word-count levels used for regular telegrams.

14–17. Mailgrams

a. *Mailgrams* are used primarily for business communications, social messages, and expressions of public opinion to government officials.

   You may originate a Mailgram message by placing a toll-free telephone call to Western Union or by delivering the message to a Western Union office or agent. The message is then routed electronically through Western Union's computerized message-switching network to one of 143 U.S. Postal Service locations. Here it is printed on a Western Union terminal and given priority sorting and handling for delivery as first-class mail on the next business day.

[5]For detailed information on services and rates, phone Western Union at its toll-free number, (800) 325-6000, or at its main office in New Jersey, (201) 818-5000.

Western Union links Mailgram service with similar services in Canada, Great Britain, Argentina, the Philippines, the Republic of Korea, and the Netherlands.

Mailgram messages permit up to 50 words in the base rate. Extra charges are incurred for each additional 50 or fewer words.

b. *Opiniongrams* are available for messages to the President, members of Congress, officials in a state capitol, and certain other officials. Priced lower than Mailgrams, regular telegrams, or overnight telegrams, these messages permit up to 20 words in the base rate. Extra charges are incurred for each additional 20 words.

14–18. Cablegrams

Western Union provides international telegram service to more than 200 overseas locations. Cablegram service is traditional operator-assisted service delivered worldwide via telephone, Telex, or mail.

GLOSSARY

Grammatical Terms Used in HOW 6

Abbreviation
A shortened form of a word or word group. Examples: *in.* for *inches* and *AMA* for *American Medical Association.*

Absolute adjective
An adjective that cannot be compared because it represents a definite and exact state. Examples: *dead, perfect,* and *full.*

Action verb
A verb that shows or represents movement. Examples: *run, talk,* and *breathe.*

Active voice
A method of constructing sentences that identifies who does what. The person or thing performing the action is the subject of the sentence. Example: The *stock-holders* rejected the proposal.

Adj.
Abbreviation of *adjective.*

Adjective
A word or word group that describes a noun or pronoun. It tells what kind, which one, or how many. Examples: *good* investment, *this* bank, and *three* employees.

Adverb
A word that describes a verb, an adjective, or another adverb. It tells when, where, how, or to what degree. Many adverbs end in *ly.* Examples: arrive *early,* come *here,* drive *carefully,* and *too* small.

Adverbial clause
A word group containing a subject and a verb that begins with a conjunctive adverb such as *if, when, since, because,* or *as.* An adverbial clause modifies the verb in the main clause. Example: *If you wish an appointment,* please *call* me.

Ampersand
A symbol (&) meaning *and* used mainly in organizational names. Example: We have signed a contract with Robert White & Associates.

Animate object
Any person, any living thing, or any group composed of persons or living things. Examples: *manager, tree, company,* and *flock* of sheep.

Antecedent
A noun (or indefinite pronoun) to which a pronoun or any number of pronouns refer. Example: Our last newsletter asked all *clients* in this area *who* are interested in bond investments to indicate *their* willingness to attend a free seminar by phoning this office.

Apostrophe
A symbol (') used to show noun possession, the omission of letters in contractions, and the beginning and ending of quotations within quotations. Examples: (1) *Car-*

ol's salary; (2) we *haven't;* and (3) He asked, "Have you read my latest article, 'Western Travels'?"

Apposition, Appositive, Appositive expression
A word or word group that renames or explains the noun or pronoun it follows. These descriptive words usually add extra information. Example: Ms. Johnson, *our new manager,* has been with the company for three years.

Article
The words *a, an,* and *the.* These words are used as adjectives. Examples: *a* method, *an* interesting tour, *the* stock market.

Being verb
A form of the verb *to be* when it is used as a main verb, that is, when it appears alone or as the last verb in a verb phrase. These forms are *am, is, was, were, be,* and *been.* Example: He has *been* our client for three years.

Being verb helper
A form of the verb *to be* when it is used in a verb phrase as a helping verb. These forms are *am, is, was, were,* and *been.* Example: Whitmore appliances *have* not *been sold* in our store for the past three years.

Cardinal number
A number such as 3 (three), 10 (ten), 32 (thirty-two), 541, or 1,856 that is used in simple counting.

Case form
A category used to classify nouns or pronouns in a sentence as subjective, objective, or possessive.

Celestial body
A planet, star, or other heavenly form. Examples: *Mars, North Star,* and *sun.*

Clause
A word group that contains a subject and a verb.

Collective noun
A noun composed of individual persons or things. Examples: *committee, team, jury, herd,* and *class.*

Colon
A punctuation mark (:) used to indicate that the following words explain further the word or word group appearing before the punctuation mark. Example: Our company specializes in the manufacture of the following women's clothing accessories: shoes, boots, handbags, and belts.

Command
A sentence in which the subject *you* is not stated but instead is implied. The sentence directs the understood subject *you* to perform an action. Example: (You) Mail this information to me as soon as possible.

Common noun
A noun that does not name a specific person, place, or thing. Examples: *supervisor, building, city council, university,* and *company.*

Common noun element
That part of a proper noun that is not a specific name. Examples: *university* in Ruttgers University, *building* in Tishman Building, and *city council* in Miami City Council.

Comparative form
The spelling or form of an adjective or an adverb when it compares two nouns or pronouns or two conditions. Compare with *superlative form.* Examples: (1) This year's sales are *greater* than last year's. (2) We have progressed *more slowly* in this area than we had hoped.

Complement pronoun
A pronoun that completes a being verb. It follows a form of the verb *to be—am, is, are, was, were, be,* and *been.* Example: The contest winners were *they,* Karen and Bill.

Complete thought
A word group that contains a subject and a verb. The word group must make sense and be able to stand alone as a complete sentence. A complete thought is also known as an *independent clause.* Example: *Mr. Reed agreed to the terms of the contract,* but *his attorney advised him not to sign it.*

Complex sentence
A sentence that contains an independent clause and a dependent clause. Example: As soon as we receive your reply, we will send you a replacement or issue a credit to your account.

Complimentary close
The first closing line of a business letter. Example: *Sincerely yours.*

Compound adjective
Two or more words acting together as a single thought to describe or modify a noun or pronoun. Example: *part-time* job.

Compound modifier
Same as *compound adjective.*

Compound noun
Two or more words used as a single unit to name a person, place, or thing. Examples: *sister-in-law, notary public, high school, community college, word processing,* and *income tax.*

Compound number
A number requiring more than one word when written in word form. Examples: *twenty-seven, ninety-eight, one hundred, two hundred fifty-three, three thousand, eight thousand five hundred fifty.*

Compound sentence
A sentence containing two independent clauses (complete thoughts) joined by (1) a semicolon; (2) a transitional expression; or (3) the conjunction *and, but, or,* or *nor.* Example: The manufacturer has promised to send us another shipment of these disks by next week, and we will fill your order immediately upon its arrival.

Compound subject
A subject that contains two or more nouns or pronouns joined by *and, or,* or *nor.* Example: *Ellen and Jack* have already reached their quotas for this month's sales.

Compound verb
Two or more words combined to produce a single thought unit that functions as a verb. Compound verbs appear as one word, as two words, or hyphenated. Examples: *upgrade, mark up, double-space.*

Compound-complex sentence
A sentence containing two independent clauses (complete thoughts) and a dependent clause. Example: This suite of offices is currently available for occupancy, and we will release the keys to you as soon as you return the signed lease agreement with a certified check for $3,000.

Conjugation
The various forms of a verb that show person. Examples: I *see,* he or she *sees,* we *see,* you *see,* they *see;* I *am,* he or she *is,* we *are,* you *are,* they *are.*

Conjunction
A part of speech that serves as a connector of words or word groups within a sentence. Examples: *and, but, or, nor, either . . . or,* and *not only . . . but also.*

Conjunctive adverb
A word that introduces a dependent adverbial clause. Examples: *if, as, when, although,* and *since.*

Conjunctive pair
A class of connecting words—conjunctions—that links contrasting or dependent ideas. These connectors consist of two parts. Examples: *either . . . or, neither . . . nor, if . . . then,* and *not only . . . but also.*

Consonant
Any letter of the alphabet other than *a, e, i, o,* and *u.*

Contingent expression
An expression that is based upon a similar expression for completion. Example: *The sooner* you take advantage of this offer, *the more often* you will be able to enjoy your personal home movie selections.

Contraction
Shortened forms that use an apostrophe to show the omission of letters or numbers. These shortened forms may be applied to certain words, verb phrases, and dates. Examples: *internat'l* for *international, doesn't* for *does not,* and *'91* for *1991.*

Coordinating conjunction
A part of speech (conjunction) that joins equal words or word groups. Examples: *and, but, or,* and *nor.*

Courtesy title
A title used to address individuals. Examples: *Mr., Ms., Mrs., Miss,* and *Dr.*

Dash
A mark of punctuation used to precede summary statements or for emphasis in setting off words or word groups. The dash is formed in typewritten or computer-based copy by keying two hyphens consecutively; no space appears before, between, or after the hyphens. Example: Sofas, chairs, bedroom suites, dining room sets--we have a large variety of styles and brands from which you may choose.

Decimal
A small dot (.) used in numbers to separate a whole number from a portion of the next number in the sequence. Examples: *12.5, 0.07, 147.38, 6.75 percent,* and *$1.4 million.*

Declarative sentence
A complete sentence appearing as a statement. Example: Our company president announced our merger with Cory Industries yesterday.

Dependent adverbial clause
A word group containing a subject and a verb that begins with a conjunctive adverb such as *if, when, since, because,* or *as.* An adverbial clause modifies the verb in the main clause. Example: Please *call* me *when the shipment arrives.*

Dependent clause
A word group containing a subject and a verb that cannot stand alone as a complete sentence. Same as a *subordinate clause.* Example: John told me last week *that he expects to win this month's sales contest.*

Direct address
The process of calling a person by name, title, or classification in written or oral communication *with that person.* Examples: (1) Thank you, *Ms. Burwell,* for

responding so promptly. (2) Yes, *Professor,* we will have this textbook available for use during the spring semester. (3) Only you, *fellow citizens,* can prevent a further decline of schools in this city.

Direct object
A noun or pronoun acted upon by the subject and verb of a sentence. Example: Our accountant mailed the *check* yesterday.

Direct quotation
The exact words spoken or written by a person or group. Example: According to the committee's report, "The property was sold in 1982 for $10,950,000."

Ellipsis
A series of three periods (. . .)—with spaces before, between, and after the periods—used to show omissions in quoted material or hesitations in other printed material. Example: According to his latest journal article, Professor Haley concludes, "Social conditions will continue to improve in this area . . . unless the government withdraws its funding commitment."

Essential subordinate clause
A word group containing a subject and a verb that cannot stand alone as a complete sentence. The word group is needed to complete the main idea of the sentence by furnishing *who, what, which one, when, why, how, whether,* or *to what degree.* An *essential subordinate clause* is the same as a *restrictive clause,* a *restrictive dependent clause,* or a *restrictive subordinate clause.* Example: John told me last week *that he expects to win this month's sales contest.*

Exclamation mark
A mark of punctuation (!) used to show strong feeling or emotion. Example: Take advantage of our free offer today--while this letter is in front of you!

First person
I or *we* used as subjects in writing or speaking. Example: After analyzing the specimen, *we* contacted several contagious disease specialists.

Fraction
A part of a whole number expressed in proportion to the whole. Example: The legislature is proposing a *1 1/2* percent increase in our state's sales tax.

Future perfect tense
A verb phrase used to express an action that will occur before a certain time in the future. This tense is formed by using the verb helpers *will have* and the past participle of a verb. Example: If donations continue to be made at this same rate, we *will have paid* for this new hospital wing before its completion.

Future progressive tense
A verb phrase used to express an action that will be ongoing into the future. This tense is formed by using the verb helpers *will be* and the present participle of a

verb. Example: Our volunteers *will be calling* other alumni during the next month to solicit donations for the newly formed college foundation.

Future tense
A verb phrase used to express an action that will be forthcoming in the future. This tense is formed by using the verb helper *will* and the present part of a verb. Example: I *will call* you next week.

Gender
A term used to refer to the sexual classification of nouns, pronouns, and their modifiers. Classifications include feminine, masculine, and neuter. Examples: (1) *Maria* lost *her* purse. (2) *He* sold all *his* stock. (3) The *company* has just purchased dental insurance for all *its* employees.

Gerund
A verb form ending in *ing* that functions as a noun in a sentence. Example: His *refusing* our offer came as a surprise to all of us.

Helping verb
A verb that appears with the present part, present participle, or past participle of another verb to form tenses. Examples: *will* go, *are* planning, *have been* employed.

Horizontal listing
A listing of items that continues across the page like ordinary text. Compare with *vertical listing.* All the sections labeled *Examples:* in this glossary are horizontal listings.

Hyphen
A mark of punctuation (-) used in some word groups to join two or more words that function as a single idea. This mark is also used to represent *through* when placed between two numbers. Examples: *mother-in-law, up-to-date,* and pages *34-5.*

Hyphenated compound
A word group joined by hyphens that functions as a single thought unit. Examples: *trade-in, self-employment, well-to-do.*

Imperative sentence, Imperative statement
A complete sentence in which the subject *you* is not stated; it is understood. Example: (You) Please mail your check in the enclosed envelope today.

Implied verb
A word group in which an intended verb is not stated. Example: If possible (If it *is* possible), we would appreciate your shipping this order by July 10.

Inanimate object
A nonliving thing. Compare with *animate object.* Examples: *computer, lease,* and *insurance.*

Indefinite pronoun
A pronoun that does not represent a specific person, place, or thing. Examples: *each, every, either, someone, anyone,* and *something.*

Independent adjective
An adjective that describes a noun without relying on other adjectives to enhance its meaning. Two or more independent adjectives modifying a noun are separated by commas. Examples: an *intelligent, conscientious* student vs. printed in *large bold* print.

Independent clause
A word group containing a subject and a verb that could stand alone as a complete sentence. An *independent clause* is the same as a *main clause.* Example: Although he was at first reluctant, *Senator Richards has agreed to seek reelection for a third term.*

Independent phrase
A word group that represents a complete sentence although it is not. Example: Now to the point.

Independent question
A word group stated in question format that stands alone as a complete sentence. Example: Who is responsible for closing the office on Friday evenings?

Indirect object
A noun or pronoun acted upon by a subject, a verb, and a direct object. Example: Chris gave *him* the check yesterday.

Indirect question
A statement that describes the content of a question or questions. Example: Several customers have asked whether we will extend our shopping hours for the holiday season.

Indirect quotation
A statement that describes the written or spoken word of another person or source but does not employ the exact words used by that person or source. Example: Sharon said that if she was not promoted within the next three months, she would begin to look for another position.

Infinitive
The present form of the verb preceded by the word *to.* Examples: You will probably need *to work* overtime *to finish* this project by its deadline date.

Infinitive phrase
A word group beginning with an infinitive and ending with a noun or pronoun. Example: *To obtain more information,* just mail the enclosed card.

Inside address
The part of a business letter that lists the addressee's name, professional title (if any), company name (if any), street address, city, state, and zip code.

Intransitive verb
A verb that does not have a direct or indirect object. Compare with *transitive.* Examples: (1) The Governor will *campaign* heavily in the southern part of the state next week. (2) Responsibility for the success of this project *lies* with the project manager. (3) Prices *rise* when manufacturers encounter increased costs.

Introductory clause, Introductory dependent clause
A word group containing a subject and a verb that begins with a conjunctive adverb such as *if, when, since, because,* or *as.* The word group begins the sentence, ends with a comma, and is followed by the main clause. Example: *Because we are unable to obtain this merchandise,* we are returning your check.

Introductory phrase
Word groups without subjects and corresponding verbs that begin with a preposition, infinitive, or participle are considered phrases. Phrases that begin a sentence and appear directly before the main clause are introductory. Examples: (1) *By this time next year,* we will have moved our home office to Louisville. (2) *To receive your free copy,* simply sign and mail the enclosed card. (3) *Lured by the promise of large profits,* investors poured millions of dollars into this fraudulent development project.

Introductory prepositional phrase
A word group that begins with a preposition and does not contain a subject or a verb. The word group begins the sentence and is followed directly by the main clause. Example: *During this time* we will need to gather more information about the economic conditions of this area.

Irregular verb
A verb that does not form its parts in the usual way, that is, by adding *ed* to the present part to form the past part and the past participle. Examples: *eat, ate, eaten; go, went, gone;* and *sing, sang, sung.*

Limiting adverb
A word or word group that restrains, confines, or negates the meaning of a verb. Examples: *not, barely, scarcely,* and *hardly.*

Limiting expression
A word group that restrains or confines another word group. Example: You may petition for a grade change, *but only for a valid reason.*

Linking verb
A form of the verb *to be* used as a main verb. Example: She *is* a conscientious employee.

Lowercase
Refers to the format of alphabetic characters; letters that are not capitalized. Examples: *a, d, m,* and *u.*

Main clause
A word group containing a subject and a verb that could stand alone as a complete sentence. A *main clause* is the same as an *independent clause.* Example: When we receive your signed contract, *we will order the equipment needed for your installation.*

Main verb
A single verb or the last verb in a verb phrase. Examples: (1) Please *call* me tomorrow. (2) The display *was* too large to fit into a suitcase. (3) Only three candidates have been *called.* (4) Our manager was *disappointed* with the results of the advertising campaign.

Main word
The most descriptive or definitive word in a compound noun. Examples: *mother*-in-law, personnel *manager, notary* public, and vice *president.*

Modifier
An *adjective* that describes a noun or pronoun. An *adverb* that describes or limits a verb, an adjective, or another adverb.

N.
An abbreviation for *noun.*

Nominative case, Nominative case form
A noun or pronoun used as the subject of a sentence, the complement of a *being* verb, or the object of the infinitive *to be* when this infinitive has no subject. Nouns always maintain the same form; pronouns require a specific form: *I, he, she, you, we, they, who, whoever.* Same as *subjective case, subjective case form.* Examples: (1) *We* called you yesterday. (2) The winner was *she,* Joyce Moore. (3) I would not want to be *he* when the mistake is discovered.

Nonaction verb
A verb that does not demonstrate action. Examples: *am, is, was,* and *were.*

Nonessential subordinate clause
A word group containing a subject and a verb that begins with a conjunctive adverb such as *if, when, as, after,* or *although* or a relative pronoun such as *who* or *which.* This word group is an additional thought unit that does not change or modify the main clause of the sentence. It is the same as a *nonrestrictive clause* or a *nonrestrictive subordinate clause.* Examples: (1) Our major advertising campaign will begin on November 1, *after all our dealers nationwide have the new product line in their stores.* (2) Jan Davidson, *who has been with our company for three years,* has been placed in charge of the project.

Nonrestrictive
A word or word group that is not essential to the meaning of the main idea.

Nonrestrictive clause
A word group containing a subject and a verb that appears with a main clause. This word group is subordinate to the main idea and does not alter its meaning. It complements the main idea by adding additional information. A *nonrestrictive clause* is the same as a *nonessential subordinate clause* or a *nonrestrictive subordinate clause.* Examples: This proposal, *as I explained to you earlier,* has not yet been approved by the Board of Directors. (2) The profit and loss statement for this project was shown in our last annual report, *which was distributed to the stockholders on March 1.*

Nonrestrictive phrase
A word group beginning with a preposition, an infinitive, or a participle and ending with a noun or pronoun. This word group does not affect the meaning of the main clause; it adds an additional idea that does not modify the main idea. Examples: (1) You cannot, *in my estimation,* expect a greater return on your investment at this time. (2) Susan and Randy, *to name at least two people,* were among those staff members in our department who were affected by the abolishment of our child care center. (3) Our president, *concerned about the steady sales decline,* has decided to invest more heavily in research and development.

Nonrestrictive subordinate clause
Same as *nonessential subordinate clause.*

Noun
A person, place, thing, animal, quality, concept, feeling, action, measure, or state. Examples: *employee, city, chair, cat, sincerity, democracy, love, swimming, inch,* and *happiness.*

Object
A noun or pronoun acted upon by another part of speech, e.g., a verb or a preposition. Examples: Scott sent *me* the *check* yesterday. (2) For the next three *months, ...*

Object of a preposition
The noun or pronoun that follows a preposition. Examples: of our *clients,* for the last few *months,* and through your *efforts.*

Objective case, Objective case form
A noun or pronoun used as the object of a verb, the object of a preposition, the subject or object of an infinitive other than *to be,* or the object of the infinitive *to be* when this infinitive has a subject. Nouns always maintain the same form; pronouns require a specific form: *me, him, her, you, us, them.* Examples: (1) You may contact *me* at this number after 3 p.m. (2) Please send this information *to me* directly. (3) I do not want *to give her* too much information about our new product. (4) I would not want our new *supervisor to be him.*

Open compound
Two or more words used to represent a single idea. The words appear as separate words and are not hyphenated. Examples: *information processing, golf club,* and *vice president.*

Ordinal number
Cardinal numbers like *3, 10,* and *246* are numbers used in counting; ordinal numbers like *first, second,* and *twenty-fourth* indicate order or position in a series. Example: Our sales report for the *fourth* quarter must be ready by January 15 for inclusion in the annual report.

Parallel structure
Words or word groups used in a similar fashion must be expressed in the same format. This principle applies to words joined by a conjunction or a conjunctive pair and those appearing in a series. Examples: (1) Our receptionist's main duties are to *answer the telephone* and *greet office visitors.* (2) You may order supplies from not only *our standard supply catalog* but also *Kalleen's Computer Supply Catalog.* (3) The whole day was spent *returning phone calls, reading the mail,* and *dictating correspondence.*

Parenthesis
A mark of punctuation signifying the beginning [( ] of a side thought and the ending [ )] of a side thought. Example: Please request copies of any ancillary materials (at least an instructor's manual and key) that may accompany the text.

Parenthetical element, Parenthetical expression, Parenthetical remark
A word or word group that does not contribute to the meaning of the clause but merely acts as a transitional thought or provides an additional idea. Examples: (1) *Therefore,* we are returning this order for credit. (2) The meeting scheduled for October 24, *as you probably already know,* has been canceled.

Participial phrase
A word group beginning with a past or present participle and consummated with a noun or pronoun. Examples: (1) *Encouraged by last month's increased sales,* our Advertising Department has decided to extend the present campaign another month. (2) *Hoping to sell the property immediately,* Mr. Rice agreed to drop the price $10,000.

Parts of a verb
The forms of a verb that are used to construct tenses, that is, those spellings of a verb used in expressing time periods. The parts of a verb include the *infinitive, present, past, present participle,* and *past participle.*

Passive voice
A form of sentence construction in which the doer of the action is not the subject of the sentence. It is used to deemphasize the person performing the action by focusing instead on the results. The passive voice is constructed by using a form of the verb *to be* as a helper and the past participle of the main verb. Example: These reports *were issued* last week.

Past part
One of the five verb parts used in constructing tenses. For most verbs this part is formed by adding *ed* to the present part, the form listed in the dictionary. The past part for verbs not following this pattern is shown in the dictionary directly after the main entry. Examples: (1) *called* (call), *discussed* (discuss), and *answered* (answer). (2) *saw* (see), *wrote* (write), and *went* (go).

Past participle
One of the five verb parts used in constructing tenses. For most verbs this part is formed by adding *ed* to the present part, the form listed in the dictionary. The past participle for verbs not following this pattern is shown in the dictionary directly after the main entry. Examples: (1) *called* (call), *discussed* (discuss), and *answered* (answer). (2) *seen* (see), *written* (write), and *gone* (go).

Past perfect tense
Used to describe a past action that has taken place before another past action. This tense is formed by using the helping verb *had* and the past participle of the main verb. Example: The applicant *had accepted* another position before he *received* our offer.

Past progressive tense
Used to describe an ongoing action that took place in the past. This tense is formed by using the helping verb *was* or *were* with the present participle of the main verb. Example: Last year our company *was hiring* additional personnel; this year the company is reducing its staff in all departments.

Past tense
Used to report a single past action or occurrence. This tense is formed by using the past part of a verb. Example: We *finished* the report last Friday.

Perfect tense
Describes the present, past, or future by using a form of *have* as a helping verb and the past participle of the main verb. Examples: *have completed, had completed,* and *will have completed*

Permanent compound
Dictionary entries consisting of more than one word to represent a single idea. Examples: *air-conditioning, high school, community college, up-to-date,* and *full-time.*

Personal pronoun
A word that substitutes for the name of a person or thing. Examples: *I, he, she, it, we, they, you, me, him, her, us,* and *them.*

Phrase
A group of two or more grammatically related words that act upon one another in a modifying, coordinating, or composite relationship. The word group does not have a subject and a verb. Examples: (1) Our sales have increased *during the past few months.* (2) Mr. Lee requested the custodial crew *to wash the windows, vacuum*

the carpeting, and *set up the chairs.* (3) Our supply *of printer ribbons* is diminishing rapidly.

Plural

More than one. Nouns, pronouns, and verbs have plural forms.

Plural noun

More than one person, place, or thing. These nouns usually require a special form and appear with a plural verb. Examples: *files* (file), *bosses* (boss), *companies* (company), *curricula* (curriculum), and *potatoes* (potato).

Polite request

A command worded like a question that requests the reader or listener to perform a specific action. Example: Will you please send us your remaining application materials by November 16.

Possessive

A noun or pronoun that shows ownership. Example: The *company's* liability in this case has not yet been determined.

Possessive case, Possessive case form

The spelling of a noun or pronoun that shows ownership. Examples: *Sally's* desk, an *accountants'* convention, *his* books, *your* paycheck, and *their* tickets.

Predicate

That part of the sentence that includes the verb or verb phrase and all its modifiers—all parts of the sentence except the complete subject. Example: All parts in this assembly *will need to be replaced within the next few months.*

Prefix

A syllable attached to the beginning of a word that forms a derivative word or an inflectional form. Compare with *suffix.* Examples: *un*able, *dis*cover, *mis*pronounce, and *ful*fill.

Preposition

A part of speech that links a noun or pronoun to another word in the sentence. Examples: *of, for, behind, in, through, during, around, above, between,* and *except.*

Prepositional phrase

A word group that begins with a preposition and ends with a noun or pronoun. The phrase modifies another noun or pronoun or a verb in the sentence. Examples: (1) Our new line *of office equipment* will be on display at the convention. (2) Do not park your car *between these posts.*

Present part

One of the five verb parts used in constructing tenses. This part is the form shown as the main dictionary entry of the verb. Examples: (1) *call, discuss, answer, see, write,* and *go.*

Present participle
One of the five verb parts used in constructing tenses. For most verbs this part is formed by adding *ing* to the present part, the form listed in the dictionary. The present participle for verbs not following this pattern is shown in the dictionary directly after the main entry. Examples: (1) *calling* (call), *discussing* (discuss), and *answering* (answer). (2) *omitting* (omit), *writing* (write), and *starring* (star).

Present perfect tense
Used to describe an action that began in the past but has continued during the time leading to the present. This tense is formed by using the helping verb *has* or *have* and the past participle of the main verb. Example: We *have sent* this client at least three reminders about his past-due account.

Present progressive tense
Used to describe an action in progress during the present time. This tense is formed by using the helping verb *am, is,* or *are* and the present participle of the main verb. Example: We *are* now *taking* applications for this position.

Present tense
Used to describe an ongoing action or an existing condition. This tense is formed by using the present part of the verb. Examples: (1) Lisa *drives* 20 miles each day to work. (2) Your company *has* too many employees.

Principal parts of a verb
Same as *parts of a verb.*

Principal word
The word in a compound noun that describes or defines the noun most explicitly, if any. Examples: *brother*-in-law, *sergeant* at arms, lieutenant *colonel,* and high *school.*

Professional title
A title related to a person's employment. Examples: *Professor* Scot Ober, *Governor* Joyce Arntson, *Dean* Marlene Friedlander, *Vice President* Norlund, *General* Rodriguez, and *Mayor* Bradley.

Progressive tenses
Used to describe actions in progress during various time periods. Describes the present, past, or future by using a form of *to be* as a helping verb and the present participle of the main verb. Examples: *are processing, were processing,* and *will be processing.*

Pronoun
A word that functions as the substitute for a noun. Examples: *I, her,* and *they; that* and *who;* and *this, each,* and *everyone.*

Proper noun
The name of a specific person, place, or thing. Examples: *Marsha Karl, San Francisco Bay Bridge,* and the *Empire State Building.*

Question mark
A mark of punctuation (?) used to end a word group or complete sentence that is a direct question. Example: Have you received any further information about the proposed project?

Quotation mark
A mark of punctuation ('') used primarily to set off the exact words spoken or written by another person. Example: As the author stated in his article, ''As interest rates decline, investments in the municipal bond market become more attractive.''

Reflexive pronoun
A pronoun that refers back to and is acted upon by another noun or pronoun in the sentence. Example: *We* can certainly give *ourselves* a pat on the back for this accomplishment.

Regular verb
A verb that forms its parts by adding standard endings to the present form; that is, by adding *ed* for the past part, *ed* for the past participle; and *ing* for the present participle. Example: *check, checked, checked, checking.*

Relative clause
A word group (containing a subject and a verb) introduced by a pronoun that refers back and relates to a noun or pronoun in the main clause. Relative clauses are most commonly introduced by *who, whom, that,* and *which.* Example: Dr. Williams is the *physician who will handle your case.*

Relative pronoun
The noun substitutes *who, whoever, whom, whomever, that,* and *which* used to introduce a clause that refers back and relates to a noun or pronoun in the main clause. Example: The *subsidiary* of our company *that* handles this product is Belegrath Tool & Die.

Relative pronoun clause
A word group containing a subject and a verb that appears with a main clause. It begins with *who, whom, whoever, whomever, that,* or *which.* Example: Heritage, Inc., is the real estate company *that is handling the sale of our Springfield warehouse.*

Restrictive
A word or word group that contributes substantially to the main idea of the sentence and is needed for it to convey the same meaning. Without the word or word group, the meaning of the sentence would be changed or incomplete.

Restrictive appositive
A word or word group used to rename or describe a previous noun or pronoun. The word or word group is needed to identify *which one.* Example: The *book The Pentagon Heroes* has been on the best-seller list for the past eight weeks.

Restrictive clause
A word group containing a subject and a verb that appears with a main clause. Although this word group is subordinate to the main idea, it does clarify, limit, or otherwise affect its meaning. A *restrictive clause* is the same as an *essential subordinate clause,* a *restrictive dependent clause,* or a *restrictive subordinate clause.* Examples: This order will be shipped *as soon as I receive approval from our Credit Department* (2) The only person *who can approve this request* is the vice president of financial services.

Restrictive dependent clause
Same as an *essential subordinate clause,* a *restrictive clause,* or a *restrictive subordinate clause.*

Restrictive phrase
A word group beginning with a preposition, an infinitive, or a participle and ending with a noun or pronoun. This word group affects the meaning of the main clause by answering such questions as *who, what, which one, when, why, how, whether,* or *to what degree.* Examples: (1) The auction will be held *on Saturday, December 4.* (2) Please mail the enclosed post card *to obtain further information.* (3) The books *lying in this corner* are yours.

Restrictive subordinate clause
Same as an *essential subordinate clause,* a *restrictive clause,* or a *restrictive dependent clause.*

Return address
In business letters not prepared on letterhead stationery, the complete address of the person writing the letter. On envelopes prepared for mailing, the complete address of the person mailing the envelope and its contents.

Roman numeral
One of a sequence of numbering based on the ancient Roman system. Used primarily for numbering the preliminary pages of a report, chapters in a report, and major divisions in an outline. Examples: *I, II, III, IV, V, VI,* and *VII.*

Salutation
The opening greeting in a business letter. Examples: *Gentlemen, Ladies and Gentlemen, Dear Dr. Gates, Dear Ms. Howell,* and *Dear Bob.*

Semicolon
A mark of punctuation (;) used primarily to join two complete thoughts in a sentence. Example: We have not received any responses to our advertisement for an administrative assistant; therefore, please do not renew our ad in the Valley Star.

Sentence fragment
A word group ending with a period, question mark, or exclamation mark that is not a complete sentence or does not represent a complete thought. Example: We are interested in sponsoring a number of spot announcements. *That describe how our services and employees benefit the community.*

Series
Three or more word groups that have the same structure within a sentence. Items in a series consist of words, phrases, or clauses. The last item is joined to the others with the coordinating conjunction *and, or,* or *nor.* Example: You may *telephone, fax,* or *mail your orders.*

Signature block
The closing lines of a business letter that contain the signature of the writer, the typewritten name of the writer, and the title of the writer, if any.

Simple fraction
Any portion of a whole number that is less than one. Examples: *1/4* or *one fourth, 2/3* or *two thirds,* and *3/5* or *three fifths.*

Simple noun
The name of a person, place, or thing that consists of one word. Examples: *Mary, computer, state,* and *manager.*

Simple sentence
A word group that contains only one subject and one verb and makes sense. Example: I received the package of materials yesterday.

Simple subject
The single word in the main clause of a sentence that answers *who* or *what* in relation to the verb. Example: All *employees* in our division *have received* copies of the employee newsletter.

Simple tenses
The present, past, and future tenses. Examples: (1) He *writes* well. (2) He *wrote* this letter yesterday. (3) He *will write* the letter tomorrow.

Singular
A mode or form of nouns, pronouns, and verbs signifying *one.* Examples: *truck* (vs. *trucks*), *she* (vs. *they*), and *drives* (vs. *drive*).

Singular noun
The form used to name a person, place, or thing that signifies *one.* Examples: *supervisor, country,* and *bank.*

Slash
A symbol (/) used primarily for expressing fractions and certain expressions. Same as a *solidus* and a *virgule.* Examples: *3 3/4, c/o (in care of),* and *and/or.*

Solidus
Same as a *slash* and a *virgule.*

Stated verb
A verb expressed orally or in written format. Compare with *implied* verb. Example: If this *is* so, please *call* me.

Statement
A word group that presents facts or ideas. It is concluded with a period. Example: Our company was established in 1953.

Subject
The word or word group in the main or subordinate clause of a sentence that answers *who* or *what* in relation to the verb. Examples: (1) The *stockholders* of the corporation *approved* the merger last month. (2) Both *answers and explanations* for this test *are contained* in the instructor's manual. (3) *We will notify* you when your *order arrives.*

Subject complement
The noun or pronoun following a being verb *(am, is, are, was, were, be, been)* that either renames or describes the subject. Examples: (1) The former *supervisor* of our department *is* the new *vice president.* (2) The *paintings* in this exhibition *are* exceptionally *valuable.*

Subject of a clause
The word or word group in the subordinate clause of a sentence that answers *who* or *what* in relation to the verb. Example: If *you are interested* in this position, please send us your resume.

Subject of a sentence
The word or word group in the main clause of a sentence that answers *who* or *what* in relation to the verb. Example: As I mentioned in my previous memorandum, any further *delays* in the completion of this contract *will cost* the company thousands of dollars.

Subject of an infinitive
A noun or pronoun that appears directly before an infinitive. Example: I did not expect *him to have* the authority to release this kind of information.

Subjective case, Subjective case form
A noun or pronoun used as the subject of a sentence, the complement of a *being* verb, or the object of the infinitive *to be* when this infinitive has no subject. Nouns always maintain the same form; pronouns require a specific form: *I, he, she, you, we, they, who, whoever.* Same as *nominative case, nominative case form.* Examples: (1) *They* signed the papers this morning. (2) The only person who responded was *he.* (3) I would not want to be *she* when our manager discovers her mistake.

Subjunctive mood
Used to describe events that cannot or probably will not happen and conditions that are not true or highly unlikely. The plural form *were* is used with *if, as if, as though,* or *wish* for singular subjects when the situation described is not true or unlikely. Examples: (1) *If* I *were* you, I would refer this letter to my attorney. (2) During the meeting Tina acted *as if* she *were* the department manager, not Ms. Elliott.

Subordinate clause
A word group containing a subject and a verb that cannot stand alone as a complete sentence. Same as a *dependent clause.* Example: Please notify our office *if you need any additional sales literature.*

Subordinate conjunction
A specific kind of conjunction used to introduce a dependent or subordinate word group that contains a subject and a verb. Examples: *if, as, when, because,* and *since.*

Suffix
A syllable attached to the ending of a word or word root that forms a derivative word or an inflectional form. Compare with *prefix.* Examples: invest*ment*, account*ing*, and fruit*ful*.

Superlative form
The spelling or form of an adjective or an adverb when it compares more than two nouns or pronouns or more than two conditions. Compare with *comparative form.* Examples: (1) Sales figures for this year are the *highest* in our company's history. (2) Your firm is the *most* highly *respected* one in the industry.

Suspending hyphen
A hyphen following the first word of a compound adjective in which the second word of the compound appears later with a compatible compound adjective. Examples: (1) This carpeting may be purchased in *10-, 12-,* and 15-foot widths. (2) Most of our automobile loans extend over a *four-* or five-year period.

Syllable
A unit of spoken language used to make up words. Syllables are marked off in main dictionary entries; a small dot separates each syllable. Written words may be divided at the end of a line only between syllables. Examples: syl·la·ble, di·vi·sion, and ir·re·vo·ca·ble.

Temporary compound
A compound adjective not appearing in the dictionary. This compound is hyphenated only when it precedes the noun it modifies. Examples: (1) These *easy-to-follow instructions* were written by one of our staff members. (2) These *instructions* are *easy to follow.*

Tense
The form of a verb that places an action or a condition in a time frame.

Transitional expression, Transitional words
A word or phrase that does not contribute to the meaning of a sentence but takes the listener or reader smoothly from one concept to another by bridging two ideas or signaling a turn in thought. Examples: (1) Our supplier is unable to obtain any additional pieces of Harwood china by Lexington; *therefore,* we are returning your deposit. (2) You may, *however,* wish to upgrade the memory of your printer to 4 megabytes.

Transitive verb

A verb that has an object. Compare with *intransitive verb.* Examples: (1) Mr. Morris *called me* yesterday. (2) Please *place the book* on the table. (3) Our supervisor *gave her* an excellent *rating.*

Uppercase

Capital letters. Examples: *A, M,* and *IBM.*

Verb

A part of speech that shows action or movement or describes a situation or condition. Examples: *write, listen, send, be, appear,* and *look.*

Verb phrase

A verb part combined with helpers such as *was, have, did,* and *will* to form tenses. Examples: *were divided, had reached, do* not *know, will have finished,* and *may be reached.*

Vertical listing

A listing of items in which each item begins a new line on the page. Compare with *horizontal listing.* The following entries are an example of a vertical listing:

First entry in the listing
Second entry in the listing
Third entry in the listing
Fourth entry in the listing
Last entry in the listing

Virgule

Same as a *slash* and a *solidus.*

Vowel

Letters of the alphabet *a, e, i, o,* and *u.*

INDEX

A

B

D

E

F

M

S

Abbreviations of States and Territories

State or Territory	*Two-Letter Abbreviation*	*Standard Abbreviation*
Alabama	AL	Ala.
Alaska	AK	——
Arizona	AZ	Ariz.
Arkansas	AR	Ark.
California	CA	Calif., Cal.
Canal Zone	CZ	C.Z.
Colorado	CO	Colo., Col.
Connecticut	CT	Conn.
Delaware	DE	Del.
District of Columbia	DC	D.C.
Florida	FL	Fla.
Georgia	GA	Ga.
Guam	GU	——
Hawaii	HI	——
Idaho	ID	——
Illinois	IL	Ill.
Indiana	IN	Ind.
Iowa	IA	——
Kansas	KS	Kans., Kan.
Kentucky	KY	Ky.
Louisiana	LA	La.
Maine	ME	——
Maryland	MD	Md.
Massachusetts	MA	Mass.
Michigan	MI	Mich.
Minnesota	MN	Minn.
Mississippi	MS	Miss.
Missouri	MO	Mo.
Montana	MT	Mont.
Nebraska	NE	Nebr., Neb.
Nevada	NV	Nev.
New Hampshire	NH	N.H.
New Jersey	NJ	N.J.
New Mexico	NM	N. Mex.
New York	NY	N.Y.
North Carolina	NC	N.C.
North Dakota	ND	N. Dak.
Ohio	OH	——
Oklahoma	OK	Okla.
Oregon	OR	Oreg., Ore.
Pennsylvania	PA	Pa., Penn., Penna.
Puerto Rico	PR	P.R.
Rhode Island	RI	R.I.
South Carolina	SC	S.C.
South Dakota	SD	S. Dak.
Tennessee	TN	Tenn.
Texas	TX	Tex.
Utah	UT	——
Vermont	VT	Vt.
Virgin Islands	VI	V.I.
Virginia	VA	Va.
Washington	WA	Wash.
West Virginia	WV	W. Va.
Wisconsin	WI	Wis., Wisc.
Wyoming	WY	Wyo.